D1809537

Alex Calder teaches New Zealand and American literature in the Department of English at the University of Auckland. He has written extensively on the literature of the cross-cultural frontier and the problems of settlement, and on the works of Herman Melville. His previous books include the non-fiction anthology *The Writing of New Zealand: Inventions and Identities* (Reed, 1993), an edition of the writings of F. E. Maning (Continuum, 2001), and he was co-editor of *Voyages and Beaches: Pacific Encounters, 1769–1840* (University of Hawai'i Press, 1999).

The Settler's Plot

How Stories Take Place in New Zealand

Alex Calder

AUCKLAND UNIVERSITY PRESS

First published 2011

Auckland University Press
University of Auckland
Private Bag 92019
Auckland 1142, New Zealand
www.auckland.ac.nz/aup

ISBN 978 1 86940 488 8

Publication is kindly assisted by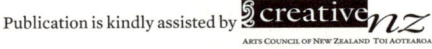

National Library of New Zealand Cataloguing-in-Publication Data
Calder, Alex.
The settler's plot : how stories take place in New Zealand
/ Alex Calder.
Includes bibliographical references and index.
ISBN 978-1-86940-488-8
1. Geography in literature. 2. Place (Philosophy) in literature.
3. New Zealand literature—History and criticism. I. Title.
NZ820.93293—dc 22

Cover design: Kalee Jackson
Cover image: 'Lakelands' map of Takapuna, c. 1911.
Courtesy North Shore Photograph Archive, Takapuna Library

Printed by 1010 Printing International Ltd

CONTENTS

Preface

This book is a study of the relationship between literature, place and the history of Pakeha settlement in New Zealand. By and large, each chapter explores one or more of the most frequently chosen settings in classic New Zealand literature – the beach, the farm, the bush or the suburb – and reflects on the plots or storylines that go with them. I believe the literary concept of setting gives us a new way of approaching Pakeha questions of place and identity. And putting setting and settlement together helps us to see that they are not uniquely our issues either – they reappear, with differences, whenever and wherever an 'old world' literary form takes a 'new world' setting.

Settings are idealised versions of many actual places. They are locations that enable certain stories to be told and around which various aspirations and values take shape, are challenged and modified. Settings also have a complex relationship to our physical geography and to what Philip Fisher calls the 'hard facts' of history. Some settings wear out and lose their magic; others are remarkably durable, revealing deeper continuities beneath our perceptions of change. Whenever a plot kicks in and events 'take place', a story will draw its own map and suggest others.

A primary purpose of this book is cartographic: I have tried to connect the way stories take shape in these settings to the actual history of Pakeha settlement. My idea comes from an illustration known as the brain homunculus: a model of the human figure spatially reorganised according to the distribution of nerve endings. From a minuscule trunk, like a genie emerging from a bottle, a large misshapen head with flabby lips and pendulous earlobes raises sunflower-sized hands from the stalks of each arm. What is the brain homunculus shape of the familiar map of New Zealand? We won't find it in any atlas, but we can imagine it insofar as poems, novels and stories are our nerve-ends.

All readers develop a sense of right relation between story and setting. A ghost story – to give a quick illustrative example – requires a haunted house, and while a New Zealand writer has a great deal of latitude as to where to situate that house, he or she is likely to follow (or pointedly disobey) a number of taken-for-granted but not always obvious rules. In our country, a haunted house is more likely to be suburban or rural than urban; no doubt this is because the inner city is culturally 'new' while ghost stories require decay and ruin. A haunted house will perhaps feature an overgrown hedge or moonlit macrocarpas along a winding driveway. All ghost stories have an affinity with remote locations; more importantly, they need a threshold to be crossed. Nor will a haunted house be the single-storey dwelling most Kiwis live in: a proper ghost story needs an attic and a cellar as well as everyday rooms. One of our best gothic novels, David Ballantyne's *Sydney Bridge Upside Down*, finds the functional equivalents of those spaces in a ruined freezing works. A haunted house must of course have a ghost – but what kind of ghost? I have not conducted a census, but if you know how ghost stories work, you might expect the greater proportion of our literary ghosts to be Maori for, as *Hamlet* reminds us, it is the function of ghosts to voice wrongs from the past. (And in fact all ghosts in this book do turn out be Maori.) Settings, in other words, are highly conventional and highly suggestive places. I have tried to be the anthropologist of the tacit cultural knowledge Pakeha have invested in the most common settings in New Zealand literature; writing a cultural history of that knowledge forms a second part of the purpose of this book.

A third aim is to read a relatively small number of classic New Zealand texts closely and well. Rather than survey the field, I have opted to examine a few illustrative case studies in the hope that one or two detailed examples are worth a hundred cursory glances. While the time span extends from the late 1820s through to the early 2000s, I have by and large focused on classic rather than contemporary literature. This is not meant to be a hard-and-fast distinction. Perhaps it suggests two always-reforming boundaries: one separating books that still have a claim on our present from those whose moment has passed; another, looking forwards, distinguishing the literature we know from the literature we are still coming to know. The first part of the book, 'Belonging', sets a pattern of treatment more or less followed by the work as a whole: one text from the 1870s and another from the 1910s, a strongly contrasting text from the 1960s, but an introduction and a conclusion that anchor the whole discussion in the present moment. Part II, 'Landing', focuses on material from and about the cross-cultural frontier and deals with narratives set on the beach or in small Maori communities. Part III, 'Settling', investigates processes of settling/unsettling the land with a chapter on land deals and another on farming; the remaining chapters examine the New Zealand pattern of early suburbanisation and the development of forms of high culture associated with urban centres. The final part of the book, 'Looming', overlaps chronologically with earlier sections, and considers the role of distance and the importance of 'overseas' as a place in New Zealand literary culture. Each of these sections is introduced separately.

The Settler's Plot is bound to relate to the notion of a canon and to received ideas about the development of New Zealand literature. Perhaps only four writers are currently regarded as irreplaceable in any book-length general consideration of New Zealand literature. They are Katherine Mansfield, Frank Sargeson, Janet Frame and Allen Curnow. That central configuration may change in time, but for the moment it seems uncontroversial to associate classic New Zealand literature first with those names, and then with several dozen other writers of considerable merit and accomplishment who are no longer living, or who are nearing the end of long and productive careers. Those four writers of course feature here, along with a necessarily restricted number from that bigger group, whose works have been chosen largely because they suit my purposes better than others. That said, I do have an ambition to 'change the canon'. Unlike most studies of New Zealand literature, *The Settler's Plot* gives considerable space to non-fiction and to writing from the nineteenth century. The default setting for most comparable books is that literature means texts in the three genres of poetry, fiction and drama. That assumption is the main reason why our nineteenth-century literature has sometimes seemed so impoverished and why the flowering of New Zealand literary culture has so often been associated with the 1930s or later. If we include non-fiction, the picture of our canonical writing alters significantly. Two very remarkable writers – F. E. Maning and Herbert Guthrie-Smith – seem to me to rank alongside or just below that central group of four. Their books are by no means unfamiliar – *Old New Zealand* and *Tutira* have remained in print almost continuously – but they have received relatively little extended critical discussion. This book addresses that lack and shows how different our literary history looks when these writers are ascribed a central and defining place.

Given its title and subject matter, *The Settler's Plot* is a Pakeha book rather than a book that actively seeks to document Maori perspectives, though the influence of Maori is strongly registered throughout. Some years ago, Pakeha were properly nervous about 'appropriating' Maori material; not quite so many years ago, Pakeha were properly nervous about failing to include a Maori perspective. Nowadays the mana of writing by Maori is evident and widely acknowledged. I have not felt obliged to add a 'special' chapter and have respectfully left most of what I might have said about the Maori contribution to New Zealand literature at one side of my point – which remains an account of Pakeha literary and cultural history from a 'Settlement Studies' perspective. A word about this academic term: it is not the same as the study of literature by early settlers. It is a form of postcolonial inquiry interested in a distinct set of problems shared by nations founded on the settlement of a 'new' – but already populated – world by modernising people from the 'old' world. Its basic premise is that the foundational problems, injustices and consequences of European settlement of this country will not disappear – though those problems can and often have been forgotten, underestimated or wished away.

Acknowledgements

I have had some fine teachers: C. K. Stead, Bill Pearson and Mac Jackson ran the graduate course in New Zealand literature at the University of Auckland when I was a student, and I have always been grateful for their inspiration and example. Leigh Davis was in that class too: he was an early and is now a much missed reader of my work. Linda Hardy is another dear friend to whom everything I write is addressed, as are my mentors-in-chief Wystan Curnow, Jonathan Lamb and Roger Horrocks. These three have all been energising collaborators over the years. Several sections in this book came out of a course on literature and settlement I co-taught with Wystan: I thank both him and the many students who will have come across earlier and often half-formed versions of these pages before. Sebastian Black, Witi Ihimaera, Peter Simpson, Terry Sturm, Stephen Turner and Albert Wendt have taught New Zealand literature with me over the years: my work on Curnow owes much to Terry, the Orakau chapter has its origins in teaching shared with Sebastian, while Stephen has been a close collaborator in the development of a local Settlement Studies.

The writing of this book was supported by periods of research leave and grants from the University of Auckland, and by the staff of the libraries of that university and the Alexander Turnbull Library. Portions of chapters have appeared in earlier and different versions in the *Journal of New Zealand Literature*, *Landfall* and two edited collections: *Settler and Creole Re-Enactment* and *Lighted Windows: Critical Essays on Robin Hyde* – my thanks to the editors and publishers of each. I would like to thank Alan Roddick, for the Estate of Charles Brasch, for permission to quote lines from 'The Islands' (ii); Christine Cole Catley, for the Frank Sargeson Trust, for permission to quote from a letter from W. L. C. Bakewell to Frank Sargeson; Paul Millar and

John Baxter, for the James K. Baxter Trust, for permission to quote work by Baxter; and Jenifer Curnow for permission to quote poems by Allen Curnow. Thanks, too, to all the staff at AUP, in particular: Sam Elworthy, Anna Hodge, Ginny Sullivan and Mike Wagg.

In more general terms, I owe an intellectual debt to Philip Fisher's *Hard Facts: Setting and Form in the American Novel*, to Franco Moretti's work on the geography of the novel, and to a network of colleagues around the world interested in Settlement Studies – not least, Simon During, who raises the national quotient of intellectual excitement every time he returns home. I am fortunate to have been able to draw on histories by James Belich and Judith Binney among others, while the earlier sections of the book would not have been imaginable without the example of Greg Dening. I have also found inspiration in the work of a group of environmental historians of the American West – William Cronon, Richard White and Rebecca Solnit, among others – and in the work of their New Zealand colleague, the late Geoff Park.

Among the many other friends, colleagues and relatives whose generosity or example leaves an imprint on these pages, I must mention: my parents, Dorothy and the late Ian Calder; June, Jen and Rob Shieff and their families; Philip Armstrong; Len Bell; Jan Bills; Tom Bishop; Anna Boswell; Mervyn and Faye Cohen; Jan Cronin; Andrea Dawe; Margaret Edgcumbe; Patrick Evans; the Ferguson family; Peter Gibbons; Melissa Gniadek; Annie Goldson; Mark Houlahan; Annamarie Jagose; John Kircher; Ken Larsen; Paul Lyons; Claudia Marquis; Paul Millar; Michael Neill; John Newton; Roger Nicholson; Bridget Orr; Chris Prentice; Geoff Sanborn; Laurence Simmons; Peter Simpson; Don Smith; Vanessa Smith; Kendrick Smithyman; Jane Stafford; Sean Sturm; Sophie Tomlinson; Lee Wallace; Lydia Wevers; Mark Williams; and Elizabeth Wilson.

Finally, though there are no words really to say it, I have oceans of love for my wife, Sarah Shieff, the first reader of every word in this book, and for my daughter Octavia Calder-Dawe. Their joyous company has, thank heavens, distracted and prolonged the writing of this book while inspiring it too. I have always wanted to write the words that follow: this book is for them.

Part I *Belonging*

CHAPTER ONE

Nature and the Question of Pakeha Turangawaewae

The hills are alive with the sound of music . . .
– Oscar Hammerstein II

NEW ZEALAND'S NUMBER-ONE CLASSIC SONG IS CALLED 'NATURE'.[1] It is not so much the words people remember – 'through falling leaves I pick my way slowly . . .' – as the radiant glory of a chorus that goes 'do-do-do doo doo do-doo, do-do-do doo'! This joyous whoop, this inarticulate refrain, this true national anthem, was recorded by a group aptly known as the Formyula. Whenever Pakeha have rejoiced in their physical presence in these islands, have felt a special sense of dispensation, of simple rightness in being here; whenever it seems the sun shines especially for us; whenever person and place are in propitious alignment, we have reached beyond inarticulateness to the simple formula: feeling good about nature equals belonging. In our holiday snapshots and in our childhood memories, in arts high and low, in all forms of advertising and publicity, and in the chatter of columnists and celebrities, it would seem we are most at home, most ourselves, somewhere outdoors, in one or another of the locations that depict New Zealand as a scenic wonderland.

Almost everything seems questionable about this. In the world of politics and the media, warm fuzzies about nature and nation are as weeds. Not only are we a predominantly suburban people, only inter-mittently in contact with dreamscapes of bush and beach, but nature itself isn't what it used to be. These days nature is as likely to be virtual as actual, managed rather than wild, and has come to seem more and more something that culture produces than a realm beyond the ideas and frameworks we have of it. Even so, it is by no means contemptible, even now, to count oneself –

A lover of the meadows and the woods,
And mountains; and of all that we behold
From this green earth; . . . well pleased to recognize
In nature and the language of the sense,
The anchor of my purest thoughts, the nurse,
The guide, the guardian of my heart, and soul
Of all my moral being.[2]

We may not put it quite like Wordsworth but we have often transplanted the sentiments. In a thousand poems and a thousand paintings, nature is a presence whose people we become.[3] With a sense of intuitive rightness, the children of settlers recognise nature as home.

This gives rise to a syndrome I call Pakeha turangawaewae. I use the word turangawaewae – a place to stand – because our relationship with place, especially with the natural world and with categories derived from nature, is at the heart of the Pakeha New Zealander's sense of belonging. We feel we have a place to stand, and we have that place because we value nature. I am generalising, of course. Not everybody has had the classic New Zealand version of Wordsworth's outdoor childhood (though I did): those barefoot days spent in nature, running like a savage through the bush on manuka-needled trails, looking down through pohutukawa to the green bay below, sand in the togs from body-surfing. I am mythologising, of course. While I necessarily take my own pulses on these issues, and while I cannot write without making assumptions about the feelings of others, it should be understood in what follows that I have polled nobody – my methods are literary, not empirical. I want to untangle some of our dominant meanings of nature, and to consider the cultural work that they do. More particularly, I am interested in why it is difficult to talk about belonging without also talking about nature, and why that might constitute a problem.

Let me come back to that ungainly term: Pakeha turangawaewae. The phrase is an oxymoron. Turangawaewae, understood in the Maori sense of belonging, of having a place to stand, is not the same as the affection for place felt by Pakeha. In addition, Pakeha are not only relative newcomers and strangers but also beneficiaries of the historical marginalisation of Maori. But, just as one can use an oxymoron like 'deafening silence' to describe a particular atmosphere, so too with Pakeha turangawaewae: it is the sort of belonging you have when you don't have turangawaewae. We Pakeha are at home here, we identify as New Zealanders, this is our place, we belong – and yet, without denying any of those things, there is another degree of belonging that we do not have that is available to Maori (or perhaps to the Maori side of you). What I am calling another degree of belonging may well have ontological and epistemological dimensions – what is it to be Maori? how does one know one is? – as well as historical and political ones, but from a Pakeha perspective that extra degree need have very little positive or coherent content at all. Even as a postulated difference, as the mere possibility of a more essential mode of belonging to this place, the prior presence of Maori has shaped the kinds of belonging Pakeha have felt and recorded in their interactions with the world of Nature. The four nature studies that follow take varying notice of the prior presence of Maori, and emphasise in turn processes of domination, rapture, identification and tourism. Any one story is bound to suggest others that might have appeared in its place. The order is chronological, but this is not a sequential history so much as a sorting through of communal memories in and around nature, of old tunes we still have in our heads.

Climb ev'ry mountain ...

In the seventeenth letter of *Station Life in New Zealand*, Mary Anne Barker complains that a lack of opportunity to experience proper hardship makes her feel like 'an impostor'. 'Ever since I came here', she writes, 'I have regretted that the rapid advance of civilisation in New Zealand precludes the possibility of being really uncomfortable.'[4] Back home, in England, her friends are likely to think of her 'with the deepest of pity, as of one cut off from the refinements and comforts of life' (125), yet she has discovered that life on an isolated South Island sheep station in 1867 holds no terrors and few inconveniences. The people she envies are the ones who got here first, in the very early days of the Canterbury colony, in what she calls those 'primitive times' – 'only sixteen years ago' (124) – when new settlers had real adventures and surmounted real challenges. In a time and place that we, in our turn, might regard as offering ample scope for settler heroism, Lady Barker's relation to official versions of derring-do and colonial resourcefulness often approaches parody. Even though this is the very same woman who sets her own broken shoulder, who digs drowned sheep out of snowdrifts with her bare hands, who says things like, 'it requires a steady head to cross a noisy stream on two slippery round poles' (98), her more characteristic note is a self-deprecating impersonation of settler hardihood. Excited by tales of stranded pioneers and backcountry bivouacs, Lady Barker plots to replicate the experience. 'I have been trying for some time past', she says in her best explorer voice, 'to excite in the breasts of our home party . . . an ardent desire to see the sun rise from the top of "Flagpole", a hill 3,000 feet above the level of the sea' (125).

The expedition to conquer Mt Flagpole begins as an amusement for house guests: Lady Barker and her husband Frederick Broome have 'new chums' to stay, and they head off late one afternoon with a couple of blankets for shelter and, in the 'commissariat department', a cold leg of lamb and a fine pigeon pie, tea, sugar, teaspoons and two bottles of whisky 'for the manufacture of toddy' (127). It is the tail end of an Indian summer but, as night falls, it becomes unseasonably, horribly, cold. No one sleeps, the wind howls, and they pass a night of thorough and intense wretchedness. 'There was no attempt at conviviality', recalls Lady Barker, 'subdued savageness was the prevailing state of mind' (132). But at last, at long last, up comes the sun. Her description of this moment corresponds very closely to a colonial paradigm – the traveller in a new land climbs to a high place and becomes 'monarch of all he surveys'[5] – yet even this very powerful experience of reorientation does not entirely subdue her feeling of displacement, of only impersonating a role.

> Presently someone called out 'There's the sea' . . . ; none of us had seen it since we landed; to all of us it is associated with the idea of going home someday: whilst we were feasting our eyes on it a golden line seemed drawn on its horizon; it spread and spread, and as all the water became flooded with a light and glory which hardly seemed to belong to this world, the blessed sun came up to restore us all to life and warmth again. In a moment, in less than a moment, all our little privations and sufferings

vanished as if they had never existed . . . . I did not know which side to turn to first. Behind me rose a giant forest in the far hills to the west – a deep shadow for miles, till the dark outline of the pines stood out against the dazzling snow of the mountains behind it . . .; then I turned round to see before me such a glow of light and beauty! For an immense distance I could see the vast Canterbury plains; to the left the Waimakiriri river, flowing in many streams . . . down to the sea. . . . Between us and the coast were green patches and tiny homesteads, but still few and far between; close under our feet, and looking like a thread beneath the shadow of the mountain, ran the Selwyn in a narrow gorge, and on its bank stood the shepherd's hut . . . that once afforded us such a good luncheon; it looked a mere toy, as if it came out of a child's box of playthings, and yet so snug for all its lonely position. On the other hand lay our own little home, with the faint wreath of smoke stealing up through the calm air. (133–35)

As the sun rises, there is a shift in her attention from things that are very big, to things that seem progressively smaller: from an immense view of the mountain ranges, to the patchwork of the plains, to villages and tiny homesteads, to a cottage she describes as 'a mere toy, as if it came from a child's box of playthings' (135). It is as if her eye is unconsciously dominating that space by partitioning it, by seeing bits of it as small and, by implication, of herself as large. In writing about this moment later, there is a tell-tale adjustment in her sense of belonging: early in the passage, the word home refers to England; at its close, as Lady Barker recalls looking down on what has previously been described as a house or a homestead, she is prompted to write of 'her snug little home'. Thus, as savage dark gives way to civilised dawn, it is as if that one night recapitulates the work of sixteen years of settlement, of the transformation of an unfamiliar, dark and unfriendly domain into a landscape they know and can name, and which has for the first time become home.

But two rather more curious pieces of behaviour complicate an apparently conventional colonial scene. First, there is a supplementary ritual: 'Our last act was to collect all the stones we could move into a huge cairn, which was built round a tall pole of totara; on the summit of this we tied securely, with flax, the largest and strongest pocket-handkerchief' (136). This ceremony has all the makings of a parody of real explorer behaviour but, in these circumstances, their mimicry of raising the Union Jack over foreign territory is not without reverence. It is a sign of their silent identification with the movement from savage night to civilised dawn, with the narrative of colonisation as it would appear from the seat of Empire; but their little ritual strikes me as overplayed to a small degree. It is as if the emotional and ideological significance of that sunrise were a little out of kilter, and required this compensating memorial. The ceremony around the cairn then concludes with the exuberance one feels when shedding a more serious role: as the party returns, 'The gentlemen began rolling huge rocks down the sides of the hills and watching them crashing and thundering into the valleys, sometimes striking another rock and then bounding high into the air' (136).

I would certainly enjoy doing that – it is not often one has an opportunity to be a hooligan on such a Herculean scale. Lady Barker does not join in on this occasion – she takes care to keep above the men, so as 'not to be crushed under a small stone of twenty tons or so' – but she understands the regressive appeal of their behaviour. She is like that herself whenever she has an opportunity to indulge 'The Exceeding Joy of Burning' (194). As far as she is concerned, nothing beats dragging a blazing stick along the grass and watching 'a great wall of fire rushing up-hill as straight as a line' (195), or the crack and flare of an exploding flax bush.

In the course of that night and in the sunrise of that splendid morning, a small drama of emplacement and displacement has been enacted. They began as impostors, as people who lack credentials as settlers or pioneers, but are then called back to themselves in an experience whose imperial overtones have prompted a style of belonging. This is something they surely believe in, yet I think they also have an inkling that the role does not quite suit them – at least, not in that place. They have metamorphosed away from metropolitan civility, and even though they try in so many ways to reproduce it, their sympathies have become rather more wild and more primitive. It would be a mistake to say they have 'gone native' – Maori barely register in *Station Life* – but one might say they have kicked over the traces and 'gone settler'. Across the Tasman, a little bit of un-English savagery and much wanton destruction of nature would qualify one as a first

Australian, but the likes of Lady Barker and Frederick Broome are rather more distant as forebears in this genealogy of Pakeha feelings of turangawaewae. This is not simply because the couple had no future here – having made an unwise land purchase, they could not recover from heavy stock losses and returned to England – but because it would take more than running a sheep station to localise in New Zealand. They are my example of a zero degree of belonging, from which other writers begin to register a more local difference by venturing a relation to Maori. But I think of them as ancestors nonetheless, for it is not their burned off and eroded hillsides we relate to, but the separate conservation estate that, as a consequence of their transformation of the environment, becomes Nature for us instead. Without settlers like Lady Barker, there would have been fewer ecological catastrophes – and fewer reserves to run wild in.

Ford ev'ry stream . . .

In the early 1910s, New Zealand's best living poet ventured up the Whanganui River in search of scenery. A nature tourist might well have been tempted to book an overnight berth on the paddle steamer from Taumarunui to Whanganui, but for the traveller interested in beauty 'rather than mere mileage', there was only one way to experience the Whanganui: to hire a native canoe and pole the twenty miles upstream from Pipiriki to Parinui.[6] Blanche Baughan, then in her late thirties, had already written most of the poems – 'The Old Place', 'A Bush Section' – which have become standard inclusions in our anthologies. She had also filed a remarkable photo-essay on the Milford Track for the London *Spectator* in 1908 – 'The Finest Walk in the World' – and followed that success with similar essays on the 'Snow Kings of the Southern Alps' and the 'Uncanny Country' of Rotorua's thermal district.[7] In these pieces, she has already developed the mannerism of taking the reader along with her in her travel writing, but in doing so, and without necessarily paying the matter much attention, she cannot write without revealing the supposed whereabouts of both writer and the person she writes for.

'A River of Pictures and Peace' begins with an account of the origins of the Whanganui River. 'Once upon a time, says an old Maori legend, two brother mountains, whose home was near Lake Taupo, in the centre of the North Island of New Zealand, fell in love with a maiden mountain living near' (157). Old Maori legends do not begin 'Once upon a time' and would not explain the whereabouts of Lake Taupo; the information cues in and points to an overseas reader. The fairy tale formula also establishes a contrast: 'The *pakeha* puts the matter much more prosaically in his geography books', she writes, and goes on to give a geography book account of the river's formation before inviting the reader to 'Choose which explanation you will!' This is not a Pakeha writing. The narrator is un-situated, at a remove from both Maori legend and Pakeha textbooks, and the reader she writes for would seem to be an armchair traveller who is also not from New Zealand. No doubt this is in keeping with the fact that she was initially writing for the readers of a London magazine, but it also signals a curious fault line that runs through her account. On one side, there is an implicit claim to extensive local knowledge; on the other, there is a strong impression that she is a visitor writing for armchair travellers from overseas. Yet in the course of telling her story, this pattern changes considerably: the tension between here and there dissolves in a rapturous merging with the landscape and results in a reorientation of both the writer and her audience as local. 'Do you remember the Maori legend of the mists?' she asks later, talking as one Kiwi to another.

This does not happen when she is writing about other scenic parts of New Zealand. Early in her study of the 'Snow Kings' she observes:

As one stands here upon this rocky-vantage point and *sees* this mountain-world, Man does not count; one does not think of him. There is no sign of visible habitation; it is the actual presence of these mighty forms that engrosses one's whole attention, not the remembrance of their scanty mortal associations; while, as for the citizen surnames imposed (often with what manifest incongruity!) upon these august majesties, far from their humanizing the landscape, the landscape has de-humanized them; warm meanings of flesh and blood they now connote no more, but stand only for splendid entities, motionless, pure, of silent rock and ice. This ocean of the snows, in brief, is so immense, the barque of human enterprise upon it so small, that the effect upon the mind at gaze is that of a quite shipless sea, a solitude still inviolate. (59)

Perhaps no other New Zealand theme has been so thoroughly mined as the idea that our natural environment – our 'scenery' – is not only splendid and imposing in its pristine isolation, but also that its grandeur inevitably marks how small, how shallow, how transient our footing on this place really is.[8] Baughan's alpine essay starts by acknowledging the lofty indifference of the New Zealand landscape to its human settlers, but unlike the cultural nationalists of the 1930s who made this a sign of an insecure cultural identity, a deficiency to be remedied by a more considered relation to settlement, Baughan develops a more radical Romantic response. The protagonist of her voyages into scenery may initially feel a sense of alienated detachment from nature, but that feeling of being at a remove from our environment, a mere consumer of the scenery we pass through, turns out to be superficial and false. Venture into nature and the haze soon falls away; the traveller is refreshed and overcome by an intense perception that human beings and nature are one: 'that the universe is nowhere dead matter, but everywhere alive and active . . . . In the solitudes of the sea, one sometimes suspects this; in these precincts of Aorangi one is sure of it' (101).

If those precincts were still known by their 'citizen surname', were still plain old Mt Cook, one wonders whether the transcendental moment would have taken hold quite so well. 'Let us allow [Mt Cook] his far more just and melodious native name', she writes earlier. 'See, is he not truly *Aorangi, Bright Light in the Sky*, where yonder to the north of our peak, he stands and shines above us?' (60). Where the European word would only name, the Maori word is like a natural sign, a word that names more truly; it is my first, although a relatively thin, example of something Maori mediating a European sense of belonging by being at one with nature. But the place Baughan writes from is not home: she writes this essay throughout as a visiting cosmopolitan romantic, as one who has the opportunity to put a thought experiment of Ruskin's into action – what would the French Alps be like if one could encounter them on their own terms, without the intervening overlay of human history? – and the reader she addresses is always situated elsewhere, is always a reader whose indulgence about local matters is sought in the invitation to imagine oneself at her side.

Baughan believed that Maori regarded the Southern Alps 'always with veneration and awe, and, fearing to profane, avoided them'

(58). She was wrong. The mountains had been extensively mapped, explored and traversed by Maori, but their maps, as Wystan Curnow has explained, were oral and imperceptible to Europeans who had 'lost their ear for cartography'.[9] The Whanganui River, on the other hand, is unmistakably linked with 'the history of both the brown man and the white'; it is 'a furrow of former violence that has brought forth peace, an old road of ruin that has become a highway of beauty' (158). The obvious historical dimension of this landscape not only helps distinguish this essay from Baughan's other studies in scenery, it also gives rise to many passages in praise of what she calls blending. A fellow passenger, for example, is described this way:

> *Pakeha* is the cut, Maori the amplitude, of that moss-green velvet coat and skirt! The lady's blouse, of Tussore silk, hangs beltless; her hat is an erection, in the latest style, of milliner's roses; she wears one earring, composed of a large shark's tooth . . . and at her neck there dangles a magnificent pendant of greenstone, probably a very ancient and valuable heirloom. What is she pulling out now from those rich recesses of her coat? A little black pipe! which she fills, with aplomb, and smokes with enjoyment; and then, putting it carefully back, she draws out a little beautifully-embroidered white handkerchief, and wipes her beautifully-tattooed mouth. There is a real 'Maori lady of the transition period' for you, if you like!
>
> And really, the river itself shows something of the same racial blend; for poplars mingle with cabbage trees and karakas on its banks, and willows, we shall find, fringe it all the way up. (165)

The Maori woman and the river are figurative as well as literal illustrations of a process of 'blending'. Both the woman and the river relate to New Zealand's 'racial' history by synecdoche, as parts standing for the whole, and each part can suggest the other through the type of blending we call metonymy, for Baughan relates the natural world to the Maori world by propinquity, and vice versa. This lacework of figurative interconnections helps give the 'blending' of Maori and European worlds, evident even in the names of the kainga on the river, a warm and positive image. At Jerusalem – 'melodised into Hiruharama' (169) – features of an older Maori world appear to combine with European constructions as if by an enchanter's wand, without edges, strain or incongruity.

> And now, fifty miles up river, set upon a hill, above a glassy bend, is Jerusalem – the largest *pa* on the river, and the picture of pleasantness. The hill is crowned by the pale-painted buildings of church and convent, standing clear against the tree-dark ranges beyond; beneath them spreads the *pa*, with its gay *whares* and *wharepunis*, yellow and red and green, its long-legged storehouses, its tall trees, fruit-groves and gardens. Men sit about on the *wharepuni* verandahs, women play with their babies, coloured clothing hangs among the trees, blue smoke rises for the evening meal; at the landing-place children and the river complete the picture. (172)

The word picture Baughan paints is remarkably still. The pa, with its harmonious mix of church and wharepuni, convent and gay whares, is seen from the middle distance, and in terms that remind me of the romanticised unreality of a pa scene painted by Lindauer. Yet Baughan is writing for people who might not be disposed to see a contemporary Maori pa in anything like so positive a light, who might well need all her adjectival nudging in order to regard this backwater as a harmonious blend of Maori and European worlds. In the 1910s Baughan is moving cultural boundaries and formulating new habits of thought and perception that our settler ancestors would need to learn, normalise and ultimately forget as obvious in a country that prided itself on having the best scenery and the best race relations in the world.[10]

As we leave the steamer for the native canoe, and as we slip further and further up the river, we are gradually invited into a space that takes the tranquillity of Hiruharama to a higher order still. 'The river is silent in its flowing, the men fall silent also. You sit poised and stirless; the notebook lies unopened on my knee. The spell of the river has fallen upon us, and our eyes are opened' (176). The power of that spell is conveyed in two phases. The first involves a multiplication of detail, of very minute detail, closely observed over several pages of her text. Each bend in the river brings a new delight: the 'cliff with all its laces and embroideries of green' (178); a pool where 'every grass-blade, every moss-coat, verdant or ruddy, of the banks, every fern frond, glint of cliff, bough-lattice, water-fall' is so perfectly reflected in the water, 'it seems as though another forest must be dwelling there' (183). After so much pool-by-pool and leaf-by-leaf perception, Baughan then steps back from the close-up. She begins to 'see deeper' and prepares 'to realise the river as a whole'.

> You see it once again the highway of a primitive people . . . catch sight of the crimson and carving of a war canoe reflected in some glassy reach, and hear the splash of its hundred paddles. . . . Then, further yet, deeper still, goes your mind's eye . . . . Surely, this river, as she moves so silently along, herself has memories, herself is musing, dreaming . . . of what? . . . . No longer do we note the beauty round us as a thing outside, no longer think the green fresh thoughts of Nature after her. Yet you cannot tell me, nor I you, what now are the thoughts we share; for something deeper than either you or I is sharing them with us, and they are less our thoughts than Its. (185–86)

'Deeper' is a very important word for Blanche Baughan. It can mean more remote, further back in time, more profound, and all three qualities dovetail with the deepest thing of all: Nature, the ultimate destination of her journey. In many ways, the view when we get there is much the same as the view presented at the end of one of her alpine pieces, but her Whanganui expedition is more 'deeply' tied to place because more deeply tied to people. The canoe is poled upstream by Paora and Tipi, her 'vivacious travel-mates' (175); Maori phrases, such as 'Kapai te waka!' soon appear, but they are not translated for the benefit of the overseas reader. It is as if, in the course of this deeper journey, the implied reader is no longer an armchair traveller but a companion in the canoe who can take local knowledge for granted, and who, along with an author who now plainly identifies herself as Pakeha, will be invited to end the excursion on the marae at Parinui.

> Perhaps you have brought with you camping accessories for the night? for my part, I mean to fling myself upon the hospitality of the natives at Parinui. . . . You are coming too? Up the hill, then, and inside the palisade of this little, lonely, but most clean and friendly *kainga*. . . . The old chief bids us a dignified, unquestioning welcome, his wife, of the fine, comely,

and most sensible old face, goes off to see that plenty of potatoes shall be scraped and steamed for the *pakeha*, and pork-ribs boiled. In the evening, we shall sit in the *wharepuni* . . . and listen to stories of the olden days, while outside, the mists gather, . . . and below the unseen river murmurs. All day we have been sharing its frank, friendly life; and now to share so naturally the naïve life of the brown man continues, do you not feel? the same melody in another key. (188–89)

Baughan's Maori hosts have become part of nature too. For some New Zealanders they still are. Pakeha have always been inclined to identify a lack in their own culture (we feel we have 'lost touch' with nature) and then to find the opposite of that lack there in abundance, in the world of Maori, through an act of projection – a sentiment on occasion redoubled when Maori embrace the role of ecologically sensitive guardians of the ancient ways. But this is to view Baughan's writing from a more contemporary moment. In her own time, she invites a reader who is expecting to camp elsewhere to follow her onto the marae. Of course, this is only the licence of a travel writer, a means of stringing the reader along in her imagination, but it is a form of border crossing nonetheless, whose most tell-tale sign is her inclination to re-assign the address of both writer and reader. Becoming local is the gain in her journey, the pay-off, and it took both nature and Maori to do this for her. She writes: 'New Zealand is always sure of the Nature-lovers' heart. Some of her aspects move one to the love that is almost worship, that excites, and that reveals unknown deeps and heights in oneself. Here, however, she is all soothing, tranquil, maternal almost . . . very loveable!' (189). The Southern Alps, where the primeval and pristine qualities of the landscape are more pronounced, also reveal 'heights in oneself'; but it is in the depths of the Whanganui, that blended river, that she first discovers that Nature is her turangawaewae.

In the only personal photograph that appears in *Studies in New Zealand Scenery*, Blanche Baughan is climbing an ice face. Crossing the paepae of Parinui may have been the greater adventure. But there is an historical irony to be observed too. Maori of the Whanganui have come to remember the early 1900s as a time of loss rather than 'blending'. It was around this time that Pakaitore – a Maori market and camping place, later called Moutua Gardens and the site of a protracted protest occupation – was taken from them. Maori blended naturally into Blanche Baughan's 'River of Pictures and Peace', but that was by no means the Maori experience of their 'assimilation' into a European world. The costs, in terms of everything that could not be translated across the border, were high; but they would also find that the more they modernised along Western lines, the more likely it was that signs of their blending-in would strike the majority of Baughan's Pakeha contemporaries as halting, incomplete and ugly. In the early 1900s, the old market of Pakaitore connected Maori to a much larger economy and to the shaping powers of the new. Across the fence, the community-minded, forward-thinking and nature-loving citizens of Whanganui may well have viewed the site differently. In a newspaper article laying out the historical background to the occupation of Moutua Gardens by the grandchildren and great-grandchildren of Baughan's hosts and guides, the historian Judith Binney explained that in all probability their ancestors had been 'booted off because the old market was considered an eyesore'.[11]

Follow ev'ry rainbow . . .

Blanche Baughan sat in the wharepuni and heard stories of the old days; James K. Baxter fashioned himself body and soul in the light of the values he found there.

> A man's body is a meeting house,
>
> Ribs, arms, for the tribe to gather under,
> And the heart must be their spring of water.[12]

And this human body, in turn, is enclosed by Nature as an overarching meeting house: looking up at night sky, the stars are 'ribs of white fire / Hung there like the underside of punga leaves / Planted for our human shelter' (567). It is common in Baxter's late poetry to begin with Maori and Pakeha at odds – 'After a dispute with one dear Maori friend / I walk all night on the road to Raetihi' – before a brilliant flash of natural detail – the silver 'underside of punga leaves' – brings the erring

Pakeha, together with the world of nature, under the ribs of a Maori sky (567). This is a new twist on an old syndrome: for earlier writers, Maori were close to nature, but for Baxter, nature itself is Maori.

This re-culturing of nature took a massive design effort, involving not only words on the page and the cultivation of a public persona, but also a pronounced rhetoric of the body. The one thing everyone knows about Hemi Baxter is what he looked like: this founder of communes was hairy, smelly and barefoot; his was a body that shed marks of adornment and discipline, that preferred clothes even the op-shop had rejected, a body that was as natural as natural can be. From the fiery torment of that 'small grey cloudy louse' nesting in his beard in the first of the *Jerusalem Sonnets*, to the satisfaction of soothing 'bruised heels on the cold grass' in the last of the *Autumn Testament* sonnets, the actions and sensations of this natural body keep getting into the later poetry – and in more ways than one.

In a copy of *Jerusalem Sonnets* inscribed for Kendrick Smithyman, Baxter traced the outline of his hand, and on each finger wrote a number of whakatauki he thought might ensure the well-being of his New Zealand tribe. They were: 'to share one's wealth; to speak the truth, not hiding one's heart from others; to love one another and show it by the embrace; to take no job where one has to lick the boss's arse; to learn from the Maori side of things'. And then on the palm of the hand he added: 'When these things are done, the soul rises to the surface of the friend's face, like a fish to the surface of the water, and the soul is always beautiful. When Maori and pakeha do these things together, the double rainbow begins to shine.'[13]

This imprint of the author's hand on a copy of his book is rather like the relic of a saint: you want to put your hand on his hand. It does not entirely disarm my resistance to Baxter's moony new-age twaddle ('the soul is always beautiful'), but the gesture, which wins me over, has something in common with writing 'A man's body is a meeting house'. It brings us one degree closer to the signs of nature. We say that smoke is a natural sign because its relation to fire is immediate and causal. Signs of the body – a blush, a smile, a tear – appear to be immediate and natural expressions of our true feelings, although they are also, of course, the resource of every con-man.

Baxter, it hardly needs saying, is as much a prophet (or con-man) as he is a poet, and in each of these roles was concerned to dramatise and exhibit the progress of a Pakeha pilgrim from his home culture over into 'the Maori side of things', to a mixed space where, as he puts it, 'the double rainbow begins to shine'.[14] There are many people who venerate Baxter's memory and example; one need not suppose them to be dewy-eyed if they are moved by the simple sincerity of that phrase and that vision. Others are more likely to associate 'the double rainbow' with shallow hippy platitudes. To the debunkers, Baxter is a facile romantic in his too copious poetry and the scourge of soft targets in his broadsides against the establishment. I propose a third position: we may view Baxter's rhetoric and self-aggrandisement positively, not as an act to be seen through, but as an experiment in self-fashioning in which references to nature and the body act as talismans in the crossing of cultural boundaries.

In one of his late sestinas, Baxter imagines himself on the road to Jerusalem.

> I want to go up the river road
> Even by starlight or moonlight
> Or no light at all, past the Parakino bridge
> Past Atene where the tarseal ends
> Past Koroniti where the cattle run in a paddock
> Past Operiki, the pa that was never taken,
>
> Past Matahiwi, Ranana, till the last step is taken
> And I can lie down at the end of the road
> Like an old horse in his own paddock
> Among the tribe of Te Hau. Then my heart will be light
> To be in the place where the hard road ends
> And my soul can walk the rainbow bridge
>
> That binds earth to sky. In his cave below the bridge
> Where big eels can be taken
> With the hinaki, and the ends
> Of willow branches trail from the edge of the road
> Onto the water, the dark one rises to the light,
> The taniwha who guards the tribal paddock

And saves men from drowning. Down to Poutini's paddock
The goats come in winter, and trucks cross the bridge
In the glitter of the evening light
Loaded with coils of wire, five dogs, and wood they have taken
From a rotten fence. On the bank above the road
At the marae my journey ends

Among the Maori houses. Indeed when my life ends
I hope they find room in the paddock
Beside the meeting house, to put my bones on a road
That goes to the Maori dead. A gap I cannot bridge,
Here in the town, like a makutu has taken
Strength from my body and robbed my soul of light,

Because this blind porangi gets his light
From Hiruharama. The darkness never ends
In Pharaoh's kingdom. God, since you have taken
Man's flesh, grant me a hut in the Maori paddock
To end my life in, with their kindness as my bridge,
Those friends who took me in from the road

Long ago. Their tears are the road of light
I need to bridge your darkness when the world ends.
To the paddock of Te Whiti let this man be taken. (589–90)

The poem is written from the city, from 'Pharoah's Kingdom'. The road of deliverance is the river road to Jerusalem and the intertwined route of several other journeys: from darkness to light, from Pakeha to Maori, from life to death and from death to eternal life. In each of these pairs, there is a gap that may or may not be bridged. It either happens, as death happens, or requires a form of assistance to cross the gap. Just as the Taniwha restores those who are drowning from the river's dark to the light of day, the poet prays for a way through God's inscrutable darkness 'when the world ends'. The bridge spanning that final darkness is woven first of Maori kindness, and second, in an image that subtly recalls the rainbow of an earlier stanza, of illuminated Maori tears – 'Their tears are the road of light / I need to bridge your darkness when the world ends'. Tears making a rainbow, tears making a bridge; it is a lovely image of reciprocity, but it might well give us pause. It is one thing to recognise that the Pakeha road is built on the suffering of Maori, quite another to make the suffering of Maori into a road for Pakeha salvation. I don't suppose Baxter seriously intends this meaning, but his religious turn of mind, his fondness for scenarios of redemption and intercession, would encourage the misappropriation if it were not for a forceful and apparently decisive closing line: 'To the paddock of Te Whiti let this man be taken'.

A prose 'Confession to the Lord Christ', written around the time of this poem, also finds Baxter thinking about what the afterlife will hold for him. He wonders: 'Perhaps [God] will make room for me in the Maori Heaven . . . Te Kooti and Te Whiti and Rua and Ratana may take me in, men with many sins who loved their people – the people I also love.'[15] If James K. Baxter is in the Maori heaven, he would have to be there as a Pakeha. It is not that conversion is an inappropriate trope for the experience of discovery in culture: many Pakeha do feel 'born-again' as they learn from the Maori side of things – but Maori identity is established through whakapapa. It is possible to use ancestry figuratively ('To the paddock of Te Whiti let this man be taken'), but if a Pakeha aspires to become Maori, whether in a restricted role or as a whole person, then at some relatively arbitrary and often-stretchable point, a literal ancestor needs to be invoked. This is not some racialist blood quotum thing: it is merely our custom.

For the Pakeha native who belongs here, a parallel but different custom applies: a relationship to the natural world may, as it were, take the part of the Maori ancestor, and that relationship is readily augmented whenever nature is seen in association with something (anything) Maori. Whenever Baxter turns to a variation of that old theme – mainstream Pakeha culture is shallow; we need to find a deeper style of belonging – his utopian alternatives almost always involve a rhetorical coupling of something natural with something Maori. In the final line of the sestina, the nouns 'paddock' and 'Te Whiti' require and intensify each other, but I think there can be no doubt which is the more primary. One could vary the proper noun in the sestina's last line with only minor contextual loss – 'To the paddock of Te Kooti let this man be taken' – but the word paddock, by contrast, is sacrosanct. Imagine, for a moment, that the sestina's rules do not apply – is there a better word than paddock? Field, farm, land, pasture – a simple substitution will not do. House is only a little better, perhaps not as good as whare, but any Maori alternative would tip a carefully balanced line. Paddock is *le mot juste* and the most complex word in the poem. It is a local word, part of our Kiwi vernacular, but as it means a fenced section of farm land, it has great potential to stand in opposition to uncultivated nature. And from a historical point of view, a paddock might also stand in opposition to Maori ownership of their land; indeed, Te Whiti's policy as a resistance leader had been to break up paddocks and knock over fences on land confiscated by the Crown.

The major contrast in this poem, however, concerns the city and the countryside, and this rhetorical framework allows all the paddocks in this poem to become untrammelled and essential sites of nature. As such, the resonance of the word builds stanza by stanza, developing from simple natural images ('cattle run in a paddock', 'like a horse in his own paddock'), to particular sections of land ('Poutini's Paddock', 'the paddock beside the meeting house'), to an actual plot of land used metaphorically ('the Maori paddock'), and finally to a usage that has no literal reference at all. Not only is Te Whiti buried at Parihaka, but also the paddock mentioned is no longer an actual plot of land at all; Te Whiti has this paddock in much the same way that the Good Shepherd has a flock. The literal meaning is held at a distance, the historical associations are suppressed, but all those earlier connotations flood back in, allowing the 'paddock of Te Whiti' to become the very sign of all that is simple, real, authentic – and indigenous.

Te Whiti names an ideal – because more natural – Maori spiritual quality, while his paddock names an ideal – because more Maori – natural quality. A rhetorical jackpot is struck in these associations. Nature, in the Western tradition, often allows us to rise above divergent values in this way: it is inclusive because it pre-exists us, outlasts us and is bigger than our puny human world. We can also trespass against it. In a secular age, it is useful that Nature is a concept very like God. And when both Nature and God look like they belong more on 'the Maori side of things', we have a form of pastoral in which good Pakeha already belong on that side too. So long as you do not actually prefer the darkness of Pharoah's kingdom, Nature gives you a quasi-indigenous form of belonging. Right feeling is all.

It should be noted that a bridge imagined from one culture to another is a feature of colonial literature: Maori had to cross it to become civilised. But a bridge is also two-way: the traffic on Baxter's rainbow bridge goes from the Pakeha city across to Maori and to Nature. It is true that it is essentially the same bridge keeping Maori on essentially the same side, yet I also have to allow that Baxter's simple signs of nature could shift cultural boundaries for both Pakeha and Maori in ways that were honoured at his funeral and that I am bound to respect. But he leaves us with a difficulty: the problem is not so much that his vision of Maori is romantic, but that his vision of Nature is.

When Baxter imagines nature as sacred source and fountainhead, he places it beyond the world of change. But let us also keep in mind that New Zealand is the last major landmass to have been settled by humans. It is tempting to imagine that our natural world, or vast tracts of it, are much as they always were: that Nature is purer and more original here than in Europe or America. But there is not a square inch of so-called pristine nature left. A thousand years of human history have wholly remade our environment; perhaps nowhere else has environmental change been so concentrated, so rapid. For Baxter, nature is a catalyst that promotes cultural exchange and is itself unchanged. But that idea of an unchanging nature is imported from nineteenth-century aesthetics and – like gorse and oxalis, like sheep and kiwifruit – it becomes an accelerant of unpredictable change. When Baxter's poem moves from a peopled landscape to a progressively more spiritualised and abstract one, it draws on much the same culturescape as every other idealisation of New Zealand as a quintessential site of nature.

... Till you find your dream

Tourism New Zealand's long-running and triumphantly successful '100% Pure' campaign has made Nature our national brand.[16] The slogan's daring promise of a landscape with no artificial additives is visually reinforced by images that draw on the myth of a pristine environment – sandy coves, gentle bush, reflecting lakes – where one may experience relaxation and rejuvenation. '100% Pure' also suggests the maximum possible, the highest dose, the very peak of achievement, and gathers a second train of imagery to do with a physically challenging environment – wild surf, rushing river, craggy mountain top – where one engages in outdoor pursuits and adventure sports. Tourist nature, then, is a mix of the pristine and the wild: it offers (frequently in the same landscape) modes of engagement with the natural world which draw on earlier formations but outpace them. Contemporary wild nature has much in common with older scenarios of taming the land, but participants will not see themselves as conquerors and quellers of an inimical environment, but as thrill seekers. Pristine nature offers joys like those Blanche Baughan encountered on the Whanganui, but she found something more than a restful vacation in a landscape that blended native and exotic, Maori and Pakeha. Yet her own Tourist Board writing reminds us that we have a long history of packaging New Zealand as a quintessential site of nature, ostensibly for overseas visitors, but also for ourselves. A century later, should nature for tourists be the same as nature for us? Is it even possible to distinguish the country Pakeha belong to from the country promoted as '100% Pure' by Tourism New Zealand since 1999?

In April 2002, Helen Clark, then Prime Minister and formerly a Minister for Conservation in the Lange government, set aside five days to host a documentary for America's Travel Channel. The idea was that Peter Greenberg, chief correspondent for the channel, should arrive as a representative tourist and be shown round the country by the Prime Minister on a whirlwind tour of scenic attractions. The trailer for the programme promised 'a fast-paced, physically active, wet and wild tour of a country that exists on the threshold of a dream. And in the Royal Tour: New Zealand, Helen Clark will deliver that dream – she will, as head of state [sic], take us on an unprecedented tour of her country, the birthplace of bungee jumping – we'll be kayaking through remote fjords, skiing down glaciers, jet boating, fishing, and mountain climbing.'[17] As we watched our own Julie Andrews climb ev'ry mountain, ford ev'ry stream and arrive at the family bach for a barbecue, it was hard not to be reminded that what we now experience as nature in New Zealand had become faintly kitsch and increasingly bound up with the promotion of tourism.

Like Blanche Baughan's writing, the television documentary was made for overseas viewers by local guides who are likely to reveal more about their own sense of identification with people and place than they mean to. Where Baughan's narrative moved from the metropolitan to the local, 'The Royal Tour' documentary set out to celebrate local belonging but became hazy and globally oriented as it did so. One way to observe this is to compare its soundtrack with its visual information. Because a television documentary has a much greater need for images than words, there is always a potential lack of fit between what we see and what we hear. 'I come from heartland New Zealand', Helen Clark says, and an opening biographical segment explains who she is by showing us where she is from in a brief narrative composed of live interview footage, archival images (the baby photo, the parents' wedding photo, a class photo from school, and so on), as well as material not shot explicitly for this scene or even this programme, but which fills out the picture in a manner viewers will ideally regard as seamless. Yet when Helen Clark in voiceover explains her opposition to the Vietnam War, the illustrative material includes stock footage of protest from the 1981 Springbok tour. A New Zealander may notice that it is the wrong date and the wrong issue, but for a target audience of Americans, the incongruity is invisible and of no significance whatsoever.

If we continue to pay attention to what we notice and what a target audience might be likely to miss, patterns emerge, as if under infrared, that can tell us a lot about how we see ourselves in relation to the natural world. For example, the usual helicopter shots of scenic waterfalls in scenic Milford Sound are accompanied by a curiously foreboding voiceover:

Helen: The waters here plunge 700 feet into the dark icy depths.
Journalist: It looks a bit eerie. Sort of reminds me of the Loch Ness.
Helen: You never know what might lurk beneath these waters. Or above them. These waterfalls are among the highest in the world.
Journalist: Beautiful!
Helen: And treacherous!

People have been bitten by mosquitoes at Milford Sound, the manoeuvres of tourist buses are a constant danger, but I do not recall the last time an erring visitor fell from a waterfall or was devoured by a sea monster. Milford Sound gives rise to this improbable version of the sublime because the programme makers wished to counter a possible misperception among Americans that New Zealand is as boring as it is beautiful. As the journalist trembles at yet another vertiginous drop, as Helen Clark gives yet another laconic assessment of danger, the programme aims to portray a country so far from dull that 'thrill therapy' has become a national pastime. 'Apparently it's good for us', the PM enthuses as the Shotover Jet gathers speed. 'We all lead these stressed lives, and we get into these thrill experiences, and really get a high off it.' The irony is that the more we cultivate this image of ourselves as distinctly outdoorsy and adventurous, the more surely we reveal ourselves to be urban hobbits in need of a mild adrenalin fix, a people more like than different from the tourists we seek to attract.

A second visual discrepancy, if I may treat the concept just a little more loosely, involves the notion of wilderness and the paradox of attracting tourists to places they cannot go and to sights they will not actually see. Relatively few tourists, and few New Zealanders for that matter, will ever be in a position to see our landscape from the exciting point of view of a helicopter as it swoops along the coastline or banks over the snow-clad alps. Yet this extraordinarily artificial and mediated view of the environment is one I can call to mind at any time; this virtual experience of nature seems as spontaneous and as true as any other personal experience. Perhaps my early and repeated viewings of *The Sound of Music* are responsible; one of the very first films to use aerial photography in this way, its opening and closing shots of the Swiss Alps have a direct descendant in the National Film Unit's *This is New Zealand* (1970), several generations of Air New Zealand and Toyota advertisements, and in 'The Royal Tour' documentary. The swooping helicopter shot has become part of what New Zealand nature means for me; it is corny, but I still enjoy the thrill of seeming to fly free as a gannet over a landscape that is conventionally sublime and without human presence.

Fiordland National Park, Helen Clark explains, as the helicopter flies over it, consists of 'three million acres of virgin rainforest'. 'What

I love about it', she adds, 'is that there are no roads – and I hope they never build any.' The target audience will naturally assume the helicopter takes us to the very heart of this unspoiled domain, but our actual destination is the start of the Hollyford Track. Most people get there by car. We carry images of a pristine natural environment in our heads, but the DOC track we must drive to is manicured for visitors. The relation between tourist nature and pristine nature is a curious one. One ought to preclude the other, but tourist nature incorporates the pristine as a myth of origin and as a selling point. It is as if our actual experience of our environment was always being topped up with feelings and images associated with the generic empty landscape as seen from the air. We are uncomfortable with a peopled nature.

This is so in the wild environment as well. The most strenuous activity that Helen and Peter undergo is a long climb up an ice face. The tubby American journalist does a fine job of demonstrating that being hot and tired and breathless and wishing it would all end can nevertheless bring a great sense of personal accomplishment. He is like any town boy learning to do a physically challenging job in the backcountry. Helen Clark, on the other hand, is like an experienced labourer who knows and enjoys the rhythms of work. 'What you have to do', she advises, as she kicks another step into the snow, 'is concentrate on where you're putting your feet. You block your whole mind to everything else. It's actually very restful.' In this particular disjunction between how things look and how things are, it is interesting that wild nature becomes a zone where leisure and work start to feel like each other. This should strike us as odd, for in a society based on extractive and pastoral economies, work is now commonly thought of as the enemy of nature. And those who settled New Zealand have worked hard: few areas of this earth have been so massively transformed by human labour and machinery. But in scenic New Zealand, in tourist nature, the ordinary human business of altering the environment is put to one side; proper work, here, is off limits. But play that looks like work, leisure activity that makes us feel alive in our bodies and alert to the terrain, is welcome.

However, as Richard White, an historian of the American West, observes, the people who have a 'deep connection' to nature are often the very people whose work transforms and – arguably – damages nature: the farmer, the forestry worker, the orchardist, the hunter and, in our case, the exerciser of Maori customary rights, the tourism operator.[18] Hence, the perennial stand-off between urban environmentalists like Helen Clark (and me), and country folk who make their living from nature. Hence, too, our urban propensity to see nature as a realm apart: a wilderness zone ransomed from an everyday world where environmental values need not apply so strictly.

Nature, for Pakeha, becomes a 'terra nullius' without history, as Geoff Park argues;[19] and, as if that weren't problematic enough, nature also becomes, in Richard White's words, a park sectioned off for visitors who 'try to know through play what workers in the woods, fields, and waters know through work'.[20] But if our relationship to nature largely consists of recreation in specially demarcated zones, an activity we value intermittently and that has much less priority than our work, the environment as a whole is likely to suffer. Richard White and Geoff Park, whose arguments I am indebted to, both write as environmentalists who are critical of received wisdom about the meanings and value of wilderness, but it seems to me that their arguments apply equally well to my questions of Pakeha turangawaewae. We fondly remember the unending golden summers of childhood, but playing in nature does not give us a place to stand.

What nature for tourists does give us is a New Zealand that is distinctive in precisely the same way as a niche market in the global economy is distinctive. 'The Royal Tour' was the second programme in a series that began with King Abdullah II of Jordan hosting a guided adventure tour of his kingdom, and was followed by other episodes filmed in other countries with other heads of state. Nature, wherever it is, becomes somewhere we all travel to, a zone set aside for rest and recreation, and, thanks to scenery that is '100%' excellent for adventures and getting away from it all, our niche point of difference. This is a poor way to know an environment at risk, but it may be that there is a positive case to be made for the notion that we are all tourists in our own country – all, in this particular and I believe unacceptable sense, New Zealanders. Philip Fisher, a cultural historian of the United States, argues that all Americans are like new immigrants in his country's melting pot because the past has no special claim on them.[21] Each new generation creatively destroys the traditions and certainties of the generation that came before; old ways of life, like old technology, become rapidly obsolete. If we really were tourists in our own country, that would be our sense of the past too. We would know it as facts in a guidebook, or with the thinness of a television documentary, where it doesn't really matter if the images match the reality so long as the right feeling comes across. Is a New Zealand that only knows the present our home too?

Helen Clark, one of the politicians responsible for the economic reforms that have, in so many respects, recast New Zealand in the mould of Fisher's ever new America, does not live there, and neither do I. I doubt even those of us who are supposedly fed up with the special consideration Maori are supposedly afforded, and who want everyone to be treated the same, live there either. Here is a simple test of any new assimilationism: would a local director make a television documentary like 'The Royal Tour' and not have a 'special' place for Maori? We have seen what such a documentary might look like: it would have Milford Sound and the Snowy Alps and the Hollyford Track and bungee jumping, and it might even, as does 'The Royal Tour', have a young Maori woman, who makes nothing special of being Maori, guiding us down a 100-metre sink-hole to a Waitomo tourist attraction aptly known as the Lost World. But inclusion of a 'Maori element' comes with the territory. Without a welcome onto the marae, without a bit of haka and poi, without some acknowledgement of the special role of Maori in the identity of this place, 'The Royal Tour' would have been a culturally incompetent documentary. It is not the adequacy of any representation of Maori that is at stake in my argument, but its necessity, its taken-for-grantedness.

So how are Maori included in Helen Clark's Royal Tour? According to the principle of disjunction, a television documentary is always likely to get from A to B via C, D, and E, but in this programme, we travel from Queenstown to Abel Tasman National Park via Rotorua for a reason. The story of the arrival of the first European prompts a segue into history and a riot of visual/verbal disjunction as the programme tries, in just a few minutes of screen time, to convey a sense of our shared past. The narrative takes us from a hostile welcome – 'Peering back at [the Dutch navigators] were the ferocious tattooed faces of the Maori' – via an acknowledgement of the consequences of colonisation – 'Over time, the Maori couldn't stop the tide of the European colonisation and ultimately they lost much of their land' – to a present-day official welcome at Whakarewarewa, where people hongi and there are friendly words in the wharenui. The marae etiquette visually reinforces Helen Clark's statement, 'As two communities we've developed processes which see us continually in search of reconciliation between two peoples', and allows the programme to move on. 'The gracious Maori have welcomed us', says the journalist, 'and given us their blessings for a safe onward journey.' We then return to Abel Tasman National Park and Helen and Peter's kayaking adventure where, the voiceover tells us, 'we paddle to a small island offshore and are met by some of the natives'. Cut to cute seals.

The programme's detour into history and Maori issues has several judder bars for the local viewer, but perhaps the bumpiest moment concerns the challenge as the official party enter the marae. There are strong connections with what we have just seen and heard of the hostile welcome afforded Tasman and the warrior who now comes bounding down the path towards Peter, flourishing the taiaha with rapid skill, eyes bulging, tongue flashing like a lizard, as he kneels and lays down the dart of challenge. 'Don't take your eyes off that Maori warrior', barks Helen. And Peter, who must respond to this challenge, does not – not for a second. He looks anxious, looks as if he believes everything he's been told: that the challenge could easily go wrong, that welcome might switch to aggression. We see the challenge through his American eyes, and those eyes are not ours. We know how the challenge works, why it is done and what happens next; we expect the conventions to be followed respectfully, but we can also be sure that in this scene the American journalist is in no danger of violence. It is as if tangata whenua and Pakeha manuhiri had exchanged winks beforehand and allowed the overseas participant a small misapprehension about a ritual we value.

Knowing these things, knowing them as a kind of second nature, much as I can't help but know the words to most of *The Sound of Music*, is what I think gives Pakeha turangawaewae here. The levels of shared cultural knowledge that I am talking about are not profound. Nor need they be. Unlike nature, which offers no purchase for belonging when packaged as an ostensibly history-free zone, as a global attraction we all visit as tourists, this low-key knowledge of ours is site-specific and based in a structure that is always open to history. As we Pakeha welcome others in our turn, we might on occasion stand with the tangata whenua; it is good that the role of manuhiri is relational, as much about where you are as who you are. But in this book, oriented as it is towards the past, to acts of arrival and deeds of settlement, the question of Pakeha turangawaewae should remain a dart laid on the paepae. Others took up the challenge before us, but there will be no once-and-for-all moment that puts the ceremony of arrival and the problems of settling behind us. We are the Pakeha: the dart of challenge is at our feet. We must pick it up and pick it up time after time.

Part II *Landing*

OUCH: A WORD FROM A SHIP'S LOG. IN THE TWO DECADES BEFORE the Treaty of Waitangi, a trading schooner out of Hobart or Sydney, with a cargo of muskets, axes, fishhooks and cloth, might touch at the Hokianga, picking up foodstuffs and flax, remaining three or four days before continuing with the cruise. What might touching lead to? This light and tentative verb anticipates the many stronger acts of connection we might find in a thesaurus of settlement: to touch, to caress, to infect, to cheat, to improve, to confiscate, to madden, to overwhelm. But in the nautical instance, touching for cargo is soon followed by the carriage and the disembarkation of passengers who are coming ashore to stay, and they make a landing place or beachhead from which other landings, other exchanges, will follow. The landing place is neither the beach of first contact nor the strand of a settled region, but a middle ground enlarged and transformed by traffic coming across it each way.[1] It is not wholly a Maori place, nor yet a Pakeha place, but a cross-cultural frontier: a beach, a verge, a perimeter moving inland.

Neither those crossing the paepae of the beach nor those waiting to receive them was a homogeneous group, though each was inclined to see the other that way. To Maori, the incomers were an unpredictable race, easily upset by trifles yet blasé about the most serious matters. But they either had, or could be instrumental in obtaining, tools and weapons that within a generation had revolutionised both agriculture and warfare, tipping the balance of economic and military power into the desperate rivalries of the Musket Wars.

31

Some Pakeha were more useful than others. Missionaries, arriving early and desirous of doing good, hammered and sawed away in their pious stockades, only venturing forth – or so it might seem – to talk nonsense to slaves and to meddle; they required tolerance and careful handling if their potential for influence was to be massaged into production. The better sort of Pakeha was a genial and flexible person who treated Maori with discernment and respect, who did not take hospitality for granted, whose acumen and fairness could be relied on, who would act as one of the family. Those fitting the bill were a mixed bunch in European eyes. They include Jacky Marmon, the convict son of convict parents, who jumped from a Sydney brig in 1823 and found protection and a new life under the sponsorship of the prominent Ngapuhi chief, Muriwai. He married Raumati's daughter, became fluent in te reo and took an active part in Hongi Hika's campaigns against southern tribes. By the mid-1820s, we hear of him as an interpreter and middleman between ship and shore; by the mid-1830s, he was a builder and landowner – a Pakeha Maori success story, but a man without a future in the coming colonial world. Luridly known to posterity as 'Cannibal Jack', he is pictured in his declining years by the poet Kendrick Smithyman as 'a heavy headed horse-faced tattooed man / who wore habitually a top hat, and scared kids. / Every Christmas he tarred his hat.'[2] The old man's memoirs were written up for local newspapers in the 1880s, the last of the surviving accounts of 'the good old days' written or dictated by Pakeha Maori.[3] For the most part, these are blunt and reticent narratives, extending beyond 'I did this' and 'I did that' only in moments of self-exculpation or in addressing the saving hand of providence. But their lives provoke the imagination.

Arthur Thomson, our first historian, felt the spell on a number of occasions. On a visit to the upper Whanganui, a chief showed him a volume of Shakespeare and a classical dictionary, as well as a stone for grinding maize into flour – 'the property of his former Pakeha Maori'.[4] What consolations might that Prospero have found in his books? Was he appreciated as a storyteller? As a cook? On the banks of the Mokau River, by the grave of another Pakeha Maori, Thomson was shown a 'tattered English Prayer-book, the only property he left, and a half-caste girl gambolling in the river, the poor man's only child'.[5] What were the prayers of that non-communicant? What were his hopes for the child? The outlines of such a life are sketched a little more fully when Thomson encounters 'a good specimen of this almost extinct class' on a journey to Taupo, in the company of Major Hume, in 1852.

His residence resembled a whaler's hut, and stood on the bank of a beautiful river, in the midst of a peach orchard. He welcomed us into his house, and told his native wife to prepare food for us. After we had finished our repast, he called five half-caste children forward, and to each gave a portion of the food remaining. When night closed in, we all sat round the fire, and the Pakeha Maori grew talkative under the influence of a glass of grog we had given him. We found he had been a sailor, once a man-of-war's man, and was wrecked in 1828 at the mouth of the Waikato river. All hands but himself on board the vessel, which was a Sydney trader, perished. With dread he approached a village, and lingered on its outskirts until hunger conquered his terror of being eaten. Here food and kindness were bestowed on him, and the villagers requested him to stay among them. Having no alternative he consented. A wife was given him from the house of a chief, food was regularly prepared for his sustenance, and he was only required to conduct the tribe's foreign trade. Fire-arms were then in great demand, and conflicts frequently occurred from which he kept aloof. The want of salt was his greatest misery, and he heard of the missionaries in the north years before any of them visited the neighbourhood.

Soon after the foundation of Auckland, his power and influence ceased, and he was obliged to cultivate food with his own hands for the support of his family. In 1838 his first wife died, leaving him three boys and a girl; but he soon got another, the wife at his side, the mother of the five youngest children. He now lived by purchasing flax, rearing pigs, and curing bacon, which his son took to the Auckland market. He had no wish to change his life, as the savage world had treated him better than the civilised. . . . Next day we left the old man's house, and gladdened his wife's heart by giving each child a present. As our canoe was paddled up the river, the Pakeha Maori stood staring at us, and Major Hume said, when a bend of the river shut him out from our view, it was a painful thing to see a civilised man turned into a savage.[6]

It takes a more tutored imagination than Major Hume's to read beyond the verge of a life as tersely represented as this. William

Satchell, in his classic historical novel, *The Greenstone Door*, gave us one view of the Pakeha Maori as a Shakespeare-reading Victorian gentleman manqué. Ian Wedde, in the best of our more recent historical novels, *Symmes Hole*, imagines the life and thought patterns of James 'Worser' Heberley, an illiterate beachcomber whose cultural backsliding into the arms of a Maori matron would have brought more pain to the likes of Major Hume. But the English officer's comments are not merely disparaging. They also point to a set of reflections inevitably prompted by the very existence of Pakeha Maori, of those men on the verge. What does civilisation mean? How is it different from savagery? Can otherwise admirable people be cannibals? Might an Englishman degenerate into a lower form of humanity? Might Maori civilisation be hurried along? Or might the island traditions of Pacific peoples be closer to a harmonious social ideal than the industrial and riven West?

No nineteenth-century writer addressed these questions with more insight or subtlety than the young Herman Melville, a downwardly mobile scion of heroes of the American Revolution, who went to sea on a whaling ship, ran away at the Marquesas Islands and wrote up his adventures in his first novel, *Typee*. (Had it not been for a gammy leg, Melville would have shipped out with his companion Toby and reached the Bay of Islands in 1842, in time to view the Stars and Stripes fluttering from the stern post of Hone Heke's war canoe – the makings of another story.) Melville, his friend Hawthorne remarked, was notable for 'his freedom of view', by which he meant a quality stronger than mere open-mindedness.[7] Some people, like Major Hume, might travel the globe without ever testing the customary assumptions and outlooks of home; others relish a taste of life on the far side of their comfort zones. Melville was like that, and so too were the unlettered Ishmaels who crossed our beach to flourish quietly as the Pakeha Maori of their adopted hapu and iwi. But educated witnesses crossed the beach too, and among those who left a written account of their experiences, three stand out for me in their Melville-like capacity to relativise and vividly render their experience of the cross-cultural frontier. They are the artist Augustus Earle, who landed at the Hokianga in October 1827 and stayed for nine months at the Bay of Islands; the Pakeha Maori trader Frederick Maning, who came ashore at the Hokianga in July 1833 and, unlike Jacky Marmon, would successfully cross from the beach to colonial respectability as a judge in the Native Land Court; and finally Edward Shortland, doctor, magistrate, government official, who arrived in March 1841, and in the course of a long career wrote the most ethnographically insightful studies of Maori from the early-to-mid-contact period.

Phrases like 'ethnographically insightful' and 'freedom of view' are not generally accorded these early- and mid-nineteenth-century reporters. We tend to treat them as if they were locked up in the ideological assumptions of their time, as proto-racialists convinced of their own superiority, as misperceivers and maligners of Maori, as the literary accomplices of British imperialism. That view seems to me as simplisitc as the view it displaced: namely, that we might open these books as we might open a filing cabinet where the true facts of the case had been stored; that merely by perusing these writings, we see Maori for what they once were. I think readers who once missed the partiality of these early accounts are still apt to find their own political certainties reflected in these texts, though the message alters with the times.

The chapters that follow pursue a different adventure in reading: at once more trustful of those earlier sources, and more willing to find complex acts of witnessing in their hesitations, contradictions and silences. I will often pause, as these commentators themselves pause, to wonder how interpretation works as things and events cross the beach and cross time, losing parts of their significance and gaining others – like sovereigns worn as cheap earrings, or fishhooks worth more than gold coins. I will try to be alert, too, in the chapters that follow, to the difficulty that lies behind good writing from the cross-cultural frontier. Any witness can give a description, but Maning, Earle and Shortland are more than usually alive to the ways in which any description is likely to fall short, and so give us narratives of epistemological suspense, incorporating their doubts, wonderings, hesitations, leaps and digressions. They write non-fiction, but it is in this genre (not poetry or fiction) that works of lasting literary value in English were written in nineteenth-century New Zealand. (Not every poem is as bad as 'God Defend New Zealand', but I mention our anthem in passing as a measure of the competition.) That changes, of course, around the turn of the century, and I end this section on the cross-cultural frontier with a discussion of *The Greenstone Door* (1914), an historical novel set between the 1830s and the 1860s: one of the first to revisit the 'good old times' before the triumph or calamity of settlement, and to associate the beach, the verge, these in-between places, with the glimmer of possible futures and the glamour of lost causes.

CHAPTER TWO

Augustus Earle and the Secret of Cannibalism

Cannibals? who is not a cannibal? I tell you it will be more tolerable for the Fejee that salted down a lean missionary in his cellar against a coming famine; it will be more tolerable for that provident Fejee, I say, in the day of judgment, than for thee, civilized and enlightened gourmand, who nailest geese to the ground and feastest on their bloated livers in thy pate-de-foie-gras.
– Herman Melville, Moby-Dick

HOW DO WE KNOW MAORI WERE CANNIBALS?[1] MOST PAKEHA WOULD say the European archive puts the question beyond doubt: from the time of Cook's voyages to the time of Titokowaru's war, every observer who was in a position to say Maori were cannibals does say they were. And Maori say so themselves: legend tells of the origins of cannibalism, oral traditions recall who ate and was eaten, and there are numerous lip-smacking references in waiata to the consumption of human flesh. Of course, relishing the idea of eating one's enemy in a song need not be understood literally, just as, in a different way, a nineteenth-century European account of cannibalism is never simply a literal report, but is bound to be coloured by cultural associations to do with savages and savagery. Today, only the unenlightened would regard Maori of the pre- and early-contact period as savages, but it remains part of our common knowledge that cannibalism was once an institutionalised and customary practice among them. Many of us will have heard a teacher explain in a matter-of-fact sort of way that Maori in the olden days were man-eaters, not because they lusted after human flesh, but only to ingest and transform the mana of a defeated enemy. If we were lucky, this piece of information might be capped by a story: about long-pig, about sailors being too salty or, my own favourite (though it comes from Fiji), about the schooner captain who, at a feast where he felt obliged 'to do as the Romans do', accepted an invitation to eat a baked hand. The captain, mastering a sensation of queasiness, began to gnaw tentatively at that fleshly part of the palm just below the thumb when, drawn by their tendons, the fingers of the cooked hand closed upon the eater's own face!

I said my story came from Fiji but I expect it is good enough to have come from anywhere. Gruesome stories about the cannibalism of others have been in circulation at least since Homer – and it is possible that our apparently objective and disinterested knowledge of the practice continues the imaginary and symbolic work performed by those older stories. Elsewhere, there has been a steady erosion of confidence in the notion that any colonised peoples were ever actually cannibals.[2] Cannibalism, it is now widely argued, is an old-world myth about new worlds. The dietary preferences of the indigenous peoples of the Americas, Africa, Asia, Australia and Oceania have all at some point been the object of grisly speculation, but the so-called facts of their cannibalism generally turn out, on a sceptical reassessment, to depend on a mélange of misinterpretation and misrepresentation, and are always refracted by the distorting haze of the reporter's cultural values. That particular argument has never taken off in New Zealand, but it has been made, on our behalf as it were, by several prominent postcolonial scholars.[3] Many New Zealanders will approach their findings with misgivings: it seems ethnocentric of those overseas experts to regard cannibalism as a slur, and perverse to doubt so tenaciously the existence of an unsurprising and well-documented practice. Eating people, we reckon, is not a big deal – it all depends on the culture you're in.

Two apparently conflicting verdicts agree on this score: if, for the New Zealander, cannibalism is an accepted part of traditional Maori culture, for the postcolonial critic, an ungrounded certainty about the cannibalism of others is a feature of Western imperialist culture. Either position finds support in an eyewitness account left by the travelling artist Augustus Earle in his *Narrative of a Nine Months' Residence in New Zealand*, a text that, on the one hand, presents the postcolonial sceptic with 'ocular proof' of Maori cannibalism, but, on the other, challenges the credulity of anyone who would take its colonialist assumptions at face value. I shall approach Earle's story from a rather different angle and with a slightly different problem in mind: it is not that I have difficulty believing cannibalism existed – it is our faith in the explanatory power of culture that I have trouble with.

Consumed by Doubt

For the postcolonial sceptic, cannibalism is an instance of a more general process by which the West's written record of other peoples overtakes the actualities it describes. In his great work *Orientalism*, Edward Said offers a suggestive analogy of this process.

> A book on how to handle a fierce lion might . . . cause a series of books to be produced on such subjects as the fierceness of lions, the origins of fierceness, and so forth. Similarly, as the focus of the text centers more narrowly on the subject – no longer lions but their fierceness – we might expect that the ways by which it is recommended that a lion's fierceness be handled will actually *increase* its fierceness, force it to be fierce since that is what it is, and that is what in essence we know or can *only* know about it.
>
> A text purporting to contain knowledge about something actual, and arising out of circumstances similar to the ones I have just described, is not easily dismissed. Expertise is attributed to it. . . . Most important, such texts can *create* not only knowledge but also the very reality they appear to describe.[4]

Said is not obliged to deny that lions can be dangerous in order to affirm that books and writing play a role in constructing their fierceness. Similarly, if we were to pursue a parallel between the cannibalism of Maori and the fierceness of lions, we needn't suppose anything about any actual practice in order to call attention to its massive overshadowing by another kind of reality altogether. Here, at the tail end of that process, is an example by Reay Tannahill that is almost all shadow.

> The aborigines of Australia – who maintained their ancient way of life until well into the twentieth century – ate human flesh for any one of a

number of reasons. It was a sacrificial ritual, it was good magic, a symbol of revenge, a sign of respect for the dead. . . . Sensitive, emotional, inclined to be gentle, the Australian aborigine differed greatly from the Maori of New Zealand, whose wars and cannibalism were marked by the same jaunty ferociousness as those of the Fijians (to whom, of course, they were related). Absorbing an enemy's strength was again the primary motive for people-eating, although one authority went so far as to suggest that the Maoris' basically vegetarian diet must undoubtedly have encouraged the despatch of raiding parties in search of stray humans to liven up the menu. . . . [But] missionaries who feared they might be popped in the cooking pot had very little to worry about. A hungry man would be more likely to go to a neighbouring tribe for his dinner, since black men had a far more agreeable flavour than white. Even so, the Maoris did manage to force a white man down occasionally. When they killed the unfortunate Captain Grant during the course of 'Heke's war', they dried and ate his flesh with the object of reducing the *mana*, or supernatural power, of the rest of his force.[5]

This extract from a 1996 study swallows its colonial sources whole and indiscriminately. The author perhaps missed Michael Pickering's 1995 investigation of some 482 colonial Australian accounts, in which he found plenty of hearsay about piles of bones but no reliable eyewitness or forensic evidence that Aboriginal peoples were ever cannibals.[6] It is not only the colonial sources that are recycled uncritically; old attitudes come through as well. Tannahill writes confidently of *the* Aborigine, *the* Maori, *the* Fijian, in a manner that owes less to the concept of culture than to an older anthropology of racial types. Cannibalism, she proposes, is a common trait of Fijians and their Maori relations – blithely muddling geography as well as genetics. Her anecdote about Captain Grant is acknowledged to come from F. E. Maning's *History of the War in the North*, a work that might seem authoritative but which is in fact a complex literary narrative that uses the persona of a native chief for satirical and polemical as well as historical and ethnographic ends.[7] The Pakeha Maori's anecdotes were regarded as gold-dust by late Victorian anthropologists, and have often been repeated, but they cannot be taken on trust. The breezy sensationalism of Tannahill's writing might also come from Maning but it is fairer to say it comes with the territory – from a popular tradition of helmeted explorers immersed in the cooking pot. Even though various alternative notions of the significance of cannibalism are introduced, this is a cartoon version of black appetite and whites on the menu.

The sceptic argues that all European accounts of cannibalism are every bit as unreliable as the example I have just quoted, relying as they do on a snowballing of rumour, credulity and prurience. If we accept that judgement, then we need no longer be impressed by the weight of opinion affirming that Maori were cannibals – most of that opinion booms in an echo-chamber and is worthless. We might also exclude from consideration any documented cases of survival cannibalism and atrocity cannibalism, which, by definition, must be exceptional, and are therefore good indications that even though acts of cannibalism might occur from time to time, as they do in the West, they do not represent the institutionalised practice of a people.

That leaves two main classes of early European document: those recounting Maori confessions of cannibalism, and eyewitness reports. These are not as numerous, or as self-evident, as might be supposed. A sceptical reader of Cook's voyages and other records of early encounter has reason to regard the many Maori admissions of cannibalism reported in those documents as untrustworthy. In response to pressing and repeated inquiry, natives the world over have denounced their evil warlike neighbours as eaters of human flesh. Cook quickly found that Maori followed this pattern, and was wise enough not to trust it. But Maori, especially when badgered or frightened or kidnapped, also confessed that they were themselves eaters of other people, and even, in a bizarre experiment on board the *Resolution* in 1773, ate a newly roasted portion of human flesh in front of the European witnesses who cooked it. In all these circumstances, the possibility of cross-cultural misunderstanding is so great, it would be unsafe to convict Maori of cannibalism on this form of evidence – and again this did not entirely escape those early European chroniclers. On the *Endeavour* voyage, for example, the crew of one boat encountered a Maori canoe and learned that a girl had recently been lost, and very possibly eaten, while a second boat met a canoe whose people admitted eating a girl the day before. Joseph Banks put two and two together: 'I am inclined to believe that our two boats . . . saw one and the same canoe and only differently interpreted the conversation of the people, as they know only a few words of the language, and eating people is now always the uppermost Idea in their heads.'[8] On the second voyage, William Wales observed how situations like these only showed 'how far we are liable to be misled by Signs, report, & prejudice'.[9] What counted was the evidence of their own senses, and on each of Cook's voyages, baskets of roasted human flesh provided it.

Yet eyewitness discoveries of cannibalism present their own special set of interpretative problems. There is usually no reason to believe the account is false or mistaken in any simple way – those are human remains, they have been cooked, the flesh has been cut away – the problem is more one of relating the 'evidence' to a context that would explain it. An early passage from Augustus Earle's *Narrative* illustrates the difficulty.

> I had not rambled far, before I witnessed a scene which forcibly reminded me of the savage country in which I then was . . . . The sight to me so appalling was, that of the remains of a human body which had been roasted, and a number of hogs and dogs were snarling and feasting upon it! I was more shocked than surprised, for I had been informed of the character of the New Zealanders long before my arrival amongst them; still, the coming suddenly and unexpectedly upon a sight like this completely sickened me of rambling, at least for that day, and I hastened back to Mr Butler's, eager to enquire into the particulars of the horrid catastrophe.
>
> That gentleman informed me that the night of the arrival of our ship, a chief had set one of his kookies (or slaves) to watch a piece of ground planted with the koomera . . . in order to prevent the hogs committing depredations upon it. The poor lad, delighted with the appearance of our vessel, was more intent on observing her come to an anchor than upon guarding his master's property, and suffered the hogs to ramble into the plantation, where they soon made dreadful havoc. In the midst of this trespass and neglect of orders, his master arrived! The result was certain; he instantly killed the unfortunate boy with a blow on the head from his stone hatchet. Then ordered a fire to be made, and the body to be dragged to it, where it was roasted and consumed.[10]

In a similar situation, many travellers – and many armchair travellers – would suppose they had been presented with evidence of cannibalism, that Earle has come across the discarded scraps of a savage meal. Mistakes of that order were commonly made: mortuary practices, the dismembering and cleaning of bones, the smoking of heads, everything to do with the Polynesian treatment of corpses, could present itself in terms of the European butchery or kitchen and yet have wholly other contexts. In this passage, Earle, quite scrupulously, does not mention the C word. The evidence is not necessarily the reality – but by choosing words like roasting and consumed, he indicates the residue of cannibalism as an interpretation that has irresistibly made sense of what he sees.

It is not just that there are often alternative explanations for what might look like the remains of a cannibal feast: on a subsequent occasion, Earle understands that rather than bury an executed slave, the body would be left as food for animals (97). The sceptic's more subtle point is that for the European observer cannibalism is like a card that cannot but be played. Even when it is played only to be discounted, having the card in one's hand still makes a difference. It is almost as if those remains were lying in wait for Earle, and in the instant before he saw them, had arranged themselves under the sign of the cannibal.

In a more elaborate version of this argument, Gananath Obeyesekere contends that 'the British *discourse* on cannibalism produced, in very complicated ways, the Maori *practice* of cannibalism'.[11] Although he believes little can be known about pre-contact practices, he suggests that Maori and other Polynesians traditionally 'did not practice cannibalism, but instead practiced an anthropophagy (displaced or real) associated with human sacrifice'.[12] This limited and highly ritualised form of 'cannibalism' might involve the singeing and consumption of body parts by a tohunga, the feigned or actual swallowing of an eyeball by a victorious chief, or other practices quite distinct from the 'horrid banquet' of European fantasy. But, by many accounts, something much closer to the banquet or ritual feast was the practice of Maori at the time of the Musket Wars. This was not, in Obeyesekere's view, an amplification of their existing practices, but a transformation in the meaning and nature of traditional anthropophagy through contact with the British. The mechanisms of this transformation are obscure, but Obeyesekere mentions 'the crucial act' of the killing and eating of Marion Du Fresne, and a year later, of the *Adventure*'s boat crew at Grass Cove – incidents he views in psychological terms as 'an introjection of the Other, in this case the power of the aggressor', and in political terms as an early act of resistance that 'resulted in a revitalization of Maori cannibalism and parallel change in its orientation into a more pronounced anthropophagy'.[13] The missionaries, in this view, were wrong about Maori cannibalism: it was not the Devil, but the British, who made them do it.

Obeyesekere is most illuminating in the way in which he takes aspects of the sceptic's argument a step or two too far. Many early European accounts of cannibalism have no place for Maori agency. Obeyesekere, among other readers, is right to redress the balance by imagining, for example, how things might have seemed to a captive Maori participant in that strange experiment on board the *Resolution*. But he sees a wishful politics of Maori resistance everywhere, as their mimicry of Euro-cannibalism becomes 'a weapon of the weak to keep European intruders away from native homes and habitations' – an unlikely development at a time when Maori would compete for the possession of European 'intruders'.[14] That the actual practice of Maori is refracted through a widespread discursive construction of cannibalism seems undeniable and consequential. The step too far is to convert discursive effects into implausible causes: the conspicuous cannibalism of the Musket Wars makes sense as an adaptation to British tools and weaponry, not as an adaptation to British discourse. Another, particularly valuable insight, is that cannibalism is a sign that travels between Europeans and Maori, and that not only are the meanings of that sign not the same on each side, they are also likely to be mutually transformed as they pass from one side to the other. As Greg Dening put it, 'Things cross the beach partially, without their fuller meanings.'[15] This is a dynamic view in which neither Europeans nor Maori are enveloped by their culture – but Obeyesekere's argument supposes such massive levels of cultural preordination, his explanations for change are correspondingly far-fetched and weak.

The art historian E. H. Gombrich maintained that 'The innocent eye sees nothing' – we see what, in one way or another, we are disposed to see.[16] The sceptical reader of cannibal discourse has this half right.

The challenge is not to prove over and over that the innocent eye sees nothing, or to suppose we see only what we are disposed to see, but to see seeing better.

The Mysterious X

On one level, what we see in Augustus Earle's *Distant View of the Bay of Islands* is like any tourist's snapshot: the image links sightseer and place in a manner that says, 'I was there'; or, as Earle puts it in his *Narrative*, 'having at length attained the summit of a hill, we beheld the Bay of Islands, stretching out in the distance'.[17] What we can also see is a disposition to see things a certain way. The whole scene – the empty grassy hills, helpful natives, the clouds picturesquely framing the traveller's destination – might be regarded as a stock representation of the colonial landscape from the viewpoint of one who is monarch of all he surveys. We have the impression that everything has been arranged for the white man who has come to take in the view.

The land that his eye dominates is empty: it stretches out before him, pliant and full of potential, as if waiting for the improving attentions of farm and plough. Our eyes are well schooled at seeing the frame of colonial values and assumptions accompanying such a representation; if we look closer, the images often turn out to be less univocal and more complex. In this painting, for instance, a carved figure gives notice of a different way of seeing. Earle describes the carving in the *Narrative*:

We had travelled all day through a country in which every object we saw was of a character that reminded us forcibly of the savage community we were with . . . . sometimes we beheld an uncouthly carved figure, daubed over with red ochre, and fixed in the ground, to give notice that one side of the road was tabooed. (73)

Whenever we refer to something on the far side of a cultural boundary as 'taboo', we are using a word that comes into English through Cook's voyages. The Maori word is tapu: a rich and resonant concept that Earle would have known partially as part of the cross-cultural pidgin of the beach. In his understanding, when crops are sown, the ground 'is *tabooed*, that is, rendered sacred, by men appointed for that service, and it is death to trample over or disturb any part of the consecrated ground' (63). Earle's carved figure carries this particular meaning and is a connotative sign of the 'savage community' he was with. But in the very height from which both landscape and the European traveller are viewed, it is obvious the landscape is seen from a zone of prohibition: from the tapu side of the road.

First, a colonial spectator's view, and now this second view, a view that sees everything the white man in the picture sees, but also sees him from the unseen – tapu – side of the road. Tapu is both in the picture and outside it as a property of its frame. What the white man in the picture doesn't see is there nonetheless; it is something that escapes and conditions his (and our) way of looking. Despite the presence of the carved figure, despite the designation 'tapu', it is not simply Maori space, and despite the obvious colonial themes, it is not simply European space either. The key detail is the way the observer is himself seen by what escapes his view. Only the European figure is affected: it takes that square-on back, viewed from a raised elevation, to connote a certain vulnerability, a blind spot, in the position of the viewer who, from this angle, is no longer monarch of all he surveys. What sees him, what sizes him up, belongs in a space derived from, but, unsettlingly, not quite of Europe. Let us call this the space of the mysterious X.

There are several aspects to this space. The mysterious X is included in the colonial view as a blind spot; it is that point beyond the painting where the protagonist is seen from a position he does not see. It is also our space: it is not inaccessible, it is on the viewer's side of the painting, as it were. Then again, it is also what is on the far side of a border – an X, an unknown value. There is an accustomed frame, but also, on the far side of a cultural boundary, there is another frame, another way of looking: you don't know what things look like from there, but you know that you are among the things taken in by that view, and the sensation is of the sort we associate with goosebumps – it might be thrilling but it might also seem distressing, even menacing. When the effect is disturbing, it can be reduced by finding a more familiar name for the mysterious X – names from the drawers labelled 'stereotypes' and 'taboos'. The mysterious X becomes less mysterious, less troubling, as soon as it starts to look like a stereotype or can be associated with responses to familiar taboo areas, such as those involving our food, our bodies and our death.

Ocular Proof

Like most travellers, Earle reached New Zealand having already 'heard a great deal respecting the splendid race of men' he was to encounter (57). He would have gathered from Cook's journals and other narratives that Maori were cannibals but, in the spirit of Enlightenment anthropology, has no difficulty pronouncing them a 'splendid race' all the same. This phrase is capable of meaning both what they look like and what they are like; in the wobble between the two are interpretative problems that not only concern Earle, but also continue to haunt subsequent assessments of races and cultures.

When Earle is explaining his motives for visiting New Zealand, he uses both 'splendid' and 'race' in particular senses. 'Splendid' is an artist's word: he has met several Maori in Sydney, and is 'anxious to see a number of them together, to judge whether (as a nation) they were finer in their proportions than the English' (57). On arrival he readily discerns, 'with the critical eye of the artist' (57), that they are. Indeed, the *Narrative* often makes us aware of that artist's eye in the many comparisons between the stature of Maori and the statuary of antiquity, in his artist's delight in an unclothed world and his contempt for the missionaries who 'obscure the finest human forms under a seaman's huge clothing' (73). When Earle refers to 'race', the term does not carry the narrower racialist meanings it would acquire later in the century, but involves distinctions that are a compound of the physical and the moral. In the following passage, for example, Earle separates various groups of people he has encountered on his travels into three 'races' or 'nations' – his own, and two others.

> I have known Indians in America from the north to the south, – the miserable idiotic Botecooda of Brazil, the fierce warrior of Canada, and the gentle and civilised Peruvian, yet in their features and complexions they are all much alike. I observed their statures altered with their different latitudes. The Chilians and the Canadians being nearly the same, in figure tall, thin, and active, their climate being nearly the same, although at the two extremes of America; while those living between the equinoxes are short, fat, and lazy. I am persuaded that these South Sea islanders, though so nearly of the same complexion, still are not of the same race; laziness being the characteristic of the American Indian from north to south, while the New Zealanders are laborious in the extreme, as their astonishing and minute carvings prove. The moment the Indian tasted intoxicating spirits his valour left him, he became an idiot and a tool in the hands of the white man. Here they have the utmost aversion to 'wine or strong drink', and very often severely take us to task for indulging in such an extraordinary and debasing propensity, or, as they call it, 'of making ourselves mad'; but both nations are equally fond of tobacco. (57–58)

These generalisations are lightly made and might have seemed tendentious in their own time, but the general categories of difference Earle employs, and their respective weightings, have the imprecision of common sense. 'Race', a vague word, is interchangeable with 'nation', another vague word: both indicate people of a common stock. In the face of human variety, what are the telling markers of commonality? Language and custom do not count for Earle – there would be thousands of American 'races' if they did. Geographic limits have some bearing on the boundaries of race, 'features and complexion' obviously need to be taken into account, but as climate can modify appearance, Earle locates the unity of a race inwardly, in terms of basic dispositions such as Indian laziness or Maori industry. Earle's choice of words for the essential characteristics of a people indicates the centrality of moral virtues and failings in the way he maps difference. The categories would seem immutable to him – laziness is the same the world over – but he is not one-sided in their application, as sober Maori are distinguished from boozy Englishmen. There is no precise way of determining the point at which mere behaviour becomes an index of essential character: a weakness for alcohol is a racial quality, but Earle does not suppose a liking for tobacco divides nation from nation. As Freud said, 'sometimes a cigar is just a cigar' – but a cannibal is never just a cannibal.

There can be many soft boundaries in a world in which races are separated from other races in terms of their essential moral characteristics. Earle, as easy a traveller as Melville, immensely enjoyed the experience of crossing these boundaries and, like Melville, invited opprobrium by condemning the doctrinaire and frosty behaviour of the missionaries. But even for the personable and cosmopolitan artist, some boundaries could never be crossed. One morning, late in January 1828, Earle learned that a runaway slave girl had been put to death and that her body was being prepared for the oven. He and Robert Duke, a whaling captain on extended shore leave, knew the girl: a pretty sixteen-year-old, who had been recently employed to collect wood at their house on Kororareka beach. When she was returned to Matauwhi Bay, the chief – 'a general favourite with us all' (114) – had tied her to a post, shot her through the heart and given orders for her body to be made ready for a feast. Earle and Captain Duke reacted, albeit belatedly, in an Indiana Jones and the Temple of Doom kind of way: they must save her! But their motives were mixed: they wanted to stop proceedings, but they were also 'resolved to witness this dreadful scene' (112). In the preceding months, the more Earle had grown to admire his Maori friends, the more he had come to doubt their cannibalism, but he now had a chance to put a controversial matter beyond doubt. A policy of commotion and confrontation would, he and Duke decided, only end in Maori denying the whole affair; so, keeping the news to themselves, the two men sneaked towards the village in search of 'ocular proof' (116). It is a curious phrase to use. It comes, of course, from Shakespeare: ocular proof – to at last believe something incredible because you have seen it with your own eyes – is what the jealous Othello demands from Iago. Yet, there is irony in Earle's use of the phrase, for Othello, as Geoffrey Sanborn points out, is easily misled through the very strength of his desire to have evidence of his wife's infidelity.[18] Can the following discovery scene be trusted, or is Earle the victim of his own horrified projections?

> As we approached, we saw evident signs of the murder which had been perpetrated; bloody mats were strewed around, and a boy was standing by them actually laughing: he put his finger to his head, and then pointed towards a bush. I approached the bush and there discovered a human head. My feelings of horror may be imagined as I recognized the features of the unfortunate girl I had seen forced from our village the preceding evening!
>
> We ran towards the fire, and there stood a man occupied in a way few would wish to see. He was preparing the four quarters of a human body for a feast; the large bones, having been taken out, were thrown aside, and the flesh being compressed, he was in the act of forcing it into the oven . . . .
>
> Here stood Captain Duke and myself, both witnesses of a scene which many travellers have related, and their relations have invariably been treated with contempt; indeed, the veracity of those who had the temerity to relate such incredible events has been every where questioned. In this instance it was no warrior's flesh to be eaten; there was no enemy's blood to drink, in order to infuriate them. They had no revenge to gratify; no plea could they make of their passions having been roused by battle, nor the excuse that they eat their enemies to perfect their triumph. This was an action of unjustifiable cannibalism. (113)

Earle and Duke then endeavoured to persuade the chief to give up his 'infernal banquet' (114). Whetoi (named Atoi in Earle's text) denied he had any such plans, but soon freely acknowledged his intention to eat the girl as soon as she was sufficiently cooked. The conversation involved a lengthy disquisition on cooking times and the desired tenderness of the flesh: come morning, Earle was told, her flesh would be 'as tender as paper' (114) – and the chief tore a piece of paper by way of illustration. But behind this frankness was a ruse, revealed when Whetoi's sister whispered in Earle's ear that the feast was timed not for the next morning but for sunset.

We left Atoi, and again strolled towards the spot where this disgust-ing mess was cooking. . . . After some time spent in contemplating the miserable scene before us, during which we gave full vent to the most passionate exclamations of disgust, we determined to spoil this intended feast . . . . I ran off to our beach . . . collecting all the white men I could . . . and each having provided himself with a shovel or a pickaxe, we repaired in a body to the spot. Atoi and his friends had by some means been informed of our intention, and they came out to prevent it. He used various threats to deter us, and seemed highly indignant; but as none of his followers appeared willing to come to blows and seemed ashamed that such a transaction should have been discovered by us, we were permitted by them to do as we chose. We accordingly dug a tolerably deep grave; then we resolutely attacked the oven. On removing the earth and leaves, the shocking spectacle was presented to our view, – the four quarters of a human body half roasted. During our work clouds of steam enveloped us, and the disgust created by our task was almost overpow-ering. (114–15)

Sanborn maintains that what Earle finds on digging up the oven is more like Iago's planted handkerchief than clear and certain evidence. It does not necessarily follow that the dismembered body has been placed in the oven in preparation for a feast, he argues, for it is 'entirely possible to read that scene as a terrorist hoax, both capitalizing and commenting on Earle's credulity'.[19] Sanborn has not plucked this theory out of the air: he has 'ocular proof' of his own that Maori of Kororareka practised that kind of deception – and from Earle himself. Two young men from Tikopia, with long tresses of bright sulphur-coloured hair, had taken passage from that overcrowded island and would have been happy to be put ashore anywhere – except Kororareka.

These poor creatures, upon landing, shook with fear, and trembled greatly when they beheld the New Zealanders, whose character for cannibalism had reached even their remote island: when our friend George went up to them, and lifted up (in order to examine closely) the curious mass of hair in which they were enveloped, they burst into a passionate fit of tears, and ran up to us for protection. The New Zealanders, with characteristic cun-ning, perceiving the horror they had created, tormented them still more cruelly, by making grotesque signs, as if they were about to commence devouring them . . . (159)

In both scenes, Sanborn argues, Maori recognise others recognising them as cannibals: they can deny the practice, but they can also manipulate the signs of cannibalism for their own ends, perhaps for amusement, perhaps as a shield of terror distracting a hostile imperial gaze – much as the Ngati Ruahine leader, Titokowaru, in his wars against the Pakeha, would later use cannibalism to inflame his enemies and so bait a trap.[20] In its own way, I suspect this resourceful argument is as much enmeshed in a Western discourse about cannibalism as the colonial understandings it seeks to dispute. Indeed, in the academies of America and Europe it may well be difficult to read Earle and not be reminded of an influential line in postcolonial thinking – concerning the mimicry of natives[21] – in a manner that recalls Said's parable about the fierceness of lions.

I do accept, however, that the postcolonial sceptic is right to insist that what Earle saw was not Maori cannibalism. What he saw was a mysterious X. Neither Earle nor I know its value as a Maori of that place and time would have known it; but, in acknowledging the common fact of difference, I am falling well short of opposing insider to outsider forms of knowledge. That opposition is often made in and around our experience of cultural difference, but although I am content to talk of local or insider knowledge, I do not believe it is ring-fenced, nor do I accept that the position of outsider is as limiting as is often supposed. When Earle, as an outsider, sees a mysterious X, we have a more complex structure made up not only of a colonial view (the simulacrum of cannibalism-as-savagery that Earle sees in the scene) but also of those elements of the scene and its frame that disclose what the viewer does not see and allow other viewers to see him seeing.

Before examining each of these aspects in turn, I would like to revisit the scene in another telling. A few days after the events Earle describes, Duke gave a verbal account to the missionary William Williams, whose diary entry for 31 January 1828 reads:

A shocking instance of cruelty was mentioned by captain Duke of the ship 'Sisters' a few days ago; to which he was witness. Atoi, a chief, had a female slave who ran away a short time before: at length he saw her sitting among some natives at Kororareka, very near her master's home: he led her away, tied her to a tree, and shot her dead. Captain Duke heard of the circumstances and went out to see what the case was; when he found the body of the girl under preparation for the native oven, the large bones of the arms and legs having been cut out. In answer to his expostulations, they said it was not his concern, and that they should act as they pleased. He returned to his dwelling to call to his assistance Mr Earl an artist from Port Jackson who is now staying with him, and returning to the spot with two spades they carried away the body without molestation, which had now been put into the oven and buried it. It was said that the people dug up the body in the night and eat it but it is not certain this was the case.[22]

Although Earle is a mere spade carrier in this account, the two stories agree in their essentials: a girl was killed, she was baked, and would have been eaten but for the interference of Pakeha who dug up the body and buried it. What Williams's account lacks is the attention to the act of witnessing that Earle's written account so vividly records. It takes the distance of third-person narration to condense Earle's many 'passionate exclamations of disgust' into the missionary's encapsulating phrase, 'a shocking instance of cruelty'. In Sanborn's view, Earle 'magnifies the signs of cannibalism in order to legitimate the tableau of humanity frozen in horror by the spectacle of savagery'.[23] No doubt this is part of the effect, but those exclamations of horror and disgust have another function too: they do not just mark the far side of a cultural boundary, separating a civilised us from a cannibal them in a frozen ideological scene, they are also uttered like spells that make it safe for an observer to be having this extreme experience in the first place. It seems to me that Earle quotes Shakespeare for precisely this reason: he is most like Othello in the extremity of his compulsion to see what he also does not want to see. Part of him wants to stay back, but disgust keeps him safe as he confronts the 'shocking spectacle' of a human being reduced to meat. It is a scenario in which every Western taboo around death is intensified: we can suppose there is true horror, true nausea, when what we most want to keep away from us – the lifeless corpse we hesitate even to touch – crosses the body's boundaries in sights and smells that catch in Earle's throat.

This is how Earle experiences cannibalism. What he doesn't see is a context in which the event occurs: or rather, he is aware of several contexts that might apply, but as none of them fits, he is left with an 'action of unjustifiable cannibalism'. Sanborn lights on the terrified Tikopians for an alternative context, but the presence of another traveller aboard that same ship in February 1828 explains why this explanation founders. Several months earlier, soon after setting Earle down at the Hokianga, the brig *Governor Macquarie* (commanded by Captain Kent) had been chartered by Captain Peter Dillon of the *Research* for a cruise to Tonga and Tikopia to return native interpreters to their islands. On the way, Kent was instructed to set down two Maori crew members at Thames. Dillon, who had a penchant for distributing grandly Irish names among his largely Polynesian crew, called them 'His Royal Highness Prince Brian Boroo' and 'His Excellency Morgan Mackmurragh'.[24] The previous year the relatives of Boroo, a high-ranking chief from the Hauraki region, were involved in the killing of a prominent Bay of Islands chief, Pomare I. When the *Research* limped into the Bay of Islands in November 1827, Boroo's presence provoked attempts by Te Whareumu (King George or Shulitea in Earle's text) and Whetoi (later known as Pomare II) to obtain utu for their relative, but Dillon's mantle of protection kept him safe aboard ship.[25] In December, the *Governor Macquarie* touched at Thames as planned but inadvertently left the area with Brian Boroo still aboard; and so, on the completion of his second cruise to the Islands in February, there he was, adding insult to injury again, on a ship in Ngapuhi waters.[26]

'Any other man than this I would have pardoned', Te Whareumu told Earle with some feeling, 'but it was only last year he killed, and helped to eat, my own uncle, whose death still remains unavenged: I cannot allow him to leave my country alive; if I did, I should be despised forever' (149).[27] A deal was struck: Boroo would not be molested if he remained on board, but Te Whareumu vowed to kill him the instant he stepped ashore. Several days later, Earle and his companions were afflicted by one of those strange bubbles of complacency that often unhinged the judgement of visiting Europeans: they invited Boroo ashore to their house and were immediately surrounded by 'fifty or sixty well armed and exasperated savages' (149). The situation was precarious. Boroo's life was forfeit, and if the Europeans strenuously resisted an attack, they might themselves be killed; however, if Te Whareumu kept his word and broke into the house, he risked losing his Europeans altogether. Captain Duke decided to bluff: they would not raise a finger to protect the unfortunate visitor, but if he were harmed, they would leave the Bay of Islands and ensure 'no other British ship would ever be seen at Ko-ro-ra-di-ka' (151). In the end, the chiefs gave Boroo leave to return to the ship so long as the Europeans guaranteed not to depart, and Te Whareumu and Whetoi mended fences further by solemnly surrendering their muskets; the day ended with a procession of young girls bearing baskets of flowers and food, and 'chanting in a low voice', says Earle, 'songs in praise of our recent exploits' (153). To the Maori, Earle and his wealthy companions required adroit and diplomatic handling; it makes no sense to suppose Maori would use a mime of cannibalism as a 'weapon of the weak' against them. Indeed, Bay of Islands Maori would not have seen themselves as weak in relation to sojourning Europeans, but they did bind their Pakeha closely to them in order to become even stronger in relation to the only enemy that then counted: other hapu, other iwi. For this reason, cannibalism was best kept out of sight – a strategy that dovetailed perfectly with their visitors' desire to know, for if Europeans were sure of one thing, it was that Maori had a secret.

These contexts throw a little more light on the cannibal scene Earle encountered. The girl died late in January 1828. Earle later reports the return of her killer and a party of men, who had been absent for 'about two months on a warlike expedition to the Thames' (155). Earle's timing is slightly out, for William Williams records Whetoi's return in his diary on 1 March. It is likely, although one cannot know for sure, that the feast Earle disrupted in late January, prepared for Whetoi and a small number of his warrior companions, was part of the ritual preparation for this southern excursion. Whetoi and his companions were conspicuously successful, for they returned, Earle reports, with 'quantities of plunder, human heads, human flesh, and many prisoners!' (154–55). The reception of those prisoners, mostly women and children – the men having been eaten, 'except some titbits, which had been packed up in baskets and brought on shore' (155) – is interesting. 'The women of Ko-ro-ra-di-ka, with their usual humanity, instantly surrounded them, and endeavoured to console them, and then shed abundance of tears over them' (155). I suspect many of those crying were themselves slaves and related to the new prisoners, and that Earle is not necessarily good at, or concerned with, distinguishing captive women from the likes of Robert Duke's consort, Te Whareumu's daughter, but he is aware that the attitudes of Ngapuhi women are not necessarily those of their menfolk. Indeed, distinctions between freewomen and slaves probably counted for less among the women themselves as the Musket Wars went relentlessly on, leaving widows and orphans, softening distinctions between concubine, wife and mother, and effecting a redistribution of affections out of step with traditional antagonisms and the masculine competition for mana.

One such slave, for example, the woman Dillon dubs Shelagh Boroo, had been taken on an earlier raid against Ngati Maru. According to Dillon, Whetoi hoped to use her as bait to tempt her intended husband Brian Boroo ashore from the *Research*. But she divulged the plan to her beloved and, with the connivance of Ngapuhi women Whetoi trusted, subsequently escaped on the *Governor Macquarie* with Boroo to Thames on 11 December.[28] Dillon adds that Whetoi was furious at the loss of 'the handsomest woman in the country', and unsuccessfully solicited a double-barrelled gun 'to dry up his tears and reconcile himself to the loss'.[29] The next month, Whetoi killed another 'runaway', the pretty sixteen-year-old whose fate Earle described. She had only gone round the point from one bay to another to visit relations – captured slaves also, whose terror and distress at the execution may be imagined. It would be a mistake to suppose their Ngapuhi captors had a uniform response to the atrocity. At that place and in that time, Whetoi was not acting beyond the pale, not committing what we would call a murder, yet even if we suppose a majority regarded the killing with approbation or indifference, there is evidence to suggest that this man's actions were not wholly approved of by the women of the beach.

Perhaps the most telling detail in Earle's account is the response of Whetoi's sister. She whispered to Earle that her brother was lying, that the feast was planned not for the following morning but for sunset. This is the nature of sisters: to be tell-tales and spoilsports. But if we pull a little harder at this thread, it may be that some of the secrets of cannibalism begin to unravel.

Whetoi, his sister and Te Whareumu all respond to Earle's response to the cannibal scene in a manner that matches secret with secret. When Whetoi denied he planned to eat the girl then lied about the timing of the feast, he made a secret of his intentions; his sister, having to whisper the truth, made another in revealing Whetoi's secret; and Te Whareumu, when reading the riot act to the reckless Pakeha, went on to convert the secret Earle thought he had discovered into the disarming form of an open secret.

'In the first place', said he, 'you did a foolish thing, which might have cost you your lives; and yet did not accomplish your purpose after all, as you merely succeeded in burying the flesh near the spot on which you found it. After you went away, it was again taken up, and every bit was eaten'; a fact I afterwards ascertained by examining the grave, and finding it empty. King George further said, 'It was an old custom, which their fathers practised before them; and you had no right to interfere with their ceremonies. I myself', added he, 'have left off eating human flesh, out of compliment to you white men; but you have no reason to expect the same compliance from all the other chiefs. What punishment have you in England for thieves and runaways?' We answered, 'After trial, flogging or hanging'. – 'Then', he replied, 'the only difference in our laws is, you flog and hang, but we shoot and eat.' (116)

In the course of this passage, a sign that reveals cannibalism becomes a sign that reveals nothing – when George says they ate the girl in keeping with an old custom, he seems to be offering an explanation for a practice, but is in fact removing the need for one. Appeals to custom (or culture) of this sort are often disguised tautologies: 'we do it because it's our custom' says little more than 'we do it because it's who we are'. Tautology – one thinks of the parent's last-ditch 'because *I say so*' – has the power to suspend a mare's nest of explanations in order to put matters on a more pragmatic plane. When cannibalism flattens out as a sign, it crosses cultural boundaries under the neutrality of a flag that allows everyone the right to his or her own customs – and, for the most part, that is how we agree to think of the cannibalism of Maori in that period today. It is an open secret, something that everybody knows, even though we may know very little about it. This form of secrecy interfaces well with the hidden secret Earle believes he uncovers. The secret seems to disclose a truer nature, a deep-down nature. Here at last, or so the revealed secret of cannibalism seems to promise, the character of Maori can be fixed in its depths, and whatever else these people may be, this is what they ultimately are. The content of the secret is not nearly so important as having the secret or (it often comes to the same thing) of seeming to have one. The secret becomes a screen, creating the illusion of something beyond it with more depth, while retaining the fixed and paltry quality of the stereotype.

But when Whetoi's sister lets the cat out of the bag, her secrecy works differently and discloses a sideways glimpse of Maori cannibalism. It is true there is not much to see: it does not disclose cannibalism as a racial or cultural characteristic of Maori, or as tautological euphemism for their difference, but merely as behaviour this one woman distances herself from, as behaviour that is both discernible in history and changing. Earle is in the picture too, seen seeing, but I do not think the horror on his face prompts the whisper from her. To say more may be fanciful, but it seems significant that Earle, a writer who barely acknowledges the presence of women in his *Narrative*, notices them most often in community-minded acts of sympathy. During the agitation over Brian Boroo, for example, the men were outside Duke's house, clamouring for utu, but the women of the village were inside, 'sitting with and trying to comfort the cause of this calamity', and 'confidently assuring him the white men would not yield up to his ferocious foes' (152). And when Boroo was returned safely to his ship, Earle received 'thanks and even blessings' from the women, who acted as if he had done each of them a personal favour. Earle is hardly surprised that the women of the village should display 'the natural kindness of heart and disinterested tenderness of the female sex' (152) – a chivalrous sentiment, and a barrier to curiosity. We can be sure, however, that Earle is speaking of Te Whareumu's daughter as she lives in the house, and I would like to suppose that another woman of much the same age and rank is with her: Whetoi's sister.

It should also be said that Whetoi, a thirty-year-old keen to assert his mana as heir to Pomare Nui, is a man with woman problems. When 'Shelagh Boroo' made her escape, his sister and her friends helped her. When one of Whetoi's wives was accused of adultery, his sister and her friends assured him nothing had happened.[30] On that occasion, Te Whareumu notified Whetoi of the rumour, and thought it prudent to be present as a peacemaker when the young chief stormed home, intent on revenge, and had to be fought to a standstill. No sooner was that problem smoothed over than a more awkward complication arrived in its train: Whetoi had assaulted the messenger from Te Whareumu who brought the bad tidings. This is the man who, Te Whareumu urged, merely followed the customs of his fathers when he shot that slave girl and gave those orders for a feast – I can imagine Whetoi looking to his honour, but I doubt his sister saw things that way.

The introduction of the musket, it is often observed, upset the balance of power between traditional enemies, and for a brief time allowed an unprecedented expansion of the scale on which victory or failure in warfare might be expressed. But I have argued that as populations were redistributed, new alliances of feeling softened boundaries between traditional enemies and traditional ranks, and that this was rather more the experience of women just as the expansion of forms of aggression towards entropy was rather more the business of men. One of the better reasons to be sceptical about cannibalism in several other parts of the world is its suspiciously rapid disappearance; white men arrive, find evidence of cannibalism, but then, as if overnight, the practice is expunged from the historical record; or rather, it moves on to the next dark place, as Obeyesekere suspects happens to a spurious New Zealand cannibalism that flourishes locally for a while and then 'migrates' to Fiji.[31]

Earle offers a different scenario. Between the lines of his outraged sensibilities, he gives an eyewitness account of cannibalism at a time when both traditionalists and innovators were modifying its occurrence and its local significance. This allows us to see cannibalism as neither Earle nor that prophet of our own common sense, Te Whareumu, see it. Cannibalism is neither lost in the maw of savage darkness nor is it quite what we euphemistically or tautologically call a custom or 'part of the culture'. All the actors in and observers of this scene see and interpret in ways that are inflected by cultural norms and expectations – that is what seeing and interpreting entail – but we and they do not act and observe as if our culture were a bubble in which we are enclosed, cutting us off from the bubbles of others we encounter. We are more open to the experience of others than that, and while their difference runs to extremes that can be as wonderful as sulphur-coloured hair or as atrocious as an execution, in the moment of encounter both we and they are ordinary and something is knowable.

Tangible Proof

I have been sceptical about sceptics – but how can I really know that poor girl was eaten? I must confess I have no 'ocular proof'. Earle has Te Whareumu's word that the feast went ahead regardless, and he can himself confirm that her body was removed from its grave. The missionary, not quick to draw conclusions from the empty graves of non-Christians, cannot be certain she was consumed, and the way he says so makes it unclear whether Duke shared this scruple. Set the bar at certainty, and Williams's doubt is a worm – yet I do not require a close-up of mastication and of swallowing in order to draw conclusions about Whetoi's intentions. There is much about this man that is opaque, but if Earle had written him as a character in a novel, one would have to say that his leading traits were impulsiveness, a strong sense of the right and proper, and a warrior's love of good fellowship. But there is one detail in Earle's *Narrative* it would have taken an extraordinary novelist to think up. When Whetoi confesses his intention to eat the girl, he goes on to explain that when she is 'sufficiently cooked', 'her flesh would be as tender as paper, which he tore in illustration of the remark' (114). There is not a food writer on earth who so persuasively describes the pleasure of eating with one's hands.

CHAPTER THREE

Maning's Demons

What, can the devil speak true?
– Macbeth, *act 3, scene 1*

F. E. MANING WROTE UNDER THE PSEUDONYM 'PAKEHA MAORI', BUT when a *History of the War in the North* came out in 1862, everyone in the north thought they knew who the author must be. 'I do not acknowledge my doings', Maning quipped, 'and only say when I am accused that it is hard no one can do anything clever but it is immediately said to be me.'[1]

Of all the accounts of life in early New Zealand, Maning's are cleverest by far. Not that this is an admirable quality, necessarily. A clever writer – Lord Byron, for instance – is likely to strike some readers as scornful, amoral and heartless. John Keats, after reading a jokey passage on cannibalism in the Shipwreck Canto of *Don Juan*, threw down the book, indignant 'that a man like Byron should have exhausted all the pleasures of the world so completely that there was nothing left for him but to laugh and gloat over the most solemn and heart-rending scenes of human misery'. The episode, Keats protested, 'is one of the most diabolical attempts ever made upon our sympathies, and I have no doubt it will fascinate thousands into extreme obduracy of heart.'[2] I doubt Keats would have cared for Maning – another laugher and gloater for whom the 'horrors' of cannibalism irresistibly give rise to a comic turn.

One afternoon, for example, the Pakeha Maori is lashing together the palisade of a new pa, and his vis-à-vis for the task is 'a respectable old warrior' whose name, in English, means 'The eater of his own relations' – which instantly prompts the aside, 'Be careful not to read rations' (111–12). The slightness of that difference tickles my fancy, nudging me to link 'the eater of his own relations' with the mental picture of a self-sufficient workman virtuously opening his own lunchbox. Like Byron, Maning likes to cajole his reader by anticipating misassumptions and teasing the civilised response – as in the anecdote of the chief who entertains two 'vagrant straggling' Pakeha one evening, and then, by way of reimbursing himself for 'his trouble and outlay', kills and cooks one of them for breakfast next morning. And why not? The Pakeha was 'a *tutua*, a nobody, a fellow not worth a spike nail; no one knew him; he had no relations, no goods, no expectations, no anything; . . . of what use on earth was he except to eat?' (101–2). 'People from the old countries', the narrator continues, owing to 'a kind of over-delicacy about them', are likely to jump to a wrong conclusion and to regard his friend the chief as 'a very rude ill-mannered person'. 'Nothing of the kind', he insists, and goes on to explain that his friend is not only respected as a warrior, an ally and an artist, but is also 'a great friend and protector of rich, well-to-do pakehas' – 'the kind of man who would not eat a *friend* on any account whatever, except he should be very hungry' (102).

So how funny is that? Consider another likely setting for the story: the gentleman's club, the businessman's lounge bar, and the haw-haw round the circle as the raconteur, unable to resist a twist to the tale, goes for the easy xenophobic laugh that incites among his listeners, as Keats might have said, a certain 'obduracy of heart'. Perhaps Maning tells Maori jokes the way Herman Goering told Jewish jokes. But it is not difficult to imagine the insider–outsider reversals working differently again, capping a double-take with a triple-take, and joking this time not at the expense of Maori but with an insider's confidence – as if rising to a high-register giggle in the manner of Billy T. James. Maning's humour is unstable: he often helps us see the funny side of a cross-cultural situation; he often seems to close sensitivities right down, hardening boundaries between Pakeha and Maori with his scorn. The latter perception is likely to be half right, but only half right; we need to be receptive to more than one message only.

One of the more 'heart-rending scenes of misery' in *Old New Zealand* involves an old woman who has been presented with the preserved head of her dead son, killed on a recent war expedition.

A number of women were standing in a row before [the head], screaming, wailing, and quivering their hands about in a most extraordinary manner, and cutting themselves dreadfully with sharp flints and shells. One old woman, in the centre of the group, was one clot of blood from head to feet, and large clots of coagulated blood lay on the ground where she stood. The sight was absolutely horrible, I thought at the time. She was singing or howling a dirge-like wail. In her right hand she held a piece of *tuhua*, or volcanic glass, as sharp as a razor: this she placed deliberately to her left wrist, drawing it slowly upwards to her left shoulder, the spouting blood following as it went; then from the left shoulder downwards, across the breast to the short ribs on the right side; then the rude but keen knife was shifted from the right hand to the left, placed to the right wrist, drawn upwards to the right shoulder, and so down across the breast to the left side, thus making a bloody cross on the breast; and so the operation went on all the time I was there, the old creature all the time howling in time and measure, and keeping time also with the knife, which at every cut was shifted from one hand to the other, as I have described. She had scored her forehead and cheeks before I came; her face and body was a mere clot of blood, and a little stream was dropping from every finger – a more hideous object could scarcely be conceived. (120–21)

Other Europeans witnessed and were disturbed by similar acts of self-mutilation among mourners. Some also wondered at the sincerity of the participants, as Maning does, when he goes on to note that 'the younger women, though they screamed as loud, did not cut near so deep as the old woman; especially about the face' (121) and, with a characteristic flourish, proceeds to lament the decay of tradition, noting that in the present day 'some degenerate hussey making believe with a piece of flint in her hand' shows 'a want of natural affection' (121). But even though Maning is, in all likelihood, either giving an eyewitness report or making a composite picture from such reports, one could hardly say that his description was reliable. He does not attempt to give a Maori perspective – the scene is viewed by a newly arrived Pakeha – yet he dwells on everything that is shocking and sensational in order to persuade the reader of the horror of life beyond the pale of civilisation. This is not a secret of the text; it wears its bias openly. 'Now if there is one thing I hate more than another it is the raw-head-and-bloody-bones style of writing', continues the narrator with self-reflexive cheek, promising to 'avoid all particular mention of battles, massacres, and onslaughts; except there be something particularly characteristic of my friend the Maori in them' (122). The satirical qualification is characteristic, but so too is the relativism that places the scene in the context of a European demand for heads as items of trade; of a propensity for 'hacking and hewing' also to be found 'in Europe, Asia, and America of late' (122); and of a closing encomium of peace.

> Hail, lovely peace, daughter of heaven! meek-eyed inventor of Armstrong guns and Enfield rifles; you of the liquid-fire-shell, hail! Shooter at 'bulls'-eyes', trainer of battalions, killer of wooden Frenchmen, hail! (A bit of fine writing does one good). Nestling under thy wing, I will scrape sharp the point of my spear with a *pipi* shell; I will carry fern-root into my pa; I will *cure* those heads which I have killed in war, or they will spoil and 'won't fetch nothin': for these are thy arts, O peace! (122)

Maning's cleverness, like Byron's, is a literary quality. It is more like a wavelength to be on than a punch line always to be got – although the tendency of the reader may well be to reduce the suggestiveness of Maning's stories, to settle too quickly and too decidedly on some mocking intention. Byron and Maning both looked to the satirists of the eighteenth century for their models, but rather than defend a central core of value in the manner of Pope or Johnson, they wrote satire from an outlook and in circumstances in which there were no sure values. Their mockery finds a target readily enough, but a sense that everything is relative can be just as fatal for some sorts of humour as it is for some sorts of philosophy. What might have been sarcasm becomes less stable as irony; a comic reversal no longer makes a moral plain but generates dramatic complexity and multiplies perspectives. What, for example, are we to make of a narrator who finds it necessary to insist: 'I love sincerity'? That dubious affirmation may well be the most characteristic sentence Maning ever wrote.

The Demon of Civilisation

Old New Zealand begins with a man making a speech.

AH! those good old times, when first I came to New Zealand, we shall never see their like again. Since then the world seems to have gone wrong somehow. A dull sort of world this now. The very sun does not seem to me to shine as bright as it used. Pigs and potatoes have degenerated; and everything seems 'flat, stale, and unprofitable'. But those were the times! – the 'good old times' – before Governors were invented, and law, and justice, and all that. When everyone did as he liked, – except when his neighbours would not let him, (the more shame for them,) – when there were no taxes, or duties, or public works, or public to require them. Who cared then whether he owned a coat? – or believed in shoes or stockings? The men were bigger and stouter in those days; and the women, – ah! Money was useless and might go a begging. A sovereign was of no use except to make a hole in and hang it in a child's ear. The few I brought went that way, and I have seen them swapped for shillings, which were thought more becoming. What cared I? A fish-hook was worth a dozen of them, and I had lots of fish-hooks. Little did I think in those days that I should ever see here towns and villages, banks and insurance offices, prime ministers and bishops; and hear sermons preached, and see men hung, and all the other plagues of civilization. I am a melancholy man. I feel somehow as if I had got older. I am no use in these dull times. I mope about in solitary places, exclaiming often, 'Oh! where are those good old times?' and echo, or some young Maori whelp from the Three Kings, answers from behind a bush, – NO HEA.

I shall not state the year in which I first saw the mountains of New Zealand appear above the sea; there is a false suspicion getting about that I am growing old. This must be looked down, so I will at present avoid dates. I always held a theory that time was of no account in New Zealand, and I do believe I was right up to the time of the arrival of the first Governor. The natives hold this opinion still, especially those who are in debt: so I will just say it was in the good old times, long ago, that, from the deck of a small trading schooner in which I had taken my passage from somewhere, I first cast eyes on Maori land. It *was* Maori land then; but alas! what is it now? Success to you, O King of Waikato. May your *mana* never be less! – long may you hold at bay the demon of civilization, though fall at last I fear you must. (93–94)

The demon of civilisation converts positives into negatives: the good old times when life was lively and men were free and women worth sighing for has closed down; in its place, 'Maori land' – a nickname for the country – has become Maori Land, an alienable commodity in these bad new times of commerce and law, clocks and calendars. But the demon of civilisation turns out to be the angel of history. Every positive from the good old days can be converted back to its negative, as if in illustration of a standard theme of Enlightenment political economy: civilisation rises from savagery through laws protecting the property and security of its members. The artless oration of the Pakeha Maori is artfully composed by an author who is not only civilised enough to quote *Hamlet*, but who probably also has Locke's 'In the beginning all was America . . . ' by heart, as well as Hobbes's strictures about life in savage times being 'nasty, brutish and short'. The unspoken meaning of the speech is that we either go with the progress of civilisation or remain sunken in savagery.

As the Pakeha Maori talks, as his explicit oppositions are decoded as the author's implied oppositions, what might have been commonalities are separated out into *either* the old ways of the Maori *or* the new ways of the Settler. All the categories of life move to one pole or the other. What makes this move different from standard colonial discourse is the invention of a voice – a voice that supposedly 'belongs to both parties' and doesn't 'care a straw which wins' (198). The bipartisanship must be a pretence – Maning knows which side he is on – but it also has to be more than a pretence for two reasons. The Pakeha Maori speaks with the voice of experience, both rhetorically and actually. Only a Pakeha Maori can explain one half of that uneasy compound to the other, because only he – so far as the narrative structure of this book is concerned – has a foot in both worlds. He has an authority the reader must trust in order to see through the charade of mixed allegiances, but the more persuasive he is – the more lively, the more vivid – the greater his capacity to exceed and outflank his own polemical intentions. Moreover, Maning actually was a Pakeha Maori, and the character's testimony draws on the author's own knowledge and experience of life on the cultural verge between Maori and Pakeha. To an active reading, his testimony opens a fuller view of the Hokianga beach where boundaries between Maori and Pakeha were loosely drawn – and where cannibals were 'respectable'.

Old New Zealand, published in Auckland in 1863 and written a year earlier, opens with a salute we might imagine being sent down the Great South Road, past a line of government redoubts and trenches dug into the Bombay Hills and the Hunua Ranges, winding along the Waikato River to the fortified pa of Rangiriri, all the way to Ngaruawahia, heart of the Kingitanga. 'Success to you, O King of Waikato', says the Pakeha Maori, 'May your *mana* never be less! – long may you hold at bay the demon of civilization, though fall at last I fear you must.' Tawhiao, the addressee of this greeting, was much occupied with a question that beset all indigenous leaders from Metacom to Sitting Bull, from Hone Heke to Titokowaru: how to resist, handle, circumvent, minimise – and finally to survive – the swamping encroachment of incomers. As long as Maori declined to sell land – and as long as Pakeha honoured the Treaty – Tawhiao could conceivably block the southward expansion of European settlement into Waikato. To Pakeha, who by the mid-1850s were more numerous than Maori but held only 5 per cent of the land, the very existence of the King Movement was a barrier to progress and an affront to the Crown; they invaded in July 1863. The writer who urged Tawhiao to resist 'the demon of civilization' while also foretelling his doom was then fifty-one years old; he had been in the country for thirty years, and had lived as a Maori among Maori, though his loyalties and sympathies were changing along with the country.

When Maning arrived in the Hokianga in the winter of 1833, he had known two worlds already: the comfortable, Irish protestant milieu of his boyhood in Dublin and, since the age of eleven, Van Diemen's Land, a colony thriving on genocide and convict labour. His father, a younger son, hoped to make good as a gentleman farmer but the land allocated to him seemed unsuitable and blighted. On driving out to inspect the block, he was appalled to find that a convict labourer had that very day shot an Aborigine with as little compunction as one might shoot a snake; the murderer thought it a great entertainment to make the fingers of the corpse move by tugging at the sinews of the arm. Maning's father revoked the land grant, abandoned all schemes for farming in the Tasmanian style and opted for the security of a position as a customs officer in Hobart town. In 1830, as able-bodied men of the colony, the Maning brothers were likely to have been involved in the infamous 'Black Line' of several thousand settlers who attempted to drive the Aborigines out of the bush – a context to be borne in mind when considering Maning's views about the likely fate of Maori after meeting 'the demon of civilization'. His brothers set up as merchants in Hobart, but Maning seems to have had little patience with collars and inkwells and the constraints of a small-town life. After a short period managing an up-country Tasmanian farm, he struck out at the age of twenty-one for the still more remote banks of the Hokianga harbour.

The hills of the Hokianga were timbered with kauri, flax was abundant, and these commodities, together with food grown for export, found a ready market in Australia. In return, Ngapuhi – then as now the largest iwi in the country – imported iron tools and guns. The trade depended on enterprising middlemen with local knowledge and chiefly contacts who could organise Maori and deliver goods on time, and who could also, from a Ngapuhi perspective, guarantee fair treatment and optimum prices from ships calling for cargo. These men were not Maori, nor were they, like most Pakeha, white strangers who kept to their own ways. Because they married into Maori families, spoke the language and adjusted to Maori ways, because they had a foot in both worlds, these men became known as Pakeha Maori.

Maning came ashore at the very tail end of the Musket Wars. A decade earlier, Ngapuhi had been all-conquering, but from 1826 on, as the balance of power levelled, their annual raids south often ended in loss and disaster. The last of these major ventures, Titore's second expedition to the Bay of Plenty, set off some months before Maning landed, but by 1833 conflict over resources and influence was rather more likely to occur at a local or inter-hapu level. One incident in particular leaves an impression on the first four chapters of *Old New Zealand*. Just prior to Maning's arrival, another trading vessel, the *Fortitude*, ran aground further up the harbour. As a consequence of this mishap, Maori custom allowed that the vessel and its cargo should be open to muru (loosely translated as plunder), and hapu from both sides of the river made the most of their opportunity. Their actions brought them into conflict with Moetara, chief of the Ngati Korokoro village at Pakanae, the first port of call for visiting ships and the most prosperous village in the Hokianga. Moetara saw himself as the protector of Pakeha and vowed to punish those up-river groups who had ransacked the *Fortitude*. In a bloody skirmish at Motukauri, both sides lost a dozen or so warriors; three Pakeha sawyers in the vicinity were then plundered to make good the losses of that battle and had to decamp for Pakanae (where they may have cheered Maning on as he wrestled with 'Melons'). Fearing an escalation of hostilities, Moetara subsequently fortified the trading post at Koutu Point and was reinforced by Ngapuhi sections led by Tamati Waka Nene and Patuone, whose numbers included Jacky Marmon, a model, perhaps, for the dubious trader in heads we meet in chapter three. Soon after Maning came ashore, Titore's war party, which included warriors related to those slain at Motukauri, returned from their southern expedition and were expected to pass through the village. Perhaps they too would require utu. It is in anticipation of these visitors that the Pakeha Maori and the Eater of His Own Relations are lashing together the posts of the pa. In the event, peace was affirmed and the taua moved on without incident.

My paragraph of standard historical information differs from the corresponding sections of *Old New Zealand* both in length (he takes four chapters) and in kind. Although we can't quite say that Moetara is not the chief who welcomes Maning ashore, or that the displaced sawyers are not among the welcoming party, we can't quite say that they *are* these persons either – the fact and the fiction are cross-contaminating categories. Second, while my account briefly puts several interconnected events in chronological order, Maning's anecdotes are neither concise nor sequential. Individuals appear as examples, events illustrate generalities and digression follows digression at the whim of a garrulous narrator who seems unable to complete the simplest description without sidetracking himself.

Although the Pakeha Maori expects to be able to tell the unvarnished truth and insists he is doing so, he gets into all sorts of tangles because of it. Take the business of arriving in New Zealand: it ought to be possible to say, 'I rowed ashore', but the narrator finds any clear and straightforward statement of fact is not only divisible into smaller and smaller microparticles of description – 'I grasped the oar' might become 'with a wobble, I sat myself down in the stern, and resolutely grasped the oar', and so on – but is also subject to endless diversionary interference from the present. It takes the narrator several pages to arrive at this point of exasperation:

> I positively vow and protest to you, gentle and patient reader, that if ever I get safe on shore, I will do my best to give you satisfaction; let me get once on shore, and I am all right: but unless I get my feet on *terra firma*, how can I ever begin my tale of the good old times? As long as I am on board ship I am cramped and crippled, and a mere slave to Greenwich time, and can't get on. Some people, I am aware, would make a dash at it, and manage the thing without the aid of boat, canoe, or life preserver; but such people are, for the most part, dealers in fiction, which I am not: my story is a true story, not 'founded on fact', but fact itself, and so I cannot manage to get on shore a moment sooner than circumstances will permit. It may be that I ought to have landed before this; but I must confess I don't know any more about the right way to tell a story, than a native minister knows how to 'come' a war dance. I declare the mention of a war dance calls up a host of reminiscences, pleasurable and painful, exhilarating and depressing, in such a way as no one but a few, a very few, pakeha Maori, can understand. Thunder! – but no . . . . On shore I will get this time, I am determined, in spite of fate – so now for it. (96)

It is not until the end of chapter two that the narrator finally makes it to shore.

This tomfoolery has several degrees of cleverness. It reminds us to distinguish between the author and the hapless narrator (a distinction qualified by the realisation that although Maning is not the narrating Pakeha Maori, he is not *not* him either). Second, we are invited to entertain distinctions between 'dealers in fiction' and purveyors of a 'true story', between a story merely 'founded upon fact' and a story consisting of 'fact itself' – all in the context of a virtuoso display of the impossibility of anyone ever narrating anything of the kind. Maning rowed ashore in 1833 – that is a simple enough fact for a history book, but we have no access to what happened in the past except through stories told about what happened in the past; any attempt to isolate the 'fact itself' can only result in another telling of the story. The 'right way to tell a story' is not something any historian can take for granted or assume neutrally – though many, of course, 'have made a dash at it'. More diabolical still: by playing on the distinction between the present time of narration and the time spoken about, between a *new* New Zealand subject to Greenwich time and an *old* New Zealand where time is 'of no account' and Maori storytellers must omit nothing, the author makes the relation between old and new a peculiar problem of his book, just as it is a defining problem of that hesitant compound of a nation we call 'Aotearoa New Zealand' and whose very name suggests two contradictory injunctions about the past.

On one hand, we Pakeha are sometimes told to forget the past: we owe it nothing, it holds us back, it makes us hidebound; we must always be updating and renovating, always looking to the new. On the other hand, we also know that if we were to consign the past to some dustbin of history, we would repeat old mistakes and continue old injustices. We cannot choose between these alternatives: we must live them simultaneously, even if, like the Pakeha Maori, it means feeling as if we were 'two different persons at the same time' (198), one side of us giving a hurrah, if not for Queen Victoria, then for modernity and globalisation; and the other side stamping a haka, if not for one's Maori tribe, then for the local against the global, for conservation against progress, for difference against homogeneity. The Pakeha Maori's difficulties in telling his own history are prophetic of everything that makes this country unsettled about settlement. Whether it is possible to bring present and past, new and old, modern and traditional into some kind of narrative order is not only an historiographical question, it is also a political one, for the very possibility of accommodation between the 'old' world of the Maori and the 'new' world of the colonisers is at stake.

Having at last come ashore, Maning first arranged to settle at Kohukohu, on the northern side of the Hokianga, where he and his business partner, Thomas Kelly, were granted land and a small house. The English adventurer Edward Markham, who stayed briefly at the cottage, left several unflattering but revealing references to Maning in his journal.

Kelly I liked, but not Manning [sic], who had come out when a Child and knew no other country than Van diemansland and his Ideas were as confined as the Country he had seen; he turned out a double faced sneaking Thief. Kelly always did what he could to please me. Manning would have done Honor to the back Woods in America.[3]

Markham, objecting to the way Maning kept house, had tried to institute a policy of keeping 'the Natives out' and noted contemptuously that Maning 'was afraid of loosing his popularity with the chiefs'.[4] The English visitor seems anxious to protect his borders, but Maning was already a man of the beach, more manoeuvrable and more flexible. From his base in Kohukohu, he traded in timber, pork and potatoes for the Australian market, and fathered a child to a woman named Harakoi. In 1837, he sold up, visited Hobart briefly, and returned to settle across the river at Onoke, where he again purchased a block of land and was soon living with a Te Hikutu woman named Moengaroa, the mother of his children, Maria (born 1842), Mary (born 1845), Hauraki (born 1846) and Susan (born 1847).

Maning's pro-Maori sympathies were caught in another spotlight of disapproval early in 1840, when the Treaty of Waitangi was formally presented to a gathering of Hokianga chiefs for their approval. Maning counselled not signing. Hobson, suspecting the sinister influence of French priests, challenged a chief to identify which Pakeha had been fomenting opposition; Maning stepped forward with an explanation. Hobson recorded that this person 'conscientiously believed that the Natives would be degraded under our influence, and that therefore he had advised them to resist; admitting at the same time that the laws of England were requisite to restrain and protect British subjects, but to British subjects alone should they be applicable' – but the arguments were treated dismissively.[5] On the day, his father-in-law Kaitoke signed, but Maning had a hand in an unexpected sequel. 'The chief . . . brought back his present of blankets', Felton Mathew recorded in his journal, 'together with a letter signed by fifty of his Tribe, in which they disavowed the act of the preceding day, and refused to acknowledge allegiance to the Queen. All this was evidently the result of European intrigue; but it is still very embarrassing, and the way it was done rendered it insulting.'⁶ No alteration was ever made to the Treaty document.

While Maning's opposition to the Treaty was not without self-interest – the new order threatened to disturb 'old settler' arrangements with Maori – his stand counted against him, for in 1841 he was denied a government post for which he was well qualified. Later in life, he sought to suppress the nature of his dissenting contribution to the Hokianga Treaty meeting. His own account of the Treaty and its difficulties appears in the opening sections of the *History of the War in the North Against the Chief Heke*. This work is narrated by an elderly Maori chief and much of the comedy lies in the author's manipulation of the rangatira's cultural misperceptions, his eye for the main chance and his lack of sympathy with European priorities. For example, the chief is astounded that English soldiers should blithely carry their own stretchers into battle – as if they had no understanding of omens whatsoever. On the other hand, the news that Governor Hobson travels all round the country with 'a very large piece of paper' is met with broad-minded puzzlement: clearly, the governor's 'chief delight' is 'to get plenty of marks and names on his paper' (23) – but to what end?

> Some of us thought the Governor wanted to bewitch all the chiefs, but our Pakeha friends laughed at this, and told us that the people of Europe did not know how to bewitch people. Some told us one thing, some another. Some said the Governor only wanted our consent to remain, to be a chief over the Pakeha people; others said he wanted to be chief over both Pakeha and Maori. We did not know what to think, but were all anxious he might come to us soon, for we were afraid that all his blankets and tobacco, and other things, would be gone before he came to our part of the country, and that he would have nothing left to pay us for making our marks on his paper. (20)

In the end, miffed at receiving only two blankets, the chief returns the 'payment' and asks for his name to be cut out from the paper. He expects 'something bad to come of this business'; it did the governor no good, for he died, 'and the paper with all its names was either buried with him, or else his relations may have kept it to lament over' (23);

whatever its fate, the chief warns it should not be kept near cooked food – 'it is a very sacred piece of paper; it is very good if it has been buried with the Governor' (23). Maning's tongue is in his cheek, of course, but behind the satirical picture of venal Maori signing a document they don't understand is a more complex view: it made a great difference then, and makes a great difference now, whether Maori ceded rangatiratanga in signing the Treaty. In Maning's *History*, they retain it. Moreover, different understandings of the Treaty and its failure to deliver what had been promised are seen as the primary cause of the war, and it is clear that Maori who fought against the so-called rebel chiefs did so as allies of the Crown rather than as subjects.

Much of Maning's *History* is pro-Maori in emphasis and sentiment, but there are other tones as well. The book is a double narrative: Maning tells the story in the chief's own words and interpolates a running series of explanatory notes and anecdotes by a Pakeha Maori editor and translator. The balance between these voices varies as the tale advances, until the garrulous chief intrudes into the narrative frame with demands for rum and accommodation and is at last unceremoniously evicted from the house and the narrative. Internal evidence indicates that this unpleasant closing frame was written shortly before publication, but we also know from letters to family in Tasmania that Maning began writing the book in 1845, shortly after one of the battles he so vividly describes. The compositional history is uncertain, but it seems likely that it began as a personal memoir – Maning was a participant in many but not all of the major incidents of the war – and developed as Ngapuhi contacts from both sides were interviewed and their anecdotes collected.[7] One of Maning's aims was to correct the official record: as he wrote to his brother, 'any one to read Despard's despatches would think that we had thrashed the natives soundly whereas they really have had the best of it on several occasions. I really begin to think it is all a mistake about our beating the French at Waterloo' (212). Another important aim was to memorialise his great friend and brother-in-law, Hauraki, who was killed at the battle of Waikare, and whose death takes up a large portion of the middle of the story, along with a waiata tangi composed by Moengaroa. At some point, Maning hit on the idea of telling the story in a Maori way, through the voice and eyes of a representative chief, a literary device that moves the *War in the North* closer to historical fiction in the conventional sense of the term. In 1862, when war once more seemed likely, it was published in pamphlet form as Maning's pointedly satirical contribution to debate over the conduct of native policy, and as a warning to new settlers who complacently underestimated Maori capacity to wage war.

The *History of the War in the North* earned Maning the friendship and patronage of former native secretary Donald McLean, who encouraged Maning to continue writing. In a revealing letter of 25 October 1862, Maning introduced his next book, *Old New Zealand*, in these terms: 'I myself believe it to be far better i.e. that is more valuable than "the war" it is ironical, satirical semipolitical with lots of fun, and many serious and striking scenes from old native life and habits, and in a word shews indirectly without ostencibly pretending to do so what sort of a creature this Maori is who we have to deal with' (213–14). His choice of phrase indicates his distance from the Maori world he had once been part of. After Moengaroa died in 1847, he sent his eldest daughter Maria to live with her grandparents in Tasmania; his remaining children spent a great deal of time with their Te Hikutu relatives and, as young adults, became increasingly estranged from their father. In the 1850s, Maning no longer worked alongside Maori but employed them in his business activities. His particular friends were old Hokianga settlers like John Webster and Spencer Von Sturmer, along with the Auckland businessman John Logan Campbell, and a number of writers and politicians associated with the *Southern Cross* newspaper. It was probably for a group of these like-minded people that Maning wrote an undated and unpublished paper on 'the Native Question' sometime in the late 1850s. Here he strikes a number of notes that he would repeat for the rest of his life: 'When Cannibals and barbarians become our rulers which they soon will if we invite them to even dream of political rights, it will be time for every man who has the self-respect of a briton to leave these shores, where degenerate Englishmen succumb to the savage' (219). Maning was becoming an expert on 'Maori-as-he-knew-them'. He maintains Maori are only nominally and superficially British subjects; in their true character they remain lawless and uncivilised – an independent people, in other words – and it would take a crushing military defeat, he believed, before they could ever acknowledge and respect the majesty of the law. Views such as these are well documented in the later letters; they offer one essential key to the political and satirical intentions of his published writings, but it should be remembered that the published works are not reducible to the letters: it is the opinions on race and politics that are reductive, not the writing – or not always.

In 1865, Maning was invited to become a judge in the Native Land Court. The Treaty's second article reserves to the Crown the exclusive right to purchase land from Maori – offering limited protection against the alienation of communally invested land. As judge, Maning's primary task was to ascertain which Maori persons could be said to 'own' some block of land, and to award freehold titles to those deemed to be owners. These people (by statute, there could be no more than ten owners) were then entitled to sell if they so wished – and could also be pressured into selling to meet their debts. Maori subsequently lost many millions of acres of tribally held land through forced and voluntary sales. The outcome of any particular case was likely to hinge, not on points of English law, but on the judge's understanding of 'The good old times before governors were invented, and law, and justice, and all that' – or what a court would more soberly term 'Maori usage and custom'. In *Old New Zealand*, the term for getting proper hold of the past is 'trying back' (167). Like the Pakeha Maori girding his narratorial loins for another effort to recapture the thread of his story, the judge also had to 'try back', to transform the digressive tellings of discrepant witnesses into the seamless historical narrative that would largely determine and establish title to the land.

In April 1871, for example, Judge Maning delivered his verdict on Ngati Haua's application for certificate of title to a large block of land called Te Aroha.[8] Ngati Haua, a Waikato iwi, based their claim on conquest, having, they argued, defeated and ousted the previous 'owners', members of the Marutuahu confederation, at the battle of Taumatawiwi, fought around 1830. But Marutuahu claimed it was they, not Ngati Haua, who were victors at the battle of Taumatawiwi, and that Te Aroha had never passed out of their possession or control. A third claimant was peremptorily considered by the court: Te Wharenui, representing Ngati Hue, 'who some generations back were owners of the land, before the Marutuahu came into possession', based his claim through descent and because the fires of his tribe 'have never been extinguished'.[9]

In order to decide the case, Maning had to put their conflicting statements into historical good order. He had to establish the nature of Marutuahu and Ngati Haua relations prior to 1830; he had to decide who won the battle of Taumatawiwi; and he had to determine whether the victors were weakened by victory, or whether their gains were decisive. Maning's legal judgment proves to be almost as complex a narrative as *Old New Zealand*. The judge, unlike the Pakeha Maori, is most assuredly cast as a reliable narrator, but closely resembles his earlier persona in that he is woefully prone to digression and has a curious way with time. The following passage, for example, concludes an account of relations between Ngati Haua and Marutuahu *prior to* the battle of Taumatawiwi. Maning wants to describe how things were over a number of years and his aim is to demonstrate that not even the Maori – 'however hardened' – could have endured conditions like these much longer.

> War had attained its most terrible and forbidden aspect; neither age nor sex was spared; agriculture was neglected; the highest duty of man was to slay and devour his neighbour; whilst the combatants fought in the front, the ovens were heating in the rear; the vigorous warrior, one moment fighting hopefully in the foremost rank, exulting in his strength, laying enemy after enemy low, thinking only of his war boasts when the victory should be won; stunned by a sudden blow, instantly dragged away, hastily quartered alive, next moment in the glowing oven; his place is vacant in the ranks, his very body can scarcely be said to exist. Whilst his flesh is roasting the battle rages on, and at night his remains furnish forth a banquet for the victors, and there is much boasting and great glory. Such things were, and the Court is obliged to recognise them . . . as evidence of title to land, according to Maori usage and custom.[10]

As Maning's focus moves from Maori in general to the still ostensive yet vividly individuated Maori warrior, his tenses also shift. The passage moves from the iterative past to the present time of narration ('the Court is obliged') by way of another mode of time altogether.

When Maning writes, 'his flesh is roasting the battle rages on', his verbs stray into the ethnographic present – a tense suited to the timeless world of an unhistorical people.

Despite Maning's own licence as a storyteller, a strict adherence to historical time is crucial to his Te Aroha judgment. He may follow 'Maori usage and custom' in awarding victory at Taumatawiwi to Ngati Haua (they possessed both the field of battle and the bodies of the enemy dead), but it is by carefully placing subsequent events in temporal succession that the victory is judged pyrrhic. Moreover, in considering Ngati Haua claims to have maintained an active use of the land, the judge subjects their iterative and ostensive statements to a withering temporal critique. One witness states, 'It is because I have lived on the land and cultivated [it] since the battle of Taumatawiwi that I say the Aroha belongs to me.' Maning wants dates, times, places and reports: 'the only example of cultivation he gives . . . was during a hasty visit to catch eels, when the Marutuahu were known to be absent, when he and his companions planted a few potatoes, which occupied them, by his own account, only two weeks (one of his companions says four days), and that having done this they went away with their eels to Matamata, and did not come back for a year, and then only to catch some more eels at a different place'.[11] In the Te Aroha judgment, 'Maori usage and custom' – the topic of Maning's blood-and-bones peroration – is an atemporal category, a category that is in every sense overtaken by the chronological history that casts Marutuahu as 'landlords', and Ngati Haua as 'stealthy and timid trespassers' with no claim to the land.[12]

'As long as I am on board ship', complains the Pakeha Maori, 'I am cramped and crippled, and a mere slave to Greenwich time' (96). Trying back, however, is not, strictly speaking, a discursive movement through the past but rather a travelling back to moments before settlement started and 'real' history began. Maning's 'good old times' are the oddest kind of setting, a non-temporal non-locus for all Maori who are unable to hold at bay the 'demon of civilization', which is time.

Demonic Possession

One day, the Pakeha Maori was walking along a stretch of coast when he came to a spot where a landslip had disturbed an old burial site. Bones were strewn about and a large skull bobbed in the water. He was travelling some distance ahead of his companions and had just finished burying the skull when the rest of the party arrived. They were dismayed and astonished, and made it plain that contact with the skull – without question the skull of one of their more famous chiefs – had turned the Pakeha Maori into a public health emergency and rendered him unfit for human company. The Pakeha Maori saw no alternative but to 'vote' himself tapu and act accordingly. Come dinner time, however, a portion of the evening meal was brought to him but placed 'at a respectful distance' from where he sat – as if he was expected to 'bob at it' without using his hands, in the manner of Maori 'kai tango atua or undertakers' (154). This, the Pakeha Maori felt, was taking things too far and, despite the warnings of his friends, he proceeded to tuck in in his usual manner.

> I declare, positively, I had no sooner done so than I felt sorry. The expression of horror, contempt, and pity, observable in their faces, convinced me that I had not only offended and hurt their feelings, but that I had lowered myself greatly in their estimation. Certainly I was a pakeha, and pakehas will do most unaccountable things, and may be, in ordinary cases excused; but this, I saw at once, was an act which, to my friends, seemed the *ne plus ultra* of abomination. I now can well understand that I must have, sitting there eating my potatoes, appeared to them a ghoul, a vampire – worse than even one of their own dreadful *atua*, who, at the command of a witch, or to avenge some breach of the *tapu*, enters into a man's body and slowly eats away his vitals. (154–55)

The ethnographic core of *Old New Zealand* is a series of digressions on the subject of tapu separated by two plot events: in chapter five, the Pakeha Maori arranges to buy some land and in chapter thirteen he describes how he himself becomes part payment. He ought to be able to move from negotiation to settlement more directly, but something about tapu impedes his narrative progress.

> If I could only get clear of this *tapu* I would 'try back'. I believe I ought to be just now completing the purchase of my estate. I am sure I have

been keeping house a long time before it is built, which is, I believe, clear against the rules, so I must get rid of this talk about the *tapu* the best way I can, after which I will start fair and try not to get before my story. (167)

A digression or two later, the narrator is 'getting tired of this *tapu*' (169), and many digressions later still, he protests, 'this *tapu* is a bore, even to write about' and vows to get rid of it 'lest it should kill my reader' (173) – presumably by having communicated too large a dose. Why can't the narrator rid himself of stories about tapu? Having handled the skull, having infected himself with this 'most horrible style of *tapu*' (154), the Pakeha Maori cheats the rituals of decontamination a little, and the suspicion remains that he 'had not been as completely purified' as he might have been (158). The narrator still carries the taint of tapu, and that is why he cannot rid himself of the topic, why he must 'try back' to an occasion chronologically prior to his contamination. Some readers might protest that Maning is just being clever, that his narrative pirouette derisively treats tapu as a form of mumbo jumbo. On the contrary, it seems to me that the Pakeha Maori really is a man possessed: by a storytelling demon, by the tapu of the Maori dead and by the demon of civilisation. Like many a bedevilled person, he is largely oblivious of his condition, and supposes that others, not himself, are in the thrall of mysterious invisible powers – powers linked, in Maning's day, to race, and in our own, to culture.

Behind all the fooling, Maning has a theory of tapu that draws on Adam Smith and anticipates structuralism's eye for binary organisation. The idea that people possessed a 'mysterious quality' that was 'extended or communicated to all their property, especially to their clothes, weapons, ornaments, and tools' (146) has a distinct utility: whereas muru and utu, he perceives, aid the transfer of goods from one person or group to another, 'the original object of the ordinary *tapu* seems to have been the preservation of property' (146).[13] Working together, muru and tapu constitute a system for the circulation of wealth in a society, while also demonstrating that primitive laws regarding property are the natural foundation of more developed social arrangements.[14] All this might be further explained in a projected book written in a mix of our two languages, to be called *Ko nga ture* – 'Of the Laws' in Maori, and punning of course on 'the law of nature' (126). The following anecdote, however, goes well beyond proving that '*tapu* is a great preserver of property' (147).

A chief of very high rank, standing and *mana*, was on a war expedition; with him were about five hundred men. His own personal *tapu* was increased two-fold, as was that of all the warriors who were with him, by the *war tapu* . . . . They were, in fact, as irreverent pakehas used to say, 'tabooed an inch thick', and as for the head chief, he was perfectly unapproachable. The expedition halted to dine. The portion of food set apart for the chief . . . was, of course, enough for two or three men, and consequently the greater part remained unconsumed. The party having dined, moved on, and soon after a party of slaves and others, who had been some mile or two in the rear, came up carrying ammunition and baggage. One of the slaves, a stout hungry fellow, seeing the chief's unfinished dinner, [ate] it up before asking any questions, and had hardly finished when he was informed by a horror-stricken individual – another slave who had remained behind when the *taua* had moved on – of the fatal act he had committed. I knew the unfortunate delinquent well. He was remarkable for courage, and had signalized himself in the wars of the tribe. . . . No sooner did he hear the fatal news than he was seized by the most extraordinary convulsions and cramps in the stomach, which never ceased till he died, about sundown the same day. He was a strong man, in the prime of life, and if any pakeha free-thinker should have said he was not killed by the *tapu* of the chief, which had been communicated to the food by contact, he would have been listened to with feelings of contempt for his ignorance and inability to understand plain and direct evidence. (147)

Could a person really keel over and die in these circumstances? It depends how far we suppose bodies can be governed by beliefs, how thoroughly we suppose behaviour is conditioned by culture. A rationalist, answering in the negative, risks underestimating the role of belief and the force of cultural difference; an affirmer of alternative realities risks buying into some of the more credulous assumptions of colonialism. Similar anecdotes can be found in every part of the colonised world: of pointing the bone in aboriginal societies, of voodoo dolls in the Caribbean, of witch doctors in Africa. As with ascriptions of cannibalism, the existence of many similar stories suggests we may be dealing with another strain of Western myth. My own hunch is that Maning is passing on a story he has been told. It sounds like a colonial version of an urban legend – a story so good it ought to be true, but which tells us more about those who believe it and pass it on.

Maning's description emphasises both the weight and gravity of the *tapu* and the strength and vitality of the transgressing slave. These points in turn highlight the workings of tapu: it is communicated to the slave by contact and, after hearing 'fatal news' of the 'fatal act', results in his succumbing to fate. But compare the following passage on the current state of the Maori, delivered not in the Pakeha Maori's usual voice, but with an authority about other worlds reminiscent of Captain Kirk making a 'star-date' entry in the log of the *S. S. Enterprise*.

> Doubting our professions of friendship, fearing our ultimate designs, led astray by false friends, possessed of that 'little learning' which is, in their case, most emphatically 'a dangerous thing', divided amongst themselves, – such are the people with whom we are now in contact, – such the people to whom, for our own safety and their preservation, we must give new laws and institutions, new habits of life, new ideas, sentiments, and information, – whom we must either civilise or by our mere contact exterminate. (137–38)

'Mere contact': the phrase occurs repeatedly in late nineteenth-century Social Darwinist texts. The anonymous author of 'Musings on Manning's [*sic*] "Old New Zealand"' (1877), for example, argues that the effects of imported disease on the native population had been much exaggerated. 'Unless the race was already "on the go" from some other reasons, real depopulation never takes place from that cause.'[15] The real cause is something else again. 'No early race of any intelligence ... was ever so petted and cared for as the Maori, but they went', says this writer,

> according to the behests of that terrible law: 'Remove thyself, that a higher than thou may take thy place, as soon as thou hast sufficiently warmed it for him'. A law so stern and inexorable, that the very means used to prevent its execution only assists it, and the efforts of the

incoming race to preserve some relics of the outgoing one only hasten its destruction.[16]

These are not the opinions of an isolated crank. Benjamin Kidd, for instance, in *Social Evolution* (1894), writes: 'The weaker races disappear before the stronger through the effects of mere contact . . . . The Anglo-Saxon, driven by forces inherent in his own civilisation, comes to develop the natural resources of the land, and the consequences appear to be inevitable.'[17] But how does 'mere contact', this strange contagion, work, and what is the nature of this grave, somewhat mysterious, quality inherent in Anglo-Saxon civilisation?

Tapu, whatever else it might be, is partly a screen onto which Maning and a racialist audience project the obscure and magical workings of Social Darwinism. When the Pakeha Maori arrives on shore in New Zealand, he travels back to an atemporal category of time variously termed savage or primitive, yet mere contact also places the indigenous culture on the first rung of historical, civilised time. The question is: will Maori rise or fall? In 'The Native Question', written in the late 1850s, Maning argues against those seeking to 'accelerate the progress of natives' (218), and would prefer 'trusting to the current of time to carry on the native race nearer and more near to a state of civilisation' (220) – yet he expected war to intervene. As an older man, he became more pessimistic still. In a letter of 1878, he wrote: 'When the waters of the sea overflow and mingle with the waters of the lake the fish become sickly and many die. The Maori are now surrounded by a medium not made for them, or such as they, as Maories were not made for, they are dying of the slow poison of civilisation.'[18] In some ways, *Old New Zealand* offers a step-by-step account. Following the digression on tapu, Maning plots the decline of Maori through a web of circumstance and innate characteristics. The Maori are warlike, they desperately require muskets, and so, in order to produce flax and timber for trade, they neglect their crops and swap their dry hilltop forts for the unhealthy dampness of the swamps. 'There', Maning writes, 'lying on the spongy soil, on beds of rushes which rotted under them – in little, low, dens of houses . . . full of noxious exhalations from the damp soil, and impossible to ventilate – they were cut off by disease in a manner absolutely frightful' (185).[19] Maning either, as in the chain of events just related, portrays the Maori in a situation of passive acquiescence before fate, or as actively willing extinction upon themselves: in wars, in the way that suicide was an 'almost daily occurrence' in the good old times (170). If the mechanisms of tapu, as of social evolution, work through contagion and mere contact, it is also clear that, for Maning, civilisation is always already more potently tapu than any native chief on the war path; and if a slave should die after eating tapu food, it only goes to show that his race has internalised the demographic instincts of the lemming.

But the Pakeha Maori has caught the infection too. After eating food with the same hands that handled the skull of a dead chief, after swallowing those demons, he returns tired and hungry, to an empty house.

> The instinct of a hungry man sent me into the kitchen; there was nothing eatable to be seen but a raw leg of pork, and the fire was out. I now began to suspect that this attempt of mine to look down the *tapu* would fail, and that I should remain excommunicated for some frightfully indefinite period. I began to think of Robinson Crusoe, and to wonder if I could hold out as well as he did. Then I looked hard at the leg of pork. . . . (A horrible misanthropy was fast taking hold of me.) Why should I not tear my leg of pork raw, like a wolf? 'I will run a muck!' – suddenly said I. 'I wonder how many I can kill before they "bag" me? I will kill, kill, kill! – but – I must have some supper.' (155)

This is the story of how the Pakeha became Maori. Because the tapu of the dead chief has been internalised, the Pakeha starts to resemble a rangatira of the good old times; that is to say, he becomes a kind of vaudeville cannibal, a creature of appetite, misanthropic, unrestrained, who will kill, kill, kill, because he must have some supper. Perhaps 'mere contact' with the tapu of the dead has opened a door; perhaps a thousand and one devils rush into him – but the mother of them all is the demon of civilisation.

In the final chapter, the Pakeha Maori, apparently confused and divided between the two halves of his identity, predicts, 'I belong to both parties, and I don't care a straw which wins; but I am sure we shall have fighting' (198). There is no confusion of identities here.

Maning believes there will be war, and his emphasis on Maori violence and skill in warfare is, as Joan Fitzgerald has argued, a warning to his possibly complacent readers.[20] But he is not merely suggesting that settlers should be on their guard; he is also convinced that war and subjugation are necessary instruments of civilisation. In a letter of October 1862, he told McLean:

I am no enemy but a friend to the natives and I know that their advancement depends in plain terms on their being <u>forced</u> in the first instance to submit to law. I have tamed wild bulls, wild horses and wild <u>men</u> in my time. There is always one struggle for natural, brutal, unprofitable, unrestrained liberty . . . and then all is over. The brute or the savage succumbs to force and afterwards willingly and with both pleasure and advantage submits to a salutary restraint. (213)

A year later, in the midst of war, and anxious about the conciliatory line taken by 'would-be-Authorities on Maori matters', he tells the same correspondent: 'it has become a dire necessity that [Maori] turbulence which has been in every way encouraged be quelled by force' (215). He never relinquished or modified that advice. As late as 1873, for example, the Sullivan murder prompted a long letter to McLean arguing that it was vital for the Europeans to amass all their power and properly subject the Waikato.[21] Later in that decade, Zulu successes reminded him of the clever way leaders like Te Whiti can 'put the onus of the first blow on Grey and the Pakeha and at the same time feeling his pulse to see if there is any fight at all in him'. 'They have found that out now', he added ominously, 'and the Maori king will act accordingly.'[22] Maning, with his bellicose alarums, joins all those figures in history who have recommended visiting destruction upon a population in order to save them from a backward ideology. If the demon of civilisation is, as I earlier suggested, an angel of history whose pointing arm is lifted towards the golden ladder of civilisation, it might be more apt to picture him, as Walter Benjamin did, as the angel whose face is turned toward the past in contemplation of the wreckage strewn about him; an angel of history whose beating wings are caught in the storm of progress, buffeting him backwards into the future, 'while the pile of debris before him grows skyward'.[23]

So far, we have dealt with tapu as a sort of demonic and transferable essence that might pass from person to person in a manner satirically intended to reveal the ingrained violence of the Maori, but which in fact displays the violence of a will to civilise others. In this respect, Maning's idea of tapu has race-like, or culture-like, attributes: once you've got it, you are stuck with it, which is why 'mere contact' with an object 'infected' by tapu resonates so strongly with the idea of 'fatal contact' in various dying race scenarios. But I have also argued that Maning's writing outflanks both his intentions and any merely corrective criticism of them. If we look less deeply but more closely still, it is apparent that tapu, even as Maning describes it, has another logic entirely. In the examples we have considered so far, tapu is an inescapable and contagious property of persons and things – the fatal touch of a Midas or a leper. But Maning also gives us many examples in which tapu requires caution as electricity requires caution. It runs through the universe, and whether its charge be concentrated or diffuse, it can be channelled or converted (made noa or 'earthed') precisely because it is so transferable.

On one occasion, the Pakeha Maori joins a large party setting off on an expedition; once the first waka departs, the remaining rangatira and warriors look about in vain for boys, women or slaves kept back to carry food into the remaining canoe; as tapu prohibits men of their consequence carrying provisions, they seem to have snookered themselves. But someone has the idea not of carrying the vital supplies, but of *hiki-ing* them – dangling the load as if it were a baby, and diverting the charge of tapu with a pun. Alternatively, in the case of a man made tapu through his work in the kumara fields, the inconvenience of tapu might be dodged by choosing to observe only the letter of the law. Tapu forbids the gardener entering the whare noa to observe the goings-on – but he is able to 'give tapu the slip' (152) by poking his head through the raupo walls of the house; and since he is outside from his feet to his shoulders, who is to say he has entered the whare? The best example, though, involves the Pakeha Maori himself. All his friends and relatives desert him in his morbidly tapu state, but eventually an old one-eyed tohunga arrives with prayers and a homeopathic basket of kumara to effect a reduction of the dangerous energies. The Pakeha Maori sputters and protests under these ministrations, and when he discovers that not only the plates, pots and pans from the infected kitchen have to be destroyed, but also the very clothes he is standing in, he becomes more savage still.

> Human patience could bear no more. . . . 'How would you prefer being killed, old ruffian? – can you do anything in this way?' (Here a pugilistic demonstration) . . . . 'Come on! – what are you waiting for', said I. In those days, when labouring under what Dickens calls the 'description of temporary insanity which arises from a sense of injury', I always involuntarily fell back on my mother tongue, which in this case was perhaps fortunate, as my necromantic old friend did not understand the full force of my eloquence. He could not, however, mistake my warlike and rebellious attitude, and could see clearly I was going into one of those most unaccountable rages that pakehas were liable to fly into, without any imaginable cause. 'Boy', said he, gravely and quietly, and without seeming to notice my very noticeable declaration of war and independence, 'don't act foolishly; don't go mad. No one will ever come near you while you have those clothes. You will be miserable here by yourself. And what is the use of being angry? – what will *anger* do for you?' The perfect coolness of my old friend, the complete disregard he paid to my explosion of wrath, as well as his reasoning, began to make me feel a little disconcerted. He evidently had come with the purpose and intention to get me out of a very awkward scrape. (157)

The tohunga is the wiser, and the more civilised, man. But although the Pakeha Maori has done a bit of 'hiki-ing' of his own – he has a strategic loss of memory about entering the main part of the house – he finds that by modifying his behaviour in the light of others' perception of him, life can return easily and smoothly to normal. And though the respectful distance with which he is treated in return indicates he has not entirely given tapu the slip, he comes to realise that 'in consideration of my being a pakeha, . . . I was let off very easy, and might therefore be supposed to retain some tinge of the dreadful infection' (158). Against all notions of ingrained racial or determined cultural qualities, against the invention of incommensurable differences between Maori and Pakeha, is the give and take of the ever-changing beach, where warring incompatibilities dissolve in the middle ground.

Speaking with Demons: Maning, Shortland and the Atua

If the living might on occasion forget the dead, the dead do not forget the living. As atua, spirits of the dead watched over Maori in the old times, punishing breaches of tapu and bringing sickness, but also sending courage to the warrior and securing prosperity for the tribe. For most Europeans of the early-contact period, they seemed a god-ridden credulous people, always ready to find an unnecessary supernatural cause behind every effect, always subjecting the future to the sway of omens, portents and the mummery of their priests. On the whole, Europeans of the 1830s and 1840s were either too pragmatic or too caught up in the reality of their own spirit world to seek conduits to another, although that was about to change in the great spiritualist revival of the mid-to-late nineteenth century, when ancient Polynesians and Sioux medicine men were at the beck and call of table rappers and trance speakers the world over.

But there are, nevertheless, several early accounts of contact with the dead. The Catholic missionary, Father Servant, had a professional's curiosity in the tenets of Maori theology, and left a valuable account of the new sect founded by Papahurihia, through whom the spirits of the Maori dead spoke to Maning at a séance in the Hokianga in 1846 (or thereabouts).[24] The voice Maning heard made 'a strange melancholy sound, like . . . wind blowing into a hollow vessel' (164). Several years earlier, further south in Matamata, the government official Edward Shortland was also struck by the voice of the atua. 'It is not like that of mortals', he recalled, 'but a mysterious kind of sound, half whistle, half whisper.'[25]

Might it be possible even now to hear that voice? In one sense yes: Te Whiowhio, the whistling cult derived from the teachings of Papahurihia, still has a few adherents in the quiet backwaters of the Hokianga, but that is not the experience I am after. In literary criticism, we sometimes talk of hearing the tone of a poem. The poem itself makes no noise, but what we might call 'reading between the lines' is an ordinary and common path to the kind of hearing I am interested in, and not only in literary circles either, for the dead, when they talk, are not always direct and to the point, and one may need to divine what they mean. Most importantly, though, whatever there is to hear in the accounts left by Maning and Shortland involves cross-cultural communication from another time that itself depends on a medium, the European commentator, whom we may suppose to be deaf to many of the frequencies that matter, but who will nonetheless have things to say.

There is a template for this kind of account, and I suppose it is not too different from the kind of report unbelieving observers like ourselves might write in similar circumstances. Like Maning and Shortland, we would have the good manners to keep our scepticism to ourselves, and we might also find the occasion to be more impressive and more challenging than we had expected. Maning, who is about to hear the voice of the recently killed warrior Hauraki, his dear friend and brother-in-law, sets the scene in these terms:

> The priest retired to the darkest corner [of the house]. All was expectation, and the silence was only broken by the sobbing of the sister, and other female relations of the dead man. . . . This state of things continued for a long time, and I began to feel . . . as if there was something real in the matter. The heart-breaking sobs of the women, and the grave and solemn silence of the men, convinced me, that to them at least, this was a serious matter. I saw the brother of the dead man now and then wiping the tears in silence from his eyes. I wished I had not come, for I felt that any unintentional symptom of incredulity on my part would shock and hurt the feelings of my friends extremely; and yet, while feeling thus, I felt myself more and more near to believing in the deception about to be practised. The real grief, and also the general undoubting faith, in all around me, had this effect. (162)

Sympathy promotes not so much a suspension as an elasticity of belief. Following the Shakespearean phrase so often quoted in these circumstances – 'There are more things in heaven and earth, Horatio, Than are dreamt of in your philosophy' – let us term this the Horatio moment. As the Horatio moment intensifies, so too does an itch to demonstrate the fraudulence of the proceedings. Shortland, impressed by the atua's uncanny knowledge of his movements in the far-off Bay of Islands, wonders if the spirit saw him also at the Hokianga – 'Yes', replied the spirit, 'in a ship with two masts.'[26] It was a good answer insofar as the Hokianga has a dangerous bar and attracted only smaller vessels, but Shortland had set a trap – he had never been to the Hokianga at all. Maning's challenge, by contrast, had a rather different outcome. Hauraki had kept a journal containing a register of births and deaths that Maning was anxious to obtain, but none of his relatives had been able to find it. When the spirit of his dead brother requested, as spirits so often do, to be asked anything, anything at all, Maning inquired after the missing book, and was told by that strange whistling voice immediately where to find it – an indication, perhaps, that the book had been not so much lost as withheld. 'What is in the book?', Maning then asked, perhaps intending to check whether the atua could divine what was on the third line of the fourth page, but the spirit of a sudden departed with stereophonic cries of farewell that seemed to come first from deep beneath the ground and then from high in the air. 'A ventriloquist', thought Maning, deeply impressed, and half-wondering if it might have been the devil himself who spoke (165).

The accounts, then, are centred on the uncanny experiences of the observer, and are ontologically driven insofar as the question of the existence of these spirits takes centre stage in the narrative. Most of the reported conversation with the atua is concerned with that point. Slightly off stage, though, is the friend, the Maori relative or companion under whose good offices the Pakeha is able to attend. If we widen the focus to include that figure, and change what is largely represented as a dialogue between two into a multiply stranded conversation, then perhaps we might also develop an ear for at least some of what the atua had to say.

Maning is surrounded by friends: most importantly, his wife, Moengaroa, 'a fine, stately, and really handsome woman of about five and twenty', sister of the slain Hauraki. As soon as the voice is heard, she runs, arms extended, into the darkness, with a cry of 'affection and despair, such as was not good to hear' (164). Straining against her other brother's arms, she collapses and lies in a faint on the ground. At the same moment, Hauraki's widow calls out, 'Is it you? – is it you? – *truly* is it you? – *aue! aue!* they hold me, they restrain me; . . . they watch me, but I go to you' (164). She too falls insensible, but not before vowing to join her husband before sunrise. After this dramatic opening, the séance proceeds as I have described, but before attention turns to the Pakeha and the question of the book, we should note that several Maori make inquiries as to how their relatives are faring in the other world.

Later that night, Maning is woken by alarms and commotion. Hauraki's widow has found a loaded musket and blown herself to pieces. Her father cradles the mangled body, not weeping, but howling and moaning in hopeless despair. Papahurihia, the medium through whom the atua spoke, sidles up to Maning and, in a calm low voice, explains that the young woman has 'followed her rangatira' (166). At this point in the narrative, something very peculiar happens. Maning turns from the scene he has been describing and addresses the reader in these terms.

> Now young ladies, I have promised not to frighten your little wits out with raw-head-and-bloody-bones stories, a sort of thing I detest, but which has been too much the fashion with folk who write of matters Maori. I have vowed not to draw a drop of blood except in a characteristic manner. But this story is tragedy, or I don't now what tragedy is, and the more tragic because, in every particular, literally true, and so if you cannot find some pity for the poor Maori girl who 'followed her lord to spirit land', I shall make it my business not to fall in love with any of you any more for I won't say how long. (166)

Something jars in this attempt at flippancy. Elsewhere, Maning is perfectly capable of seeing the funny side of, say, the fate of a pipe-smoking Maori who pokes his head into a gunpowder barrel, and there is a sense in which he asks us to see the young woman who has thrown her life away as characteristic of Maori of her time. Hers is one of many deaths suggesting that Maori have a careless and slender hold on life, and that the population at large has internalised a strange instinct for destruction. But this anecdote, with its melodrama and bizarre shift in tone, seems motivated by emotions that the writer is not fully in control of, as if feelings associated with genuine loss – fear, rage, denial, self-reproach – stalk this attempt to lighten his narrative.

It seems to me that the young woman who dies is a composite figure, part Hauraki's widow, part representative Maori, but also Maning's own wife, the sister of Hauraki – and it is worth noting that it is a sister rather than a wife who pines to death out of grief for her brother in an earlier telling of the obsequies surrounding Hauraki's death.[27] Moengaroa actually died in 1847 – we have no information as to the circumstances, but possibly there were complications following the birth of her fourth child. And so, as Maning tells the story of the séance, we might suspect that a response to her death and a response to her grieving are intertwined in a tragedy that is at once impersonal and deeply private, and at once distanced through an uneasy lurch into humour and accurately named as 'true tragedy' in the text.

Insofar as Maning's theme is death and loss, he also suggests the missing half of the conversation – what the atua actually said when he wasn't talking to the Pakeha about Hauraki's book. The atua and his audience speak mostly about the dead – have you seen x? have you seen y? – 'Yes', the spirit assures them, 'they are all with me' (164). It is always difficult to imagine what it would be like to live through a period of severe and sudden population collapse – especially in an oral culture that preserves far fewer traces of a subjective response than are available in our own. But we know from other times and places – the rise of spiritualism in the United States after the Civil War, and in Europe during and after the Great War, for example – that people will search for explanations for suffering by bringing the worlds of the living and the dead into communicative alignment.

Papahurihia was an expert in these matters. According to Father Servant, his tutelary spirit as a medium was Te Nakahi, the serpent, no less, of the book of Genesis and of Moses's rod. Although Papahurihia was inspired by the Bible, he drew considerably more on traditional beliefs about lizards, especially those called upon by tohunga as messengers – aria – between the realms of life and death. One of these lizard atua was specifically associated with the new epidemics. 'This [atua] is evil', Servant reports, 'he comes from foreign countries to kill Maoris.'[28] The serpent who spoke to Eve becomes cargo, to use a Pacific metaphor, a sign that travels across cross-cultural boundaries, keeping some meanings and losing others in an unpredictable process of revaluation and transformation. On one hand, the lizard can become the spiritual personification of new epidemics and sickness, and on the other, the nearest thing to a lizard in the Bible can become Papahurihia's familiar. One of the first biblical passages translated into Maori comes from John's gospel: 'And just as Moses lifted up the serpent in the wilderness, so must the Son of Man be lifted up, that whoever believes in him may have eternal life.'[29] Against the lizard god of the missionaries and the epidemics, Papahurihia lifted up the serpent, Te Nakahi, and brought news of eternal life: 'how is so and so getting on in that place?' he was asked at the séance, and he might have replied in these words, ventriloquised here in Father Servant's account of his teachings:

When a good man has left this life, which is but darkness, he goes into . . . the dwelling place of the good; there one feels neither the rigours of the cold, nor those of hunger, nor thirst; one enjoys endless light. There, all is in abundance: flour, sugar, muskets, ships – there also reign murder and voluptuousness.[30]

While Papahurihia was an inveterate enemy of the protestant missionaries – in their heaven, he reckoned, all you could do was eat books – Wiremu Tamihana Tarapipipi, Edward Shortland's friend, was on the side of the new religion. Shortland met the recent convert in 1842, at a time when members of Ngati Haua, his tribe, were much divided in their religious sympathies. As in the north, many attributed a climbing death rate and new forms of sickness to Christianity, and the decision of their leading chief to become baptised was greeted with dismay by many of his people.[31] One old priest was so disgusted, he challenged the young man to confront the atua, and Tarapipipi, Lady Martin informs us, 'half fearfully, half willingly agreed'.

He went into the house where the old priest was lying wrapped up in a blanket. Suddenly, as he sat by him, a shrill whistling cry came from the roof of the house. [Tarapipipi] darted out to see if any one were outside, but no one was near. On his return, he plucked up courage to cry out: 'You are a false and lying spirit, perhaps', and a low voice answered from the roof: 'No, no! I am a true god!' Poor [Tarapipipi] was greatly scared, especially when the old priest warned him that his Atua Maori would destroy him. But after a while, finding he did not die, he took heart again. He, however, still thought it was Satan's voice.[32]

A year or so later, following a conversation about atua one morning, Tarapipipi invited Shortland to attend a séance. They hoped to keep their plans private and to arrive without warning at the house of an old woman who had the power to summon the dead, but on their way fell in with Tarapipipi's cousin, Tuakaraina, who was of the anti-Christian faction, and who insisted on joining them. While Tarapipipi remains outside, Tuakaraina encourages the medium to contact the spirits, and when nothing happens, calls out to them himself, beating the earth with his fists, and demanding not only that they appear but also that they punish the Pakeha for his presumed scorn of the Atua Maori. It is only when Tarapipipi looks in to assure the medium, who also has recently become 'mikonari', that he is not opposed to the proceedings, that the first of three spirits arrives. Something heavy seems to drop onto the thatched roof of the hut; it moves along the ridgepole and stops above the old woman, who then begins to channel, in a whistling voice, the spirit of Tarapipipi's own father.

The reported conversations largely concern attempts by both Shortland and Tuakaraina to persuade the atua to make himself visible: Shortland is warned it would be dangerous if the atua approached, but Tuakaraina urges the spirit to teach the Pakeha a lesson. The atua, however, disdains to become present in an embodied form, and as Shortland can tell the woman is doing the whistling, his Horatio moment centres on the mystery of the object that appears to drop with impeccable timing on the roof of the hut. Tarapipipi is outside, and Shortland, confident that his friend would not be party to a deception, can find no explanation for the uncanny harbinger of the spirits' arrival; in the face of mystery, the light of reason comes to his aid with an observation on the similarity between Tuakaraina calling for his god and the ancient Hebrew worshippers of Baal. The wonder of the experience is thus transferred to wonder at the survival of an archaic religious practice without apparent modification in the isolation of Aotearoa.

If we bring Tarapipipi back into the picture, a number of rather different points come into focus. Shortland reckoned Tarapipipi probably thought of Christ as a superior sort of atua, more powerful and better natured than those of the Maori, who were no longer regarded with dread but were treated with due circumspection nonetheless.

It seems to me that Tarapipipi initiates the meeting and sets experimental conditions because he has found a sympathetic investigator in Shortland. Perhaps Christian scruple keeps him outside the hut, perhaps a political line of demarcation is being observed; either way, his position works to isolate the medium. His side of the conversation with the atua is worth following closely: when the spirit of his father arrives, it reveals something apparently known only to his wife and himself. Round one to the atua perhaps. But Tarapipipi then leans in and quietly asks Shortland to put his hand over the mouth of the medium: something he personally might not have been able to do without causing offence, but which a Pakeha might well get away with. Shortland discovers the sound is being made by the old woman. From this point on, everything that Tarapipipi says is accompanied by laughter: when his father asks for a present – perhaps a cask of tobacco or a coat – Tarapipipi wonders what use a spirit has for a coat: 'how will you be able to put it on?', he asks shrewdly.[33] The third spirit is an infant, summoned at Tuakaraina's behest, because such spirits are known to be capricious and malevolent, and it is their role to punish offences against tapu of the sort Tuakaraina alleges Shortland has recently committed. By the time this spirit arrives, it is as if the old woman's cover is blown and she and Tarapipipi are quietly having fun at his cousin's expense: Tarapipipi chuckles at everything the infant says, but the atua responds to Tuakaraina's request for utu with an insult, 'tou rokeroke' – a phrase Shortland regards as 'not sufficiently delicate for translation'.[34]

The missionaries and Shortland expected Tarapipipi to believe in atua; his heathen upbringing is a taint that baptism would not quite overcome. In more up-to-date terms, we might observe that Christianity had to become part of Maori culture before Maori became Christians. But Tarapipipi's role in the séance he attended with Shortland suggests a less determined picture, one in which beliefs about belief are undergoing rapid change, as well as the beliefs themselves. A Maori of his village tried to explain this to Alfred Brown, the missionary. 'The belief of a native', he said, 'was no part of himself like his head . . . it was rather a hat which could be taken off or put on at pleasure.'[35] As different belief systems encounter each other along the cross-cultural frontier, we not only find forms of syncretism such as

Papahurihia's anti-Christian reading of the Bible, but also more generally that an experience of rapid change accompanied by population collapse promotes both a search for belief and an instrumental attitude to questions of belief.

In the mid-1840s, missionaries in Tarapipipi's district were complaining about the baleful influence of wahuism – a form of spiritualist faith healing practised by 'Wahu Maori' – Hawaiians from the island of Oahu who had come ashore from a whaling ship. One of their number, Brown complained, was 'deceiving the people by pretending to work their cures in the case of extreme sickness', and later lamented the 'sad falling off' of numbers at Divine Service, many of whom had been 'led from the simplicity of the Gospels by the lying wonders of the wahu natives'.[36] Perhaps this counter-missionary was the person Cowan identifies as Friday the Kahuna, a boat-steerer on a New Bedford whaler who came ashore at Kororareka, travelled south, and eventually settled with the people of Rangiuru Bay, in the northern Bay of Plenty.[37] James Cowan – no Maning but he tries – spins a yarn about deadly makutu, picturing the Hawaiian tohunga twitching the wands of life and death as he chants incantations through the night, eyes ablaze as 'his form shivered with intensity of the thought waves he directed at the unseen and unseeing object of his sorcery'.[38] The victim sees it all happen in a dream and is dead within days – 'the fatalism of his race, killed him as surely as ever bullet or tomahawk blade could kill'.[39] Colonial balderdash? Certainly, but more than that too. Perhaps 'the Wahoo Man' was a confidence trickster come ashore off a whaler, perhaps he was a true tohunga; either way, I am sure he too talked with the atua, for if there is one place that atua flourish, it is surely between worlds.

CHAPTER FOUR

A Small Plot at Orakau

All plots tend to move deathward.
– Don DeLillo, White Noise

L AST SUMMER I WENT TO ORAKAU. I WANTED TO WALK OVER GROUND where, all those years ago, Maori resisting the invasion of the Waikato made what has come to be called their 'Last Stand'. Over several days in 1864, 300 Maori defenders of the pa repulsed the repeated attacks of about 1000 troops. Out of water, out of bullets, encircled by the British army, their situation seemed hopeless, but they refused an offer of surrender with the famous words, 'E Hoa, ka whawhai tonu ahau ki a koe! Ake! Ake! Ake!' – 'Friend, I will fight against you forever and forever!' – and later made a gallant escape through the encircling army. The story of this 'great moment in New Zealand history' has been told dozens of times, often with the emphasis one finds in the rolling title of Rudall Hayward's 1940 film *The Last Stand*.

In New Zealand after the Maori Wars of the sixties, men of famous British regiments took up land and became soldier settlers. Near one of the towns they founded – Te Awamutu – the townspeople filmed recently, these pages from rough-hewn history, re-enacting on the actual locations, the parts played by their pioneering forefathers. In the struggle for possession of this land of promise the 'Pakehas' (white men), found the Maoris tough and chivalrous fighters, who were often defeated by sheer weight of arms, but were never conquered. Today, the slowly blending races of white men and brown live in peace and equality as one people . . . the New Zealanders.[1]

Although Orakau is an important place in our history, the actual site near Kihikihi is unlikely to attract visitors. A small monument marking the fiftieth anniversary of the battle is situated on what one would normally call the side of the road. You stop the car, walk over, see what there is to see – but there is no parting of the swirling mists of time, no intimation of the smoke and stir of battle, only the pelting roar of cars and logging trucks. You discover a small plaque with a map of the engagement. The engraving is a little indistinct and it is a neck-twisting puzzle trying to orient the faint lines of a diagram to anything in the landscape. What you see is ordinary farmland: fences, hedges, cows, hay barns, tractors, buildings. You learn that on the other side of the cutting, a macrocarpa indicates the mass grave of Maori who fell that day, but you guess much of it would have been bulldozed when they put the road through. A visit to this small plot of ground turns out to be a very ordinary New Zealand experience: you come to a place where you might expect the past to be remembered, but what you actually encounter is the record of a kind of forgetting going on.

In 1914, the same year as the Orakau monument was erected, William Satchell published *The Greenstone Door*, a literary narrative centring on the historic episode. A monument casts a briefly imposing shadow before settling into the unnoticed background – alas for books! How short the afterburn of their celebrity, how rapid the decline from display to discharged item, from back bedroom bookshelf to unpicked item on the picked-over charity stall. Few novels have plumbed obscurity more quickly than *The Greenstone Door*. In the first year of the Great War, it must have seemed odd for a writer to make so much of a small local skirmish; the book was ignored, briefly revived, and ignored all over again. Copies are still obtainable on shelves where books wash up – perhaps in the edition bearing the Ozymandian legend, 'New Zealand Classic'. My own copy was a school prize; for years unread, yet – as it turned out – very far from unreadable, even though it has something of the drawn-out and stilted quality of an Edwardian historical romance.

Satchell wanted it to be a New Zealand take on *The Last of the Mohicans*, which in turn was modelled on the historical novels of Sir Walter Scott – another influence on Satchell. Both *The Greenstone Door* and *The Last of the Mohicans* have noble warriors and beautiful half-caste maidens; Hawkeye, the white frontiersman, fights alongside his Indian brothers much as Purcell, the Pakeha Maori, fights for his adopted tribe against the Crown; both books lament the vanishing wilderness and the closing of the cross-cultural frontier. The similarities may go further. Magua, Cooper's revengeful villain, is modelled, Geoffrey Sanborn has recently argued, on the unjustly whipped Te Pahi and the affair known in our history as the 'Burning of the *Boyd*'.[2] And yet, despite these many parallels, and despite Satchell's best intentions, his plot goes haywire. This is not the same as going nowhere – the fate of an earlier colonial epic, Alfred Domett's *Ranolf and Amohia*, a long poem aspiring to be the *Hiawatha* of our literature. It might have been a trophy in the cupboard had its author not taken two wrong turns: he thought frequent stops for scenic word painting and digressive tours into philosophy would lend interest to a stock cross-cultural romance; he was wrong. Yet Domett is probably as able a writer as Satchell – both are ambitious, both look to the best American and European models. The key difference is that Satchell is both more interested in history and more concerned with plot. As a result, Domett's transplanted epic suffocates in alien soil while Satchell's novel becomes what botanists call a sport.

By following the plot of *The Greenstone Door*, you get to know something of the history of the battle, but plainly – as with Maning and Earle – there are silences and many absent voices. In its own way, the novel commemorates the valiant Maori dead while putting the literary equivalent of a road through the kind of plot in which bodies might lie. But what if we were to put those monuments together: the small plot at Orakau has the advantage of occupying actual space; a novel, on the other hand, can only take place in a represented landscape, but yields information and atmosphere. What would happen if my eye were more able to connect the spaces a book represents with the actual places it describes? Will I be left in that stock New Zealand pose, map spread on the car bonnet, gaping at an absence that was history; or might trying to read this novel geographically be a way of recovering memory, of unsealing those acts of forgetting embedded within our memorials of settlement?

The Greenstone Door is narrated by Cedric Tregarthen, a waverer in the tradition of Sir Walter Scott's Waverley heroes, who is torn between loyalties to his Maori tribe, and to civilisation as represented by Sir George Grey and his ward, the beautiful Helenora Wilde, with whom Cedric is in love.[3] Cedric's foster-father, the Pakeha Maori trader Purcell, has decided to side with his wife's people, an honourable choice that will lead him to be on the wrong side when the conflicted loyalties of wavering characters are resolved at the battle of Orakau. Most of the named Maori characters die bravely in this conflict, and Purcell is shot for treason soon after. The various outcomes and alle-giances of the novel can be plotted by tracing a spatial and temporal division between three zones: a metropolitan zone, a semi-civilised zone and a savage zone – a division also found in history novels by Walter Scott and James Fenimore Cooper. In *The Greenstone Door*, Auckland constitutes a first zone; it is civilised and advanced. At some distance from it are two neighbouring zones: a semi-civilised, inter-mediary, agricultural zone which is home to Purcell and progressive Maori; and, beyond that, a mountainous third zone, where old-time Maori exist in a savage state under their cannibal chief, Te Huata.

The zones are readily located in actual space. Suppose you are standing on the Bombay Hills with Auckland at your back and the Waikato plains before you. Once you see the Waikato River, follow it as far as Ngaruawahia where two rivers join, then follow the Waipa River further south in the direction of Otorohanga. On the way, looking west, are the mountains of Pirongia. Purcell's pa is at Matakini, an invented place, but we are told it is on the Waipa River, and we also know that twelve miles to the west, high on a terrace that is one of the foothills of Pirongia, stands Te Huata's pa. Since, from this pa, you have a view of Kawhia harbour, Purcell's settlement must be somewhere between Puhenui and Waipa. It is not remote: anyone who has taken the back road from Ngaruawahia to Otorohanga has been thereabouts often.

But now take an actual historical view as you look south from the Bombay Hill. A boundary between the first two zones separates the Auckland district from the Waikato just below you at Pokeno, and extends eastward (through a line of redoubts) just south of the Hunua forest. We may take this line to represent the southern limit of Auckland influence in mid-1863, when Grey ordered all South Auckland Maori either to take an oath of allegiance or to move south of the Waikato River. A second line follows a division between the flat river country and the high and rugged mountain ranges to the west and east. Only the western border need concern us: it runs from the high country south and west of Auckland down to Pirongia. On the inland side of that mountainous border, we have land Maori and Pakeha fought over in a series of battles moving south over successive months towards Orakau in April 1864. This is the intermediary Waikato zone. In the novel, it consists of land made fertile and brought into production by the combined efforts of Maori and Pakeha; it is geographically close to, but ideologically distinct from, the mountainous/savage Pirongia zone. So far as this third zone is concerned, it is essential to realise that Maori did not live where Satchell's novel puts them: there are no major pa sites on Pirongia; birds were hunted in these rugged forests, but their hunters lived on the river flats and around the harbours, on land that, after Orakau, was soon lost to European confiscation and settlement.

Satchell needs to place Maori in the mountains for several reasons. Mountains are useful insofar as they highlight the passage across a boundary that is psychological and temporal as well as physical. Those three zones are a correlative of the Victorian ladder of progress: a present world of the city and trade; a sort of middle ages of farming and small settlement; and a dark old world of the iwi or tribe. Cedric can walk across the border from Purcell's settlement to Te Huata's mountain pa in a day; as Franco Moretti says of Walter Scott's Highlands, 'a distance of just a few miles, and people belong to different epochs'.[4] In terms of the psychology of difference, it also helps to have some Maori off in those mountains in order that others may be brought closer. In the world of this novel, Cedric and his friend Rangiora, though different, though far from equal, can be imagined as brothers partly through a contrast between them and a group of degenerate natives over yonder in a zone of absolute otherness.

These divisions are familiar and over-determined, and not so very different from the run-of-the-mill historical novel of the period. But in making his *Atlas of the European Novel*, Moretti noted something rather more surprising: stylistic choices also turn out to be determined by proximity to one of these borders – and again, *The Greenstone Door* follows this pattern exactly. The further away from Auckland you get, and the closer to Pirongia you get, the more figurative, stilted and melodramatic the language becomes. 'I should like to meet your foster father', says Governor Grey in Auckland (174).⁵ But in Pirongia we are apt to get: 'Thumb! . . . said I not to you years ago that in the day you brought more pakeha to the village you should go to the oven? . . . . Begone, you and the White Man who barks like a dog!' (101). Savage chiefs the world over talk much like that. They speak in tired metaphors and contorted syntax in order show how unfamiliar things must be in a world across the border – but without troubling the reader's familiar categories of reference. Across a second internal border, in the Waikato zone, the language conforms on the whole to a realist norm, with one exception. Maori characters associated with this zone will always sound like natural poets: 'Sweet have you made the hour of my freedom' (64), says Rangiora, thanking Cedric's sister Puhi-Huia for her company, as if he were Shakespeare in love. The same principle applies somewhat differently thirty years later in *The Last Stand*. As the camera takes us across a boundary into a Maori village – 'favourite calling place of war parties moving north to attack British settlements' – the film runs over a stylistic judder bar. Out of the blue, a voiceover describes traditional pastimes taking place – 'there were games to test the rhythmic skill of the Maori maidens' – and the characters we see playing the stick games no longer belong to a fictional past, but have crossed into the 'ethnographic present' of mid-century anthropology, much as if the pages of an old *National Geographic* magazine had somehow come to life.

The outcome of Sir Walter Scott's historical novels, Moretti argues, is the incorporation of the Scottish Highlands into the larger unit of the state and the replacement of figurative language, which tends to be associated with zones not assimilable to Western knowledge, by the norms of realism. *The Greenstone Door* follows but does not quite fit this dominant pattern. After Orakau, most of the Maori identified characters are dead: not just Te Huata and his uncompromising savages, but more importantly the characters most closely associated with the mixed-race Waikato zone: Purcell, Rangiora and Puhi-Huia. The reader may feel it was glamorous of them to die for a lost cause, but in this battle between old and new, between tribal and national loyalties, there is no doubt which side ought and must prevail. Yet when Maori leave this zone of disputed land, they open a space not for 'good settlers' who might honour their memory, but for negatively portrayed characters like the Bromparts, who are corrupt, shallow and venal. It is conventional enough for the European historical novel to feature some overly zealous or unlikeable representatives of a new order, not common to so plainly award them the future.

An unusual level of discomfort with the colonial takeover is marked in other ways too. It may not be evident on a first reading, but Cedric, the narrator, who never sounds more than middle-aged, actually turns out to be an astonishingly old man – he is some seventy years older than the teenager who made an eternal bond of friendship with Rangiora by 'closing the greenstone door behind them' in the early chapters of the book. It seems to me that Satchell is drawn to put so much distance between story-time and the time of narration because he identifies as a novelist not with the growth of the nation but with something much bigger still: the inevitable working out of social evolution. As the novel's spokesman for history, Sir George Grey, puts it: 'it's the germs; the infinitesimal little things that fill the air where white men and brown men meet . . . . My mind sits up aloft and watches the making of the tide' (p. 298). The author is drawn to include as much time as he can because the novel is imagined from a loftier and more distant perspective than is afforded by the boosterising nationalism of so many of his contemporaries. Where they see the rise and progress of a colony towards nationhood, he observes the clash of people and cultures as if they were bacteria multiplying on a petri dish.

I have said Satchell kills off almost everyone in the Waikato and Pirongia zones. It is his way of declaring a part of history to be over: the tide was not only against the old Maori, it was also taking with it the efflorescence of two cultures meeting in a brief but inventive moment before the more powerful inevitably swamped the weaker. Most European and American historical novels set on the frontier end with the passing of the old or mixed order. *The Last Stand* ends like that too, with the death of Ariana in the white hero's arms.[6] But *The Greenstone Door* winds up peculiarly, the melodrama increases and the novel seems to bifurcate into two genres with barely compatible endings.

A little plot summary is in order. One of the main baddies in the book, the tohunga, Te Atua Mangu, has the power to turn Maori who annoy him into zombies obedient to his will, and Cedric, after escaping from the tohunga's clutches, has been hunted high and low by an implacable zombie-like figure called 'The Idiot'. After Orakau and the execution of Purcell, which might have made a normal ending for the book, Cedric suffers a nervous breakdown, and himself becomes an Idiot figure, fleeing from all human contact into the wilds of Pirongia. In this guise, Cedric is an early anticipation of what we have come to call the man alone figure, the double of the alienated settler artist, whose authenticity is radically tested, away from the falseness of towns, in a mortal confrontation with nature. Once again, one can imagine the novel reaching what would later become a normative ending along these lines. But Satchell now turns to another genre altogether: the imperial romance, and in particular, to a journey up a mighty big river to recover the lost European, be he Kurtz or Lord Greystoke. Cedric becomes the feminised object of Helenora's quest, and her share in the novel's plot, if we were to represent it visually, would be a line joining London to a distant colonial port, and from there following a river inland – in Conrad's words, like 'an immense snake uncoiled . . . its tail lost in the depths of the land'.[7]

But *The Greenstone Door* lacks the metropolitan neatness of those novels written from Europe. Cedric's plot line zigzags all across the country, and it is significant that he is rescued not from his home in the Waikato zone, but from Pirongia (to which, in his madness, he feels inescapably and mysteriously drawn), and that while his own position resembles that of the driven Maori Idiot character, he also confuses his rescuer with that very figure and runs from her. When at last Helenora catches up with him, she offers food and a line of poetry.

> 'I was thou neighbour once, thou rugged Pile.'
> 'Wordsworth.'
> 'What do you know of Wordsworth?'
> 'Wordsworth', I repeated, frowning. 'Wordsworth. He was a chief of the Ngapuhi.' . . . .
> 'Then what does he mean by his '"rugged Pile"'?'
> 'A pile, creature', said I, 'is the block used for the support of a food-store to preserve its contents from rats.' (394)

Cedric recovers from compulsive hybridisation soon enough, and the novel will at last reach its conclusion as the two lovers turn their backs on Pirongia and 'follow the trail for home through the golden lights and leafy shadows of the bush'.

> 'You remember', I said, 'the image of the Greenstone Door?'
> She nodded, and lifted her lips mutely to mine.
> And so at last for us two also the Greenstone Door was closed. (398)

Closing the Greenstone Door has earlier meant peace and fraternity between Maori and Pakeha, and its concluding reformation as a pact between two Pakeha is in keeping with the normal ending of an historical novel in which an old form of society is supplanted by a new. Yet Satchell has taken us there very indirectly, only after having presented Cedric as a character with Maori knowledge and affinities who needs to be rescued from a Maori zone by a character who is herself mistaken for a Maori. If this were a colonial romance pure and simple, the rationale of that ending would be much as Moretti describes it in his *Atlas of the European Novel*. Making Cedric an idiot captive allows him to be saved, converting what might have been a story of conquest into a story of liberation, and sidelining what might have been a story about the invasion of rich farming land into a story more about mountains. But Satchell can't let it rest there either. It is in the sheer strain of his ending, in its massive un-convincingness, in the very lengths to which his imagination is prepared to go to find an ending that gets rid of Maori while somehow saving 'them' by proxy as well, that *The Greenstone Door* is most deeply a Pakeha novel.

Part III *Settling*

IN 1843, THE LONDON FIRM OF SMITH, ELDER & CO. PUBLISHED a selection of testimonials from settlers of the Wellington, Whanganui, Nelson and New Plymouth districts. A resident of the 'city' of Wellington (pop. approx. 2000) declared 'there cannot be a finer climate, or a more healthy, or productive one in the world'.[1] Across the Strait, a correspondent from Nelson drew the inevitable comparison: 'As regards the climate here, I never saw anything more delightful, or a greater contrast to [Wellington]. Instead of being tormented with winds here, we have absolutely almost too little wind, if such a thing is possible' (83). In Nelson's un-buffeted clime, one could look forward to growing 'peas, cabbage, and turnips' all winter long (83). Not to be outdone, a settler from Whanganui declared his district was not only 'decidedly superior' to both Nelson and Wellington in terms of climate and healthfulness, but also more abundant: 'in my own garden, I have growing, amongst other things, peaches, apricots, plums, melons, strawberries . . . cabbage, peas, beans, broccoli, carrots, cauliflowers, turnips, sweet herbs, &c, &c.; in short, I can truly say, "Here one can live in ease, without care or trouble, in one of the most genial and healthy climates in the world, and where it only requires the hand of man to make a Paradise"'(51–52). Yet the palm for the pioneer who most looked on the bright side must surely go to the Waitara resident who wrote: 'From becoming blind so soon after my arrival at New Plymouth, I could not see much of the interior; but . . . I heard that the country was beautiful beyond description and that there were many miles of the flax growing in all directions.' Waitara, he noted with satisfaction, 'was allowed to be the finest flax district in the country' – indeed, he added, 'I am not aware of any place in the world, for size, with so many running streams, or so well calculated to turn mills of every kind' (181). Some of these New Zealand Company settlers would go on to found fortunes and dynasties, but the correspondent from Waitara reminds us that settlement is also a process by which blind men are led to swamps.

Phrases formed out of words like salubrious, abundant, opportunity, advantage and profitable generate an effulgent rhetoric of settlement from Albuquerque to Auckland, from Illinois to Illawarra. But settlers, for all their boosting, inevitably arrive in a place that will confound their expectations. A settlement is always – in Allen Curnow's words – 'something different, something Nobody counted on'.[2] Local conditions must produce difference, yet, as Frederick Jackson Turner first argued in his essay on 'The Significance of the Frontier in American History' (1893), the processes by which cross-cultural frontiers become settled regions are not only similar, they repeat themselves from one frontier to another.[3] Though we would no longer describe those operations in social evolutionary terms or draw conclusions about 'national character' from them, it remains the case that a few powerfully simple social and economic factors articulate the transformation of most new-world environments, including our own. The editors of *Under an Open Sky: Rethinking America's Western Past* describe these processes of transformation under a parsimonious group of five headings: species shifting; market making; land taking; boundary setting; state forming and self-shaping.[4] Each operates more or less simultaneously, with cumulative and sometimes delayed impact, and each is amply illustrated even by a sample as small as those 90 letters written from settlements only recently established by the New Zealand Company.

A letter from Wellington brings news of an agricultural society formed 'to promote the more rapid introduction into the colony of those fruits and flowers usually cultivated in England, and also to render the productions of New Zealand better known in the Mother-country, by sending home from time to time, as opportunity might offer, favourable specimens of our ornamental woods, plants, &c' (38). Most histories of settlement are human centred, but – as

Guthrie-Smith reminds us in *Tutira* – the massive transfer of plants and animals and microorganisms massively reshapes the indigenous environment; each peach stone, each tuberculosis germ, is also a settler. A writer from New Plymouth is confident that 'we shall have no difficulty in finding 200,000 acres of fine land within a reasonable distance of the town' (144). Letter after letter assumes the ready availability of land and anticipates the profits to be made by an early investment in an upside-down economy in which land can be bought for a song and menial farm labour is richly rewarded. Land taking – whether through purchase or swindling, invasion or treaty – not only brought violence and injustice to indigenous peoples in the past, it also leaves a legacy of cruelty and unfairness that unsettles – though often fails to disturb – its beneficiaries. The ongoing complexities of this process, and the difficulties writers have in representing it, are the subject of the opening chapter in this section, dealing with land transactions in narratives dating from 1863, 1953 and 1993; the first – by F. E. Maning – is arguably more perceptive than either of the ostensibly more sympathetic narratives that follow.

A Wellington correspondent, with an interest in the whaling trade, advises potential investors back home that merchants in Sydney are paying £16 a ton for oil, and £85 for whalebone. 'Why should not a Company be got up in Glasgow, and form a settlement connected with New Zealand, . . . and secure to Scotland a part at least of the trade?', he asks (21). Whaling is just one example of how small local arrangements, made between Maori and Pakeha to their mutual benefit and in their joint control, are connected to and will eventually be overtaken by the operations of a global economy. 'In the long run', as an American historian observes, 'the very markets that brought [Native] and European traders together eventually helped drive them apart'.[5] Later still, Pakeha-dominated extractive industries would themselves prove vulnerable to collapse; markets make ghost towns as well as temples of commerce. Guthrie-Smith, the sage of *Tutira*, has a particularly shrewd understanding of how his sheep station has been shaped not only by wind and rain and the upheavals of the earth, not only by the introduction of alien flora and fauna, but has also been as effectively moulded by rises and falls in distant marketplaces.

Boundary setting, we know from *Old New Zealand*, is a pervasive process of settlement – as of all cultural life. Maning's book involves the assertion of hard boundaries out of once-fluid arrangements, and is one marker of the settler population's increasing power to define the boundaries that matter, whether spatially, through the conversion of land into property, or interpersonally, through legal and cultural constraints on behaviour. Boundary setting takes place within the settler population as well. 'Those who come thinking of being gentlemen, without any exertion on their part, had much better stop at home', advises a Nelson settler (95) – giving warning that metropolitan expectations about class should not be tolerated in the new society. Self-fashioning is no longer constrained by the expectations and horizons of the homeland; Jane Crocker, writing from Taranaki, says approvingly of her cousin, 'If her father was to see her he would not know her' (131). And the settlers who celebrate the first anniversary of their landing with boat races and sack races, with 'running a wheelbarrow blindfold', are shaping themselves as a community too, and it is with this kind of settlement process, rather than the legal, political and military processes of state forming, that literature is most intimately associated.

Self-shaping and state forming come together in our literature's prolonged engagement with problems of national identity: do we have one, have we lost it, would we know what it looked like if we saw it again? A study of literature and settlement could be told as a narrative about the growth of a national identity, but while I need to find an angle that can take nationalism as its object without determining the kind of story that is to be told, I don't want to be so free from nationalist preoccupations that I forgo my own attachment to place. An analogy from the world of cuisine may help put these issues in perspective. A programme on the Food Channel, *Great British Menu*, pits chefs against each other in a battle to conceive and cook the perfect menu for a grand occasion like the Queen's eightieth birthday dinner. Britishness is naturally important to the *Great British Menu*, but what Britishness means to the cooks and judges is variable: it may be registered by locally sourced produce, or by a twist on heritage dishes, or simply by reflecting what is happening in the nation's trendiest restaurants. Suppose the programme were to be remade in all the Anglophone settler regions of the world – how different would each national cuisine turn out to be? What literary anthologists used to call local colour will always and necessarily constitute superficial points of difference, but in terms of format and even of the actual food prepared, I would expect the local and the particular to be outweighed by transnational similarities. Moreover, we would also find that these apparently distinctive national cuisines had comparable histories – pioneer resourcefulness, the cooption of indigenous ingredients, the nostalgia for half-forgotten brands, the liberating influence of new migrants, the wine industry, the overcoming of cultural cringes – and that these would be common way-stations on each nation's triumphal progress from culinary blandness to the 'vibrancy' that is so often said to characterise an achieved expression of cultural identity.

Yet where food comes from does make a difference. What the French call *terroir* is actual space – a sub-national region defined by soil, microclimate and produce; and also something more than actual space – a complex geo-cultural entity whose modes of existence are legal, commercial and ideological, and give rise to the imagined community of those who believe in them. The concept of *terroir* throws some useful sidelights on the not dissimilar concept of nation. Firstly, a *terroir* is somewhat like a nation in its association with a defined territory, but somewhat unlike a nation in that it is not a sovereign entity. It seems to me that in New Zealand, unlike much of the first world and unlike much of the third world, it may be useful to think of our literature as if it were the expression of something more like a *terroir* than a nation. With the exception of Maori sovereignty movements, the nation as a polity has never been especially important to local varieties of nationalism; in this respect, we offer a counter-example to Ernest Gellner's generalisation that nationalism comes before nations.[6] When Allen Curnow ends one of his sonnets: 'Not I, some child born in a marvellous year, / Will learn the trick of standing upright here', he expresses this oddly proleptic quality of a settler society's post-national nationalism. Secondly, *terroir* is a marketing tool – I am encouraged to believe in the New Zealandness of our literature just as I am encouraged to believe in the Gimblett gravelness of that wine region. But third, and for my purposes, most importantly, *terroir* implies a more direct, though not unmediated, relation to actual space than talking about national literatures generally allows. When it comes to actual space, nationalist literary discourse is either not really about physical space at all – its currency is 'myths, memories, values, symbols'[7] – or else is crudely deterministic about space, as in the notion that a hard clear light registers distinctly on New Zealand canvasses.[8]

What varieties of *terroir*, then, have shaped New Zealand literature? In earlier sections, we have considered the relation between Nature as a setting and Pakeha styles of belonging, as well as the marae and the beach of the cross-cultural frontier. This section examines two further settings that, in my view, are most important in terms of late-nineteenth and early-to-mid-century stories of settlement: the farm and the suburb. The final chapter in this section examines a third, Bohemia, a somewhat clumsy name for a number of emergent spaces. The autodidact's study, the small-town library, the inner-city boarding house, the student flat, the alternative lifestyle block are settings that register the problems concerning the value of art in the pragmatic and allegedly philistine society formed by settlement. The stresses involved are often explored in our literature, but most artfully in Frank Sargeson's comic masterpiece, *Memoirs of a Peon*.

Frederick Jackson Turner's essay of 1893 is also famous for declaring the American frontier closed. The decisive event occurred three years earlier, when the US Census Bureau announced there was no longer a westward-moving line of American settlement – except for a few inland pockets of Indian territory, the continent had been filled in. One might argue that the New Zealand frontier closed in 1883, when the King Country finally became accessible to Pakeha, but I would nominate an event that occurred three years later. Tongariro, New Zealand's first national park, was gifted to the nation in 1887 by Te Heuheu Tukino in order to preserve the mana and tapu of the mountain and to forestall subdivision and sale of the surrounding land to Pakeha farmers. Our frontier closes – if it ever did close – with an act of resistance to settlement. Many New Zealanders look forward to finally turning the page on the problems of settlement – but that is to mistake the nature of those problems. They are not a phase to outgrow or a problem to be superseded so much as a set of relations that persist, even as we are conscious of inheriting a world that is no longer new, and not of our making.

CHAPTER FIVE

Taking Place

Grab this land! Take it, hold it, my brothers, make it, my brothers, shake it, squeeze it, turn it, twist it, beat it, kick it, kiss it, whip it, stomp it, dig it, plow it, seed it, reap it, rent it, buy it, sell it, own it, build it, multiply it, and pass it on – can you hear me? Pass it on!
– *Toni Morrison,* Song of Solomon

IN EVIDENCE PRESENTED TO A PARLIAMENTARY SELECT COMMITTEE on the Disposal of Land in the British Colonies, Edward Gibbon Wakefield complained of the 'slovenly, and scrambling, and disgraceful' manner in which New Zealand was being colonised. 'Adventurers', he fumed, 'go from New South Wales and Van Diemen's land, and make a treaty with a native chief, . . . the poor chief not understanding a single word about it: they make a contract upon parchment with a great seal: for a few trinkets and a little gunpowder they obtain land.'[1] Coming from the founder of the New Zealand Company, whose own paper schemes would require vast acres of land somehow to become available at almost no cost, this protest is rich, yet simple representations of grossly unequal exchange – land for gunpowder and trinkets – constitute one of the self-serving myths about settlement. Much as its invocation aids Wakefield's efforts to supplant the haphazard colonisation of New Zealand with his own more concerted but essentially similar scheme, 'small inoculations of acknowledged evil' in the very distant past have long improved the immunity of settler memory to ongoing historical injustice.[2]

But as soon as even a little more is said or portrayed, the represented land purchase generally loses this simple mythical charge; it is no longer pure enough, or reductive enough, to function quite in this way. It is not that our writers and film-makers are at all averse to understanding the processes of settlement through simple moralising tableaus. Often, they plainly would like to, but the alienation of land from native peoples is a problem whose implications and legacies are difficult to apprehend, let alone resolve; and when land changes hands in a narrative, the consequences are often more troubling than their authors may suppose. In tracing the reverberations of land transactions through three texts – F. E. Maning's *Old New Zealand* (1863), Maurice Shadbolt's story 'The People Before' (1963) and Jane Campion's *The Piano* (1993) – I hope to show how the results of land changing hands can sometimes be registered as a disturbance in story-telling in ways that raise questions concerning the relativity of cultures, the conventionality of justice and the completion of settlement.

On the third of September 1839, one of those 'adventurers' from Van Diemen's Land drew up a document 'to let all Men Know that we the undersigned New Zealand Chiefs have sold to Frederick Edward Maning his heirs and Assigns for ever A Tract of land . . . . Known by the name of Onoke.'[3] The undersigned chiefs did indeed make their marks, and a bill of sale lists the various items – tobacco, blankets, cash, muskets, gunpowder – for which the land was exchanged. The early European settlement of New Zealand is performed in encounters like these and in documents like these. A year later, another such document, the Treaty of Waitangi (1840), guaranteed Maori the full, exclusive and undisturbed possession of their lands, but by the turn of the century customary native title had been extinguished over about 85 per cent of the country.

Maning's semi-fictional account of his land purchase, one of the great set pieces of *Old New Zealand*, occupies a turning point in that history: it was written in 1862, a year after the faulty Waitara purchase led to war in Taranaki and a year before the invasion of the Waikato in 1863. Maning tells the story of how he purchased his 'estate' in two sharply contrasting phases, the first of which seems calculated to bolster the impatience and prejudices of settlers hungry for land.

> I really can't tell to the present day who I purchased the land from, for there were about fifty different claimants, every one of whom assured me that the other forty-nine were 'humbugs', and had no right whatever.

The nature of the different titles of the different claimants were various. One man said his ancestors had killed off the first owners; another declared his ancestors had driven off the second party; another man, who seemed to be listened to with more respect than ordinary, declared that his ancestor had been the first possessor of all, and had never been ousted, and that this ancestor was a huge lizard that lived in a cave on the land many ages ago, and sure enough there was the cave to prove it. Besides the principal claims there were an immense number of secondary ones – a sort of latent equities – which had lain dormant until it was known the pakeha had his eye on the land. Some of them seemed to me at the time odd enough. One man required payment because his ancestors, as he affirmed, had exercised the right of catching rats on it, but which he (the claimant) had never done, for the best of reasons, *i.e.*, there were no rats to catch, except indeed pakeha rats, which were plenty enough, but this variety of rodent was not counted as game. Another claimed because his grandfather had been murdered on the land, and – as I am a veracious pakeha – another claimed payment because *his* grandfather had committed the murder! Then half the country claimed payments of various value, from one fig of tobacco to a musket, on account of a certain *wahi tapu*, or ancient burying-ground, which was on the land, and in which every one almost had had relations or rather ancestors buried, as they could clearly make out, in old times, though no one had been deposited in it for about two hundred years, and the bones of the others had been (as they said) removed long ago to a *torere* in the mountains. It seemed an awkward circumstance that there was some difference of opinion as to where this same *wahi tapu* was situated, being, and lying, for in case of my buying the land it was stipulated that I should fence it round and make no use of it, although I had paid for it. (I, however, have put off fencing till the exact boundaries have been made out; and indeed I don't think I shall ever be called on to do so, the fencing proviso having been made, as I now believe, to give a stronger look of reality to the existence of the sacred spot, it having been observed that I had some doubts on the subject. No mention was ever made of it after the payments had been all made, and so I think I may venture to affirm that the existence of the said *wahi tapu* is of very doubtful authenticity, though it certainly cost me a round 'lot of trade'.)

. . . . The day being now come on which I was to make the payment, and all parties present, I then and there handed over to the assembled mob the price of the land, consisting of a great lot of blankets, muskets, tomahawks, tobacco, spades, axes, &c., &c.; and received in return a very dirty piece of paper with all their marks on it, I having written the terms of transfer on it in English to my own perfect satisfaction. (127–29)

The bent of this passage seems clear enough: Maori, it would appear, cannot be said to own land as the English understand ownership, but the ragtag and bobtail of Maoridom will be sure to discover a relation to the land in order to milk the hapless settler for all he is worth. To a Pakeha ear, their claims will sound spurious, resting either on superstition – lizard ancestors! – or on something, like rat catching or murder, that Maning's first readers are likely to perceive as ridiculous. Yet we cannot say the narrator is lying exactly: having stories about the land, having utilised it as a food resource, having a relation to it through utu – all this is part and parcel of having a tie to the land, but those ties are treated in a comic and dismissive way.

Maning's more serious aim is to raise doubts as to the possibility of anyone ever making an authentic purchase of land in these circumstances. The Pakeha Maori has a deed written in English that *he* is perfectly satisfied with, but rather than insist on the validity of any such document, he implies it is only to be expected that whatever is written in the purchase agreement will not match what the purchasers suppose they have relinquished. Perhaps he has purchased this land for ever (hoko whenua), perhaps he has only obtained the use of it (tuku whenua)[4] – his grubby piece of paper supplants any concern with such niceties, for the document's most significant function is not to convey property from one owner to another but to convert land from one form of ownership to another. As if to dramatise these differences, these gaps in translation, Maning hurls a barrage of legal words at us. He mentions claims and claimants, latent equities and provisos, evidence is affirmed, and a wahi tapu is said to be 'situated, being, and lying'. As he warms to his subject, though, we find there is a twist in store.

While I am on the subject of land and land titles, I may as well here mention that many years after the purchase of my land I received notice to appear before certain persons called 'Land Commissioners', who were part and parcel of the new inventions which had come up soon after the arrival of the first governor, and which are still a trouble to the land. I was informed that I must appear and prove my title to the land I have mentioned, on pain of forfeiture of the same. Now I could not see what right any one could have to plague me in this way, and if I had had no one but the commissioners and two or three hundred men of their tribe to deal with, I should have put my pa in fighting order, and told them to 'come on'; for before this time I had had occasion to build a pa, (a little misunderstanding), and being a regularly naturalised member of a strong tribe, could raise men to defend it at the shortest notice. But somehow these people had cunningly managed to mix up the name of Queen Victoria, God bless her! . . . in the matter; and I, though a pakeha Maori, am a loyal subject to her Majesty, and will stick up and fight for her as long as ever I can muster a good imitation of courage or a leg to stand upon. This being the case, I made a very unwilling appearance at the court, and explained and defended my title to the land in an oration of four hours' and a half duration; and which, though I was much out of practice, I flatter myself was a good specimen of English rhetoric, and which, for its own merits as well as for another reason which I was not aware of at the time, was listened to by the court with the greatest patience. When I had concluded, and having been asked 'if I had any more to say?' I saw the commissioner beginning to count my words, which had all been written I suppose in shorthand; and having ascertained how many thousand I had spoken, he handed me a bill, in which I was charged by the word, for every word I had spoken, at the rate of one farthing and one twentieth per word. Oh, Cicero! Oh, Demosthenes! Oh, Pitt, Fox, Burke, Sheridan! Oh, Daniel O'Connell! what would have become of you, if such a stopper had been clapt on your jawing tackle? . . . . For my part I have never recovered the shock. I have since that time become taciturn, and have adopted a Spartan brevity when forced to speak, and I fear I shall never again have the full swing of my mother tongue. (129–30)

Clearly we have a reversal. There have been changes from the written to the oral, from legalese to speeches of four-and-a-half hours' duration. And there are protests, not at the spurious authenticity of Maori claims to land, but at the meddlesome ways of the law. Once again, Maning is not lying exactly. According to the Treaty, only the

Crown could extinguish native title, and it fell to the Crown to determine whether or not native title had properly been extinguished in pre-Treaty transactions. Maning's 'alleged purchase' of 200 acres was duly confirmed as a Crown grant in 1843, and the schedule of fees actually did include a charge of half a crown for '100 additional words over and above 100'.[5] As the acreage of land claimed was obviously a round number, with inexact borders, Maning's title was subsequently called in; a survey reduced his estimated 200 acres to an actual 99, and a replacement title was finally issued in 1861. For reasons like these, the law may well be 'a trouble to the land', but even as Maning offers a supposedly 'Maori' view of the matter, he makes clear there is no alternative to the rule of British law. The broad effect of this reversal, then, is to demonstrate and qualify a particular kind of relativism: Maori and Pakeha think very differently about land, there are problems of translation in between, and therefore, or even so, the tendency of Maning's satire is to distinguish between protections afforded by a civilised legal system and tribal ways that amount to putting one's pa in fighting order and challenging one's enemy to come on.

It would be an error to regard Maning's position as an example of an outworn ideology characteristic of the early days of settlement. For much of our history, there have been law-centric and culture-centric ways of making much the same point as Maning. The law-centric position – call it a Crown position – would regard Maning's story as an allegory about the relationship of the English common law to tribal societies.[6] The latter may only enter the discursive universe of the law by being conquered or, as in New Zealand, by treaty, by the cession of sovereignty, by the striking of a bargain. There are two sides to this bargain, one of which is preserved fully, the other of which – call it the untold Maori side of the story – is only refracted through the European record, and has an alternative existence in oral traditions that the Crown regards as beyond proof or disproof by empirical means.

A Crown reading is sensitive to injustice; indeed, the Crown wishes above all to be just, to place the foundation of settlement within the law. But that wish has the violence of an imposition. The Pakeha Maori's 'very dirty piece of paper with all their marks on it' may part Maori from land they never intended to let go, just as, in that larger piece of paper, the Treaty itself, Maori cede sovereignty only in the English wording. The Maori version cedes kawanatanga but reserves rangatiratanga. The former, a word coined for the occasion from the transliteration of 'governor', is intended to mean governance; the latter means chiefly authority and responsibility, and thus, arguably, the notion of sovereignty itself. But that is not an argument the Crown (in this definition) can ever hear: its own assumption of sovereignty is foundational. The Crown finds itself, therefore, in the position of maintaining that the problems of settlement can be settled within the discursive universe of settlement, while insisting, with force if need be, that the discourses of the settler are the ones that pertain. One actual nineteenth-century outcome ran as follows: if Maori in 1840 were a community beyond the community of law, in 1877, Justice Prendergast could retrospectively regard the Treaty as a simple nullity, a contract made with those who, by circular definition, could not enter into a contract. If this was legal positivism in full armour, it should not be forgotten that even today, when the Waitangi Tribunal seeks to redress past failures to include Maori within the community of settler law, it works under the discipline of presuming to apply the 'principles' of the Treaty while delivering findings that must be historian-proof and judge-proof even before they are politician-proof.

A Crown approach to Maning's story of how he purchased his estate would allow a judge to determine – but only within prescribed limits – whether or not a bona fide purchase had been made. What I shall call a culture-centred or 'revisionist' approach to the problem would agree with the implication in Maning that no purchase could ever legitimately be made. Maning, so the interpretation might run, understands there is no culturally neutral approach to the question of Maori ownership of their land, with the difference that his relativism works not according to culture but according to time. He believes in civilisation's ladder of progress: while Europeans have made their way up that ladder and have the advantage of the law, the more primitive Maori belong on a lower rung, perhaps on a par with Germanic tribesmen in the days of Julius Caesar, who were similarly 'warlike' and held land in common.

In another writer, this routine ethnocentricism might have informed a plea to hasten the peaceful advancement of Maori; the way Maning sees it, there can be no colonialism without violence, and any 'Maori doctor' who thinks otherwise is likely to be deluded as to his own motives as well as underestimating the Maori will to independence. Maning and his revisionist interpreter would not have the same attitudes to that violence – Maning believed Maori required a crushing military defeat to save them from extermination – but both are apt to conceive the relations between coloniser and colonised in roughly similar terms: one's iron engine of progress is the other's imperial juggernaut. And while Maning and his 'revisionist' critic do not have compatible understandings of cultural difference, they are both likely to exaggerate the coherence and discreteness of the cultures that are said to be different. For instance, where a Crown reading must rely on the written and largely European record, a revisionist reading would stress the Eurocentrism of all European records, the fundamental and thoroughgoing untrustworthiness of documents claiming to represent other cultures. Maning's text, it might then be supposed, can only present Maori attitudes to land in the form of a vicious travesty. But what was understood by Maori making an arrangement about land? For the revisionist, a Maori side of the story is at once an epistemological empty set and the possible object of an immediate, sacred knowledge; a knowledge the weak and the poor may only mumble, but out of which those with the right rhetoric can make thrilling, righteous and politic affirmations of their identity.

Neither the Crown reading nor the revisionist one questions the central obviousness of Maning's text: that Maori and Pakeha have fundamentally different attitudes to land, or, as we would now say, fundamentally different cultures. The incommensurability between those cultures has been the central interpretative problem of the positions I've sketched so far. The differences supposedly ring-fencing them are things Maning might still persuade many New Zealanders about today. A reader of *Potiki* or *the bone people* might suppose that because Maori attitudes to land are so much more 'spiritual', and because European ones are so much more legalistic and materialistic, there is bound to be a stand-off between them. But Maning also helps us see why this cultural division between Maori and Pakeha is not so much a problem as itself a solution, a simplifying answer to the problem of boundary construction in conditions where borders had been permeable. What Maning accomplishes with his book is the construction of an incompatibility: between whenua and property, between utu and law, between old and new, between Maori and Pakeha. As I've argued earlier, we need to see past those stark oppositions and recover the transactional, mutually transformative, space between cultures that Maning's text nonetheless also records. Perhaps the following passage illustrates my point sufficiently.

> When I purchased my land the payment was made on the ground, and immediately divided and subdivided amongst the different sellers. . . . One old *rangatira*, before whom a considerable portion of the payment had been laid as his share of the spoil, gave it a slight shove with his foot, expressive of refusal, and said, 'I will not accept any of the payment; I will have the pakeha' . . . . I consequently was therefore a part, and by no means an inconsiderable one, of the payment for my own land. (174)

The old rangatira prefers the Pakeha to his goods much as anyone might prefer a goose to its eggs, and Maning's satire goes on to enumerate the various arrangements whereby a Pakeha Maori could expect to be 'plucked'. The rangatira, although plainly a caricature in Maning's text, is partly modelled on Kaitoke, the principal chief from whom Maning purchased land in 1839, and who was a senior relative of Moengaroa and Hauraki, Maning's future wife and her brother. What Kaitoke got out of this sale, allocation or gift of land was access to trade on favourable terms; what Maning himself purchased was never only the land but also whanau, a family, a set of relations and obligations binding him to the tribe. By the time Maning became a Pakeha Maori in print, Moengaroa and Hauraki were long dead and those wider relationships had become encumbrances. Writing the book was his ticket out of a backwater. It earned him cachet as a no-nonsense expert on things Maori, and would lead to his appointment as a judge in the Native Land Court overseeing the transfer of Maori land to various forms of individual title. *Old New Zealand* presents the trend towards property owned by individuals as the working out of an ineluctable plan, but the ironies and complexities of the book run deeper than Maning might himself have supposed. Settlement requires not only access to land, but also rituals of belonging. Maning, the mobile *Pakeha* Maori, may have been a pioneer most of all in discovering there is much to be said for a strategic indigenisation of one's settler identity.

Maurice Shadbolt's 'The People Before' is the story of a family who farm a remote stretch of river flat in the 1920s and 1930s.[7] The father 'got the place for a song' (140), as he likes to say, because others walked off the property before him. Those first pioneers burnt the bush and set about building a hill-country sheep station, but all their work came to nothing. They have been gone since the turn of the century. No one knows much about 'the people before' – a derelict farmhouse overtaken by manuka and fern is their barely perceptible memorial. So far as the father is concerned, 'history only began the day he first set foot on the land. It was his, by sweat and legal title: that was all that mattered. That was all that could matter' (142). He saw that the land's real potential lay not in sheep but in dairy: there is a decent spread of level ground running down to the river, accessible by a launch that comes as regularly as any milk tanker. In a fury of accomplishment, the farmer improves his property, making good on a promise he'd made himself in 1915 when under fire at Gallipoli, that if he ever got out of the war alive, he'd find himself a piece of land he could call his own. He is the type of nuggety dourly practical bloke the late Martyn Sanderson specialised in playing: when visitors call, he takes the menfolk on a tour of the property, laconically drawing attention to the new milking shed or water-pump; at rugby games, his is the voice that rises out of the crowd with a mordant comment at the expense of a softie who falls off a tackle. Most of all, he is proud of the results he has achieved on the farm: 'I've made it pay, and pay well. I've made this land worth something. I could sell out for a packet. Why don't I?' (146). The question is not one he could give an answer to.

The story is narrated by the elder of two sons. He takes after his father; the younger brother, Jim, is his mother's child. While the narrator helps with the milking morning and night, and is pulled from school to work on the farm, the younger brother – a softie – reads books and continues with his education. One night Jim returns with two pieces of greenish triangular stone: greenstone, the father reckons, and possibly worth something – 'Maori stuff. Some people'll buy anything' (147). Few Maori now live on their part of the river but there is a small settlement down on the coast. Jim becomes intrigued that Maori once lived on their land and soon discovers that the country round about had been confiscated after the wars. Later, exploring a cave, the two boys find another sign of an earlier occupation: a human skull on a ledge – 'it just sat there sightless, shadows dancing in its sockets' (149).

These discoveries are made during the Depression, when the father's attitude to the farm has begun to change. Prices have collapsed; the property's value has fallen. The father becomes 'gripped by the idea that he might have failed' (148) – just as the previous owners had failed – and though he endeavours to talk himself out of the notion, the possibility nags away like a fever dream, without resolution. One day there is a telephone call from 'the people before'. They would like to visit the farm and the father wonders if they might now want to buy the property off him for a song. But the visitors turn out to be Maori from the coast. An old man, almost a hundred years old, has been carried back to see the land on which he was born. With him are two kuia, carrying green palm fronds and singing waiata; also, a young man named Tom Taikaha, who does the talking for the group. The father is astonished: 'No Maori ever owned this place. I'd have known' (153). Even more astounding, Tom, who has never been up the river in his life, immediately identifies a pa site and tells story after story about the hills, the landing place, the arrival of the first musket and battles fought over the years – 'Until there was a day when it was no use fighting any more. That was when we left' (156). There is an awkward pause as the family realises Tom is referring to the confiscation of their land. While his father continues to ring the changes on expressions like 'what do you know' and 'I never knew', Jim quietly goes into the house and returns with the two pounamu adzes which he offers to return – 'these are really yours', he says, doing the right thing, though reluctant to part with his treasures. Tom refuses, saying 'you better keep them, eh? They're yours now. You find, you keep. We got no claims here any more. This is your father's land now' (157). It seems he too is doing the right thing, though it is evident he would like to have kept the greenstone.

The visitors stay the night at the old pa, but when they return, the old man is not with them. The father is riled: 'you can't just leave dead people lying around' – not on his land. He gets the police in, the health department, but no trace of the kaumatua's body is ever found. 'But we knew', says the narrator, 'we knew every night we looked up at the hills that he was there, somewhere.' The farmer now feels 'the land itself had heaped some final indignity on him, made a fool of him' (161). As soon as butter prices recover, he sells out and moves on.

The story is in the mode of standard Kiwi realism, and the points it makes about settler amnesia and the contrast between owning and belonging, between knowing and really knowing the land, are distinctly made. Shadbolt could well have ended his story with the farmer making a new start on a farm ripe for subdivision, still confusing value with price, still unable to come to terms with the ongoing presence of 'the people before'. It would be a simple allegory of settlement. That reading is not withdrawn but it is complicated by a twist. The narrator and Jim both saw action in North Africa during the war, and the elder boy, remembering how his father found he was less scared if he focused on the idea of having a farm, tried to think of something of his own to hold on to, but nothing ever came to mind. Jim, on the other hand, explains how the same trick worked for him.

'I thought of the old place . . . by the river. Where', he added, and his face puckered into a grin, 'where they buried that old Maori. And where I found those greenstones. I've still got it at home you know, up on the mantelpiece. I seem to remember trying to give it away once, to those Maoris. Now I'm glad I didn't. It's my only souvenir from there, the only thing that makes that place still live for me'. He paused. 'Well, anyway, that's what I thought about. That old place of ours'.

I had a sharp pain. I felt the dismay of a long distance runner who, coasting confidently to victory, imagining himself well ahead of the field, finds himself overtaken and the tape snapped at the very moment he leans forward to breast it. For one black moment it seemed I had been robbed of something which was rightfully mine.

I don't think I'll ever forgive him. (162)

Prior to this moment, every detail in the story has been neatly marshalled into a series of comparisons between the Pakeha father and 'the people before'. Had Shadbolt left it at that, with those Maning-like oppositions, the story would seem tidy and unchallenging, as if he had been unable to imagine our history without a scapegoat tethered securely, but instead he has found a way to a conclusion that is neither safe nor transparent. I see two contradictory lines of interpretation. Perhaps the ending works against the narrator, who discovers at this moment just how much he is his father's son, and how thoroughly he has failed to form any kind of deep attachment to place. Jim, with his burnished greenstone, with his ear tuned to Maori priorities, trumps his brother just as surely as the people of the land trumped his father, effectively dispossessing the settler with evidence of a more intimate and enduring relation to place. Like the skull in the cave, like the presence of the old man's bones, a piece of greenstone on the mantelpiece can become a powerful sign – 'a mysterious X' – that animates the past and indicates the presence of other frameworks. All of a sudden, something overlooked, that didn't seem to count, has an unsuspected power to reveal a deficiency in an accustomed view. One label for the annoyance the narrator feels might be 'affronted monoculturalism'.

Then again, the ending might be on the side of the narrator. Jim, now a university lecturer in the city, makes a point of helping out with the milking on his brother's farm during holiday visits, but he is sentimentally refashioning his own childhood, and overlooking the fact that it was his brother who was the worker, that his education came at the expense of opportunities foreclosed to another. Perhaps the narrator feels something of the annoyance anyone might feel when someone steals a march on you through political correctness; perhaps the narrator becomes like 'the people before' in finding himself marginalised by a self-serving narrative about one's relation to place – it's as if his memories of 'the old place' are about to be absorbed and displaced by the narrative of his brother. Another name for what irks the narrator might be 'Jim's bicultural smugness'.

I don't believe it is possible to decide between these two readings without making assumptions about the deal Tom and Jim make about the greenstone, which itself can't be decided without also making assumptions about the rightful ownership of confiscated land. If the ending is on Jim's side, then Tom's not accepting the pounamu might be treated as a gift re-given and bestowed with a blessing. But if the ending is on the narrator's side, then Jim is merely the beneficiary of Tom's acknowledgement that 'we got no claims here any more. This is your father's land.' This cannot be a judgement the story endorses: the story's major patterns all click into place insofar as the father's values are found wanting, and insofar as 'the people before' behave as if land they no longer possess has always, in a more fundamental sense, never been let go. Yet an interpretation that requires us to read the statement, 'this is your father's land', as if it could more deeply mean its opposite, is hardly an adequate response to the fact of confiscation.

'The People Before' becomes a small masterpiece thanks to the calculated disturbance of its ending. What might have been a palatable allegory of the injustices of settlement, told from a distance, and with a sorry shake of the head at the inadequacies of our settler forebears, becomes resistant to easy interpretation as soon as the narrator ventures his own relation to the past. His sense of what is at stake is not easily articulated, but he gives a very precise idea of how it feels to be a runner coasting to victory, the only one in the race – when, out of nowhere, comes punctured illusion and the chagrin of displacement. History can creep up on Pakeha like that. There are other ways in which the past comes alive for us, but whenever Pakeha are compelled to register an injustice of settlement, you cannot help but notice that 'affronted monoculturalism' and 'smug biculturalism' have a large share in the usual furore.

When Jane Campion's *The Piano* appeared to international acclaim in 1993, its local reception hinged on an appreciation of the pitfalls awaiting an expatriate Pakeha director whose material required her to take notice of Maori perspectives on settler history. Elsewhere, this was a feminist art movie that succeeded as a multiplex romance; in New Zealand at this period, Pakeha were becoming nervous about their mode of access to Maori material, sensitive to accusations of hogging the stage, and wary of being thought disrespectful, mercenary or pious. *The Piano* is a glorious film, and my own impression as an overwhelmed first-time viewer was that Campion had succeeded as few others had done in making an adroit and careful representation of our history. It wasn't noble savages or unreconstructed Kiwi nationalism; the director had gone to some trouble to make things look authentic and, with the help of Maori cultural advisors, managed not to press too many wrong buttons. In a note on the making of the film, Jane Campion recalled:

> Even though it's a European story, which is what I am – European – I determined that it would involve having Maori people in the film. Cross-cultural collaborations are sensitive, and for me it was a pretty scary endeavour. It wasn't without tears and difficulty. But I think people were actually pleased to have a position where there could be a meeting. You just don't get opportunities to experience that in everyday kiwi society. In the end the cross-cultural quality of it was one of the deeply moving aspects of being on the production for all of us, cast and crew.[8]

Nowadays, few Pakeha would feel comfortable with the term 'European', or quite so removed from the 'cross-cultural quality' of ordinary life, yet the expatriate director did make a deeply Pakeha film. As such, it has a great deal in common with representations of early contact from other settler cultures, as Linda Hardy, in a brilliant essay, was the first to point out. She argues that when the heirs of settler colonialism come to tell stories of national origin, in stories like *The Piano*, or Ian Wedde's *Symmes Hole* or Patrick White's *A Fringe of Leaves*, the central characters don't so much come to possess the new land as to dispossess themselves of the old. There is generally some rite of passage whereby the politics of colonial domination can be displaced and reworked as a different kind of problem to do with what Hardy calls an 'erotic and aesthetic deficiency in European culture': 'To surrender the furnishings of a culture both European and bourgeois', she writes, 'is to come into the sensuality of a "natural occupancy" of the new land. The pleasure afforded by these fictions is that they allow the heirs of a settler society to imagine our unhistoric origin as the (possibility of the) making of a settlement without a colony.'[9]

What Hardy suggests is an imaginary difference between colonist as interloper on the one hand and settler as natural occupant on the other is strikingly expressed in the contrast between Sam Neill's Stewart – an angular, virginal Bluebeard, chopping off fingers and hammering in survey posts – and Harvey Keitel's rubbery, roly-poly,

Baines, the inarticulate Pakeha Maori whose moko is a sign already of his distance from European ways. In Hardy's terms, the fantasy of difference between colonist and settler is not only marked by who gets the girl, but is supported more subtly by the piano's dual role as item of European furniture, consigned, like Prospero's books, to the deep, deep sea, and as the not entirely sublimated expression of a will to sexuality whose evocation in music and in flesh is the evident sign of Ada's and Baine's natural occupancy.

I've outlined Linda Hardy's argument not only because I am indebted to her, but also because I would like to make a similar point somewhat differently. Among the many silences of the film, there is a silence concerning land. Baines has 80 acres which he will give to Stewart in return for the piano; in turn, Baines will allow Ada to purchase her piano in instalments, key by key, in return for peeks and caresses. While these two plots – the land sub-plot and the love main plot – are intercut for much of the film, the land plot gradually thins out and eventually disappears, although traces of it survive in a published script that does not always match what we see on the screen.

There are three related questions I wish to pursue. What does having a plot involving a land deal accomplish? What does curtailing the land plot accomplish? And what does the land plot suggest about natural occupancy and the politics of the film's ending? I can begin to answer my first question by noting some similarities between the land plot and the love plot. In the love plot, Stewart, Ada's husband, has a dodgy but nonetheless legal title to the piano: Ada may feel that it is her piano, that it has travelled all the way from Scotland with her and is less a possession than an extension of herself; but so far as her husband is concerned, a marriage is a contract and all her property belongs to him. The piano is to the love plot what Baines's 80 acres of land is to the sub-plot. Since the land cannot always have belonged to Baines, in what sense is it his, and what right does he have to sell it? By and large, these are questions the film raises but cannot answer. It is a gap in its and our knowledge. Possibly, the land deal we see negotiated in the film concerns those 80 acres, which would imply that so far as its Maori owners are concerned, the land was not sold, merely allocated to Baines, and Stewart, like Maning before him, must negotiate with everyone who has a claim to the land. Alternatively, it is possible that

Stewart already owns Baines's land, the transaction having proceeded without complication, and he is now negotiating to purchase a further block, with the assistance of Baines as a middleman. Either scenario is possible: the more salient point is that while the plot requires land to change hands, its memory regarding the ownership of land is vague and incomplete.

We do see negotiations occurring, however, and have some sense of their outcome. In true Maning fashion, Stewart's offer is first refused by the Maori. A chief explains: 'The rivers and burial caves of our ancestors lie within these lands . . . are you saying we should sell our ancestor's bones? . . . . There's no price you can pay.' In the next scene, Stewart then acts as if a bargain had been made, telling Baines, 'we might as well mark [the land] out, as we agreed'. Baines nods in doubtful agreement, and it is clear that by putting in survey pegs in advance of any secured agreement, he and Stewart are taking liberties. Later we hear that Baines has been 'plundered' – or rather, he has become subject to muru, a form of utu in which a transgression or misfortune is redressed by a semi-ritual plundering of goods and property. This may be an undisclosed reason why, a little later, Stewart's own house is invaded, and why he in turn fortifies it against the obscurely 'restless' natives. In the film, the land plot goes no further than this. So long as the land deal establishes a routine contrast between Maori and Pakeha attitudes to land, its symbolic work ought to be over and done with. But in the 1990s, in the post-Waitangi Tribunal era, things to do with land are not quite so simple.

Both the love plot and the land plot involve this-for-that exchanges, and it is not clear to all parties precisely what *this* and what *that* will entail. In the love plot, Ada plays for keys, for title to her piano; in return, Baines says he will do things while she plays – but what Baines has in mind by doing things goes further than Ada expected. And the results of this exchange are unpredictable: Baines alienates Ada; Ada alienates her daughter; Flora comes close to gaining a father in Stewart; Stewart gets the land, but loses his self-respect and Ada. For all characters involved, the this-for-that love plot is rather like a treaty in which something agreed to in the past comes to have a life or force of its own; it is an exchange in which what once looked to be bargains prove costly, and in which notions about what is real become uncertain for all the characters involved. Similarly, in the foreshortened land plot, exchange involves understandings that are hard to discern, whose effects are hard to predict, whose momentum is not easy to control.

However, something else soon happens and another kind of exchange intervenes. Baines *gives* the piano to Ada. In return, Ada gives herself to Baines, and Stewart, who seemed bent on revenge, makes a delayed and perhaps redundant gift of Ada to Baines. Gift exchange is not the same as this-for-that exchange: in the love plot, giving seems in the end to work positively, propelling the characters into a new relationship and securing for them a kind of natural occupancy. The political function of the land plot lies in the implied contrast between gift-giving and more venal modes of exchange. The implication is that in our present relation to our past, we should be wary of a this-for-that approach to questions of exchange in the way the wrongs of the past are counted and recompense made. Rather than cut out victims who can't meet high standards of historical proof, or who don't belong to the right iwi, rather than deal in 'fiscal envelopes' or *x*-pounds-then-equals-*y* dollars-now calculations, or in timetables that propose an endpoint to settling colonial injustice, the film suggests that better outcomes can happen when exchange is put on a different footing: along the lines of the gift, say. There is much to be said for wishing Maori and Pakeha were bound by the politics of the gift rather than the contractual obligations of Treaty partners, but I fear the true allure of the notion is to make multi-faceted problems seem capable of grandly simple solutions.

Here is a scene from Jane Campion's published screenplay that does not appear in the final cut of the film. Baines is about to leave with Ada, and a Maori woman, Hira, says to him:

> *Peini*, I miss you, you are human like us. The *pakeha* man, they have no heart, they think only of land . . . . I worry for us, *Peini*. *Pakeha* cunning like the wind, KNOCK you over, yet you not see it. Some they say, 'How can *pakeha* get our land if we won't sell it? . . . . They wrong, *Peini*. Today our enamee he sell some land for heapah guns. Now, we too buy guns. We must sell our land to fight for our land.[10]

And later:

In the end, can we lose? No, we turn the *pakeha* gun on the *pakeha* and get our land back. Pow! Pow![11]

I do not know why these fragments of an untold Maori story did not appear. Perhaps they were reluctantly sacrificed, but my hunch is they were found to strike a wrong note or cluttered the movement towards the film's conclusion. One unfortunate consequence is that the Bluebeard scene, where the film's symbolism is most concentrated, no longer quite works. In lantern-lit dumb show, an axe descends on a hand holding a key, but Maori in the audience mistake a piece of stage violence for the real thing, and rush the stage. It is a peculiarly unconvincing moment. Without being able to draw on those references in the land plot intimating future Maori violence, the scene loses part of its rationale, and can no longer suggest the anger that comes when what you thought to be real turns out to be someone else's legal fiction.

The film's rejigged ending is typical, in its way, of New Zealand in the post-1984 settlement era. Injustices over land can no longer simply be ignored, but it seems they can't be dealt with expeditiously or efficiently either – hence the attraction, I have suggested, of submerging the land plot to highlight alternatives to regular modes of exchange.

Submerging: the film will end under the sea, and it is curious that the land itself has an underwater look throughout the film. According to Stuart Dryburg, the cinematographer, this was part of the director's brief: '"Bottom of the fish tank" was the description we used for ourselves to help define what we were looking for.'[12] What then, might land have to do with the haunting closing image of the film, which is itself the final movement of an elaborate, three-phased conclusion? You will recall that Ada goes down with her piano but chooses life; in the next scene, all of a sudden, and with no explanation whatsoever, it seems Baines and Ada are prosperous, they have a new house, a new piano, Flora does cartwheels; Ada has a tin finger and is learning to speak; she has entered a happier world of exchange in the way a lotto winner might, through luck. 'What a chance', she says, 'what a surprise, my will has chosen life.' Then, there is the powerfully imagined fantasy of Ada's umbilical attachment to the drowned piano, and her voice speaking of silence in a strange undersea world of silence. Campion is evoking the ecstatic narcissistic pull of Ada's involvement with the piano, and she does so by showing Ada in a state of radical completion, a self so at one with its environment, it is as if the water around her were somehow amniotic and the piano had become a placenta – the Maori word for which, by the way, is whenua, which also means land. Ada naturally occupies this desired place under the sea, the supplement and impossible underside of good or pure settlement. Let me quote from the screenplay:

> At night I think of my piano in its ocean grave, and sometimes of myself floating above it. Down there everything is so still and silent that it lulls me to sleep. It is a weird lullaby and so it is; it is mine.

> *ADA's piano on the sea bed, its lid fallen away. Above floats ADA, her hair and arms stretched out in a gesture of surrender, her body slowly turning on the end of a rope.*[13]

What is she doing down there? Perhaps she is waiting for Maui, fisher of islands.

The Plots of *Tutira*

Nations trek from progress.
– Wilfred Owen

Man marks the earth with ruin.
– Lord Byron

THE SUMMER OF 1924 CONTINUED DRY INTO MARCH ON TUTIRA station and was broken at last with an almighty thunderstorm. Lightning started at five in the morning and continued without pause until six in the evening. Fifteen inches of rain fell that day, eight inches (20 centimetres) in just three hours. At the Guthrie-Smith homestead, which is overhung by an amphitheatre of hills, water ran in a torrent as high as the kitchen windowsill. From the veranda next morning, Guthrie-Smith looked across at the steeply sloping ranges on the far side of the lake and counted two hundred slips across two miles of hillside. 'Eastern Tutira', he wrote, 'appears to have been weeping mud. . . . New red-raw wounds smear the green slopes, scalp-shaped patches detach themselves, slipping downward in slush and turf. Sometimes a whole hillside will wrinkle and slide like snow melting off a roof, . . . smothering and smashing the wretched sheep, half or wholly burying them in every posture.'[1]

The weather is often our news. Nowadays, television reporters would be on the scene quickly, interviewing those in the disaster area about their lucky escapes, tragic losses, comic predicaments. The overall story would be the big clean-up: what roads would have to be fixed, when the electricity would be back on, which houses could be put right and which condemned. In this common scenario, a 'natural disaster' visits ruin and destruction upon a portion of the world, and humans struggle to restore the balance. Obviously, another story might be told: of clear-felling and erosion, of marginal high country unwisely brought into pasture, of once spongy hillsides, as Guthrie-Smith put it, 'transformed . . . into slate' (196). In this alternative but equally well-known scenario, the human impact on nature brings ruin and destruction to what had been a balanced ecosystem.

These double understandings of a catastrophe like the deluge of 1924 are associated with two major plots of settlement, identified by the American environmental historian William Cronon as progressive accounts of improvement and development on the one hand, and retrogressive stories of loss and impairment on the other.[2] Improvement narratives are heroic and uplifting: pioneers arrive to a wilderness and eventually bequeath a nation of farms, cities and nature reserves. Thomas Bracken, for example, imagines Canterbury's first settlers crossing the Port Hills.

> They saw, from yonder mountain's brow
> Plains yearning for the spade and plough;
> And where naked rivers ran,
> Vales waiting to be dressed by man;
> Their help all Nature seemed to woo,
> 'Neath speckless skies of sunny blue.
>
> They gave the breeze that fann'd the foam
> Sweet farewell sighs to carry Home; –
> But though old Albion was dear,
> They saw a fairer England here
> Awaiting them, the dauntless few,
> 'Neath speckless skies of sunny blue.
>
> Behold their work! Revere their names!
> Green pictures set in golden frames,
> Around the City of the Stream,
> Fulfil the Pilgrims' brightest dream;
> With them a fairer England grew
> 'Neath speckless skies of sunny blue.[3]

If one were to develop a novel or film treatment based on Bracken's outline, the protagonist, probably a settler allied with a particular district, would face deluges and droughts and be tested by adversity, but his future would not only turn out well, it would also represent a significant advance over more primitive times. In stories of improvement, William Cronon explains, the narrative arc 'gradually ascends towards an ending that is somehow more positive – happier, richer, freer, better – than the beginning'.[4]

Narratives of improvement in our historical and political discourse are legion, but we will find remarkably few literary examples outside the boosterism of Bracken's poetry. It is not that we lack family sagas or historical romances – genres that ought to be especially hospitable to this patterning of events – but those we still read and remember refuse this storyline. By and large, it takes a distinct drop in literary value, to the level of the 'Mills and Boon' sheep station romance, say, before one comes across numerous episodes of the handsome farmer musing positively about changes wrought and benefits to come. Cultural value is overwhelmingly associated with an alternative patterning of events. The ruination plot, as I shall call it, follows the downward path typical of tragedy.[5] It is a story of hubris and comeuppance, of ignorance leading to painful knowledge. The optimism characteristic of the improvement plot now becomes a tragic flaw: our blind faith in progress ends in environmental degradation – not paradise made, but paradise lost.

Almost all the New Zealand literature we value follows or assumes this plot line in one or another of its many variations, and it is striking that it occurs routinely much earlier than the 1930s, when writers like Fairburn, Curnow, Sargeson and Glover elaborated an environmentally minded critique of settlement we sometimes mistake as foundational. In 'The Passing of the Forest' (1898), for example, William Pember Reeves called for clouds 'To hide the scars that every season brings, / The fire's black smirch, the landslip's gaping wound', and invited readers to –

> ... Scan
> The blackened forest ruined in a night,
> A sylvan Parthenon that God will plan

But builds not twice. Ah, bitter price to pay
For Man's dominion – beauty swept away.[6]

In verses like these, the settler has his progress and laments it too; it is a compromise form of the ruination plot. In yet another compromise form – call it the *Frankenstein* variation – we learn that it is always a terrible mistake to meddle with nature. There is a *Toll of the Bush*, as the title of one of William Satchell's novels has it, and the bush-destroying pioneer who pays that toll with his life has the precise symbolic function of the scapegoat: a figure who carries the wrongs of a community, and whose sacrifice maintains a relationship with nature as a sort of injured deity. Even novels that might otherwise seem narratives of improvement, such as Jane Mander's *The Story of a New Zealand River*, are qualified by their treatment of the masculine agent of environmental change. Tom Roland owns a sawmill; he is the entrepreneurial force behind the progress and development of his community, but like many characters representing those forces – *Man Alone*'s Stenning, Stewart in *The Piano* – he is a rural brute. When Tom fells a mighty kauri, his wife shudders and thinks of her marriage bed; when Stewart can't break in his wife, he cuts off her finger with an axe.

In American narratives of improvement, such as *The Virginian*, the cowboy equivalent of our inarticulate bloke in a black singlet is eminently marriable and will be led to culture as to the altar by his more sophisticated fiancée; in our narratives of ruination, the character who stands for progress and the conquest of nature is more likely to be an obstacle to love. Both *The Piano* and *The Story of a New Zealand River* end happily, with new marriages in new settlements, but before that can happen, the heroines must escape the pioneering brute. Ada ditches Stewart for the pseudo-indigenous Baines, while Tom Roland is killed, with a crush of dramatic irony, under a kauri log.

Narratives of improvement are particularly fond of prolepsis. Bracken, for example, uses the perspective of settlers looking across the empty plains and seeing the 'fairer England' of farms, towns and cities that will one day be established there. For those starting to feel at home in these new places, the imagination was more often drawn the other way. Ursula Bethell, pausing from earnestly digging her garden, looked across the agronomic patchwork of the Canterbury plains to the snow peaks of the vast alpine ranges.

> It is only a little while since this hillside
> Lay untrammelled likewise,
> Unceasingly swept by transmarine winds.
>
> In a very little while, it may be,
> When our impulsive limbs and our superior skulls
> Have to the soil restored several ounces of fertilizer,
>
> The Mother of all will take charge again
> And soon wipe away with her elements
> Our small fond human enclosures.[7]

The imaginative journey of the poem, from her garden out to wild nature, from wild nature back to the small enclosures of garden and grave, is a prolepsis in reverse: the future anticipated here belongs to the past, to the uncultivated natural environment. Bethell's fondness for perspectives that erase marks of human presence is a gesture characteristic of settler creoles everywhere.[8] It is an expression of the misgivings that accompany the transformation of new-world environments, of reservations that have as their literal monument those islands out of time we call national parks.

Yet our cultural disquiet over narratives of improvement, expressed in all our major art forms for almost all our settlement history and playing on the heartstrings of a nature-loving majority, has always had a disproportionably slight impact on actual states of affairs. One of the more brazen ironies of our '100% Pure' slogan is that New Zealand is not only one of the most altered environments in the world: we also have 'one of the worst records of native biodiversity loss' – nearly a third of all land and freshwater birds have become extinct since the arrival of humans, and about a thousand plant, animal and fungi species and subspecies are currently considered threatened.[9] Historians of this familiar story invariably mention the role of acclimatisation societies in the latter part of the nineteenth century, and point to the kind of whimsical folly that resulted in, say, the introduction of the possum and gorse with catastrophic results (in 1994 the possum population of New Zealand was estimated at 70 million).[10] But we need to be careful of what Michael André Bernstein calls backshadowing: 'a kind of retroactive foreshadowing in which the shared knowledge of the outcome of a series of events by narrator and listener is used to judge participants in those events *as though they too should have known what was to come*'.[11] Bernstein draws his examples from writing about the Shoah, but there are many New Zealand instances. It is scarcely possible, for example, to learn that Maori were once regarded as a dying race without hearing an accompanying snicker at the folly of so rash a prophecy. This is the complacency of hindsight, and a sideways glance at what was happening to indigenous people in Tasmania or California in the mid-to-late nineteenth century should correct it. Because backshadowing thrives in scenarios of catastrophe and apocalypse, it is particularly common in environmental literature, especially when the writing becomes figurative – as, for example, in such classic works as *The Invasion of New Zealand by People, Plants and Animals*, a book which is given to imagining 'armies' of 'invading' animals, as if possums by the million were already massed in their landing craft.[12]

It is misleading to think of early settlers as environmental vandals. Much like ourselves, they tended to be conservationists and developers both, and their legacy is not so much an awareness that the contradictions between those roles are so difficult to resolve in practice, but that we continue to act as if those contradictions had little real grip on us. It seems to me that the discourses of improvement and ruination, with all their potential for friction, are easily compartmentalised in the mind, much as nature reserves are compartmentalised in the workaday landscape. There may be many reasons why we so easily tolerate a division of sympathies, but I suspect we do so at least partly because the idealisation of nature associated with the ruination plot is in deep and fundamental accord with fatalistic assumptions about historical change in the plot of improvement. From this angle, works lamenting environmental degradation belong rather more to a dominant than to an oppositional ideology. Narratives of ruination are a dime a dozen: it is much rarer to find writing that illuminates tensions between progress and despoliation in order to look past them.

Writing *Tutira*

Herbert Guthrie-Smith's *Tutira: The Story of a New Zealand Sheep Station* is seldom commended for the magnetic interest of its plot. This very lengthy work, written over several decades and appearing in the successively revised and expanded editions of 1921, 1926 and 1953, is 'a record of minute alterations noted on one patch of land' (xvii–xviii). How minute? Perhaps I might best convey the scale of this work by noting that the introduction of weeds on the sheep station is discussed across eight chapters, loosely organised by their probable method of arrival: Stowaways, Garden Escapes, Children of the Church, Burdens of Sin, Fire and Flood Weeds, Pedestrians, the New Jerusalem and Late-comers – the chapter titles signalling a wry note of comparison with patterns of human settlement and displacement. The following passage is representative:

> To my backwoodsman's heart, there is . . . something austere, distin-
> guished even, in the brotherhood of weeds. They are the MacGregors of
> our artificial highlands seizing as of right – these hard faced children of
> the wilderness – conditions they must yet despise – leaf-mould, sieved
> peats, sharp sands, and shredded sods. . . . Centuries of condemnation
> and oppression have made them what they are . . . . Theirs has been that
> sad sharpening of perception that comes to dwellers beyond the pale, to
> creatures proscribed, to whom discovery is death. Who can doubt but
> that in the process of natural selection and the survival of the fittest, . . .
> that garden cress however circumvently gripped has added a new fury to
> its seed ejaculation, that petty spurge beneath its decapitated head has
> developed a more sure and certain stem reduplication, that mouse-ear
> carast has evolved a more profoundly furtive concealment in the heart of
> his host? Such are the lowly ways whereby humble folk may face adver-
> sity and perpetuate themselves amongst ill-wishers. (297–98)

These exuberant anthropomorphisms perhaps unfold a parable of settlement, but it would be more accurate to say that they are in the service of an historical vision in which the distributions of both humans and weeds are of equal interest and are complexly interre-lated, requiring alternatives to the usual compromises by which we reconcile the scenarios of improvement and ruination.

Guthrie-Smith came to these alternatives in the course of writing *Tutira*. They are the result of a prolonged adventure in writing as well as in the discovery that there was indeed something to write about in the interaction of humans, animals and plants, in one place, over half a century. It is a book one needs to read with an eye to how it, as well as the land it describes, is a record of changes, and changes of mind about the nature of change.

The 1921 edition of *Tutira* has a preface and thirty-eight chapters; these range, more or less chronologically, from the geology and primordial vegetation of the run, to its history and ecology following Maori settlement, to the tapestry of interlocking changes wrought by European agriculture and the wholesale introduction of alien species. The second edition has an index and an additional preface; the latter partly develops new perspectives but mostly updates points of botanical and zoological information. The new front and back pages enclose a text that is largely unchanged: some minor corrections are made but some errors are preserved; pagination and page layout for the body of the text are identical. Proofs for an expanded third edition were received from the publishers in 1940, shortly before the author's death. With the help of a small army of proofreaders and fact checkers, Guthrie-Smith's daughter, Barbara Absolom, saw the book through to publication in 1953. It is a different work. Once again, factual material is updated, but Guthrie-Smith had also added eight new chapters and made significant alterations to many others. The 1926 edition's preface now appears in a truncated form: the more factual material has been distributed through the body of the text, and two key sentences are transferred to a new third preface which, along with a new concluding chapter, now reorient the work.

The opening and closing strategies of the 1921 and 1953 editions are worth comparing. The concluding chapter of the first edition, 'Vicissitudes', deals with the recent legal and economic history of the run. It explains how the land passed from Maori leasehold to private title and ends with the author's decision to subdivide his empire of grass into smaller units. There are only two paragraphs of conclusion. The penultimate advises 'any youthful readers to go forth also into the wilds and possess lands and flocks of their own' (399), and modulates into a hymn in praise of New Zealand: 'in the sowing of the nations other emigrants have sought homes of easier attainment, the heaviest grain has been the furthest flung' (399) – a cultivation metaphor entirely in keeping with a narrative of improvement that seems unqualified at this point. A final paragraph then reads as follows:

> One last word: he hopes that his readers have played the game, that they have not indulged in the practice of skipping. If this has not been done, if every chapter has been read, they can rest assured that in examination, as it were under the microscope, of one sheep station, they have discovered what is to be found in all . . . . Every station in Hawkes Bay has been moulded by a great rainfall; possesses legends and relics of a splendid aboriginal race; has been clothed with forest, flax, and fern; has been subdued by pioneers in desperate straits for cash and its equilibrium; has had its surface mapped by stock, its rivers affected by scour, and, lastly, has been or is in the process of being subdivided into smaller holdings. (423)

The reader who has not skipped, who has read 'unflinchingly', as a word inserted in the third edition has it, will not only see how the local example tells a larger story of human settlement and environmental transformation, but, like a reader of Proust, will come away from a masterpiece of sustained narrative in which the creation of an unusually rich perspective on 'lost time' has little to do with the actual content of the story, which is itself quite ordinary, but is largely dependent on the storyteller's sensibility and style. Moreover, as in Proust, the reader will discover that the narrator's shifting judgements and assumptions about time and change are at the heart of *Tutira*. In the original preface, the author commends his book because it preserves a record of irreversible change: 'A virgin countryside cannot be restocked; the vicissitudes of its pioneers cannot be re-enacted; its invasion by alien plants, animals, and birds cannot be repeated; its ancient vegetation cannot be resuscitated' (xvii). 'Alas', says the conservationist; 'it had to be', replies the improver; the linear plots of improvement and ruination, which are locked in debate for much of *Tutira*, would seem to settle into a vision of linear and irreversible, necessary but regrettable, change.

In some respects, the binaries of development and conservation are preserved and even emphasised in the opening and closing passages of the 1953 edition. They are personified in the ancestral promptings of two grandmothers, the one a canny and tenacious Scot, the other an easy-going Irishwoman; the one admonishing, 'Destroy your fern! Clear off your woods', the other urging, 'Oh be content to leave alone'. These are the 'melancholy musings that perplex a sheep farmer in concern for his soul', who looks back on a life's work with the discomforting question, 'have I then for sixty years desecrated God's earth and dubbed it improvement?' (xiii). These starkly posed alternatives invite us to weigh the book and its author in the balance, but they may not have been the right questions to ask, and do not seem adequate to the more complex vision of change that *Tutira* also recounts.

One indication of a change of mind is the inclusion of a new chapter on the regeneration of bush. In the earlier editions, the clock of progress could not be turned back, but the old farmer now believes it is possible to restore 'pristine conditions existent ere Tasman, Cook, Banks and Solander were born or thought of' (329). This may seem another of those compromise narratives of ruination, a reverse prolepsis of the sort performed by Bethell's poem or publicity for national parks, but the vision of change and history belongs to an emergent storyline, one hinted at in those two sentences cut and pasted from the preface to the second edition, and which now conclude the third preface. I give both versions:

> . . . the writer himself has been compelled to side against what he would fain cherish and protect. There is no escape for a man from his environment, from his own era, he is drawn like dust into the draught, like water into the whirlpool. (1926)

> In palliation of his offence he may say with the lady in the song that he 'fell, but unwillingly fell'. It is impossible in fact for an individual to withstand the stream of tendency, to divaricate from lines eons ago laid down. He is drawn like water into the whirlpool, like dust into the draught. (1953)

Both versions suggest that the question of 'desecrating God's earth' or improving it has been too egocentrically posed; the individual is part of a larger pattern that is not of his making, a pattern that shapes him. But there are subtle differences between the two phrasings: in the earlier, the writer is compelled by environmental circumstances; in the revised version, the writer is caught up in them. In 1926, our attention is drawn to the complexity of the present – 'his own era' – while in 1953, the phrase 'lines eons ago laid down' suggests influence from the past. What makes the passage come alive, of course, are the similes, and we may readily understand that a writer casting off much of his second preface would go out of his way not to lose them. But it took a writer of unusual sharpness to see that it was better to reverse their 1926 order to read 'drawn like water into the whirlpool, like dust into the draught'. First, the power of a vortex, then specks of the very small: at a stroke, the incipient linearity of 'lines eons ago laid down' is thrown to the wind. The suggestion now is that if one follows the tendency of one's times, it is not because events are determined, but because systems are chaotic.

That may seem to place undue weight on a nicety of style, but style is precisely what distinguishes *Tutira* from the thousand other works that might otherwise resemble it. There are many studies of New Zealand flora and fauna, many works of regional history, but by and large they are written in a serviceable prose that does not draw attention to itself. In *Tutira* writing itself becomes an instrument of discrimination. Looking back, the first chapters to be written, those on the geomorphology and natural history of the station, seem relatively matter of fact and can be marred by summarising conclusions; on the whole, the book's complexity of texture and tone increased as the project grew and as new material was added, especially in the third edition. One might say Guthrie-Smith grew into his performance, that his book became more ostentatiously literary as time passed, but passages of wordy brilliance occur from the first. Indeed, he had always been a writer, and of all the adaptations of organism to environment noted in the book, not the least is that of the author himself, whose career in literature began with the verse drama *Crispus* (1891) – set in the palaces of the Holy Roman Empire but written by candlelight in a corrugated-iron hut – progressed to short stories with rural New Zealand settings, and only then to natural history with *Birds of Water, Wood and Waste* (1910) and *Mutton Birds and Other Birds* (1914).

'Every man has his idiosyncrasy', Guthrie-Smith wrote in the 1921 preface to *Tutira*; 'it has been that of the writer for half a lifetime to note small things; it has interested him.' As a work of natural history, *Tutira* rests not only on observational skill – noting small things most people would overlook – but also on seeing through to the patterns they suggest. The problem his writing everywhere confronts is that those small things – weeds, sheep, sparrows, hillsides – are always familiar to us; in order to convey the interest he finds in them, he needs to wrench his subjects free from the blanket of habitual perception. It would be a mistake to suppose that his elaborate and formal syntax is old-fashioned, the verbose residue, as it were, of his Latinate education at Rugby College; on the contrary, he writes like a modernist. In an early chapter on geology and erosion, for example, he wants to explain how, from an original flat uplifted plateau, a comb-like succession of ridges and valleys was formed. The valleys of Tutira, he explains, were not carved by streams but by water percolating its way under the topmost layer of earth, forming parallel ridgelines over time. Guthrie-Smith calls it 'subcutaneous' erosion and compares the process to 'the dissolution of a dead beast when first the flesh decays, then the skin shrinks and shrivels, whilst only at the last do the bones protrude' (26). His analogy has the violence of defamiliarisation: the grisly fate of sheep scenically dotting the ridges and gullies of our rural high country is intimated in the rib-like contours of the land.

One indication that his thinking has moved on in the 1953 edition is the inclusion of several new chapters, most notably those dealing with earthquakes, and those (to be discussed later) concerning the microhistory of a section of regenerating bush. In the earlier editions of *Tutira*, the opening chapters on geology reveal steady and incremental processes of change that have determined the appearance and potential productivity of the land. Although evidence of seismic upheavals was everywhere apparent in the fault lines and seaward tilt of the hills, Guthrie-Smith always thought it poor form in a geologist to conjure up an earthquake when accounting for puzzling features in the landscape. Explaining everything, earthquakes explained nothing. In 1931, however, there occurred 'a brief wrinkling of the epidermis of the earth, as evanescent as the shrug and stamp of a fly-pestered ox' (42) – and the city of Napier was levelled by an earthquake. Fourteen or so miles away, out in the paddock, Guthrie-Smith was himself momentarily 'shaken like a pebble in a box' (42), but remained unaware of the magnitude of what was taking place around him. Returning home to scenes of devastation, the fact that the whole countryside had been uplifted several feet was not observable, but it was the micro-patterns of disturbance that most challenged his sense of the possible. How was it, for example, that a hundredweight block falling from the chimney could be tossed clear of the veranda roof, pass between the posts and railings of the veranda to crash through the veranda floorboards, then extricate itself, flying once again between the roof and railings before embedding itself some yards away in the lawn? It requires several dumbfounded reiterations of the startling facts – there is the hole in floorboards; there, perfectly intact, is the veranda roof and the veranda railings – before more exact analogies are found. The forces involved remind him of juggling a pole in the palm of one's hand, and the path of the block, domesticated to reason at last, is like that of a girl catching and tossing an apple in the lap of her dress (49).

But the earthquake also made it possible to read the landscape differently. He had often wondered why, after heavy rain, the eels of Lake Tutira congregated en masse at a particular end of the lake, as if 'eagerly scrutinising the margin' (43). Two hundred yards away, an elongated depression preserved the outline of a shallow creek. To one not versed in earthquakes, there could be no connection between the imprint of a distant dry watercourse and the congregation of eels; post-1931, 'what had been inexplicable, in a flash became crystal clear' (42): the intervening hummock of land had been uplifted, stranding the eels that in times of flood would once have been flushed out to sea. Their thwarted migratory instinct had endured for at least a thousand years.[13] Earthquakes, then, were important to Guthrie-Smith because they enlarged his historian's sense of the room needed for unlikely and singular events.

This was not wholly a new discovery. Major sections of the book that appear largely unrevised in 1953, to do with the settlement of the land by Maori and then by European settlers and their sheep, may seem unpromising avenues for historiographic innovation, but they too indicate a fine appreciation of the lack of reasonableness in history. In a chapter introducing the pioneering period – called 'The Lure of Improvements' – Guthrie-Smith compares an actual diary of early station life with reflections on the motivation of the new settlers. The diary itself, from 1878, is a prosaic record of numbers of sheep mustered and drafted and shorn, of fencing erected and bracken burnt off; a pause for heavy rain is followed by the comment, 'found lame bull bogged in the drain where the bridge formerly was' (131). This apparently dreary and repetitive work proceeded, Guthrie-Smith assures us, under a golden haze of single-minded devotion to the farm that was to be. 'In those times, to think of an improvement to the station was to be in love', he writes. 'A thousand anticipations of happiness rushed upon the mind – the emerald sward that was to paint the alluvial flats, . . . the spurs over which the fencing was to run, its shining wire, its mighty strainers; . . . the glory of the grass that was to be' (135–36). These pictures of the perfect farm might indeed come from advertisements for grass seed or fencing wire, and are exaggerated a little in the writing so as to emphasise the siren call of improvement, while not entirely deflating the joy that devotion to an ideal can bring. 'Oh, those were happy days, . . . when every thought was for the run, when every penny that could be scraped together was to be spent on the adornment of that heavenly mistress' (136).

And to what end? The original developers of the station went bust and received from its new purchasers, H. Guthrie-Smith and partner, the exact sum owed to the mortgage company. The cycle began over, money and labour were again invested, and improvements lovingly made, but the finances of the run quickly passed from marginal to impossible. Guthrie-Smith eventually took over his partner's half-share in the debt-laden property for the sum of five shillings. He stood, he writes, 'with head barely above water' on the 'carcasses' of those who had 'spent all and gone under' (163). The point Guthrie-Smith is making is ostensibly an economic one: improvements, while necessary, do not bring an immediate return; and the future development of the property would involve a delicate balance between spending and not spending, between adding value and sitting tight. But the word carcasses is one of many terms in an extended comparison between humans and those other unmindful pioneers of the wilderness: sheep.

Wool over the Eyes

The first priority of a pioneering sheep farmer was pasture. In the 1880s, the once-forested hills of Tutira were a tangle of fern and bracken. On a hot day in late summer, the hillsides were set ablaze and grass subsequently sown in the black and fertile clearings. Come spring, the fern would shoot away again, but the tender fronds, if not exactly palatable to sheep, were at least edible. By crowding sheep onto a portion of land, a battalion of mowing jaws would keep the fern closely nibbled and allow the grasses to come on. It sounds simple in theory but was murderously difficult in practice. Fern-grinding, as the process was known, not only meant overstocking the land and wearing the sheep into 'greyhound lankness' (142), it also broke another fundamental rule of stock management: never to move sheep from good country to bad, from dry land to wet – and from a sheep's point of view, no previous home could be worse than Tutira. 'All sheep suffer from nostalgia', wrote Guthrie-Smith, 'but the merino is perhaps the most miserably homesick beast on earth.'

> Liberated in strange country, a mob of merinos will lie against the barrier – cliff, river, fence, whatever it may be – blocking their homeward route. Night after night, day after day, week after week, there they will camp, resigned to starvation. They will hug the fence-line that debars them from return to their old haunts till their droppings are inches deep, until their lank frames reveal every bone. (141)

But the rugged high country of Tutira offered many opportunities for sheep to escape: they drowned fording swift rivers, fell into crevasses, were snared in thickets of prickly scrub and bogged in quagmires. And not singly, for sheep are followers: a dart by one sparked ten in its train, each misjudged leap had an imitator. In the early years of the run, annual losses of 30 per cent or more were common.

In an early unfortunate leap of their own, Guthrie-Smith and his partner chose to invest in well-bred rams from South Canterbury in the hope of improving the hardihood of the flock; they lost three-quarters of these newcomers in a year. Because their predecessors, benefiting from exceptional conditions following the first firing of the land, had once shorn 9000 sheep in a season, they made the mistake of attempting to restock at that level. With too many sheep over too many acres, the grazing area contracted as the bracken gradually got away. With it came plagues of lungworm and footrot, and all because the young farmers were determined to do things by the book, and not set a cleansing fire until the bracken was tall enough to ensure a good burn. Just as sheep, when introduced into new territory, map it out through trails leading to bogs and crevices as well as green pastures, so too with the farmer; inexperience leads to failure, loss and wastage promote adaptation as conditions change. What might, in retrospect, look like a narrative of steady improvement, of mistakes corrected and right paths eventually found, turns out to have been the by-product of repetition and chance. This is not adaptation in a strict evolutionary sense, for the farmer's plans of course are deliberately made, but the role of intention in the historical patterning of events is much reduced in *Tutira*. Unconscious behaviour – the sorts of things we do when operating on automatic pilot – and unplanned outcomes play a greater role in accounting for change.

In this anti-teleological view of history, there is a sense in which humans transform the land in much the same way that sheep corrugate the hillside with their trails and sleeping shelves. A sheep, retiring for the night, turns round three or four times before finally settling, with hooves dug in downwards to take pressure. Through the repetition of insignificant action, they build platforms jutting like a pouting lower lip from the side of the hill. In a similar manner, their trails over the property evolve like a river into rapid and pool formations; their current of movement is diverted by larger obstacles, braids into ribbons at open ground or forms a single stream where a pocket of bush funnels the animals into close file. A sheep track might meander into a long bend for no apparent reason – unless, like Guthrie-Smith, you happen to remember the rotting corpse of a horse that long ago forced a diversion to windward. The very grass growing on the hilltops of the station was likewise produced through an unpredictable combination of circumstances. At one period, the hilltops were covered in sparse bracken; at another, they showed crowns of red sand; later still, a cover of luxuriant grass. Merino were the inadvertent agents of these changes. As it is the instinct of these easily startled animals to seek higher ground, they soon make their nightly camp on a hilltop. They chew off the bracken, their hooves loosen the soil and the wind carries it away, leaving the tops bare for a period of years; meanwhile, their faeces and urine are washed by the rain to fertilise grasses that slowly spread upwards to recolonise the tops. Meanwhile, in wet weather, the reticulated paths and hollows made by the sheep act as open drains, rushing off rainwater, and contributing to the transformation of the countryside from an absorbent sponge to a hard slate vulnerable to slips and the erosion of topsoil. As the turf gradually lost quality, hardier varieties of sheep had to be introduced. 'It would be easy to stretch the links of cause and effect', writes Guthrie-Smith. Having inadvertently made his hills less porous –

> . . . the settler growls as, tipping his correspondence from mailbag on to verandah floor, he opens an epistle demanding an increase in rates owing to the destruction of bridges. Stock trample hard a countryside 12,000 miles from the great cities of Europe; carpets are softer to the tread – the coarser Lincoln fleece has been supplanted by the finer wool of the Romney Marsh. (200)

The vision of *Tutira* is everywhere one of subtle and interactive change, of an environment transformed through 'the cumulative result of trivialities' (195).

Whenua

The intertwined story of Maori and Pakeha is as central to the story *Tutira* tells as it is to the history of the country as a whole. But it is told from an unusual angle. Human beings are moved from the centre spotlight: a human story of 'early failure' and 'ultimate acclimatisation' (xvii) has a place, Guthrie-Smith notes in his original preface, but it is a place we share with sparrows and rabbits. We are a migrating species whose anthropocentric priorities are dwarfed by our role as agents of concomitant biological change. But a history of Maori and Pakeha told only in terms of natural history would be reductive: it would risk seeing things so much under the eye of evolution that the problems of settling a land already inhabited by others would be viewed distantly, as in Satchell's *The Greenstone Door*, where conflict between Maori and Pakeha follows the inevitable course of an adaptive process arising out of 'the germs, the infinitesimal little things that fill the air where white men and brown men meet' (298).

The story shapes of ruination and improvement have near relatives in simple narratives of colonisation, which alternately propose settlers arriving to start over (improvement) and invaders arriving to take over (ruin). But there are no necessities in Guthrie-Smith's view of change. And far from viewing natives or native species as doomed, he came to entertain an opposite theory: given time, the native will always reassert itself. He was talking about people as well as birds, trees and grasses.

The Maori material in *Tutira* is spread across several sections of the book. A number of early chapters concern the fortunes of a particular hapu in the pre-contact period. The author refers to 'Ngai-Tatara' as the 'bygone inhabitants of Tutira', and advises the reader to 'accept for the nonce the ethics of the Stone Age, to imagine themselves bare-limbed, bare-headed, brown, the *pake* of everyday wear thrown over their shoulders, on high days and holidays clad in soft mats of woven flax, plumes in the hair, and *taiaha* in their hands' (65). This dissolve into the past is in keeping with the primitivism of early twentieth-century ethnography, and is associated with a generalised narrative of progress and improvement. But there are several complicating features that are less common in the anthropology of the time. Firstly, Guthrie-Smith refers to named informants, three particular friends, in whose company he has often walked the trails of Tutira, and he organises his material as a series of walks and talks along these trails: from the coast to the station, around the lake and from the lake to the inland ranges. Secondly, the information he presents reflects Maori priorities rather than European ones. Warning the reader about the seeming redundancy in coming chapters of seemingly irrelevant names, he asks:

> What does it avail to know that Tataramoa was the father and Porangi the mother of the damsel Tukanoi – all of them by the way descendants of Kohipipi – in her love affair with the gallant, the gay, red-headed Te-Whatu-i-Apiti? Why, it just matters everything; for after that fashion

for ages have these stories been transmitted. It is proper, therefore, that in that exact shape they shall be crystallized in print. (66)

Not only are people identified along with their named ancestors, but also eel weirs, fishing grounds and the like are all given their proper names, conveying a landscape that is thoroughly known and utilised. Finally, it might also be noted that Maori in the pre-contact period are not placed in a timeless past in *Tutira*, but are very much in history, being affected by their environment and modifying it in their turn. The pre-contact chapters end with the observation that while Tutira had attracted the envy of invaders for centuries, 'according to its annalists . . . the Ngai-Tatara were always victorious, so much so indeed that the station became famous in the land as *Tutira upoko pipi* – Tutira where heads become soft' (103).

Looking back, Guthrie-Smith wonders what on earth induced a soft-headed young farmer like himself to attempt running a sheep station in a place like Tutira.

The tenure of these runs was leasehold, and native leasehold at that; without exception the titles were flawed; the land was devoid of grass, the climate was wet, the access bad, the soil ungrateful and poor. There was no compensation for improvements. It seems impossible now that any reasonable soul could have believed there was either money or reputation to be made out of them.

The truth is that [we] were not reasonable, that [we] did not think at all. . . . To this day indeed I am unsure whether we were splendid young Britons, empire builders and so forth . . . or asses of the purest water. (153)

The latter case, we have seen, is made in convincing detail, but so too is the satisfaction to be found in breaking in new country and making marginal land productive. A similar division of sympathy is also found among the Maori owners of Tutira, some of whom would not sign leases on principle or, in the early days of the run, sought court orders, nonsensical to a young farmer leasing the land, forbidding the burning of bracken or banning drainage, 'on the ground it might affect the welfare of the eels in the lake' (225); but a majority were content to have the land farmed, while they themselves retained title and kept improvements without paying for them.

Guthrie-Smith's account of the recent history of the run, involving problems to do with farming leasehold land and its eventual conversion to freehold, is one of the most comical in the book. It does not, of course, offer a Maori perspective on the processes through which so much of their land was alienated, but it would be unfair to find fault with the writer on that score. What seems most valuable in Guthrie-Smith's account is his equanimity in the face of irritations and challenges that would have reddened the necks of his less tolerant countrymen, and that is perhaps as rare now as it was then. Let me give one or two examples.

Requests for an advance on the next year's rent were common. Funerals and weddings often produced a run of such appeals, which meant Guthrie-Smith would pass a new bridal display in the Napier shops with dismay, and be greeted as a friend and benefactor by all the undertakers of the town. And then there were solicitations like the following. The author invites us to imagine 'an English landlord writing to his tenant – the duke of Westminster, say – in the following terms: "Dear sir Wroting you these few lines . . . for I am very sick I am not well . . . Please don't for get to give me some money if you send just £3-10 that is good enough that will do for me"' (224).

The health of the landlords was indeed a cause for concern. An elderly Maori passed away:

> We regretted his demise of course, but the greater grief was his eleven successors, three of whom inherited one-sixth each of the original share, three one-twelfth each, three one-eighteenth each, two one twenty-fourth each. Well we were hardly out of mourning for this sad event, when bang would go another landlord . . . . Again we were sorry, of course, but the bitterest pang of all was the fourteen successors of the deceased. (222)

The politics, as well as the administration, of these highly fragmented native titles was by no means easy, and Guthrie-Smith paints a picture of perpetual litigation between sub-groups of Maori, the land boards representing them and farmers like himself. He recalls one particular occasion when 'the eyes of [his] landlords turned Tutira-wards':

> The plan [to dispute the Tutira lease] had many advantages . . . . It would raise the mana of Tutira to a height hitherto unattained. I feel sure that on the Maoris' part there was no malice. . . . They thought, not perhaps that I would actually enjoy a law suit, but that, as with themselves, it would dissipate ennui and boredom and provide me with a subject for thought and varied speculation. (404)

As a result of this particular court case, the lease was confirmed, but a block of station land reverted to native title, rents were quadrupled, and a new block of unimproved land had to be found and burnt off to replace the pasture lost. The complexity of interconnection between, in this case, an effort by Maori to consolidate their land holdings and the broader history of ecological damage to the region is typical of *Tutira*, and in principle not unlike that cliché of chaos theory in which a butterfly flapping its wings over China brings a cyclone to the North Island of New Zealand. The upshot, so far as the author of *Tutira* is concerned, returns us with a difference to the central dilemmas between improvement and ruination that we have noted so often.

In accordance with Guthrie-Smith's wishes, Lake Tutira is now a bird sanctuary and wildlife preserve; the foreshore is a public domain, open for camping and fishing; and the residue of the property provides outdoor education and practical training in farming. Behind the homestead, a trail zigzags up through the hanger – a term for a steep wooded hillside – which is now managed as a native reserve alongside a recently developed arboretum planted in exotics. There are two chapters about the hanger in *Tutira*, both written for the final edition of the book. In the 1880s, the hanger, like much of the station in pre-European times, was covered in the dense bracken that burgeoned in the wake of forest fires many centuries ago. Several attempts were made to burn off the fern but the newly sown grasses were crowded out in the spring rush. The third time this happened, owing to the cumulative effect of small changes elsewhere on the farm, a small and somewhat spindly tree, manuka, competed with the bracken for light and space, and within a decade, had largely displaced its forebear.

Guthrie-Smith saw the potential for a biological experiment and let the land alone. For twenty or so years, the hillside was densely covered in manuka: 'a grove of sombre green during eleven months of the year, a sheet of hawthorn white during the twelfth' (324). But conditions were subtly changing beneath the canopy. Millions of tiny spores and seeds responded to small chinks of light, and boring insects and wind eventually took their toll on weakening top branches of manuka, opening small light wells around which arose 'an incipient forest' of tree seedlings, creepers and ferns (324). In a word, the primeval forest was awakening, and would in turn over-shade and destroy the manuka, creating the 'mixed woodland of green-leafed trees, tall shrubs, tree ferns innumerable, creepers, ground ferns, and small terrestrial orchids' that is the hanger today (325).

Earlier, Guthrie-Smith had seen environmental change as irreversible: 'A virgin countryside cannot be restocked; . . . its invasion by alien plants, animals, and birds cannot be repeated; its ancient vegetation cannot be resuscitated' (xvii); but he now had a new rule: 'primordial conditions reassert themselves if given a chance' (320). Natural history could, as it were, be re-enacted. The second chapter on the hanger is a hypothetical study of what would happen if a great fire destroyed the forest for a second time. Bracken, manuka and green leaf tree seedlings would have their chance again; within months, a luxuriant foot-high forest would cover the blackened earth but, within this 'Lilliputian Eden, . . . as in the first garden of old, the Serpent, too, would be present twining and writhing in the form of honeysuckle and convolvulus' (328). He estimated that within four years, 'the greater part of the hanger would have become a tangle of suffocating honeysuckle coils, long bramble shoots, sprays of rose, and twining ropes of convolvulus' (328). What to do? Guthrie-Smith supposed that if one were to mass-plant a fast-growing exotic like macrocarpa, and faithfully keep the growing trees clear of honeysuckle, blackberry and other opportunists, they would eventually shade out the creepers and restore a forest of completely alien trees. Ringbarking these aliens would so manage the distribution of light to the forest floor that, in a new phase of regeneration, the hanger would be restored once again to 'pristine conditions ere Tasman, Cook, Banks, and Solander were born or thought of' (329).

There is an anticipation in this thought experiment of a kind of puritanical nativism that one finds both in literary works and in government policy: in *the bone people*, for instance, Kerewin snarls, 'Bloody pines, . . . this land isn't suitable for immigrants from Monterey or bloody wherever.'[14] Consider, too, the Department of Conservation's emphasis on recreating ecosystems found in pre-human times. A portion of Tutira is now designated a Mainland Island – that is to say, a reserve, in which scientists aim to restore primordial conditions by reproducing the ecological security that is characteristic of an offshore island.[15] It is not that I object to a preference for native trees, or to setting ambitious conservation goals, but I would wish to disconnect my liking for such things from ahistorical myths of a pristine environment, and from historical models that can conceive of change only in terms of development or disaster. Guthrie-Smith leaves us instead with a sense of the interconnectedness of all living things, and of humans as organisms whose migrations from one landmass to another are only to be expected, but who settle the land in much the same way as sheep explore a hillside run, in strings and stragglings that are both unpredictable and highly patterned, and whose actions shape and are shaped by the new world in a dynamic that poses a fundamental problem of perspective. In the last paragraph of 'The Hanger', one of the last chapters composed for *Tutira*, Guthrie-Smith writes:

When a block of land passes, as it may do through the hands of ten holders in half a century, how can long views be taken of its rights? Who under these conditions can give his acres their due?

Aue, taukari e, ano te kuware o te pakeha kahoro nei i whakaaro ki to mauri o te whenua. Alas! Alas! That the pakeha should so neglect the rights of the land, so forget the traditions of the Maori race, a people who recognised in it something more than the ability to grow meat and wool. (325)

What makes his lament different from the usual compromise, whereby we accept the benefits of land development while mourning its results, is the historical vision that emerges from taking a long view of the history of this sheep station and rues the amnesia that accompanies a foreshortening of time in the new place. Looking back, nothing has turned out quite as expected, unintended results have been at least as important as planned actions and the future has never been inevitable; neither have individuals, whether sheep, sparrows or humans, been able to 'withstand the stream of tendency' (xiii). The individual is 'drawn like water into the whirlpool, like dust into the draught' (xiii). But this 'stream of tendency' is not a juggernaut of progress or ruination moving irresistibly, like a locomotive, along its iron track; a tendency is irresistible not because it is powerful, not because it is massive, but precisely because it is an aggregation of very small and insignificant pieces of behaviour. 'If this volume has a value', he writes, 'it is because of [its] insistence on the cumulative effects of trivialities' (320). It is a long view that allows us to see the settlement of New Zealand by Europeans on the same stage as its set- tlement by rabbits and weasels, bumblebees and trout, and in terms of processes and tendencies that resist reduction to the cartoon binaries of colonist or invader, improvement or ruination.

Coming back to the weather, it is a long view that would allow us to see the rainstorm of 1924 not as a singularity, but along a continuum that stretches from years of drought to the equally impressive deluges of 1938 or of Cyclone Bola in 1988. Seeing the big picture helps, but Guthrie-Smith's passion for noticing small things also reminds us that we live among close-ups, with perspectives that reflect our own priorities and the refracted priorities of others. After all, not even the weatherman expects a twenty-year rainstorm in the next three weeks.

CHAPTER SEVEN

Suburbs, Settlers, Souls

> . . . *what great gloom*
> *Stands in a land of settlers*
> *With never a soul at home.*
> *– Allen Curnow, 'House and Land'*

372 Karori Road

In 1909, a young Katherine Mansfield, fearing that life had given her nothing to write about, addressed a poem to a writer from the old world who had been blessed with the opposite problem. Stanislaw Wyspianski, born into the non-state of Poland, was as provincial as she, but she had been born in 'a little island and with no history' among 'people [who] have had nought to contend with'.[1] The European writer, by contrast, not only had centuries of political struggle and national-ist yearning to draw on, but there were also heroes ready-made from folklore and history to populate his imagination. In his writings, he seemed a virile great-hearted giant – and what was she? Merely 'a woman, with the taint of the pioneer in [her] blood'.[2] The word 'taint' is wonderfully ambivalent, and has excited much commentary, but the word 'pioneer' is also surprising. The Beauchamps of Wellington hardly qualify as a pioneering family: they were townspeople recently across from Australia. They did not hack farms from the bush, and if any of them 'handled the clay with rude fingers' it would have been figuratively, in the gold mines of Ballarat or Bendigo. But Katherine Mansfield's family, like their fictional avatars the Burnells and the Sheridans, were pioneers nonetheless, pioneers of suburbia, and she would become one of the first writers in the world to put a very new kind of place on the map.

The suburbs of the ancient and medieval world were shanty-like areas beneath and beyond the safety of a city's walls. 'In the suburbes of a toun', warns Chaucer's Yeoman, 'lurkynge . . . in lanes blynde', amidst the desperate and anonymous poor, all sorts of shady characters have their 'pryvee fereful residence'.[3] Suburbs kept those unwholesome connotations until the mid-to-late nineteenth century; all the good addresses were in town. The first suburbanites in our modern sense of the word were factory owners from the industrial midlands of Great Britain. A comedian of the period once offered this solution to the problems of urban blight: 'let us build the city in the country – the air is so much purer there!' And that is precisely what the mill-owners of Manchester did, building family-sized homes in park-like gardens a carriage ride – later several tram-stops – away from the inner-city slums. Garden suburbs on this pattern soon followed in the larger cities of the northeastern United States, but a distinctively new-world pattern of suburbanisation, which we share with Australia, Canada and much of the United States, would involve no escape from the crowded and unsanitary tenements of the metropolis, and would involve cities that never developed much of a centre at all.

The Burnell family, moving from Thorndon to Karori, leave behind their Jewish neighbour, Mrs Samuel Josephs, and a town centre that is mapped by the author of 'Prelude' in only the faintest of ways: it is the location of Stanley's office and also of a 'Chinaman's shop'. Are the Burnells fleeing ethnic diversity? One feels they would if they could, but the family lights out for new territory for the oldest of reasons.

'The thing that pleases me', said Stanley, . . . 'is that I've got the place dirt cheap . . . I was talking about it to little Wally Bell today and he said he simply could not understand why they had accepted my figure. You see land about here is bound to become more and more valuable . . . in about ten years time . . . of course we shall have to go very slow and cut down on expenses as fine as possible.'[4]

Stanley is 'mortgaged to the tonsils' – to borrow a phrase from *Foreskin's Lament*.[5] The house is 'a good six and a half miles' from his office in town, far enough for Linda to dread the 'very high pressure' of her husband's early-morning start, but not so far as to make a daily commute impracticable (26). The one character who is aware of distance is the teenager, Beryl. She tells her elder sister:

'Oh yes, I like the house immensely and the garden is beautiful, but it feels very far away from everything to me. I can't imagine people coming out from town to see us in that dreadful jolting bus, and I am sure there is not anyone here to come and call' . . .

'But there's the buggy', said Linda. 'Pat can drive you into town whenever you like.' (31)

A suburb has always been a place where adults underestimate a teenager's transport needs. Not that any of these characters think of Karori as a suburb: on the way home from work, Stanley thinks to himself: 'Ah, it was splendid to live in the country – to get right out of that hole of a town once the office was closed; and this drive in the fresh warm air, knowing all the while that his own house was at the other end, with its garden and paddocks, its three tip-top cows, and enough fowls and duck to keep them in poultry, was splendid too' (35).

The word 'country' in this passage comes from a real estate agent's lexicon; the Burnell property is the exact equivalent of what we would today call a lifestyle block. There is a working dairy farm next door, but the 'big louts of boys' and the 'two dreadful females with rabbit teeth' who welcome the newcomers with scones on moving day will meet no neighbourly reciprocity from the Burnells. Their closest local contacts are their relatives, the Trouts, who live a mile away and 'don't know a soul here' (55–56); other friends, like Stanley's tennis-playing chums from the office, are expected to visit. Beryl may feel the pangs of exile from 'the giddy whirl of town', but the adults of the family are keeping their town-oriented social world intact. Stanley's so-called 'house in the country' is the outpost of the suburb that will come to surround it.

For many readers, the Burnell and Sheridan families of Katherine Mansfield's New Zealand stories represent a phase in our national story when people regarded Britain as 'Home'. These characters are like old Miss Wilson in Allen Curnow's poem 'House and Land', 'Taking tea from a silver pot / For fear the house might fall', and their superficiality is often regarded as a symptom of a lack of connection between custom and place, of their not having become real New Zealanders yet.[6] We should neither underestimate nor disparage the ties immigrants and their descendants have felt for 'the old country'. It is a sentiment commonly expressed by settlers in all new-world environments, but whether it is New England or New Zealand, historians of those places have tended to misdiagnose those old-world attachments as a deficiency, and have overestimated the explanatory value of an inauthentic attachment to home when unfolding their nations' foundational narratives. When Beryl's heart sinks because the afternoon tea looks ugly and common, when Stanley resists an egalitarian impulse to share his cherries with an employee, when Mrs Sheridan forgets the flags for the sandwiches, when Laura ponders the aesthetic placement of the marquee, these characters are reproducing English forms of genteel class-consciousness, but this is by no means a sign of a diminished or suspect relation to place. These people are identifying with 'Home' less in the sense of where they've come from than in terms of where they think they've arrived: home, but a good notch up. Their gentility celebrates a settler ideology of progress and improvement and is a sign that they have a stake, or perhaps a picket fence, firmly planted in a land that has been true to its promise.

A more telling symptom of dislocation is the attitude of these characters to the town. Wellington, in Mansfield's stories, often seems both bigger and more crowded than a small city of under 50,000 souls would have been.[7] I have mentioned Beryl's wistful mock reference to the 'giddy whirl of town', but she goes on to refer to the previous house – call it 25 Tinakori Road – as that 'awful cubby hole in town' (55). And as Stanley drives home, his lungs expand in the rural air while he rejoices in the contrast between 'that hole of a town' (35) and the new-found spaciousness of 372 Karori Road. In colonial Wellington, there were no tenements as Manchester, Glasgow or New York had tenements, but Mansfield often shows her middle-class characters acting as if they were in an enclave surrounded by urban blight. In 'The Garden Party', the little cottages of Thorndon are really 'far too near' the Sheridans' imposing residence at, shall we say, 75 Tinakori Road:

They were the greatest possible eyesore and they had no right to be in that neighbourhood at all. They were little mean dwellings painted a chocolate brown. . . . The very smoke coming out of their chimneys was poverty-stricken. . . . Children swarmed. When the Sheridans were little they were forbidden to set foot there because of the revolting language and of what they might catch. (254)

The Sheridan family needs to draw these boundaries so firmly because of a peculiarity in New Zealand's local geography. In early Auckland and early Wellington, as now, property values followed the sun; expensive houses were on the top of ridges, facing north, often with a view and with all-day sun. The cheapest housing could be very close by, but the sections weren't as sunny and the houses would be cold and damp in the wintertime. (Franklin Road in Ponsonby is perhaps the classic surviving example of this pattern: two-storey mansions at the top, then villas, then little cottages towards the bottom of the hill.) In upper Tinakori Road, though, the proximity of working people's cottages to the Sheridans' home encourages an exaggerated perception of difference: it is as if all the horrors of London's East End were to be found just a stone's throw away, in the insalubrious shade of a working man's section.

Mansfield gives her characters sentiments like these not because she is interested in suburbs per se, but because she is very much interested in the gender and intergenerational patterns with which these settings will become associated. The latter need just a word here, as fiction focused through children often presents an exception to the generalisations I shall be making. Suburban children do not share adult work, as they do in rural settings, nor do they require the oversight of adults, as they do in urban settings. The more suburban space is idealised, the more children's worlds and adult worlds are parallel universes. In the garden and paddocks of their big Karori house, Kezia and Lottie and Isabel, Pip, Rags and their much tormented dog, Snooker, run wild. It is true we glimpse the adult each child will grow into; it is true they are little savages, little beasts; but theirs is the paradise of the great unsupervised New Zealand childhood – a paradise available to me along the shorelines and mudflats of Beachhaven, and that would extend past my own suburban childhood until 'the end of the golden weather' – a date possibly marked by the introduction of compulsory bike helmets.

Beryl and Linda Burnell, on the other hand, point to another great plot line with which suburbs are associated: the proverbial 'great place to bring up children' was also a kind of Sargasso Sea for the stranded women of the house. Beryl admires her hair in the mirror – 'you really are a lovely little thing' (58), she says to herself – but feels the falseness of her performance as she does so, as if she is always playing a part and keeping it up for Stanley's benefit. The real Beryl, she feels, is a shadow, 'faint and unsubstantial' (59). Her married sister cannot fully find herself in the roles of wife and mother, but those roles shape the sense of self she has. Hers is the double bind of wanting what her husband wants for her – to be desirable to men, to have children, to make a happy home – yet she also does not want those things and, like one of Chekhov's hemmed-in heroines, yearns for something more. Characters like Linda and Beryl present us with such familiar psychological predicaments, and open such well-worn lines of feminist critique, it is easy to miss the way those stories rely on a suburban setting. By absorbing (among other things) Chekhov's stock situations and tone – those Russians stuck in the provinces, those yearnings and resignations – and transposing them all to provincial Wellington (as well as to the 'absolutely satisfactory house and garden' (96) of a London story like 'Bliss'), Mansfield found that she did, after all, come from a new sort of place that gave her a new sort of subject matter of her own.

Many writers, from Sinclair Lewis to Janet Frame, from Maurice Gee to Richard Ford, would open new doors in the suburbs, but this is not a history of expanding innovation. It is striking how little and how slowly the basic moves in suburban literature do change, and how fully the possibilities of that setting are anticipated in just a handful of Katherine Mansfield's best stories.

14 Esmonde Road

A section on Lakelands Estate, one of the first subdivisions in the new suburb of Takapuna, could be purchased in 1910 for £46, on a 'new easy term plan' of £10 down and £1 per month at 5.5 per cent interest.[8] It had to be good buying. Advertisements for the adjacent Shakespeare Estate offered 'Sea-side homes 20 minutes from Queen

Street' – a Phileas Fogg of the day would have taken one of the super-fast steam trams along Lake Road and down Bayswater Road to the wharf, where a waiting ferry would whisk him across the harbour in almost no time at all. The Lakeland subdivision called itself 'the most accessible and yet the most secluded Estate in the district'. Perhaps Takapuna's accessibility was exaggerated by a minute or two, but there was no doubting what public transport was going to do to land values. The Davey family purchased their property at 14 Esmonde Road in the mid-1920s for between £400 and £500, but they were not among those who would build the villas and bungalows of the suburb.[9] In a small way, the Daveys were property investors who trusted that their land would gain in value while they enjoyed summer holidays in an inexpensive and temporary bach. As things turned out, the property would never be a retirement nest egg for them, but having a one-room creosoted shack of his own would make all the difference in the world to their bohemian scapegrace of a son, Frank Sargeson.

In 1931, when Sargeson moved in, Esmonde Road was a quiet cul-de-sac running down to the mangroves of the inner Waitemata harbour. The bach was rotted and ramshackle, cold in winter, without electricity or running water. To an unloving eye, it was a hovel and a health risk; the council soon wanted it demolished. After a long and gallant rearguard action, Sargeson at last had no option but to comply, and in 1948 built the modest fibrolite cottage that is now preserved by the Sargeson Trust; a plaque outside says, 'Here a truly New Zealand literature had its beginnings'. Much as I honour Sargeson, I see the beginnings of a 'truly' New Zealand literature rather less national-istically than the sign indicates, but I do think those 'beginnings', as they are alleged to have occurred in the 1930s, are largely suburban in origin, and have a relation to suburbs in keeping with Sargeson's own dismayed reaction to subsequent patterns of development on the North Shore.

'Thank God I'm still able to live in my flimsy bach and cultivate my citrus trees, my tomatoes, sweet corn and rock melons', he wrote to his publisher back in the golden days of 1941. 'It can be damned miserable and uncomfortable sometimes in winter, but I don't miss the hundred and one pseudo-comforts that I've never experienced anyhow.'[10] Soon after the new bach was completed, feeling 'almost penthouse' in the new place, Sargeson told another correspondent, 'I really must send you some snaps of the new house. With electric hot water, stove ditto, indeed everything that opens and shuts, I feel that some hostile daemon must be lying in wait somewhere to bring me a cropper.'[11] Meanwhile, Takapuna had become a well-to-do and rather genteel suburb, while to the west, from Glenfield to Beachhaven, another standardised pattern was emerging with the low-cost housing developments of the 1950s. Then, in 1959, with the opening of the Harbour Bridge, the waiting daemon struck: Esmonde Road became a roaring motorway feeder. By the 1970s, as new suburbs spread further north, infill housing and ugly sausage-block developments began to despoil the older, once-graceful suburbs. Behind Frank's barbarian hedge, books were still produced, tomatoes, sweet corn and peppers were still cultivated; the little bach on 14 Esmonde Road may have become surrounded, but for those who came to drink the fabled Lemora wine and talk books, it remained a non-conforming oasis in a desert of respectability and pseudo-improvement. I share those sentiments but had better acknowledge a paradox: there is nothing more suburban than our antipathy to suburbia.

'City and Suburban' is one of Sargeson's late stories. In this period, he was exploring what he could do with verbose and highly self-conscious narrators, with autodidacts whose wide reading and cultural ambitions are in advance of a community whose interests range from the philistine to the barely middlebrow. The narrator of the story is an accountant who has included some Arts papers in his Bachelor of Commerce degree. He would like nothing better than to devote himself full time to the study of history, but can only fantasise about swapping his professional career for the undemanding milk-round that would give him time to pursue his intellectual interests. His problem is that he has been educated just enough to feel always that there must be more to life. He sees himself as representing the 'new average': 'the latter-day common man, the runner among the ruck in the urban rat race', with a wife, 'two youngsters a home of my own and of course the car'.[12] This is how he presents his most recent crisis:

It *would* be on a day like this . . . that our youngsters should come up the beach at low tide, and bring with them the finger they had found in one of their favourite rock pools.

Mummy, look! That was our boy, Happy. The pair of them had been disagreeing over who was to carry their find, which was cupped by Glad in her two hands. To me, it was as though I had never seen a finger so astonishingly large despite the wrinkles. The nail was intact and all had been washed white and clean. As an object composed of alabaster or translucent wax it could have been attractive – but there was no mistaking what it was.

As usual Pam was quicker than I was, and her technique within its own limitations couldn't be faulted. While she whipped out a handkerchief she agreed with the young 'uns that they had found something very precious (Why! of all things! a new kind of shell – a *finger*-shell! Well!), and at the same time quite desperately fragile. Mummy would keep it for them. . . . And as the handkerchief-draped horror went into the picnic bag, out came the transparent packet of chocolate biscuits.

In the meantime, I had been trying very hard to rid myself of the impression that what our children had found was somebody's severed phallus; and I recovered my speech only to say a thing which to Pam would be irritating and silly, and which in the circumstances she was quite right to ignore.

For God's sake, Pam, I said, why ever in the name of heaven and earth did you insist they be called Happy and Glad? (286–87)

The story soon sets out on a series of digressions in which the narrator ponders how many times Athenians, camel drivers and other studs of the ancient world were required to 'service' their wives; and after various protests at his wife's excessive expectations of himself in that regard, and after bemoaning the cruel way nature allows males to hit the top of their sexual form in their teens while women reach their peak only in their thirties – after all this 'Reader's Digest' sexology, he concludes:

But what in the name of all that's sub specie aeternitatis would she have made of me if I had confessed the simple shocking truth – that even from her and my closest friends I conceal the melancholy which is induced in me by the afternoon slope of the summer sun? And that sex, Kinsey, and what have you are all the easiest kind of stuff to take compared to that horror? (291)

Why Happy and Glad? The author has given the children those names because suburban life involves a conspiracy to cushion out anything difficult or unpleasant life throws in our way. The narrator, like so many of the male protagonists of suburban fiction from George Babbit to Truman Burbank, doubts and dissents from that rosy consensus. Most suburban fiction with a male protagonist is built on the joists of a familiar plot: someone with just a little more vision than usual, shackled to an efficient but shallow wife and suffering the ennui of the modern consumer, becomes restless and dissatisfied, and will either 'light out for the territory' or, as here, in a tragicomic mode, stare grimly at the setting sun, aware of how paltry his life looks under the eye of eternity.

Pam is negatively depicted by the author as the carrier of social values, the mum with the 'transparent' bag of chocolate biscuits. But he also allows the narrator this comment:

> I will say at once that I have no petty complaints about my wife. . . . Pam is nicely put together, and I am confident about wearing qualities which should ensure that she remains for many years easy on the eyes. Also, being one hundred percent woman, I can never see her landed in my own sort of jam. (286)

The narrator's self-ironising patter seems intended to be read as a symptom of the way he has opted for a lifestyle instead of a life. But the suburban home is also the place where the woman's place is. And as this story from the Holyoake years jokes about sexual boredom and the payment of the marital debt, it perhaps gestures uneasily toward a second wave of feminist critiques of the suburb that are just around the corner, and that will upset Sargeson's equation of suburban malaise with emasculating wives.

Ian Wedde has described the characters of Sargeson's *Collected Stories* as a 'secret army', a 'Chaplinesque fifth column' of misfits and malcontents at war with mainstream suburban values.[13] The family home is the most common setting for these confrontations, often explicitly – as when 'The House that Jack Built' becomes 'The Hole that Jack Dug' – but also as the disapproving silent partner of the inner-city boarding houses of 'That Summer', 'A Final Cure' or 'An International Occasion'. The boarding houses of Ponsonby and Grafton are embryonic urban spaces in Sargeson's stories; their kitchens and bedrooms have the jostling function of streets and hotel rooms in the conventional big city, where people meet by chance and in privacy, where things frowned on in the suburb become alluring. Yet the suburb, rather than the city, is Sargeson's privileged setting because it articulates a tension in society between the promise of security, the charm of building a cosy little nest, and the complacency, the narrow horizons, the homogenising and deadly conformity, that can result from playing life so safe. Sargeson's target in all this is often thought to be religious and secular forms of Puritanism, those conformist, timid, life-constricting ideologies that, as analysed in such major works of criticism as Bill Pearson's 'Fretful Sleepers' (1952) or Robert Chapman's 'Fiction and the Social Pattern' (1953), seem not so much to have shaped as deformed so much of our social history. Yet the emphasis in those studies of the secularisation of puritan values obscures a point that seems as unlikely as it is peculiar: insofar as the target of anti-suburban critique is consumerism or materialism, writers and readers must somehow imagine that middle-class souls have been impoverished by their affluence.[14]

In stories about early settlers, as Linda Hardy has argued, we often find contrasts between the settler who establishes 'natural occupancy' by casting off pianos and other old-world paraphernalia, and colonists who make a baggage-laden but less adaptable landfall.[15] The protagonists of suburban fiction, burdened by their materialism, want to throw off encumbrances and find a simpler and more authentic relation to place too. Theirs is a 'sentimental dispossession', to borrow a phrase from a recent American study.[16] Beryl and Linda in 'Prelude' are perhaps early examples of the woe that is in wealth, the pain that is in privilege, and of the often hard-to-pin-down, somewhat uncertain, partly sympathetic, partly satirical, point of view authors tend to evince in relating their characters' discontent. And just as Linda Hardy's so-called natural settler is only wishfully distinct from the colonial type, so too with the restless and bored narrator of Sargeson's story: he may seem to serve as a critic of suburban values – chafing at them, disdainful of them – but this character's alienation poses no challenge to mainstream suburban existence; on the contrary, it is its very essence.

Loomis

It is not difficult to imagine the narrator of 'City and Suburban' growing sideboards in the seventies, taking up pottery, buying Hotere in the eighties, drinking Cloudy Bay into the nineties and morphing into the retired public servant who looks back with some dissatisfaction on a life of safe options in Maurice Gee's novel *Going West* (1992). This is a novel of 'territories, places': Castor Bay, Kelburn, Ngaio and a fictional suburb Gee has made his own:

> West of Auckland, out towards the ranges. Purple evening hills with a sunset like an open wound. We both knew that margin to our world, Rex from New Lynn, I from Loomis.[17]

The narrator, in his first go at 'doing' the landscape, unconsciously picks up a simile – 'like an open wound' – from a description of the half-settled countryside in 'Man Alone'. As this is a novel about our literary tradition, we can be sure Maurice Gee knows where the image comes from while hinting that his narrator, Jack Skeat, is more than an anagram away from poetic greatness. *Going West* is also the story of the narrator's envied best friend, Rex Petley, whose mysterious drowning haunts the narrative, and who (for my purposes) is interesting as an attempt to imagine a first-rate poet who writes in an unfussy, natural-as-breathing way about the sacred sites of childhood and small moments of domestic felicity in the suburbs. There is no 'great gloom' in a bundle of Rex's late unpublished poems that Jack takes home in a plastic supermarket bag.

> Happy poems. They won't please everyone. Some people are going to say, Where's the tension? Some are even going to say, there's nothing here, no content. But it seems like poetry to me, even though it rarely gets off the property.[18] (277)

Maurice Gee spares us chunks of Rex's poetry, but its suggested qualities are those realised by the novel itself. A drive through Loomis, then and now:

> Down again, along, through, into. Here is Loomis under the hills. A glass and tile front, traffic lights and carparks and people. He wants the town of empty dusty streets and broken hedges. It's in behind and a long way back. He drives down the shopping streets and turns left into industry and commerce – where once a little square-built jam factory had stood – and passes through a district of panel-beating shops and coal and firewood yards and boarded-up stores until, at a straggly line, Loomis is residential. (46–47)

No 'content', just the poetry of place. And of property:

> They had once made an offer on a villa in Worser Bay where the salt spray in southerlies would rattle like hail on the window panes – it rattled on the day they inspected the house, the trees thrashed, wind boomed in the ceilings – but someone else saw it and offered more . . . it was like losing a baby. (15)

The novel is notable, too, for its frequent use of terms of belonging: characters speak of 'roots', of 'blood attachment', of being a 'true Aucklander', and – shades of Henry James – the novel considers the charms of Wellington as might be seen by a Wellingtonian versus the charms of Wellington as might be seen through the consciousness of an exile from Auckland who has lived there twenty years. This is a novel that is very confident of its grounding in place.

A half century earlier, Allen Curnow's poem 'House and Land' invoked an 'Awareness of what great gloom / Stands in a land of settlers / With never a soul at home'.[19] Curnow was the leading voice in that generation of writers who first asked what it would take for New Zealanders to be at home in their country and to define this as an ongoing problem for the Pakeha majority. The question of being at home, the theory ran, was not something a householder might simply take for granted, but something artists and citizens might spend a lifetime trying to work out. One of the longer-running squabbles in our literary history began when a group of younger Wellington poets misidentified Curnow's argument, and took him to be affirming a literary determinism of his own, which assumed that the writer's 'adventures in search of reality' were to be found in the nation's past rather than its present, and in a natural rather than an urban or suburban setting.[20] But for all the Wellington Group's talk of engaging the commonplace suburban world in which most of us actually live, these 'anti-nationalists' were of the 'great gloom' school too.

In Baxter's 'Ballad of Calvary Street':

> The afternoon goes by, goes by,
> The angels harp above a cloud;
> A son-in-law with spotted tie
> And daughter Alice fat and loud
> Discuss the virtues of insurance
> And stuff their tripes with trained endurance.[21]

It is a limitation in Baxter that his suburbs are caricatures not only when they need to be, but also in more earnestly imagined poems about dropouts, suicides, neurotic housewives and the like. It is much the same with the dissatisfied personae of Louis Johnson's poems. In 'There was Something Wrong with My Life', the wife of a cheating husband speaks of 'An emptiness, something lacking, I couldn't / Put my finger on it'. Johnson fills out her sense of isolation and abandonment with images drawn from a desolate new subdivision – 'standing under a tree on an empty allotment / Wind in my hair and the rain crying over me' – and closes with a gothic touch:

> . . . he wouldn't be there
> Nor on the road I took back to the house,
> Nor in the kitchen when I took the knife
> From the drawer to go and attend to the children.[22]

It is striking how closely suburbs are associated with caricature, hyberbolic misery and gory endings. And then, remarkably suddenly, everything changes: in the 1990s there are grounded novels of unabashed prosperity like *Going West*, where the character of Rex Petley, curiously enough, writes exactly the kind of post-nationalist poems of belonging that the Wellington Group envisaged but failed to write, while Jack, the untalented poet, is a natural on real estate but labours to describe the view out the window. The Skeats's Wellington house is a renovator's dream:

> We made it beautiful, as it had been before the time of yellow paint, partitions, lowered ceilings and seventeen students crammed in. We restored the barge boards and the fretwork and raised new finials and all the while I felt that I restored our marriage and pulled off ugly bits I had tacked on. I thinned the trees and opened up the view. We looked across the city and Oriental Bay . . . . I've seen the white ships shine like icebergs coming from the south, while over beyond the entrance, beyond the reefs, the shelves of Baring Head, planed as smooth as timber and shining like fields of wheat, lay in the sun, an untouched, warm, impossible new land.
>
> I can't do lyricism and shouldn't try, but the Central Terrace view moves me still, even though poles and insulators and sagging wires lie across the front of it. (198–99)

There are some lightly ironic nudges at the expense of his narrator – a phrase like 'untouched, warm, impossible new land' repeats more history than Jack knows – but Maurice Gee is also remarkably adept at using the built-up suburban landscape and its distinctive terminology to evoke place, time and memory with accuracy. Searching for a house he once new, Jack 'walks along the footpath reading the numbers and works out which house it must have been: a bungalow, with a bow window, and a roof of decromastic tile out of keeping with the weather-boards' (233). 'Decromastic' waited some time to become, in this sentence, *le mot juste*.

Despite the rural setting of Allen Curnow's 'House and Land', the 'great gloom' he complains of might well be characterised as a form of suburban blues: in the 1930s – and through to the early 1980s – it is settlers in the suburbs who are conformist, soulless and dull, who suffer from a loss of reality and a lack of belonging. His critics, the younger poets of the 1950s, who spoke of transnational perspectives, who wanted literature to pay attention to ordinary life in the suburbs, are every bit as concerned as he was with the homelessness of homeowners. I referred earlier to 'sentimental dispossession': the spiritual and cultural impoverishment of the prosperous. It is a syndrome in which the very things that generally do function as signs of our belonging – houses, views, possessions, the commonplace environment of what we have and where we are – come to be regarded as signs of a deficiency in belonging. In both our literary nationalism and the transnational literature of the suburb, the things that conventionally stand for home are used to signal a problem with being at home. To find those signs empty is a first lesson in the art of 'standing upright here' or coming to terms with 'something' that is wrong with one's life.[23] But what looks like an injunction to discover a deeper national identity or a quest to find your own authentic self turns out to be more like a self-inflicted cup and ball trick. Where you think the ball ought to be is precisely where it's not, and though not finding it puts you in the game, it must have been under the cup all along.

By the early 1990s the situation of the represented suburb had changed. It is home – or, more accurately, becomes home. At the beginning of *Going West*, Jack's wife 'lets herself boil over now and then on the subject of belonging in a place'.

> 'Roots', Harry says, without a blush. The house and suburban Castor Bay, they are not home, but the city on the isthmus, and the wild west coast out there, and the blue gulf in her view, and the beaches and the mangroves and the mud – Harry belongs. (15)

This looks like another example of 'Pakeha turangawaewae' – belonging through nature. Yet Jack's journey into his past, like George Plumb's before him, will involve discovery and healing and a richer sense of home: there is a difficulty in the marriage to be repaired, and a right relation to place turns out to depend on Jack's openness to the past and the reclamation work of memory – including those decromastic tiles. The novel ends with a moment Rex Petley might have written a poem about:

> When the weather is fine we walk on Takapuna Beach. If it rains – it rains a lot in Auckland but the wind doesn't blow like Wellington's – we

run for our car, holding hands. We bring home Chinese take-aways and eat watching the news. (278–79)

But why the change, why do serious writers begin to imagine scenes of suburban bliss after so many years of doing precisely the opposite? An answer can have nothing to do with actual changes in people's lives: whatever the annual quotient of happiness or misery in the suburb, it has no direct relation to the purposes to which those emotions are put. For most of our history, writers have come up with variations on an early Curnow theme: the 'never a soul at home'-ness of the comfortably housed. Yet I suspect that from the 1930s through to the 1970s, few Pakeha readers of 'House and Land' would have posed the startling questions – whose house? whose land? – as these questions had yet to have any conceivable legal purchase.

Given the challenges to Pakeha assumptions about land in the post-Waitangi Tribunal era, it is perhaps not surprising to find older styles of alienation being replaced by new expressions of belonging in an upswing of identity-claiming as steep as house values would rise. Put baldly like this, and at what is a high level of generalisation, it may seem as if I am suggesting that the recent turnaround in representations of suburbia was a simple case of cause and effect, but the relation between story and place is much more complex than that, more like our subconscious sensation of spatial position than flight and fright in response to a threat. Nor am I describing anything new: the shift in representations of suburbia returns us to old and ordinary problems of settlement: someone was here first, people still are, others are coming too. We see this in *Going West*, when Jack realises that these days he only knows part of Auckland: whole suburbs are now unmapped regions for him, and when he visits the most sacred site of his childhood, the Loomis creek, it is only to find it has become a scummy swimming hole frequented by Maori toughs in league jerseys. Jack worries they might break into his car. The scene could be replayed with a difference in Philip Roth's Newark, with black youths making Nathan Zuckerman feel uneasy. Or it might be viewed the other way round, as when Grace in Alan Duff's *Once Were Warriors* stares into the lighted windows of a house in a wealthier suburb. Nowadays, the cheek-by-jowl divisions between rich and poor that we found in Mansfield's 'The Garden Party' have long since been dispersed across distant suburbs with differential patterns of housing stock. But perhaps the paradoxes of the suburb have another twist in them yet: the characters in *Going West* do belong in their suburbs, but their suburb is starting to look like a gated community.

CHAPTER EIGHT

Glorious Phantoms: Frank Sargeson in Bohemia

Though this island seem to be desert...
– The Tempest, *act 2, scene 1, line 35*

*Bohemia is a fairy land upon the hard earth. It is Arcadia in
New York or London, Paris or Rome. Hereabouts, you may
find it in painters' studios, and in the rooms of authors....
Respectability is the converse of the Bohemian idea. There
are plenty of men among them worthy of respect – but none
who are technically respectable. If they are the lees of society,
as has been injuriously argued, then they are the richness
which settles at the bottom of the cup. Respectability is the
pale, thin, emasculated liquor that floats upon the surface
and is easily seen through. Bohemia is the nimble essence, the
fat substantiality, which 'ascends into the brain' and begets
there glorious phantoms.*
–Harpers Monthly Magazine, *1859*

I N 1912, JANE MANDER LEFT NEW ZEALAND TO BECOME THE FIRST
woman student at the Columbia University School of Journalism
in New York. She took with her a novel that had been rejected by
publishers four times. Over the next ten years, writes a biographer,
she worked on it intermittently, while also 'addressing meetings in
the campaign for women's franchise, lecturing, doing research work
at Sing Sing Prison for prison reformers, coaching junior students,
writing magazine articles, managing a hostel for workers and teachers during vacation periods, ... and working on drafts of two other
novels'.[1] It is *la vie bohème*, Greenwich Village style. Later, in the 1920s,

she moved to Paris, where she read manuscripts for Glenway Westcott and Monroe Wheeler, an openly gay couple who ran the Harrison Press and were friends of Gertrude Stein and Ernest Hemingway. Encore *la vie bohème*. And while she was living the kind of existence now memorialised for tourists by the Shakespeare Bookshop or the Chelsea Hotel, that first novel did get published; but in her home town, *The Story of a New Zealand River* – allegedly a 'sex novel' – could be borrowed from the Whangarei public library only with the special permission of the head librarian. As Mander says of Alice, the straight-laced heroine of her novel, 'no wandering vibration of the Zeitgeist' had been felt in that quarter (50).

Yet the 'wandering vibrations' and 'glorious phantoms' of the bohemian life do reach and inspire the restless young in the cultural outposts of the world. Mander was born in Ramarama and grew up in the Kaipara; the dishy Glenway Westcott himself came from Kewaskum, Wisconsin. No one is born a bohemian. But what of the artistic soul who, amidst the great gloom, feels the siren call but is unable to migrate to Paris or New York, or whose portal into the zeit-geist is dimmed by the likes of the head librarian of the Whangarei public library? How does the would-be bohemian 'live for art' when there is, as it were, not even enough culture to be counter to?

The comic potential of small-town bohemianism and the strained pursuit of what Wystan Curnow has memorably called 'high culture in a small province' are the subject of Frank Sargeson's widely unread masterpiece, *Memoirs of a Peon*.[2] The title is taken from A. L. Coleman-Thompson's *Talks with a Bodgie*, a work Sargeson has made up, and which ostensibly features an establishment figure in conversation with a member of our first fully fledged urban sub-culture: a so-called bodgie (fem. widgie), whose local styles came from James Dean movies by way of Darlinghurst, Sydney, in the early 1950s.[3] Older folk thought these young originals were merely conformists aping the latest American fad; the respectable went into vapours at the prospect of their supposed moral delinquency. The Mazengarb Report on teenage promiscuity, released in 1954, opens with a policeman giving evidence in a 'carnal knowledge' trial. His investigations 'revealed a shocking degree of immoral conduct which spread into sexual orgies perpetrated in several private homes during the absence of parents, and in several second rate Hutt Valley theatres'; 'in many cases', the officer added, 'the children came from excellent homes'.[4]

Sargeson had himself been arraigned on an 'indecency' charge and he knew the deadening perils of those 'excellent homes'. In story after story, one of his 'good boys' has a glimpse of life on the other side of the tracks – and prefers it. Sargeson's best-known works feature transvestites, misfits, vagrants, sex-murderers, suicides; the protagonists are mostly men alone, or men in pairs, perhaps living in temporary accommodation, perhaps on the move. In 'The Hole that Jack Dug', Mrs Parker has her ladies' book group over for tea; her husband comes in from the garden, 'looking awfully hairy and sweaty but not too naked on account of his dark colour', to 'spout' poetry amidst the rattling teacups.[5] Jack, we learn, has relinquished the marital bed for a 'camp stretcher in the little room off the back verandah' (246). It is his anti-domestic anti-suburban enclave, an interstitial space like the three upstairs bedrooms Mrs Clegg lets to Terry, Maggie and the narrator of 'That Summer'. 'You paid for your bed and had to get your meals out' (147), but 'out' has no enchantment in this setting. 'I didn't know what to do', says the narrator describing a typical evening; 'I didn't know whether to blow in a bob on a talkie or not, so to put off trying to decide I thought I'd go and have a lie-down on my bed' (163). Had the story been set in San Francisco, a character on the verge of adventure might climb into a taxi and say, 'Follow that car!'; 'That Summer' has an urban plot, and the narrator will take a walk on the wild side, but in this Auckland novella of the 1930s, adventure begins with a decision to have an early night.

By the 1950s, the small smoke has come to seem bigger. In another decade or so, once inner-city housing stock became available en masse to cheap rentals, small cities like Auckland, Wellington or Dunedin developed what might conceivably pass for a 'scene', but in the meantime, there were bohemians, there was a demimonde, but their habitat was circumscribed. Sargeson for a time allowed the army hut at the back of his section to be used by the bodgies and widgies and beatniks of the North Shore. He approved their liking for books and art and music – and took a degree of prurient interest in their nocturnal couplings. The story 'Just Trespassing, Thanks' draws on those times and relationships and suggests that while Sargeson would eventually tire of picking up after teenagers – he later burnt the hut to the ground – he saw the blissful young as enjoying a dawn not available to him in the Hamilton of his youth. A second friendship bears on the writing of *Peon*. Every fortnight or so since the late 1940s, it had been Sargeson's habit to spend an evening in the company of William Levenet Bakewell, a retired bank manager. 'Bake', burly and verbose, owned the best stereo system on the North Shore. The flavour of his conversation comes through in the way a neighbourly invitation to drop by for music, booktalk and Lemora swells into the following:

My dear Frank,
The news in the 'Herald' this morning of change of sex by means of registration has perturbed me deeply; a dreadful fear clutches my heart. The question is, does such a change appeal to you? I do not suggest you are 'predominantly' female but certain of your characteristics are not 'predominantly' male. Your kindness of heart, your maternal care for your old friend Jim, your culinary gifts, the confidence with which females stop the night with you and rise in the morning, possibly disappointed, but undefiled – all these things, in view of the news this morning, makes me morbidly doubtful.

I must admit at once to you that my fears are based on selfishness – a 'predominantly' male attribute. For should you make the change it would mean the end of our long friendship. My past reputation as a 'predominant' male precludes the visit of females to me, even in the daytime. Further, my imagination pictures your arrival here minus the old knapsack but with a natty suitcase clutched in a gloved hand, your head-gear no longer the dashing sombrero you sometimes wear but a toque-like contraption somewhat similar to that worn by the late Queen Mary . . . . No it could not – it shall not be: if the change be made, we part forever.

Mind you, I do not for a moment doubt but that you would behave and conduct yourself as a perfect lady. No loud belches or resounding farts for you – even when alone; but a shapely hand to mouth and a soundless emission accompanied by an 'excuse me' and – <u>sneakers</u>, detestable things. In any case, 'perfect ladies' have never appealed to me. Give me "The girl who eats brown bread and farts aloud like thunder, who drops a turd like the deep sea lead and screams out 'Stand from under.'"

I know not on what facts the doctor makes his 'statutory declaration': what number of florins . . . must or must not be swept from a kitchen table: the length or diameter of a 'donger' whether dormant or expectant – these matters do not interest me. But shall my old friend still be Francisco or known as Florenca – this <u>does</u> interest me.

I do not ask for a written answer and I am ever diffident in pressing for an early visit, but the occasion demands I toss diffidence to the four winds. I beg of you a visit on next Wednesday night. Come with the old knapsack, the beard, the sombrero, and come, beyond all things, the old Francisco.

(subscribed herewith a la Boswell)

I have the honour to be,

  With affectionate veneration,

    My dear Sir,

      Your most humble faithful servant,

        Bake.[6]

Immensely likeable, ribald, fluent and learned, Bake was also in some respects a rube. 'In conversation', recalled Sargeson, 'his choice of words besides being comically sumptuous could often be surprisingly right and apt', yet he might also deliver 'heavily derivative' philosophical chestnuts 'with a curiously solemn air of originality' or share 'the many odd corners and dead ends' of his 'haphazard' reading.[7] Without the 'powerful sympathy' Sargeson felt for his autodidactic friend, he allowed that Bake might well have been 'a bore' (86). Yet something about Bake prompted 'a hazy notion about the biggest novel of my life' (86). 'What fascinated me', he recalls in his memoir, 'was an uncommon richness of material all concentrated into one identity'. The raconteur's voice, 'with its unfailing choice of polysyllabic words', had possibilities as a touchstone for diction and tone, while Bake's distinctive combination of bawdiness and literary pedantry, subtly re-imagined, prompted the invention of a character who would 'serve . . . in a required double capacity: I mean as a first person narrator who would be as well a focus-figure of the largest dimension' (86).

Sargeson's novel is told by a retired insurance executive, Michael Newhouse, who recollects his youthful attempts to realise the destiny that inheres in the Italian version of his name: Casanova. Much as

Michael fancies himself as a suave and seductive libertine in training, he feels like a person in the wrong body: he not only lacks the curls and profile of a Lord Byron, he has the misfortune to develop the lantern-jawed, Neanderthal look of a tight-head prop, while his early upbringing, home-schooled at the hands of elderly and bookish English grandparents, has equipped him with a vocabulary more suited to an earlier century and a distant hemisphere. 'I can still hear myself the day I was out walking with my grandmother, and three urchins were pelting each other with handfuls of mud scraped from the gutter: I stared, repelled yet fascinated by their game, and as we passed I said, "They seem to be three merry young ruffians, don't they Granny?"'[8] Later, as a university student sitting his English examination, Michael takes it into his head to answer all questions in a style adapted to the period; an answer on Milton, for instance, refers to 'hyse musick' – 'an affectation of which I was at first very proud despite its orthographic extravagance, but which afterwards did not strike me as an altogether happy touch' (118). Michael's failure resonates with one of Allen Curnow's frostier verdicts on a literature that has lost its relation to place. In the 'sickly' verse of the *Kowhai Gold* school, 'imported insipidities' mixed with 'puerilities of local origin' pointed to 'extreme confusions of taste' – confusions against which a writer like Robin Hyde, with her 'passionate crush on poetry', had continuously to struggle in an effort to 'free her vision from its literary swathings'.[9] Sargeson, as he is familiar to us from the short stories, is the writer most in the vanguard of his generation's search for a sparse and unornamented prose style that at least sought to register something real. *Memoirs of a Peon* is a radical departure; it sticks with 'the passionate crushes' and the 'literary swathings' and, piling confusion upon confusion, turns literary space inside out. The city – the *little* city – becomes a new frontier of sexual and artistic misadventure, while rural, suburban and small-town New Zealand becomes a respectable hinterland peopled here and there by isolated and often loveable bohemian eccentrics.

After the death of his grandparents, Michael returns to his family in Hamilton. The guardian angels of his youth are his English teacher, the 'not at all feminine' Miss Ryland, and her bachelor friend, Ernie 'Horseface' Clayton, a self-taught barrister who, having attained those qualifications only to avenge a social slight, prefers to run a confectionery shop inherited from his mother and to devote his free time to books, or – as he himself would put it – 'fodder for one's headpiece' (32). 'Ernie's years of study had proved his undoing', writes Michael:

> He had taken a look into the world of learning and decided that he was a citizen of that world by vocation. Not that he could be described as anything but a smatterer, he used to say; but who could be anything more in such a country where one was lucky to lay hands on about ten out of every hundred books one wanted to read? Perhaps Ernie was rather like the French encyclopaedists. He wished to achieve all-round enlightenment so that he might hope to fit together all the jig-saw pieces of chaos, and discover to his great satisfaction that he had made a picture of universal order. As I remember him, he did not greatly discriminate between what might be valuable or not: all the odds-and-ends might come in handy, so they had to be collected. (31)

Ernie is part Bake and his kind, part a figure drawn from Sargeson's own possible future had he remained a closeted non-writing non-practising Hamilton solicitor whose self-education would see books piled above and beside the overstuffed shelves, until every room in the house resembled the dilapidated stores from which they had been furnished. A bach full of books can be a kind of paradise, yet there are 'overt signs of frustration in Ernie' who, we learn, 'might have preferred a very different life from the one he had' (37). Ernie has 'never seen the inside of a university' and could not 'conceal his curiosity and perhaps his envy' (37). For all his stockpiling, Ernie remains off-centre and incomplete. Characters like Ernie, as Melissa Gniadek has pointed out, belong to the literary tradition of the grotesque; they are creatures swollen with appetite, ungainly, distorted – the product of 'an unfinished metamorphosis'.[10] Sargeson was right to associate these figures cobwebbed in literary swathings not with gloom but with carnival – a mode not only suited to the Don Juan tradition of *Peon* but also congenial to the comic gothic imagination of that small-town autodidact, Hawera's own Ronald Hugh Morrieson, whose best book begins with a sentence faultlessly combining an admiration for the prose of Robert Louis Stevenson with the sensationalism of a shilling shocker: 'The same week our fowls were stolen, Daphne Moran had her throat cut.'[11]

Sargeson's spinster and bachelor bohemians can have no development in the small town or in the country. The more someone like Ernie reads, the more he is destined to become like himself. By the end of the novel, he has acquired an enormous armchair for support whilst reading; it dominates the lounge and encourages his 'habit of speaking *ex cathedra*' (273). Michael's eldest brother is Ernie's rural counterpart as a self-educated man. Besides running the old family farm, he takes an interest in the sciences of composting and cross-breeding. At the novel's end, he has become a pastoral sage quietly thwarting a real estate brother's plan to realise a profit on the sale of the property; a sign, 'Dad's Den, Beware!' points to another of those anti-domestic anti-suburban oases in which Sargeson's eccentrics grow into themselves. Michael's career as a rake and a litterateur, by contrast, requires a move to the city and access to private sexual and cultural space sponsored by one or another of those figures from the traditional libertine plot: the cuckolded husband, the rich widow or the wealthy father.

The comedy of Michael's successive failures and misfirings, and the little humiliations and torments that accompany his eventual successes with women far cleverer than he, entertain the reader through much of *Memoirs of a Peon*. Among his difficulties, for example, Michael, on holiday with a wealthy Remuera family, contrives to escape the 'mutual chaperonage' (94) exercised by Betty and Amelia Gower-Johnson, while the mother and daughter each conspire to part Michael from the many books that are his own preferred companions. Michael – alone at last! – is reading his way through Hobbes on the state of nature when Betty returns ahead of her parents from an evening engagement. The young Casanova is soon on his knees before the porcelain beauty, and just as he is wishing Betty might cease to repulse his 'manual explorations . . . of her bosom's geometry', in walks Amelia with a trilling, 'Oh, hello, children!'

> I had not, it is true, been caught *mountant*; but Betty's frock had tightened as she turned away in her agitation to hide her face from her approaching parent, and some assistance was required from Mrs Gower-Johnson

before I could release my imprisoned hand: and although I must risk falling into *clichés* by saying that I could have conveniently dropped dead, I
must also insist that this extraordinary matron retained my hand in her
own while she tenderly put her other to the region where mine had been,
murmuring as she did so words of endearing solicitation to her daughter.
I am not prepared to reproduce her revolting baby-talk in detail; but
pretending that Providence had fortuitously directed her footsteps to
Betty's couch of illness, she pleaded to be told the symptoms, referring
to the tum-tum and the little heart and finally suggesting the cucumber
salad we had consumed that evening as the possible source of an attack
of indigestion. (98)

Soon, the voluptuous Mrs Gower-Johnson has Michael to herself in
the car, where the young man, much to his chagrin, is too abashed to
play the required part.

This farcical scene works insofar as we appreciate the discrepancy
between the comedy of action and the comedy of its verbal presenta-
tion. As action, the episode might be played with the coy smuttiness of
a 'Carry On' movie, but the writing is more Henry than Sid James; to be
precise: it is arch and orotund in the manner of an eighteenth-century
picaresque novel. A style as artificial as *Peon*'s ought to be camp, but
the affect is more one of an author effortlessly securing the literary
capital his autodidacts would like to possess through this mastery of
a faux-period style. Moreover, if stylistic display were all there was to
Peon, the book would be a sort of glorious folly, but few works from
this period are as responsive to the situation of high culture in a settled
post-colony.

Maurice Duggan's story 'Along Rideout Road that Summer' comes
close, as does *All Visitors Ashore*, C. K. Stead's brilliant reconstruction
of *la vie bohème* in the Takapuna of the 1950s. All three works seize
on the potential of a bohemian plot to refocus an essential problem
of defining what is different about New Zealand Literature. A generation earlier, writers had struck out for literary independence, but
bohemians can 'live for art' only by fashioning themselves after a prior
literary model. Life has copied art in every bohemian neighbourhood
since the likes of Baudelaire and Courbet frequented the Café Momus,
and scenes from Henry Murger's popular stage play about them were

mimicked by the fashionable young throughout the capitals of Europe. For the young writers of the 1930s, the syndrome of an art that didn't know its own place seemed amenable to resolution through the project of discovering New Zealand, but after two decades of accomplishment, that sense of a disjunction between old world and new world hadn't so much faded as become one of the richer veins of experience a writer might wish to explore. Take Buster O'Leary, 'shouting "Kubla Khan" . . . from the seat of a clattering old Ferguson tractor, doing a steady five miles an hour in a cloud of seagulls, getting to the bit about the damsel with a dulcimer and looking up to see the reputedly wild Hohepa girl, perched on the gate, feet hooked in the bars, ribbons fluttering from her ukulele'.[12] Duggan's story is about 'a problem of connexion' (196): dulcimer and ukulele to be sure, but also, and despite the narrator's protest to the contrary, Buster and (the aptly named) Fanny. One might regard Buster's love affair with Coleridge as a lodestone of value in a story of escape from entanglements and respectability; one might also regard the liaison with Fanny as a deflationary factor in this story of a Pakeha trifler lost in his own Xanadu. Each interpretation crosses the other, and the tension between them is only resolved if we suppose Buster, the mature narrator who so pompously addresses himself to a club of gentlemen, to have made *two* regrettable life choices: no girl and no opium-wafted poetry either.

Sargeson has a richer set of disjunctions to play with. The memoirs of Michael Newhouse and the memoirs of Casanova are bound to be in a relation of comic disproportion, while the old- and new-world associations of their names open a deeper layer of thematic possibilities. Stylistically, as we have seen, Sargeson relishes the opportunity to render low farce in high prose. Added to this, the Casanova side of things takes on spin from the fact that a retelling of what Bake might with some understatement have called a 'predominantly male' story is patently the work of his queer friend with the beard and sombrero.[13] Perhaps the most important of the bookish tutelary figures in Michael's life is his Uncle Hilary: disfigured, alcoholic, homosexual, he lives in a room full of books upstairs in the Wynyard Street house of Michael's grandparents. Michael visits him as a child for Latin lessons. As the story continues, Michael will often meet people who remind him of his Uncle Hilary: after meeting Margaret Ryland, for example, it occurs to him that Hilary 'should have been the woman and she the man' – but he afterwards learns 'never to make these mental corrections to the work of nature' (29). Hilary is at the centre of two of the novel's major plot arcs. The most obvious comes from the eighteenth-century picaresque convention, and concerns the fortunes of a hero who has lost his estate and must somehow contrive to recapture it or marry into another. The other comes from *The Tempest*.

The Wynyard Street house is one of those large two- or three-storey villas that, until not so long ago, housed various departments of the University of Auckland. (I believe it was the largest and most beautiful of those demolished to make way for Arts 1.) Sargeson, quite pointedly, associates the house with an island of bohemian splendour – an 'isle full of noises, sounds and sweet airs'.[14] Michael, having decided to leave Hamilton, visits his Uncle Hilary in the hope of finding a friendly welcome and an offer of accommodation. 'Mr Chelton's in Blighty, mate', says the sailor-like man who answers the door, but invites Michael in to meet 'Mister'. The familiar books still line the grandmother's old sitting room, but her German piano, when Michael sounds a note, is quite out of tune. As the note disappears on the air,

> I heard myself greeted in the most resonant, most beautifully articulated and modulated voice which I had ever heard at close quarters. The owner of the voice was a tall man in middle age with a fine head of thick grey hair; he wore a plum-coloured velvet jacket and a shirt of pleated silk with a large bow tie. (40)

The usurping John Morgan, having sent Michael on his way, returns late in the novel as the producer of a training college production of *The Tempest*. Michael, cast as Caliban, has his own ideas about the histrionic potential of the role, but after chafing against the director's sense of theatrical balance and order, reluctantly submits to Morgan's Prospero-like discipline. Newhouse's skimpy costume, altered at the last minute by a vengeful girlfriend who has discovered his affair with an 'island girl', androgynously features 'two monstrous dugs which were also flabby and pendulous' (244). With that outfit, comments Morgan approvingly, Michael has 'the opportunity for a magnificently restrained performance', but his Caliban needs no such warning: on the night, Michael both looks and acts like 'a zombie too lately resurrected to have reacquired any powers of audible speech' (244).

Michael is also cast as Caliban in relation to Hilary's Wynyard Street house. Morgan has indicated that Michael should wait for an invitation before visiting Hilary, but one night Michael clambers over the back fence, and on hearing music and party noise within, resolves to visit his uncle. Silence follows Michael's policeman-like knock. The door opens a crack, and Bobby the sailor man, clad only in a tablecloth, escorts him upstairs to Hilary's study; the name Caliban is uttered in explanation from behind closed doors as the party resumes and Michael is led into a room remembered from his childhood.

> A courteous scholarly man with a table lamp arranged to illuminate the book on his knee sat quietly at his ease in an armchair with books at his elbow: more books were scattered about the floor and many more climbed the surrounding walls: it was Ernie all over again or Margaret or my grandmother: and it was with a recaptured sense of timeless peace and security that I recognized a world where nothing monstrous beyond the capacity of the human spirit to endure could ever be admitted, unless first confined to paper and hence reduced to entirely manageable proportions. (238)

When their conversation comes round to *The Tempest*, Hilary remarks that nobody in that play 'could be counted a real person' – a point, he suggests, 'which could make all the difference between a successful performance and a failure if it was intelligently kept in mind' (239). Indeed, in *Memoirs of a Peon*, roles from the play are suggested without regard to 'real' persons: Michael has been a Caliban and might prove a Ferdinand; John Morgan is at times an Antonio/Alonso figure, at times a Prospero, a role Hilary in his sorcerer's cave obviously portrays despite the disfigurement which also marks him as a grotesque. *The Tempest* might have been a master text offering a simple key to Sargeson's novel, but *Memoirs of a Peon* draws on a deeper magic than that. As with the Casanova plot, Sargeson has found a way to restage Shakespeare's 'isle full of noises, sounds and sweet airs' in a manner that not only resonates with the cultural uncertainties of our own 'brave new world', but is also a spur to further modes of carnival, transvestism and metamorphosis. As Miranda might have said, 'It's a mixed up muddled up shook up world that has such people in it.'

When Hilary dies, the news is brought to Michael by Ariel – or rather, by the actor who played that role in John Morgan's production. We learn that the house has been left to Bobby who, when Michael visits, allows him to select a single book of his choice as a memento; Michael leaves with Charles Lamb's *Tales of Shakespeare*, an unread gift from his childhood. Ariel also brings Michael up to date with some facts about his uncle and the house. Hilary's facial deformity, which requires the application of a putty-like filler, turns out to have been the result of a misunderstanding with some rough trade in the Canary Islands. 'It just shows you', says the sprite, 'how careful you have to be when living among people who inhabit islands' (253). And islands can undergo strange transformations: thanks to the grandfather's activities as a herbalist, the back section of the house is now a jungle of marijuana plants – invisible to respectable eyes – and the enlivening factor in those parties held behind closed curtains for the gorgeous and promiscuous young. While Michael has ineptly pursued his fortunes as Casanova among the Gower-Johnsons of Remuera, he has missed Grafton's best parties. As he reflects on how Ariel's cautionary remark about islands might apply to the country at large, and how the Wyndham Street house will always be an enchanted island to him, I cannot but recall Sargeson's own milieu in this period, when he was interested in theatre, and when he and Chris Cathcart as director and Colin McCahon as designer wrote and put on plays for 'The New Independent Theatre'. The small house at Esmonde Road, he recalled, 'was often as never before chock-a-block, [with] noisy and arguing young people, male and female, in new clothes and non-clothes'.[15] I trust I do not forget Hilary's advice on the nature of theatrical performance if I suggest that, as Michael visits 'the courteous scholarly man with a table lamp arranged to illuminate the book on his knee', we glimpse a night portrait of Sargeson musing in his reading chair – master of these revels.

Part IV *Looming*

Remindingly beside the quays the white
Ships lie smoking; and from their haunted bay
The godwits vanish toward another summer.
Everywhere in light and calm the murmuring
Shadow of departure; distance looks our way . . .
– Charles Brasch, 'The Islands' (ii)

NEW ZEALAND STORIES ARE SHAPED BY AND GIVE SHAPE TO A number of special places – the beach, the farm, the bush, the suburb – but there is one setting that is at least as important as any of these, although it is not, strictly speaking, part of our physical environment. 'Overseas' might be a word for it, but what I have in mind is not so much a destination as the gap distance opens out between here and there. It is this gap that leads Charles Brasch to see the white passenger ships 'remindingly' – as if drawn, like any godwit, by the instinctive pull of a compass bearing north of here, out of here. Fifty years ago, in a contribution to a Winter Lecture series on this theme, C. K. Stead noted that 'A tension exists in the mind of every New Zealander between here and there.'[1] Despite a thousand countervailing influences, that tension still exists. The year 1960, when Stead gave his lecture, was the first of television and the last of the flying boat service; overseas telegrams were still transmitted in Morse. When Stead referred to our distinctive 'combination of physical remoteness and *insignificance*',[2] he described a condition that – against all predictions – did not turn out to be a phase we would ever progress beyond. Rather, in a networked world, we have come to share our condition with more people in more places, and a sense of isolation and insignificance characterises our geo-cultural location as profoundly as ever.

'There', of course, is less predominantly the 'Home' of British settlers. 'There' could be as big as China or as small as a poppy on a distant war grave; 'there' might be the Louvre, the Met or the anywhere-else-but-here yearned for by the stifled young. 'There' might (at various times) be as close as Sydney or Melbourne, but not Brisbane or Adelaide, and not Canberra either. By 'there', I mean anywhere in the big wide world that makes 'here' seem outlying or negligible in comparison. (Hence one of the differences between Maori and Pakeha literature. Stories of departure and return, of the distance between 'here' and 'there', are perhaps even more character-istic of Maori writing, but 'there' is usually the city of the post-World War II urban migration, while 'here' is typically the small rural com-munity, such as Witi Ihimaera's 'Waituhi' or Hone Kouka's 'Waiora'.)[3] Gertrude Stein, writing of her home town of Oakland (which is how Americans hear Auckland), thought it a drawback that 'there was no there there'.[4] We recognise the feeling, but a New Zealander's prob-lem is a little different. Our problem is that there is simultaneously so much there *here*. While the global wash of migration sweeps vil-lagers and townspeople like ourselves to the larger metropolises of the world, the majority of those arriving or returning to these islands will have forsaken a more populous situation for the unManhattan-like challenges of life on a smaller scale – and memories of that bigger brighter place bed down here too. Yet if New Zealanders feel notably peripheral and inconsequential as a nation – touchy, others say, about our lack of stature – we have also, for all our modern history, experi-enced an erosion of distance from the cultural and financial centres of the world. Travel times to London have dropped from a plateau of months to weeks to days to hours, while a series of communica-tion revolutions from the clipper ship to the telegraph to the satellite have exponentially increased the speed and bandwidth of incoming information. It seems we cannot both believe in progress *and* feel cut off from the rest of the world. In 1910, a newcomer from the British Isles, downsizing to a town as desolate as Auckland, might have been consoled by a well-stocked public library and could expect to keep in touch with London newspapers scarcely six weeks old. Now, in 2010, any major newspaper can be delivered to my laptop; I attend 'live in HD' performances from the Metropolitan Opera's current season at my local cinema – yet all such details are destined to become quaint. Twenty years ago, before computers, the International Film Festival brought that same oddly mixed sensation of distance from and bounding proximity to the exciting places of the world. So much from there has always been coming here, but in a manner that is out of step and season, at a remove, virtual – which is never the same as *being there*.

Janet Frame began *The Carpathians*, her last novel, with a narrator's note announcing the existence of an astronomical phenomenon termed the Gravity Star.[5] Her idea was that a distant galaxy might seem impossibly remote on one observation, light years closer on another, the variation disclosing the existence of a hidden star whose gravitational field bent light first one way then the other, oscillating backward and forward, as if in the shimmer of an intergalactic heat mirage, and overturning all customary distinctions of near and far. The early settlers, crossing the chasm between there and here on a lengthy sea voyage, might have encountered a similar phenomenon: looming. A hull-down vessel usually disappears gradually below the horizon, but looming might bring it back again, larger and more distinct, only to vanish in a moment, as if the ship really had fallen off the edge of the world. In 1822, one captain 'recognized his father's ship, the *Fame*, by an inverted image in the air, though it was subsequently found to have been at the time thirty miles distant, and seventeen miles beyond the horizon'.[6] I myself, looking east in misty cloud illuminated by the late afternoon sun, have seen the Waitakere Ranges loom above the quarry cliffs at Auckland Grammar School – a suburb-leaping projection that was a wonder to behold, though not as astonishing as the occasion, near the English town of Hastings in 1798 (the year of an invasion scare), when the cliffs of the French coast, normally far out of sight, were distinctly visible just a few miles off: 'by the aid of a telescope, small vessels were plainly seen at anchor in the French harbours and buildings on the heights beyond were distinctly visible'.[7] Janet Frame's novel looms further than those fifty miles: the Carpathian mountains on the Transylvanian edge of Eastern Europe shift towards the Tararua Ranges, and in the late-night darkness of her room, Mattina Brecon senses the breath and gleaming eyes of a presence old and dangerous: 'whatever it was, it was warm, either warmed by the sun or by its own blood; and alive' (80).

Janet Frame's extraordinary hemispheric shifts mobilise a powerful meditation on the problems of relating here to there, but before turning to her work, I would like to consider three other exemplary stories, each of which involves a particular sub-genre of narrative that has been shaped by our connection to the big wide world. The first, *Passport to Hell*, is a war story that involves the traumatic experiences of a returned serviceman and the imprint of the war on a generation of New Zealand women who grew up it in its shadow. *Man Alone* – generally regarded as one of New Zealand's first authentically local novels – also begins with talk about war, but I am interested here in how a story written by an author who thought of himself as 'a man of two countries' – New Zealand and England – turns out to have been mediated by the hidden force of a gravity star: the popular Western. My third story comes from the 1970s, when (for most people) any travel to the fabled cities and landscapes of Europe still had the quality of the proverbial Big OE, insofar as the trip was likely to have been long anticipated, of an extended duration and likely to happen only once or twice in one's lifetime. When Allen Curnow first visited Italy he was in his mid-sixties, towards the end (one might have thought) of a writing and academic career that had been intensely engaged with literary nationalism and conspicuously receptive to modernist – and largely American – refurbishments of poetry. How then might such a determinedly new-world writer encounter the deeper time and older places of Europe? In each case, I hope to show how metaphors of looming offer a better account of the place of these texts than those proposed either by our traditional 'here' narratives – the discovery, growth and maturation of a distinct cultural identity – or by post-nationalist postmodern alternatives that are themselves cultural imports, often arriving from there to here on an updating mission, as if without precedent, and as if the distortions of looming were not themselves real, and had not – like Frame's Gravity Star – always already unfixed our relation to space and to time.

CHAPTER NINE

There and Back: Robin Hyde's *Passport to Hell*

*She knew, had always known, why Stark exasperated her. He
troubled the depths, making her remember things she wanted
to set aside. He was an unsolved problem limping about, and
his ghosts were on nodding terms with her ghosts.*
— Robin Hyde, Nor the Years Condemn

Little new zealand, 'punching above its weight' as always,
is often said to have contributed disproportionately to the major
military struggles of the last century – though we probably share
this conviction with our larger Anzac partner. Like the Australians,
we have a sizeable shelf of war literature, and a similar inclination to
associate defeat at Gallipoli with national coming-of-age stories.[1] Boys
of my generation grew up with imported English war comics set in
the Second World War. Any assiduous reader of 'Commando' or 'War
Picture Library' will be able to visualise, even now, a page depicting
the stock action scene of taking out an enemy machine-gun nest: the
creeping up, the pin pulled on a grenade, the 'Donner und Blitzen!' a
German soldier always says when surprised – but I doubt any of us
would ever recall an issue featuring a protagonist from New Zealand.
A Kiwi war comic would have seemed as outlandish as Karangahape
Road on a Monopoly set. The unrealism went with the irrelevant
'Biggles' values; local references would only have challenged the
happy mindlessness of the genre, tipping it towards other modes of
representation that taught even impressionable young comic readers
that war was hell.

The 'grown-up' war novels I began to read in the 1970s were different. Following World War II, a number of young American novelists
had begun to do something unusual. *Mister Roberts* (1946), *The Naked*

Dead (1948), *From Here to Eternity* (1951), *The Caine Mutiny* (1951), *Catch-22* (1961) are all realistic novels written by servicemen who saw action in the war, but – as Stephen Fender points out – in every instance, the enemy is not the Germans or the Japanese, not an enemy the Americans actually fought, but an enemy within: 'usually superior officers, sometimes buddies in the ranks'.[2] I offer no candidates for a similarly distinctive New Zealand war genre, but I have noticed that for every sober and taciturn memoir of combat – such as Alexander Aitken's superb *Gallipoli to the Somme* – there must be dozens of narratives involving servicemen who bring the war home with them. In Janet Frame's *Intensive Care*, for example, the narrator remembers her father's war looming in their own backyard.

> All was so quiet on the Western Front, and do you know why? Because the war had gone away from the Western Front, it was home, at home in our house at Eagle Street, and when we looked out of the window at the pine trees in the valley we the saw the War and the soldiers, and when the trees died in a storm and the branches fell we saw the dead soldiers, and when we walked in the pine plantation in the valley we walked up to our ankles in blood, all among the dead, and no one but us knew.[3]

The hybrid domestic-war novel, ubiquitous since Vietnam, cannot be ours alone, but it is emphatically ours, and it becomes so as early as the aftermath of the First World War, when the emphasis in Europe lay rather more with 'sorrow and pity' treatments of trench warfare by combatants like Graves and Sassoon, Remarque and Jünger, along with a broader re-assessment of what progress and civilisation amounted to after four years of mechanised mass slaughter. In New Zealand, though, the pre-eminent literary representations of the Great War were achieved less by returned servicemen like John A. Lee – his *Civilian into Soldier* appeared in 1937 – than by the wives, daughters and sons of those silent, damaged, family men.

In the winter of 1935, the chaplain of Auckland's Mt Eden Prison gave a young journalist named Iris Wilkinson (her pen name is Robin Hyde) an account, written in an old school exercise book, of the war experiences of a former inmate: bomber James Douglas Stark, known to all as Starkie. Hyde soon called at Starkie's house and found the likeable ex-soldier had dozens of good stories, but no job prospects and a string of convictions for drunkenness, petty theft and assault. Psychologically troubled, and with shot-up lungs, Starkie had never been able to settle back into civilian life; there had been problems before the war too: no school except borstal would have him, and he made the first of his many court appearances as a twelve-year-old.[4]

In Hyde's novelised biography of Starkie's childhood and experiences in the First World War, we encounter a man whose pathological and half-splendid indifference to authority brought about one disciplinary crisis after another. During the war, he managed to be court-martialled nine times and amassed sentences totalling 35 years' penal servitude, most of which were cancelled for conspicuous gallantry in action. Private Stark had cheek and charisma as well as bravery, and wore the stars of a captain of infantry tattooed on his shoulders – an indelible 'fuck you' to those in authority. Despite his insubordinate attitude, he kept the respect of his often exasperated commanding officers and was a man his comrades looked up to – at least some of the time. He embodied those 'larrikin' qualities the Anzacs prided themselves on and that have since become legendary in both countries, but he embodied them to excess.

Passport to Hell, so keenly interested in male institutions like the prison and the army, was written from another such place, 'The Grey Lodge', a voluntary ward of Auckland Mental Hospital at Avondale, where Hyde found 'a room of her own' in which to write. Her book leans on her reading in and around Freudian psychoanalysis during this period, and *Passport to Hell* is as much a psychological case study of Starkie as a novel of his war experience, as much an analysis of the social patterning behind Starkie's manifest contradictions as a biography of them. While in jail, Starkie had given an account of his war experiences to a fellow prisoner who planned to ghost-write a book, but anecdotes that could be vivid in his oral telling died on the page. Nor did Hyde simply do a journalist's job of turning her interview notes into decent non-fiction prose. Like the 'new journalism' of the 1960s, *Passport to Hell* is a thoroughly imagined work that uses the resources of fiction to tell a non-fictional story. On publication, it attracted amazement from old soldiers like John A. Lee that a woman in her late twenties, who had never left New Zealand, could describe the horrors of war so vividly, along with brickbats from an officer in Stark's battalion who, overstating as well as missing the point, complained that factual inaccuracies made the book 'worthless as a record of truth'.[5] Hyde explained how the war loomed for her in a letter to Lee:

> The realism is because when people talk about things they have seen and known I can see 'em like little pictures, or think I can – maybe it's only an unusually clear knack with words taking shape so quickly that it seems like a visual image – Anyhow that is how it worked with Starkie – I tried getting him to make notes – it was hopeless, no marrow in it at all. When he talked though ... I seemed to get it without difficulty.[6]

He talks, she listens; pictures form in her mind, pictures that will later be reconstituted back into words. She seems like a recording device plugged into the visual display of Starkie's own memories and dreams, but the imagery can only be derived from the public visual memory of the war: newsreels, photographs, war paintings. The closer she is to Starkie, the further she is away. It would be more accurate to see *Passport to Hell* as a double story – both his and hers – refracted through a double masquerade. As the editors of its sequel, *Nor the Years Condemn*, put it:

> Not only is Iris Wilkinson 'repeating' what was told her by a man, she has also devised a signature whose gender is ambiguous, and which puns on a word which itself means concealment or disappearance (Hyde/hide). 'Robin Hyde' was the name she both gave to, and borrowed from, her dead son, thereby both inventing and effacing herself in an act of maternal identification with her child.[7]

Passport to Hell is certainly Starkie's story, but the author has folded her own response to the war into the narrative. She was ten years old when her father left with the New Zealand Expeditionary Force in 1916, returning without injury as a stranger to the family in 1918. One of her uncles was killed at Gallipoli; men of her acquaintance only eight years older than herself were likely to have fought in the Great War. In her unpublished autobiography, written in 1934, she recalls what it was like to grow up in the shadow of the war, to become someone who saw herself as part of a generation who 'gave to that grim uniform the unthinking hero worship which may have helped all modern men to despise all modern women'.[8] We half expect the predictable insight: unthinking hero worship contributes to the madness of war; yet her comment asserts there is a connection between the soldiers' experience of war overseas and the 'battle of the sexes' at home. But to perceive the full effect of this looming, we must first encounter the extraordinary war experiences of 8/2142 Private J. D. Stark.

In July 1916, in the trenches in front of Armentières, the soldiers in Starkie's division blackened their faces and embarked on a night raid across No Man's Land to capture outlying German trenches. One member of his platoon was a boy named Jackie MacKenzie who had enlisted several years underage. The older soldiers admired the lad's pluck, and afforded Jackie the unofficial rank and duties of a mascot. The men anticipated heavy casualties that night, so, with the connivance of their captain, Starkie discretely knocked the lad unconscious and left him behind in their dugout. The raid proved calamitous. The men were shelled, caught in wire, machine-gunned down. Of 280 Kiwis in the vanguard of the attack, only seven completed the 150-yard dash across No Man's Land to the position they intended to occupy; 133 were killed or wounded. Starkie made several trips back across No Man's Land, bringing in the wounded and the dying, but in the morning, when he got back to the trenches, there was no sign of Jackie. Rushing along the trench and anxious for news, he called out to a mortar crew – but they had not seen him. He ran a little further, then turned back to ask them to help get up a search party. But the mortar crew were not there; a shell had burst right where they were standing.

Starkie went back into No Man's Land again – in Hyde's words, 'this time out to get even' (130). A German machine gun was picking off the wounded as they crawled back; Starkie wriggled toward it through the mud and the wire and tossed in a grenade. He continued to look for Jackie, turning over bodies one after the other, until he found a white face among the grotesque boot-blackened corpses. Jackie had been shot clean through the heart. Starkie carried the body back to the lines and laid the boy down, not in the casualty area, but in his own dugout. The narrative continues:

> The kid didn't look any different now from when, just a few hours ago, Starkie had knocked him out and left him wrapped up in the blankets. 'If you'd only stayed here, you poor, game little fool!' he shouted; but the merry brown eyes didn't open to laugh at him. He ran out of the dug-out and blundered across No Man's Land.
>
> There was a German maxim-gun . . . that in the rising dawn made merry across No Man's Land, telling the story of a raid that got cut to pieces before it reached the lines. But as the maxim sang there was a shout overhead and a terrible figure crashed down upon it. The figure wore a tunic torn open at its waist, clotted and dyed and hideous with blood. Blood dripped from its nose and open mouth, blood stained its nightmare club – a great axe-handle with an iron cog nailed to one end . . . . So much the three German gunners had time to see before the figure uttered a madman's shriek, and with a madman's strength leapt down on them. The axe-handle swung twice, and twice the iron cog came away with hair and blood sticking to it. Then the butt end was thrust into the third gunner's face as he turned to run. The three lay in the pit. The figure groped forward with great brown hands, swung the machine-gun round until its muzzle pointed directly at the gunners. Then the rattle of bullets began. The maxim sang again and its gunners lay on the ground, their bodies impaled by the sharp little tusks of lead.
>
> The terrible figure met an officer from the Otago lines as it dragged the maxim towards the British wire. The officer, a Major, stopped and said: 'Good work, Starkie!' Starkie stared at him, a red world swimming before his eyes. (131)

Although Starkie is in a panic about Jackie from the start, the trigger that sends him out of control is the shock of being with the mortar crew one minute, then running back an instant later to find them blown to pieces. He has himself escaped death by a moment, by chance. In his work on shell-shocked soldiers, Freud noticed that it was uncanny experiences of precisely this sort that tended to push people over the edge. Curiously, soldiers who were not seriously wounded were worst affected; those who had escaped death or injury by a whisker were often compelled to relive the traumatic event in repetitive nightmares and daydreams.[9] Freud reckoned they were stuck on automatic – driven to come back to the incident in a forlorn effort to recover the moment before the psychic shock happened, and so to master it retrospectively. On a much reduced scale, most people have had the sleep-depriving experience of endlessly rehearsing and replaying the circumstances in which we suffered some little assault on our self-worth. It is like what happens when a record gets stuck: the needle should be going forward, but it hits a scratch and bounces back and hits a scratch and bounces back. It is as if trying to get over the moment of trauma – past the record's scratch – bumps you back into it all the time.

Starkie was living a nightmare rather than having one, but he may have been in the grip of a similar compulsion when he went back into No Man's Land. Hyde says he set out 'to get even'. But getting even is a phrase we use for something that is not consciously thought about in terms of revenge, but is radically impulsive – in much the same way that lashing out with a punch is not the product of deliberation, but of a state of rage. Perhaps really outstanding and exceptional courage in war requires a surrender to rage of this sort. Rage knows no other time but the present – the future in which you might get yourself killed doesn't exist subjectively – but even as rage is focused so intensely on the present, it is caught up in cycles of repetition. Like that stuck record, Starkie will keep firing that maxim gun, keep killing, until the energy driving that impulse is finally expended. We observe a similar kind of repetitive behaviour in the tantrums of children, or in the behaviour of people who go ballistic over some trifling obstacle: a bit of inconsiderate driving, the refusal of some mechanical object to function properly. When people are in a rage, they are stuck in an unbearable present and gripped by a compulsion to repeat. Basil Fawlty can make this spectacle of rage very funny indeed, but anyone who has been caught up in the strange energies of a tantrum will know that it is horrible to be out of control like that, to be 'beside yourself', as we say, with rage.

After this episode, Starkie hoisted Jackie onto his shoulders and carried the dead body miles down the line to the public cemetery at Armentières, where he obtained a coffin and 'dug a grave in consecrated soil among the weather-worn old French tombs' (132). He then took a photo to send to Jackie's folks, and was promptly arrested for espionage. On this occasion his commanding officer dismissed the charge, but there is a pattern in the way, from an official point of view, Starkie's behaviour is commendable one minute and meretricious the next. Starkie might be recommended for a medal one day, but the next might find him drunk on absinthe, firing bullets through the locked door of the sergeants' latrine. The irony is obvious: the very qualities that, in the eyes of the army, make Starkie a delinquent, a nuisance and a criminal, are the very qualities that also make him the perfect soldier in combat. But so far as Antipodean men are concerned, there is also a sort of charismatic larrikinism in Starkie's antipathy to discipline that we identify with too. We don't like authority, we're easy-going, we bridle under petty forms of discipline, we pride ourselves on our egalitarian matiness – and so forth.

Where might these values have their origin? One conceivable answer that Robin Hyde explores involves Starkie's childhood in the great outdoors and his feelings for the natural landscape. 'The New Zealand bush world was as disorderly as himself' (17), she writes, and goes on to paint a Huckleberry Finn picture of a boy playing hooky from school to catch eels, a boy to whom boots were anathema, a boy whose toes 'enjoyed an Arcadian existence of muddy freedom' (17). These settings are ubiquitous in our culture: we 'belong' to an ideal-ised natural environment, and idealised depictions of the Kiwi male generally take place in nature.[10] By the light of these associations, the problem with Starkie would be that he embodies 'natural' values to such a degree that he is forever getting into trouble for being consti-tutionally unable to compromise on them. Hyde also allows us to look beyond this mythology. Starkie, ostensibly from a mixed Spanish and Native American background, ought to be an odd fish in provincial New Zealand, but he is a character who moves from his Marist school to a job on a coastal steamer, from the workplace to jail, from jail to the army, from the ranks to military prison, from his circle of mates to the killing fields, with seamless ease.[11] If we saw only the mythology, we might say that Starkie brings a set of irrepressible natural male qualities to all these very different environments, but the opposite is in fact true: Starkie fits in everywhere because the settings through which he moves are fundamentally similar. They are all places where people are knocked into shape.

His first job on a ship and his first days in the army involve learning official and unofficial boundaries, and it is striking how much in common these spaces of easy male camaraderie have with the jail and the military prison. In the training camp's Tent 8, there is a circle of mates and, as part of what bonds them together as a group, a dogsbody, a youngster who carries the can, who makes up for his junior status by being especially daring and game, who might be teased and knocked about but is under the mantle of the group's protection as well. In 1914, Starkie had this function among the scapegraces of Tent 8. He is of lower status, an informal subordinate to the rest of the men for two reasons: he is young and he is coloured. His role inside the tent is not so very different from his role as a recidivist offender in the army; in the tent, having a mascot makes for a tighter group of pals, just as having someone to make an example of builds group cohesion in the army. The role of mascot and the role of scapegoat work to similar ends.

Learning, in all these environments, follows a similar pattern as well. You use violence to get your lesson across, but you don't teach a lesson, you teach the violence. Starkie's elder brother George is the book's prime example. Whenever Starkie steps out of line, or is in danger of stepping out of line, George belts him one. But what is George trying to teach? It is not until very late in the book, when Starkie reflects on his own feelings for Jackie MacKenzie, that he comes to realise that his older brother, though handy with his fists, though obliged 'as a matter of policy and duty' to smack a younger brother's head from time to time, has always hated fighting, and his violence isn't bullying or hardness but something else: a mix of responsibility and 'the feeling one has for a younger man' (137). Needless to say, communicating that love by means of violence is not an optimum strategy. George has made mistakes and wants his younger brother to learn from them, but the more George says, don't follow my example and sends the lesson home with a clip about the ears, the more surely his younger brother copies the behaviour and continues the cycle.

On the morning of 15 September 1916, there was another futile and disastrous attack on German lines. George Stark's battalion had been in the first wave, Starkie's in the second. A wounded soldier drew Starkie's attention to a body lying nearby; once again, I will need to quote at some length.

A horrible foreboding curiosity tore at him. He fell on his knees beside the thing and turned it over. There wasn't much of it, only a head and shoulders. The legs that should have belonged to it sprawled fifty yards away, and there wasn't any middle at all – the shell had ripped it in half. But the head and shoulders belonged to his brother George . . . . *Where had George gone to?* The eyes, open and agonized, couldn't tell him. But the thing might have been important to George, so Starkie scooped it up and carried it over to the fragmentary trunk. Then he started to dig a shallow pit in No Man's Land, tearing at the soil like a dog, sometimes with his bayonet, sometimes with his naked hands . . . . He put the awful contorted bits of George into the pit, but he couldn't make them look like a body. So he tore off his tunic and hid what he could with that; and then, denting the pillow of the earth as George a night before had dented his own pillow for him, found that the head, lying back in the brown soil, looked comparatively peaceful. . . . Then he took to his heels, sobs tearing at him in hiccoughing gusts. In half an hour he had rejoined his own battalion, but the men didn't know him. When he tried to talk he stammered. An officer pulled out a flask and poured out a tin pannikin of rum, filling it to the brim. Starkie drank it down and started out to kill. It wasn't so much vengeance as a desire to find George. Somewhere at the back of the sodden field, straining before him, George might be. He wanted to slash his way through.

The Somme attack was going well on the British side. The German prisoners were already pouring in, squads of a dozen at a time. . . . A little line of prisoners came in sight shepherded by their guard, a New Zealand officer. Starkie emptied his revolver into the field-grey. The guard yelled at him, and he swung his revolver round at the angry man in khaki and told him to shut his mouth or he'd put five rounds into it. Then that group was gone. He was stumbling over a dug-out, a big cave filled with wounded and exhausted Germans. A face stared up, white and young. He asked, 'How many down there?' and the German answered something – it sounded like sixty. Then Starkie drew the pin out of a Mills bomb and flung it into the dug-out. He didn't wait to see what might crawl out of the cascade of mud and brushwood. Fragments of men . . . fragments of George. (139–40)

What is the difference between killing unarmed prisoners and crawling back into No Man's Land 'to get even'? Each episode involves Starkie giving in to reckless rage; each seems caught up in destructive cycles of repetition that are very difficult to stop; each carries the imprint of occasions where violence is an expression of love. Each might have ended as the other did, with talk of a Victoria Cross – or with eyes turned away from a war crime. But there is a small difference in the sequence of events that strikes me as suggestive. George is buried before a surrender to rage; Jackie after. And whereas Jackie has a neat bullet wound, leaving him looking as if he might be asleep, with George, Starkie finds a body that is not a body, that is his brother and is not his brother either. The uncanny nature of the encounter spins him out of control; once again, Starkie goes berserk, and this time sixty or so German prisoners die.

Yet the way Starkie looks after Jackie and tries to look after George suggests that burying the dead can offer some hope, some way out from these cycles of repetition. By way of contrast, I place Hyde's observation on the ease with which soldiers accustomed themselves to the horrors of the battlefield. After a particularly graphic and gruesome description of dead bodies awaiting burial on Gallipoli – 'the sun had caused each body to swell enormously, until the great threatening carcases were three times the size of a man, and their skins had the bursting blackness of grapes' (84) – Hyde remarks that the men soon came to regard the chore of burying the dead without nausea or emotion. Within a month, 'The men thought . . . so little of the corpses on No Man's Land that money belts were unbuckled as rotting corpses were rolled into the pits of death. It was only afterwards, after the war, . . . that every twisted limb, every blackened face waiting in those gullies, came back into memory once again, and forever repeated the protest the tortured body uttered after its death' (85). Perhaps this is the reason why societies need a tomb of the unknown soldier: only the right sort of burial brings closure.

Robin Hyde took up Starkie's story because she believed in the underdog and in the possibility of change. 'I'd like to run a column called "For the Defence"', she told Eileen Duggan while writing the book, 'and tell something of the other side of the world that's so continually hectored by the police and the Nine Hundred and Ninety Nine amendments to the Ten Commandments.'[12] Although Hyde began writing as an advocate for Starkie the war-damaged veteran, her purposes soon developed beyond the goals of crusading journalism. Like many of her contemporaries, she found a counterpoint to the horror and the waste of war by relating Starkie's experiences to a new found sense of a New Zealander's place in the world. We hear something of this every Anzac Day: soldiers who left as subjects of the British Empire, who were eager to fight for 'King and Country', who then went on to discover that these geographical abstractions were disconnected from the homes they missed and the farms and towns they returned to. Hyde registers – or rather promotes – this reorientation in a highly unusual reconstruction of the evacuation from Gallipoli. It occurs to her that the departing soldiers might well have wanted to sing a Maori lament. Odder still, Hyde then interpolates several backgrounding paragraphs on waiata, in which she pictures a row of Maori girls on the banks of the Whanganui River singing:

> Now ... ees ... the time
> When I ... mus' say ... farewell,
> Soon ... you'll be sail-eeng
> Far away ... from me. ...
> [...]
> When you return, you'll find me
> Wait-eeng here. (103)

These maidens are given the full picture-postcard treatment – complexion, figure, hair, bodices and skirts are lovingly enumerated and described; we will learn the girls' names, even how to pronounce them, before this strange puff of expository wind pushes on to a rhetorical climax.

> O, listening dead upon the hillsides of Gallipoli and in the deep gullies of the little bitter-tasting bushes! – it is the voice of your country that is bidding you farewell.

They are going now, with that music on their lips, to slay and to be slain, in other fields . . . . Listening dead, one day a man will come back to you and learn the answer to that song of farewell. He will not stumble away, blind and hopeless, into the deeper pools of blood and filth. For you, speaking out of the knowledge bought by travail, will tell him what paths he must take. (104)

Hyde – a precociously accomplished writer for most of this book – has plunged into one of her treacle-pit lows. The coming generation of the 1930s – the likes of Curnow, Glover and Sargeson – disdained the flabby rhetoric and sentimentality of much of Hyde's writing then available to them, and were apt to use words like 'a schoolgirl crush on literature' or 'hysterical' to account for the unevenness of her work.[13] Perhaps they assumed a woman as flighty as Hyde might be expected to write indulgently, but their more telling diagnosis is that she cannot discern – or does not care about – these effusive lapses in her writing. Let us concede the badness of the passages quoted above in the hope of finding a better explanation – not 'hysteria', not carelessness – for their presence. What has happened?

My hunch is that Hyde, picturing the evacuation as Starkie described it, imagined the weary lines of retreating soldiers as if to a film music accompaniment and then went on to specify it. In fact, the retreat from Gallipoli actually took place under the cover of darkness and in the strictest silence – a chorus of song would have been answered by artillery and gunfire trained on the beach. (Indeed, the Allied position was so exposed, troops rehearsed long spells of silence in the days before the evacuation in order to spring a trap on the probing Turks, who came to regard silence as a ruse.)[14] Rebounding from these actualities, Hyde's imagination has been drawn to music because she needs to close the Gallipoli episode with the right tone; to waiata because she feels the need of something indigenous; and to 'Po Atarau' because it is apt for the occasion and expressive of the nation. This traditional waiata had been put to a popular melody – 'Swiss Cradle Song' – in 1913, and was subsequently sung as a farewell to Maori troops leaving for the war. The song as we know it today is associated rather more with the Second World War, and with the international hit recordings by Gracie Fields and Bing Crosby that followed soon after. In the mid-1930s, when Hyde cites it, the English lyrics have yet to stabilise, but as the 'Haere Ra Waltz', the tune was beginning to enter the national repertoire. In the dancehall, it was invariably the last waltz of the evening, and on the passenger wharf, 'Now is the Hour' – or words to that effect – would be sung by those holding streamers as the white hull eased away from the wharf. Hyde has turned to this popular expression of the sorrows of distance – before the song has become kitsch – because she knows in her heart there is no more appropriate way to leave the New Zealand dead at Gallipoli, her own uncle among them. The dead loom for her, and – perhaps this is already a step too far – she imagines their native complement, the maidens of the river-bank, looming back, singing a farewell for brothers and fathers and sweethearts who will not return.

But an effect of actual distance derails the passage. People reading her work in England (where the book will be published) will not know what a waiata is, and so she has to explain herself, has to fall back on a misplaced section of 'This is New Zealand' travelogue. Her final apostrophe to the 'listening dead', by contrast, is perhaps too local in its impulses to be easily followed. There is a hint of a reference to the paths taken by the dead to Te Reinga; a hint also of a motif emergent in poems by Brasch and Curnow from this period, which similarly imagine a future New Zealander one day learning 'the trick of standing upright here'.[15] Perhaps the figure she and they conjure is a prophecy of those who annually crowd the beaches of Gallipoli on their OE, young people the age of the fallen soldiers, on the point of discovering that 'the answer to that song of farewell' lies in the realisation that home for them will always be 'wait-eeng here'.

When that moustachioed and emphatically pointing icon of empire Lord Kitchener drowned in 1916, Hyde's mother, writes Derek Challis, 'on hearing the news, rested her face on outstretched arms and mourned with tears in her eyes: "My poor country. Oh my poor country. What has she done to deserve it".'[16] Mrs Wilkinson never set foot in England. Her pronounced Anglophile sentiments – common enough at the time – are likely to strike us as extravagantly misplaced. In our histories, sentiments like hers are generally regarded with wonder as a mass delusion of the late colonial period, an 18,000-kil-ometre-wide literal demonstration of how ideology, in the classic

Marxist definition, offers its subjects an imaginary relation to their real conditions of existence. Critics generally make the point with a visual metaphor: from the 1880s to the 1920s, New Zealand-born settlers, it is said, saw their homeland through English eyes, as if with oddly tinted spectacles, and as if clarity of vision might be restored with a simple substitution of the lenses. Critical nationalists like Allen Curnow – and critics of his settler nationalism in their turn – often spoke of the need for 'true vision', for the restoration of a local reality that ought to have been more plainly in sight.[17] I don't suppose Hyde's mother is any less 'at home' in her world than I was as a boy with my head in English war comics – or any more bewildered by distance than the young journalist who sends a waiata halfway round the world to be implausibly sung on the shores of Gallipoli. Rather than deplore these hemispheric illusions, these shifty confusions of here and there, it is worth remembering that it is only natural for things from beyond the horizon to appear upside down in the air.

Hyde's own more sustained analysis of the powers of looming involves the impact of the war on relations between the sexes, and what may seem an unpromising insight: that women like herself were brought up to regard the 'grim uniform' of the Anzacs with an 'unthinking hero-worship' that has encouraged 'all modern men to despise all modern women'.[18] *Passport to Hell* is mostly written as a conventional third-person narrative, presenting Starkie's point of view, but always with the potential to manifest Hyde's own perspective through patterns of imagery, narrator's commentary and the inclusion of imaginary episodes.[19] Two contrasting departure scenes might serve as illustrations. In the first, Starkie is one of a draft of newly enlisted soldiers about to leave on the train from Invercargill when suddenly a young woman, 'healthy as a sheepdog' (55), throws her arms around him, kisses him passionately on the mouth; eyes streaming with tears, she offers the startled and aroused soldier a sewing kit and moves on to repeat the entire performance with another man. Starkie feels 'furiously jealous and contemptuous. It takes a war to get some of them [to feel] like that about the whole world of men' (55). In his own manuscript, Starkie merely notes that an elderly woman handed out sewing kits at the railway station. Presumably, Hyde has elaborated the scene to exemplify her thesis about what happens when women buy into the romance of soldiers in uniform, and she is also setting up a pattern in which sexual excitement is converted to feelings of anger, frustration and disgust.

The second departure scene takes place in Wellington, as wives, children and sweethearts gather on the wharf to farewell the troopship. Hyde described much the same episode on several occasions, drawing on her own experience of seeing her father off to war as a ten-year-old. In one version, she recalls cries of 'Goodbye old girl, goodbye Betty'; she remembers 'lines of tears' on 'wet faces', and people 'smiling still, smiling and shouting foolish things'.[20] This version is a straightforward report, looking and sounding rather like a moment caught in the semi-propaganda of the 'Movietone News'. *Passport to Hell* renders that scene in an expressionist style – demonstrating, in this instance, how short of the mark a diagnosis of hysterical overwriting could be.

The entire shipload of men . . . pressed against the deck-rails and portholes. Starkie, looking down on a crowded wharf in which he had no desire to single out any one person, was suddenly startled by the dreadful expression on the faces of the women. Those faces, ordinary enough in daily life, seemed torn right in two like paper masks. Mouths, wide open, made gashes in them, the eyes . . . were shadowed so that they looked huge as the eye-sockets in skulls . . . . Those hollow faces, pitted with the dreadful fear of a final parting, the upstretched arms, which looked like roots torn from the flesh of the black-clad bodies, communicated to the men their own foreboding. Sobs began to break out from the wharf and ship, a convulsion of sound. All uptorn, the voices, the faces, the straining arms . . . . They had barely known that they were one flesh, but they knew it now. Torn apart, they would never be joined together again, and consequently they were destroyed. The individuality of the women had become fused with that of the men; it wasn't only their partners who were taken from them, it was themselves: their flesh and spirit and their secret buried thoughts – the thoughts you do bury in a man when you wake in the morning and find him at your side, his sleeping face a profile upturned in the pale light from between drawn window-curtains, one hand helplessly uncurled on the white counterpane. Father, lover, son, all drawn together in the one person, and the receptacle of your secret thoughts – in God's name, how can you lose that and remain the same? How could the men on the ship expect to come back to the same women when, departing, they had destroyed them? (64–65)

The women are left behind, exactly as the dead on the battlefield will be left behind, while soldiers off to war are pictured as if they had yet to wake to the morning of departure. Hyde's deftly imagined reversals run counter to the usual prescription for these scenes: not 'Goodbye, Betty, goodbye, old girl', not even the undercurrent of foreboding and sorrow that dampens faces in *The Godwits Fly*, but a homing in on a female experience of what it is like to be fused with another person, and then to have that intimacy destroyed.

Starkie's experience and perspective is naturally always in the foreground, but Hyde is able to introduce qualifying sidelights from two angles. One – illustrated by the Invercargill episode – involves the layering of point of view, offering in effect a woman's view of a man's view of a woman's view of the war. The embarkation from Wellington, by contrast, bypasses all mediation through Starkie to directly embed a feminine perspective in counterpoint to the largely male experience the book more obviously records. The combined potential of these approaches is most fully utilised in what, for Hyde, is one of the more revealing engagements of the war: the battle of the Wazir, Cairo's red-light district. In the bars of the 'Wazza', boys from Mosgiel and Fendalton would get to see the cancan danced naked; in the brothels, some 34,000 licensed prostitutes, each displaying a certificate of health updated thrice-weekly, offered their services to the soldiery. Hyde calls her chapter 'Conjuror and Pigeon', and uses the extended metaphor of an illusionist's trick – a robed magician bites the head off a pigeon and shows the bleeding stump; in a whirl of silks and drumbeats, the bird comes fluttering to life – to suggest the relation between the glamour of the quarter and its flyblown underside: 'a rotting pile of fungus and disease, infecting the ancient stones' (73). Starkie happens to be alone in a square when it suddenly fills with onrushing soldiers.

Starkie ran with them, yelling as they yelled, without the faintest idea why he ran and yelled. The Wazza began to glare with the pattern of flames against the windows of seven-storeyed houses. There were shrieks and crashes as women and *souteneurs* were thrown down from the upper windows of those tall-balconied rat-holes. Furniture was tossed out and battered into splinters. A soldier reeled into a doorway with a Gippo knife sunk to the haft in his belly, and sat there retching and coughing, a bright red foam on his lips. (75)

Next morning, having spent the night with a girl in the cellar of a brothel, Starkie returns late to camp – 'red-eyed, unshaven, singed' – with a story that he had been hit on the head and 'rescued by a young lady' (76–77).

Hyde has her own theory about why the pimps and whores of the Wazza were targeted. On parade, when an officer demands an explanation from the lines of disgraced soldiers, a voice yells out, 'they was better off dead' (77). She calls this 'from the psychological point of view . . . one of the most remarkable sentences spoken in the history of the War' and analyses it as follows. In the Wazza:

> . . . there was no pretence that one soldier's face differed from the rest. The men were used, especially the colonial soldiers whose countries supported no licensed houses, to more regard for their vanity . . . . In the Wazza they were nobody; male embracing heterogeneous female. The first shock of this faded from their consciousness, but it waited in hiding – a resentment that they hardly realized, but that could not be placated except by vengeance. The convict becomes accustomed to the loss of his name and citizenship, but the surface resentment wears down into his deeper hatred of Society. So it was with the soldiers in the Wazza. The place stole their sexual identity from them. They had to revenge themselves. The women who had deprived them, the *souteneurs* who shared the spoils, the houses where they had waited, were – in the phrase of that inspired and hysterical soldier – better off dead. (77–78)

One of the consequences of battle is a loss of personal identity; one thinks of what happened to George, or of occasions when Starkie crawls out into No Man's Land with a wooden cross carved with his name strapped to his back – as Hyde puts it, 'there was a horror of the unnamed graves of No Man's land' (136). And the anonymous encounters of the Wazza generate horrors too, similarly depriving men of their identity and generating behaviour they might themselves explain in terms of 'vengeance', of 'getting even', but which Hyde sees in terms of the logic of 'deferred action'.[21] In the bordello, as on the battlefield, a 'first shock' fades from consciousness but its wave persists into the present, relaying impulses and defences proper to the past to a new setting that telescopes beyond the broken windows and upturned bars of the Wazza.

There are two reasons, then, behind Hyde's hunch that women brought up to venerate the Anzac legend inadvertently fuel men's disdain for women. Starkie is an extreme instance of the Anzac who is intimate with violence and radically disinvested in military ideals of valour; who can only despise those who believe and maintain what Wilfred Owen called 'The old Lie', that it is sweet to die for one's country.[22] Starkie is also an extreme instance of the damaged soldier in flight from intimacy, for whom women are either angels like the aptly named Nurse Sunshine – Starkie worries he may have used bad language in her presence while delirious – or else whores and good-time girls, who not only pass on their own form of disinvestment in chivalric ideals, but who also duplicate the pattern of war trauma by setting in train the return of unconscious feelings of fear, rage and disgust.

Hyde, of course, is not so much analysing how things are, as how she thinks men think they are, if only they knew it. I doubt she needed to have read Freud to form her view, but her reading of the most up-to-date psychology then available has evidently influenced the way she conceives 'deferred action' as a special kind of looming. The other thread, her own perspective as distinct from that mediated through Starkie, has no obvious precedent in the standard war books. A month into writing *Passport*, she told a correspondent, 'I wrote the book because I had to write it when I heard his story, and because it's an illustration of Walt Whitman's line – "There is to me something profoundly affecting in large masses of men following the lead of those who do not believe in man".'[23] The majority of books about the First World War invariably celebrate the courage of the ordinary soldier going over the top, men plodding forward through barrages and the fire of machine guns, to be cut down as surely as cattle in their thousands and hundreds of thousands. Yet Whitman's emphasis on the fate of 'large masses' is not especially highlighted in Hyde's text. Her book is necessarily too involved in the psychopathology of Starkie to mine that vein of pathos successfully – though we do see her trying for this effect in her embroidered account of the evacuation of Gallipoli. On the whole, alternatives to Starkie's particularised forms of courage are associated with the surprising number of women who populate the borders of its battlefields: the nuns, the nurses, the sturdy and compassionate women of France. Hyde portrays them as models of compassion, endurance and *savoir faire*:

> You could never forget them – the solid-hipped, red-cheeked women who came into the estaminets, still smelling of the clean faint fragrance of soil and cow-byre, and served out the heavy mugs of beer across the little table. . . . The big arms that girdled a New Zealand soldier's shoulders were casual, really, thinking no more of it than of patting a useful dog who'd done his bit turning the water-wheel. Their eyes, when you really looked into them, were stern and proud. Their hands were strong as a man's hands. Starkie wondered why the Frenchmen always seemed so much smaller than their women. Odd to think of one of these Hecubas surrendering herself to a *gendarme* with a waxed moustache and patent-leather hair. (114)

This setting of farms and estaminets is some distance from the Wazza, a place that turns conventional male desire into a kind of nightmare. But the genre in which to frame this alternative glimpse of ordinary life in the proximity of war is not the action movie of violence and atrocity but domestic comedy interrupted by tragedy. It is almost off limits for a book of this sort, but Hyde takes us there in the difference between the scene described above and another in which a farmhouse estaminet popular with the soldiers suffers a direct hit from a German bomber.

> And – well, that jagged hole in the ground was all. The old French couple, gran'père and gran'mère, Val's golden plaits and the two kid sisters, hadn't even fragmentary existence. Saved burial expenses, the Hun flier did; and blotted out at one shot all the fun, the gentleness, and

the laughter that had waited for the men when they climbed out of the stinking pits of the tunnels. (150)

This passage looms in our direction. It seems like an incident from a more modern war because the 'large masses' Whitman spoke of turn out to be civilians, and because Starkie, like a CNN journalist, reports on the size of the crater in a voice that has trouble taking in the significance of an obliteration that leaves nothing behind, nothing to bury.

Our story about what Robin Hyde made of Starkie's journey to and from the war, of the trauma he carried back, of its looming significance for relations on the domestic front, has a predictable postscript. Starkie fell in love with Robin Hyde. He proposed marriage to her, mooned about, wrote passionate letters and made a general nuisance of himself. On 5 April 1935, she wrote in her journal:

Starkie is worrying me terribly – not by wanting money, . . . but by wanting all the desperate faraway things people do seem to want. . . . . Of course he's trying to attach himself to me. Equally of course I shan't let him do so in any vital sense. But to use stern measures seems so impossible – like kicking a stray dog that *wants* to be well-groomed and beautiful and always your very faithful servant . . . . They're all such babies, the physical and earthbound type of men.[24]

CHAPTER TEN

Western Swing: John Mulgan's *Man Alone*

The silence of a falling star
Lights up a purple sky . . .
– Hank Williams, 'I'm So Lonesome I Could Cry'

IN JUNE 1944, JOHN MULGAN WAS LIAISING WITH PARTISANS IN THE scrubby high country of Nazi-occupied Greece. Reaching out in a letter to his five-year-old son back home in New Zealand, he described how he spent much of the day singing to himself on horseback. If the youngster did not know 'I've Got Spurs that Jingle Jangle [Jingle]', Mulgan suggested the boy should get his mother to teach him. The tune – 'largely featured' in radio broadcasts by Duke Ellington's band – had been Mulgan's 'favourite song of 1943'. 'The other song I sing when I am riding', he confessed, 'is called "Deep in the Heart of Texas".' They are both, as he said, 'simple and beautiful songs', and I like to think of him singing them as he rode out on his horse Heroniko – Gene Autry, for a moment, in a John Wayne kind of war.[1]

From the days of Tex Morton to the 'Huntly and Western' of the Topp Twins, New Zealanders have been singing, strumming and yodelling country music. Country, one might say, is the natal music of all settler societies, while its literary counterpart, the popular Western, is the major form for the conversion of settler experience into romance and myth. In Australia, for example, we recognise the standard plots and motifs of the American Western in a popular 'outback' tradition of bushrangers, drovers and faithful Aboriginal trackers, while high cultural revisions of the 'bush novel', such as Patrick White's *Voss*, are regarded as defining landmarks in the Australian literary canon. It is not surprising that this should be so: historians of settlement from Frederick Jackson Turner to James Belich remind us that the processes by which frontiers become settled regions work in similar ways to somewhat different ends in very different regions. Land is taken from indigenous peoples; introduced species and technologies remake the environment; markets emerge and capital flows in; economies cycle through boom and bust. Once the capacity to transfer goods, people and information to and from the old world reaches a certain threshold, Belich argues, those frontier territories will grow and modernise quickly. Within only a few decades, they expand into populous, civil and independent centres, while the threads joining each former colony to its homeland will simultaneously have been woven more thickly.[2] Settlers have similar experiences of those processes wherever they have occurred; their dreams, disappointments and predicaments take comparable narrative shape, however sharply individualised their experience. Whether it is the forlorn and rootless poetry of a Hank Williams song or the major discursive structures that organise beliefs about progress and ruination, we should not only expect to find story patterns repeating across the sites of new-world settlement, we should also be able to explain why any particular genre might fail to transplant, and why apparently singular hybrids appear.

Oddly, New Zealand seems to have got 'Country' without the 'Western'. *The Oxford Companion to New Zealand Literature* has no heading for Westerns (it has one for Weston, Jesse). Our enduring stereotypes of rural masculinity were developed in the comic yarns and sketches of Frank S. Anthony, Barry Crump, and others, but our 'good keen men' – the likes of Gus Tomlins, Sam Cash or Fred Dagg – belong to a rosy world of bachelor comedy. These laconic raconteurs are like Bertie Wooster in a black singlet, and their search for a Sheila-free haven is about as far from the melodrama and darkness of the true Western as the Drones' Club.

Although New Zealanders have produced 'Mills & Boon' titles at a remarkable rate, although we are strong in the family saga, although Ngaio Marsh is eminent in detective fiction, we would seem to be consumers, not producers, of a popular form that ought to have been especially resonant for us. James Cowan is an exception. One of the first comparatively minded historians of settlement, his two-volume *History of the New Zealand Wars and the Pioneering Period* (1922 and 1923) leans more on Turner's Frontier Thesis than on British imperial history, and he went on to write dozens of magazine items that borrow extensively from the popular histories and novels of the American West. His *Tales of the Maori Bush* (1935), for example, refers to gulches rather than gullies, prairies rather than plains, and Cowan draws an unlikely portrait of Te Kooti as a 'bold bandit-like figure, with two revolvers at his side and a high pointed soft black hat on his head'.[3] One of his anecdotes, 'The Bush Court Martial', is the basis for our most notable achievement in the Western as a film genre, Geoff Murphy's *Utu* (1983), which transposes a formulaic story of retribution to the Ureweras and a quirkily revisionist 'bicultural' perspective. Beyond these examples, we may point to writers of ephemera, like the extraordinary Tex Morton – 'The Yodelling Boundary Rider' – who was not only good enough to open for Hank Williams in America, and not only popular enough to outsell the likes of Bing Crosby in New Zealand, but also co-wrote a 'Wild West' comic strip that, according to one source, had a trans-Tasman print run of 100,000 copies; yet we have no Louis L'Amour and no Cormac McCarthy.[4] Perhaps our most significant writer of Westerns will turn out to have been Witi Ihimaera, who wrote *Bulibasha* because his father asked him to write a cowboy book. This is a backcountry novel about tough men who work closely with animals; who have strong codes of honour and loyalty; who, Lone Ranger fashion, can pluck a maiden up onto the back of a prancing white steed; who match strength and skills in 'The Golden Fleece' shearing contest (which might conceivably pass as a Kiwi form of rodeo). Ihimaera's Maori shearers are every inch the New Zealand version of the cowboy, but his novel is not deeply a Western. It is its own inimitable hybrid, part rural pastoral and part duelling banjos, but also part teen rebel movie and part Book of Mormon; most of all, it is a sentimental comedy about the importance of whanau – a novel of showdowns and escalating feuds in which the family ranch is likely to be saved not by some rangy gunslinger, but by a bunch of hockey-loving transvestites home on the bus from Wellington.

While we have no obviously significant Western tradition, this popular import looms most strongly where we might least expect to find it: in classic works of cultural nationalism from the 1930s, and with John Mulgan's *Man Alone* in particular. The title of that novel certainly sounds as if it ought to belong to a Western: the existential drama of 'man alone' under an unforgiving desert sky transposed to our green dripping bush, to swollen rivers and strength-sapping hills, to nature as refuge and destroyer. Suppose that, and every teacher of English from Kaitaia to the Bluff will pounce to correct you: far from celebrating black-singlet values, *Man Alone* is generally thought to espouse social commitment and fraternity – qualities the novel finds absent in the anomic rural heartland, where success in life is a farmer retiring on a capital gain, and 'she'll be right' attitudes reconcile the majority to pinched and impoverished lives. At the end of the novel, Johnson, the protagonist, is in a train carriage with other volunteers off to fight in the Spanish Civil War, and he speaks of the importance of solidarity to the bearded university student seated beside him:

'I've only felt like this sometimes', he said, 'going somewhere with people I liked, doing something together. It's a fine feeling. Most of the time a man spends too much alone.' (205)[5]

Later, after a difficult night on the Pyrenees, as the men cross the frontier into danger, 'the sun came out for a moment as they were coming down the mountain-side into Spain' (206). One might suppose that the sun shines approval on the novel's explicit statement of its theme, but what this sentence actually validates is the physical sensations it both describes and impels. Visualise the moment, and perhaps you are Johnson, looking up from a band of comrades to the sky, but it seems to me the sentence is calling for cinemascope, for the wide shot filling the screen with sunlight and mountainside, and placing the purposive action of men (on what must surely be a trail) against the larger horizon of Nature.

Man Alone often used to be mentioned as one of the first 'truly' New Zealand novels; it was boldly critical in its realism, it looked hard at self-deceiving settler myths of progress and the virtues of farming 'God's Own Country', much as those other writers of the New Zealand Renaissance, Curnow, Fairburn, Glover, Mason and Sargeson, had done in their poems and short stories. Nowadays, the 'homegrown' qualities of the book are much underplayed in academic circles; it is generally regarded as an engaged political novel of the 1930s, indelibly linked to the international Marxism of the period and to the pervasive influence of Ernest Hemingway's prose style.[6] Mulgan's readers, though, are nonetheless struck by the power of the chapters set in the Kaimanawa Ranges, where Johnson takes to the bush after accidentally killing his lover's husband.

The bush journey was carefully mapped. Mulgan could draw on memories of student tramping-club trips to Ruapehu for the first leg, when Johnson follows the old Blythe Track up the mountain from Ohakune. With the aid of a large-scale map of the North Island, Mulgan then worked out a route from the Blythe Hut round the mountain to the moonscape of Rangipo, down through tussock country to the Desert Road and eastward across the plateau to the 6000-foot mountains beyond; his protagonist then follows creeks into the high country, crossing ridge after ridge as far as the Rangitikei River, and traversing Ngamatea Station country to emerge at Bill Crawley's hut in the hills above Kuripapango, where the road comes in from Hawke's Bay.[7] The geographical accuracy is matched by vividly evocative descriptions of making one's way with difficulty through 'real' bush: 'deep, thick, and matted, great trees going up to the sky, and beneath them a tangle of ferns and bush-lawyer and undergrowth, the ground heavy with layers of rotting leaves and mould' (139). Johnson crashes through trackless bush for months on end, but his experience of immersion in its colours and smells, together with a sense of wetness, of steep never-endingness, of claggy-booted exhaustion, is within my own reach towards the end of a day tramp on a DOC trail. Although much of the novel's physical world has, like six o'clock closing, gone the way of history, Mulgan's description of the bush, by contrast, seems timeless and a natural ground of identification.[8] Little wonder that a 'man alone' myth soon crystallised around the book, despite its pointed statement of a contrary theme.

It is not unusual for a book to pull in several directions at once. Mulgan wrote the novel in Oxford and had been away from home since 1933. Vincent O'Sullivan, noting the thematic inconsistencies, suggests 'there was more emotional montage in the novel than a present-day reader might easily detect'.[9] The stunted, puritanical dystopia Mulgan portrayed in the novel is not 'easily disentangled', O'Sullivan suggests, 'from the Britain he now lived in', while the novel's socialism is a response to European storm clouds rather than being determined by conditions at home.[10] C. K. Stead, in a superb essay on Mulgan, has argued that the contradictions at the heart of the novel are more than a reflex of Mulgan's expatriate experience; they are, he suggests, determined by a fundamental New Zealand 'problem of identity' and by the competing claims of 'here' and 'there'.[11] For much of the novel, Stead explains, Mulgan offers a textbook Marxist analysis of the economic basis of New Zealand society. Johnson, the drifter, serves as a traditional picaresque hero moving the action and the analysis from place to place, and also as an ideological dupe. 'There isn't any better country than this', he philosophises, 'not where a man can go about and get work, and stop when he wants to, and make money when he needs it, and take a holiday when he feels ready for one' (36). But there is a flaw in his system: the economic 'base' of a society is its fundamental reality, and the coming Depression exposes the limits of Johnson's freedom. A 'man alone' can't change things; a spontaneous revolution like the Queen Street riots will be contained, but purposeful collective action offers a way forward. Mulgan's rather schematic analysis is then derailed by what Stead, with an eye on his own first novel, calls the appeal of 'Smith's Dream' – the temptation to withdraw from all social ties in search of a more essential freedom and a more radical self-reliance. For most people, 'Smith's Dream' might mean opting for an alternative lifestyle, but it is a form of escape whose mythological extreme is Johnson going bush.

The contradictions of *Man Alone*, Stead argues, could not be resolved by Mulgan, and are not likely to be resolved in our fiction, he believes, 'so long as it remains a contradiction fundamental to our sense of ourselves – so long, that is, as our collective sense of identity is something imported, while our individual sense is shaped in childhood in direct relation to the particular physical environment of these islands'.[12] What might an imported collective sense of identity be? Some readers might suppose Stead has in mind his usual suspects: 'isms' – like the Marxism of the 1930s or the feminism of the 1970s or the postcolonialism of the 1980s – that reach our shores on waves of modish theory, turning us into members of a strident collective; but on this occasion he is drawing another bow altogether. Our sense of who *we* are, he suggests, is likely to be mediated by an import from elsewhere (the very name of our country is thus mediated), while my sense of who *I* am is immediately experienced and known in the fibre of my being. If those who live in the very large cities or the very isolated villages of the world might be supposed to have a certain self-sufficiency in the available modes of identification, we New Zealanders are bound to look elsewhere; it is a corollary of our distant connections, of the gap between here and there.

Yet my mind glazes over whenever anyone talks about the importance of a 'New Zealand identity'. I can form no conception of what they might mean, though they are clearly describing something valuable. Perhaps it is a rare and ineffable quality, drawn earthwards through the meditations of our more sensitive artists; perhaps, like the smell of himself that a pig might enjoy, it is more robust, a tang; perhaps it is a sovereign assertion of us-ness – 'we are who we are' – a tautology chest-thumped to the winds. Yet if identity is an incoherent concept, identification is not. In psychological terms, identification is the process by which a person 'assimilates an aspect, property or attribute of the other and is transformed, wholly or partially, after the model the other provides'.[13] A little boy playing with a toy car is becoming a driver just like his Mum or Dad, though he is also modelling himself on other children and their toys, and (though he is just going 'vrim-vrim' or squealing round a corner) patterning himself after what a car is like too. If identity – the name on a driving licence, the nationality on a passport – is singular, any person so identified is an assemblage of many identifications. Books are like that too. An often-told back story to *Man Alone* involves two complex strands of identification: the relation of a son to his father, and of a New Zealander to English literary models.

John Mulgan's father, Alan, born in 1881, was a journalist, novelist, poet, playwright, critic, historian, autobiographer, editor – a one-man Readers and Writers Festival. His tastes were formed before the twentieth century got under way. For him, books taught life's little lessons and broadened the mind with facts about people and places. He wrote patriotic verse on the nation's progress – 'Further the plough's quest, fresh fields breaking; / New life, new hope, new nation in the making' – and urged younger New Zealand writers to portray 'not what was *wrong* with a country but what was *right* with it'.[14] Even so, as Vincent O'Sullivan notes, 'it was his pen that most fervently attempted to "bind us to Britain and her established order; her politics, her Navy and Army, her Empire, her literature, her ways of thought"'.[15] Alan Mulgan was born in modest circumstances in Katikati; a scholarship took him as far as Auckland Grammar, but he lacked the means to attend university or venture overseas; having to stay home, journalism seemed the best path for his talents. While he lacked the background of an English man of letters, he fashioned himself after the model, becoming a literary all-rounder, columnist and broadcaster – the J. B. Priestley of the *Auckland Star* and National Radio. John, his golden boy, not only went to university, but – after failing to win the Rhodes scholarship he seemed destined for – also continued to Oxford on funds borrowed by his father. After taking a degree in English, young Mulgan joined Oxford University Press as an editor, and was soon immersed in the world of books and authors and ideas, much like his father, though a good step up, in the heart of metropolitan culture.

We know that children who identify with their parents' dreams often have a hard time of it. Their lives can seem overly scripted; they wonder who they are; the success others struggle for comes easily to them, and ambivalently. If there is one word for what they suffer from, they would usually say it is emptiness. Yet Mulgan had a steady enough relationship with his father to be able, on the one hand, to deal kindly and loyally in assisting Alan with the publication, in England, of his books, and on the other, to pinpoint their limitations across a well-negotiated generation gap. The strongest impression one takes from Vincent O'Sullivan's biography is that John Mulgan was a well-adjusted person, a little serious and inclined to moderate bouts of depression, but far from fragile. He seems capable, humorous, fun-loving, courageous. And then comes the shock of his suicide, at the age of thirty-three, in a Cairo Hotel room, on Anzac Day 1945. One should always distrust how an event like that backlights the past; signs that were never portents can begin to loom, and one would wish to avoid, as O'Sullivan scrupulously does, the presumption that Mulgan's suicide was ordained or susceptible to our ready understanding.

That said, O'Sullivan mentions several things that recur often enough to be suggestive about Mulgan's personality, though not in any strongly individuated sense, but in ways that strike me as representative of his generation, and as adding public context both to the problems of identification noted above and to the novel as a cultural and literary sounding board for them. Mulgan, we learn, liked nothing better than to talk to veterans of the First World War. The original title of *Man Alone* was 'Talking of War', and the novel begins with a frame narrator, who has no experience of war, endeavoring to get an older man, Johnson, to open up on the subject. The actual origins of the novel go back to a poem written on exactly this theme several years earlier, called 'Old Wars':

> Thinking there would be war again
> I said to Johnson, old-timer,
> sitting in the sun half-sleeping
> Tell me of the war that you fought in,
> tell me of the long campaigning
> in Suvla, Lemnos and Passchendaele . . . .
>
> Tell me of the war days, I asked him,
> Not of the camps and laughter that I know,
> but tell me of the trenches and the fighting
> and the men you killed when you were young.[16]

As in the novel, Johnson won't speak of the war, but remembers as more significant 'the bush we cleared and burned, / the rata, rimu and black matai', and recalls dead companions memorialised in a half-settled landscape of 'dark paddocks', pine shelter belts, and 'grass, green, heavy with richness'. The speaker of the poem hopes to unlock an older man's unspoken knowledge of violence and death, but the poem itself gestures towards the charismatic silence of the landscape, and ends with the two men sharing it:

> . . . And we turned then and silent went westward,
> away from the sun,
> and silent we came to the homestead
> low down in the pines.

The 1930s were great days for theorists and talkers, particularly in left-wing university circles. In Auckland, and subsequently in Oxford,

Mulgan knew socialists, Trotskyites, Moscow-line communists and fellow-travellers; he could talk, half-jokingly, of his Oedipus complex; and, with fellow expatriates, endlessly pick over responsibilities towards a distant home with the nearer and more pressing claims of the coming anti-fascist war. But time and again, in letters and journals, Mulgan expresses impatience with the universe of talk and the emptiness of social forms and distinctions. He ached for something more solid, more real:

> More and more I begin to feel that the world is divided into two classes . . . I find that I am content talking and living with people like my farming friends, with men I meet in the pubs, with my friends here . . . and I feel that all these very different people have some quality in common, something which I would call reality or sincerity – and the world is fairly barren outside them.[17]

It seemed there was limitless scope in England for barrenness: the class system, the politics of appeasement, the complacencies of the common room, were full of it. As the war approached, his disdain for 'over-intellectualised man' became more pronounced, and the word 'action' enters his vocabulary as another lodestone of value.[18] As Vincent O'Sullivan explains, 'he no longer much wanted the society of teachers, or of "writers for writing's sake" – he preferred the comradeship of people who made a difference, like his friend, the political reporter Geoffrey Cox, with whom he co-authored "Behind the Cables", a series of columns on the situation behind the European headlines'.[19] Another of his friends, Ian Milner, then an ardent thirties-style communist, thought Mulgan was 'distrustful of generalised schemes of thinking', and spoke of his empirical cast of mind and 'natural reticence'.[20] Mulgan was also acquainted with several very accomplished women, but his letters home reveal not just 'natural reticence' but an aversion to uphill conversations with them; Robert Graves's niece, for example, was said to be 'nice' but 'too intelligent to be pleasant company'.[21] Later, when he and his wife Gabrielle were separated by the war, she would write him letters that spoke of her loneliness and difficulties, asking anxiously after his own feelings for her and the child. He would generally fumble a sentence or two of assurance in reply, but the tenor of his response, in Vincent O'Sullivan's paraphrase, was: 'It was a tough world; lousy things like separation and sadness happened. There was no point much in going on about it.'[22] Another old friend was disconcerted by Mulgan's atheism: 'When we died, we went phut like a candle', Mulgan maintained, and could imagine circumstances in which the 'permanent sleep' of death might be 'preferable to being alive'.[23] With nothingness after, and barrenness all about, what was most valuable was authenticity, intensity and resistance – 'a nobility', as he put in his preface to *Poems of Freedom* (1938), 'which causes men to go forward and when they can no longer go forward, to die'.[24] These are only incidentally the words of a future suicide, but they complete a sketch of Mulgan as a generational type: the proto-existentialist.

As a student, he once tried to interest his philosophy lecturer Dick Anschutz and his wife Jean in Westerns, dragging his friends off to a cowboy movie at the Roxy Theatre in Queen Street, but the eyes of those cosmopolitan intellectuals, lovers of Stravinsky and Joyce, remained closed.[25] His friends might have seen a film about a sheriff fronting up to a band of whiskery outlaws, a wagon train circled by whooping Indians, a posse of riders galloping toward the screen in a storm of dust – any of the clichés of a popular, conservative and escapist genre. If so, they missed what many readers of *Man Alone* also miss: the existential dimensions of the genre's setting and deep structure. In the words of Louis L'Amour: 'There are times in life when the fancy words and pretty actions don't count for much, when it's blood and death and a cold wind blowing and a gun in the hand and you know suddenly you're just an animal with guts and blood that wants to live, love and mate, and die in your own good time.'[26] According to Jane Tompkins, the literary anthropologist of the genre, Westerns 'satisfy a hunger to be in touch with something absolutely real'.[27] Like all forms of pastoral, the Western is an urban (or suburban) genre, and the pleasure we take in imaginatively inhabiting its untrammelled spaces signals, she believes, 'a powerful need for self-transformation. The desert light and the desert space, the creak of saddle leather and the sun beating down, the horse's energy and force – these things promise a translation of the self into something purer and more authentic, more intense, more real.'[28] The Kaimanawa chapters of *Man Alone* are hardly 'big sky country', but their enclosed world taps just as strongly into this structure of feeling: 'he was going . . . into bush country, where for a hundred miles no-one lived or travelled, where there were no paths nor animals except birds, but only high bush-hills and rivers going down to the sea' (130). What may be less apparent is that the novel as a whole – and despite the absence of wagon trains, gunfighters, cattle drives and the like – resonates powerfully with the preoccupations of the traditional Western: land, silence, gender, death.

Johnson is generally regarded as a flat character whose primary function is to move from place to place, allowing Mulgan to portray various economic conditions and to examine the effects of settlement on a range of people. But a lack of psychological depth can work in other ways too. On screen, leading men like John Wayne or Clint Eastwood seldom give depth to a Western hero; they bring presence, not personality, to the role. Novels in the genre become lavishly physical in their own way, too, telling us what it is like to see with those crinkled eyes, to move with those aching muscles, to be inside that skin. When Johnson is on the run after the Queen Street riots, for example, sentence after sentence does little more than register a bodily action or impression.

> He rested, taking his breath. It was not long before he grew cold again and, with the cold, stiffness returned to his legs and the throbbing to his head. He would have to move on, but first of all he felt through his pockets and found his tin of tobacco and papers. He rolled himself a cigarette clumsily in the darkness and smoked it carefully between thickened and dry lips while he made his plans. (63)

Sentences like these seem generated from a checklist of possible physical sensations. The artfulness comes in the way events are rolled out as little strings of action and perception: not 'having a cigarette', but fumbling through pockets for tin and papers and pausing to note the hydration of the lips. These assemblies of micro-mapped sensation are particularly well suited to imagining the body under strain, which is one reason why the larger plot arcs of the genre, as in *Man Alone*, so often involve extended sequences of pursuit or escape. The typical Western finds the hero trapped in a life-threatening situation that will require a monumental effort on his part to overcome. He has to be persistent, ingenious, iron-willed; in the face of total exhaustion and overwhelming odds, the hero, like Johnson in the Kaimanawas, comes through. The novel ends with the words: 'There are some men, this fellow said, you can't kill' (207). Some readers of the novel might find a moral in that, but it is always an error to suppose the outcome of a Western counts for much. The good guy will always win; the obstacles thrown in his way are far more important, and the writer must ensure that our disembodied attention is gripped by the perils that grip the hero.

The purer the Western, the purer the struggle; whether it is man against man or man against the elements, the consciousness of the hero – and of his proxy, the reader or viewer – is fully immersed in the present moment. Ordinarily, we are not so engaged; in tennis, I toss the ball up for a serve, but I remain my own commentator and encourager; I am not wholly given over to the action. If I were playing supremely well, I would be in the groove and just do it. When the action hero is given over to the present moment, he risks losing himself in another sense too. His unselfconsciousness, a form of heightened awareness, ought to be sharply distinct from loss of consciousness, yet in the Western these states move close to each other, as if they were two sides of the one ideal. Johnson, for example, at the end of his tether, glimpses a hut on the next ridge. It is in view for just a minute before the clouds lower again, and a 'fine, wet, chilling mist' drives in against him (147). The action is now goal oriented; he must reach that hut or die. A first effort fails; he cuts up from the river too soon, arriving above the mark. A second attempt, described considerably more slowly, begins as darkness falls.

He began to go forward up the side of the valley again, often crawling and climbing on hands and knees, while the bush grew dark around him. His head was at first very clear and his senses seemed alert and over-sensitivized so that he could hear each sound from the patter of rain in the leaves to the rustle of small birds. But as time went on he began to talk aloud, arguing softly with himself, murmuring over each obstruction as he came to it. He went on, unable and not caring to stop, until the full pitch blackness of night was really around him and the rain still falling steadily. He planned not to stop consciously, but as he went on he could feel the strength of his resistance to unconsciousness lessening. The sense of reality that he had had began to go from him until he was struggling with ferns and creepers in dreams that succeeded each other.

He stopped suddenly, not realizing what was strange to him, and then, collecting himself, knew that he was in a clearing of some kind, that for the moment there was nothing in front of his groping hands. . . . He stood up and stepped forward, feeling with his arms outstretched until he met the trees again, then back until he had placed them on the other side. He was on a track of some kind. (148)

The novelist now finds a new moment of danger in the proximity of safety: should Johnson go up the track or down? – up it is, and there is the clearing and light from a window. The action sequence comes to a close with another deftly interpolated detail. Under the automatism of great stress, Johnson is allowed a superfluous moment of politeness as, 'Dropping the small axe which he had carried all this time from his hand he knocked on the door and without waiting threw it open and went inside' (149). It matters relatively little that Johnson's journey to this point has been harrowing. Every pang of tiredness, every goad of exertion, is in service to the suspenseful drive towards an ending and to the corresponding drama of a consciousness saturated in the present moment and staggering towards oblivion.[29]

At the outset of his journey, Johnson tells himself he will need 'patience and endurance' to survive (130), qualities externalised in the hills that 'close round and over him' (139), in the shaping of water on rock and in the massive overhanging trees. To survive, Johnson has to become less like a person and more like the land. Its remoteness is the counterpart of his ability to stand isolation; its abidingness, his self-sufficiency; its indifference, his hardness. When he is 'farther than anyone could ever follow him', he feels 'surrounded and drowned in the hills and bush, safe and alone and submerged' (139). The word 'submerged' (encountered earlier in a discussion of *The Piano*) suggests the danger as well as the attractions of this refuge. The elemental struggle with nature takes all Johnson's attention and immerses him in the present moment, yet the deeper into this experience he goes, the more he risks losing awareness altogether. Tired and half-starved in his winter cave, Johnson struggles with 'a desire never to move from where he was', and sits for hours in 'dreams that were half sleep' (142); later, in the final effort to reach the hut, he feels his hold on reality lessening, and only rallies when his mind catches up with his body's knowledge that he has reached a track. Like Robert Frost's traveller in 'Stopping by Woods on a Snowy Evening', he must resist the impulse to cease. Mulgan never quite gives us the poetry of 'The woods are lovely, dark, and deep / But I have promises to keep, / And miles to go before I sleep', but the attraction of stopping, of falling back into nature, is implicit in the way Johnson struggles with lethargy as a 'weakness . . . he could only fight by going on', and in his reluctance to stir from a 'rough shelter . . . more comforting to him than most homes had been' (142).

Death, in the Western, is usually violent and over quickly – you just go 'phut like a candle', as Mulgan put it. But there is also the siren call of oblivion, evidenced in the matching-up of masculine qualities with the enduring majesty and silence of the land, and in the entropic desire 'to become the ground, become the water, become the trees, mix with the whole thing' – as a cowboy in Owen Wister's *The Virginian* lyrically puts it.[30] Robert Frost and Ernest Hemingway work this territory too, and while the latter is a direct and acknowledged influence on Mulgan – the title of the novel comes from the closing words of *To Have and Have Not* – we risk contextual losses in making too much of the narrower literary connection. The male romanticism all these writers share moves on a broad cultural front, acting in concert against the triple perils of feminism, Christianity and domesticity.

The anti-type of the Western is the popular family saga: fictions centred on home, on the civilising role of women, on community-mindedness, on generational ties. The anti-type of *Man Alone* might be found in any of the novels of Nelle Scanlan, the best-selling New Zealand novelist of the decade (and a Mulgan family friend), but – in terms of novels that are remembered today – might also be illustrated by Jane Mander's *The Story of a New Zealand River* (1920). Alice has a marriage of convenience with the timber-mill operator, Tom Roland. In an old-fashioned Western, Tom Roland would be the sturdy patriarch of a cattle ranch – Lorne Greene from *Bonanza*, say – but in Mander's hands, the River's first settler makes Alice's life a misery through sexual insensitivity and the never-ending drudgery of labour round the house. Alice is eventually rescued by the male love interest, the cultivated David Bruce, working below his class as Tom's right-hand man, but Bruce must first be saved for femininity by forgoing the demon drink and renouncing his footloose ways. Towards the end of the novel, Alice and David reverse the normal plot direction of a frontier narrative by moving back to Auckland. Their ideal setting turns out to be the parlour of a town house, with art on the walls, Beethoven on the music stand, white lace cloths on the polished side-table. But in *Man Alone*, as in all Westerns, the plot takes us out of town, and towards rural or wilderness settings where the power and presence of women is reduced.

Given its title, it is perhaps appropriate that the most feminine character in *Man Alone* is a slightly built bloke with a Mexican moustache named Scotty. He befriends Johnson early in the novel, and they are mates together on an established Waikato farm, then on a marginal concern hacked out of hill country, and finally in Auckland during the Depression. Scotty is a feminine character (in Western terms) not so much because he likes to take care of the cooking and tidy the hut, but because there are three far worse strikes against him: he knows nothing of war, he talks too much and he wants to settle down. Mulgan's original title, 'Talking of War' is in fact an oxymoron. As Johnson explains, there is nothing to be said about war: 'You wouldn't understand it unless you saw it. If you did see it, you wouldn't understand it' (6). As in the traditional Western, silence is opposed to speech as doing is opposed to talking: the saloon braggart is exposed early, the tenderfoot's theory is always mistaken and, just as surely, Scotty, holding forth confidently about taking a partners' share in Thompson's remote farm, boosts their prospects on land that will swallow all their labour and yield nothing. As Scotty prattles on about the farm, 'the thin man who owned it, said nothing' (24), yet Thompson's capacity to draw on the power of this silence has been damaged. Most properties in the district have been taken up by returned soldiers, but Thompson is the only one who wants to speak of the war, tiresomely rehearsing campaigns until he gives up on his auditors and talks like a nutcase to himself. Pederson, the skipper of a coastal scow, is more the novel's communicative ideal: with the *Sea-Spray* tied up of an evening and the deck moving with the swell, he and Johnson 'would sit there and smoke and talk, though not much, and watch the moon coming up in the sky and the lights ashore, and the riding lights of the yachts and their own light on the mast-head shaking slowly across the sky' (35). The physical sensations and lulling repetitions outweigh the 'not much' of their talk – a bias towards companionable silence capped, only a few sentences later, with the assurance that the old sea-dog 'talked about men he had met and places he had seen sometimes, *but not very often*' (35, my emphasis).

The masculine values of silence extend to Mulgan's treatment of politics and economics. It is a count against Roach, the Cockney union organiser, that he 'talks endlessly, volubly' (51), and against Scotty, too, who has developed an interest in currency reform. An older man says of him: 'That bloody social creditor, . . . if he talked less, I'd listen more' (49). Money is similarly opposed to silence. Like words themselves, money is not real, it only stands for things. It is an artificial system of representation that rewards those who can manipulate its language – buying a farm on credit, making a capital gain, retiring on the proceeds – but men like farmer Blakeway are defined by their property and their meanness, not by anything that is authentic and manly and immediate. Johnson is largely content to work for his keep and a little pocket money, and many of his best days are spent labouring for nothing. Stenning, for example, can't pay him a wage, but rewards his employee with egalitarian silence.

> Johnson could not like Stenning . . . but he liked working with him. He admired his great forearms and his skill with an axe, and the way he drove at the work in a fury of accomplishment. He was good towards Johnson and treated him equally and fairly. When they first went out in the bad days of rain and snow he made it so that Johnson seemed to come of his own accord because he could not leave Stenning to work alone. They worked without talking except sometimes as they ate, and then little; they would work sometimes half a mile apart and not meet all day until Johnson would hear Stenning call and look up to see him leading the horses over for the home ride.
>
> On good days, when the sun shone and the ground perhaps was hard and sharp with frost, it seemed the best life in the world. (88–89)

The mute proximity of his boss lifts Johnson's work into a form of parallel play. It is a vision of unalienated labour, but no revolution of the proletariat ushered it in, just the power of manly silence. The unemployed workers' march up Queen Street is perhaps the key expression of the novel's political theme, but even here, Mulgan seems to require a vocabulary of voicelessness to assert the value of solidarity.

It was a very silent procession that marched, without bands or songs or shouting. Johnson going with them felt this change. He lost the sense of waste and frustration that had been with him. Instead he felt that he had a part in something. What it was he could not have said, but only that he was with men who shared his lack of fortune, who were the same as he was and had the same purpose; that they were going forward together . . . . The same feeling had changed even Roach who marched beside him so that he no longer talked and joked and grumbled, but marched silently with his head up looking forward, and Scotty was no longer ill, but well-looking. (53–54)

If there is a tear in the fabric of this novel, it is not, as Stead argued, to be found in the difference between collective purposeful action and the values of independence and self-reliance. Just as there is no contradiction between the cowboy alone in the desert and the hero on the trail with his 'pardner', just as there is no contradiction between the bloke off pig hunting and the bloke in the pub with his mates, there is really no contradiction between the ideals of 'man alone' and of 'men moving forward together'. But there is a considerable tension between the many passages of quasi-Marxist critique – to do with relief work, currency reform, the 'boom' economy – and Mulgan's unreconstructed belief in the revolutionary power of male silence and the idealised homosociality of the workplace – if I may be permitted these locutions for the inexpressive noun 'real'. While a sub-genre of anti-capitalist Western is conceivable – the smallholder against the unscrupulous cattle baron – *Man Alone* has much more in common with the genre's standard treatment of labour relations and the language of men. The Western uses words to assert the value of everything-that-goes-without-saying in an economy in which the bond between rancher and hired hand is its own reward, and in which money is just one of the false currencies of the town.

A town's limits are a key boundary for the Western. A town has saloons, of course, and maybe prostitutes with hearts of gold, but although the cowboy may be drawn there awhile, he moves out as fast as he can, for its attractions represent everything that might seduce, tie down and entrap him.[31] A sheriff, of course, necessarily lives in the town as the protector of women and children, shopkeepers and teachers, but he has no truck with the unmanly civility of the town. The action will either bring some piece of the frontier – a 'wild bunch' – into a settlement to suspend its meanings, or can only properly begin once the hero leaves Main Street in search of outlaws or Indians. Once again, *Man Alone* lacks the trappings of the genre but is plotted along an identical trail. When Johnson arrives in Auckland from the Great War, he spends only a day and a night before the character's counter is moved across the Bombay Hills to the Waikato. Most of the city action takes place in bars. A good-time girl befriends the newcomer, but the risks she presents to penis and pocket are evaded and Johnson spends his evening swilling – and feeling bloated by – the local brew: 'No-one got merry with the drinking. There was a quietness and sickness over everything and over the other men in the bar' (9). Next morning, as he gazes morosely at the pink floral wallpaper and the faded yellow curtains of his room, he vows, 'I'll get out of this town . . . that's one thing I'll do' (16). It takes the economic slump to bring him back – but Auckland is still no place to be. His partner Scotty says, 'These towns never did me any good', and Johnson replies, 'It's a hell of a way to live, . . . I've got a feeling it's always this way in town' (44). Later, on relief work building the Scenic Drive through the Waitakeres, as Johnson pulls on his 'wet, clay heavy' trousers, he grumbles, 'this comes of living in towns, I'll get to hell out of here the first thing I can, it can't be worse in the country' (46). The Queen Street riots propel his second flight from the city, and before Auckland features again as the scene of a third escape, Johnson's movements follow a circuit through the Central Plateau to Hawke's Bay, and back to 'The Queen of the North' via Hamilton, another town with another woman holding a threat to the hero and his freedom. The fugitive is recognised by the wife of the man he has killed – and he must hightail it out of there.

If it were not for one key difference, Rua, Stenning's wife, could be inserted into any Western not obligated to end with a heterosexual embrace. As the bored and slatternly wife of an older man, she is the novel's main, but by no means its only, emblem of marital entrapment. Her attractions, such as they are, wear out quickly. Johnson tells her, after they first make love, 'There'll be trouble, . . . and trouble's not worth having, not even for you' (109). But of course women bring trouble. Rua becomes pesky and careless, and no sooner has Johnson decided to move on than a flagrant piece of idiocy on her part propels a crisis in which Johnson fights for his life with her crazed, gun-toting husband. The difference is that Rua is Maori. American Westerns of the mid-twentieth century would not countenance a Native American woman in her role – indeed, the genre at its height scarcely features Indians as characters at all. When present, they function, as Jane Tompkins points out, as 'props, bits of local colour, textural effects' – more a 'dangerous form of wildlife' than the characters with motivation and personality, however stereotyped, that one finds prior to the genre's emergence in the novels of James Fenimore Cooper or, after its decline, in revisionist works such as Larry McMurtry's *Lonesome Dove* series.[32]

One of the minor achievements of *Man Alone* is that Mulgan makes neither too little nor too much of the small Maori community Rua comes from. Stenning regards his in-laws with bemused contempt, limiting hospitality to a cup of tea when they come to visit, and remaining aloof from the family. We find him venturing the standard semi-racist opinions of the period – 'They're damn poor farmers' (94), 'Who'll pay for that beer of theirs, nobody knows' (99), and so on – but the Pakeha farmer's point of view is not echoed by Johnson; nor is it strongly undercut by all that might have been made of the contrast between Rua's life in the bosom of the whanau and her lonely misery on Stenning's farm. Mulgan has tried to give an uninflected portrayal of a community, somewhat distanced, that avoids weighing Maori with tendentiously positive qualities, and avoids overcorrecting to the anti-romantic 'realism' of, say, Henry Lawson's 'Daughter of Maoriland'.[33] I do not wish to imply that Mulgan is especially percipient for his time, but I do think the manner of his incorporation of Maori characters into *Man Alone* explains why the Western would never develop a copycat form in New Zealand. Elsewhere, in the USA and Australia, the Western is a genre set in a mythical past that erases the actual past. The memory of genocide, swamping, contagion, the theft of land, the legacy of broken treaties – all of that history fades to the whoop of hostile Indians round a wagon train, or the Tonto figure, helpfully reading tracks for the white lawman in a wilderness nobody owns. There is a half-truth in the notion that New Zealand in the mid-twentieth century could pride itself on having the best race relations in the world: *Man Alone* reminds us that intermarriage and an easy fraternisation were indeed more common here than elsewhere; but had the Maori population been less numerous and more overlookable, our Westerns might have been more like those of our settler cousins than is palatable to admit.

I have no nostalgia for the lost glamour of the Western, for those strong silent types, those 'hard men bred to a hard land' and their dark aura of intimacy with struggle, violence and death. But I still like Westerns, and for much the same reason as I like Western swing, the country music of the jazz era: the books are as readable as the music is danceable. Action does that for you: the grip of a plot is immensely purposive, and for some hours at least, you are plugged into goal-oriented thoughtlessness – for most of us, a 180-degree change from life's usual setting of preoccupied pointlessness. And I also find Westerns interesting historically. The 1930s were a time when a major modern art form – jazz – was the popular music of the day, and it is like that too, in the relation between the tough modern prose styles and attitudes of a Hemingway or a Mulgan and the hard-boiled popular genres of the decade, the Western, and its urban confrère, the crime novel.

The cultural history of 1930s New Zealand is, it seems to me, too often viewed as if a rather earnest and narrowly focused nationalism was all there was to say about it, and as if the only other part of the world that might be mentioned in this connection was the England Alan Mulgan longed to be part of. Apart from *Man Alone*, I might have looked to the poems of Denis Glover, another decorated war hero, to fill out my picture of the New Zealand Western. Here is Arawata Bill, the gold prospector, making a river crossing and heading for the tops:

There's no horse this time,
Going's too rough.
It's a man with an eighty-pound pack,
And that's more than enough.
> Always the colour, in quartz or the river,
> Never the nuggets, as large as a liver.[34]

Or there's Harry, the high-country shepherd and drifter, who leaves 'good land to moulder' and the 'fences sagging' to follow his 'wild thoughts / away over the hill':

Mustering is the life:
Freed of fears and hopes
I watch the sheep like a pestilence
Pouring over the slopes,
> *Sings Harry.*
And the past is thistledown planted on the wind.[35]

Thistledown is white and puffy like sheep coming over the slopes, but I can easily transpose them to the tumbleweed of 'big sky country' and – though the tune will stick like a burr – I might happen to recall a song in praise of the drifter's life called 'Tumbling Tumbleweeds' (by Bob Nolan and the Sons of the Pioneers). This Western swing number became famous thanks to a 1935 Gene Autry movie of the same name; I'd bet my last dollar John Mulgan saw it. But his father's Anglophile loomings are also a continuing part of our story. Douglas Lilburn, setting the 'Harry' poems to music, is infallibly reminded of A. E. Housman's 'A Shropshire Lad' and the English Art Song tradition. No matter who sings them, those songs in that setting sound pompous and lardy. Like *Man Alone*, they belong to another version of pastoral.

CHAPTER ELEVEN

Cathedral Rock: Allen Curnow in Italy

> *The carriages followed a prescribed course . . . past the Badia and*
> *the Bargello, beneath the great tessellated cliffs of the Cathedral*
> *. . . and out into ten minutes' sunshine beside the Arno.*
> *– Henry James,* Italian Hours

IN TURNER'S PAINTING *APPROACH TO VENICE*, THE SERENE CITY OF palaces and domes floats on the horizon as if in a mirage, backlit in a wash of gold and creamy light between the blue of the sky and sea. Proust wrote of that unearthly city, 'When I went to Venice, I found that my dream had become – incredibly but quite simply – my address.'[1] For a more recent visitor, the dream is like a Fellini movie: I am sitting with a guidebook at a café table when, glimpsed between and above the buildings across the canal, a cruise ship glides past, impossibly large and close, and the water half a minute later 'slap-slops' against the steps in an afterthought of wake. As Lord Byron said, 'Venice pleases me as much as I expected – and I expected much – it is one of those places which I know before I see them – and has always haunted me.'[2] Italy is always likely to do strange things to a visitor's accustomed sense of novelty and familiarity, anticipation and realisation, but on this occasion, the uncanniness comes, I soon realise, from a poem by Allen Curnow. It begins with him sitting 'at Nico's tables / on Zattare' on a sunny April morning in 1978; the passing Chioggia car ferry makes the water 'slap-slop to the feet of the old / angler who trolls / past the Geusati church', while the poet, 'deciphering' his newspaper, follows developments in the police hunt for the kidnapped politician, Aldo Moro.

Allen Curnow came late to Italy. He was 63, two years away from retirement and on his last university leave, when he and his wife Jeny first arrived, by ship, in February 1974. An unusual amount of 'Italian luggage' would have accompanied them: a canon of prior literary responses from Goethe and Byron through Ruskin and Henry James to Proust and Pound, not to mention all the art books, operas and concertos, the travel guides, the anecdotes and tips of friends, even the kind of memories one has from watching Kenneth Clark's *Civilisation* on colour TV. And with the luggage a question: can a place as old as Italy be 'something different, something / Nobody counted on'?[3]

After a first week in Florence, Jeny was called home to attend a family emergency; Allen stayed with his brother in Geneva until she returned, three weeks later. They then spent three weeks in Venice, staying at Ruskin's old house, had a week in Ravenna, and returned to Florence in mid-April, for a further two weeks. They were in Sicily for most of May and concluded the Italian leg of their trip with two weeks in Rome. After briefer visits to Geneva and France, they based themselves in London for three months and returned home in December after a six-week stay in the United States. Almost half of a full year's leave had been devoted to Italy; Florence, the first and then the midpoint of their visit, would have been special for all the usual reasons, but as they were there at Easter time, they made a point of observing the celebration of High Mass in the Duomo.[4]

The poem 'In the Duomo' is part of a sequence entitled *An Incorrigible Music*, published in book form in 1979, but appearing in the literary journal *Islands* a year earlier as one of three poems excerpted from a sequence of the same name. Those three poems – 'Canst Thou Draw Out Leviathan with an Hook?', 'In the Duomo' and 'Bring Your Own Victim' – formed a series of interconnecting poems in the manner of Curnow's most recently published work, the sequence *Trees, Effigies, Moving Objects* (1972). In *Islands*, the three poems appeared without punctuation – a practice that places stress on syntax and the management of line endings – but Curnow subsequently thought better of that experiment and introduced the usual commas and full stops in the final version. I have counted over two dozen tinkering changes between the first and second appearance of these poems, but none of the revisions is especially significant. Each of the poems that appeared in *Islands* is only a whisker away from its final published form, and is already part of a fully conceived and titled longer work. Indeed, all the poems in *An Incorrigible Music* except one had been written before the Curnows left for a second trip to Italy, early in April 1978.

The three poems published in *Islands* – one set at Karekare, one set in fifteenth-century Florence and a third connecting the themes of the other two – are the ridgepole of the original sequence. Others radiate like rafters from that central line of thematic continuity. But the centrepiece of the published book is undoubtedly 'Moro Assassinato' – a poem in nine sections, and by some pages the longest of the individual poems or mini-sequences that make up the volume. Although it reads as if it might have been the single key poem that prompted the writing of others, 'Moro Assassinato' was in fact the uncanny postscript to an already completed work. The post-retirement trip to Italy had been long planned: besides the simple joy of returning, Curnow needed to check up on details and make final revisions to the longer version of the sequence announced in *Islands*. But he arrived to find that the sacrificial themes and political violence he had been writing about were unfolding in a real-life drama involving one of Italy's most senior politicians, Aldo Moro. The former prime minister had been abducted by the Red Brigade on 16 March and was still being held at a secret location when the Curnows arrived. The press reported daily on the ineffective police efforts to find him; from time to time, they also published pleas from Moro's wife, a series of increasingly anguished letters from Moro himself, as well as weekly communiqués from his captors, the last of which announced that Moro's execution had taken place on 9 May. Almost exactly 500 years earlier, the ruling Medici family had been targeted by assassins, and those events – the so-called Pazzi conspiracy – had been the subject of 'In the Duomo', the historical lynchpin of the earlier version of the sequence. The poem's setting moves between worlds, as Karekare beach dissolves into and out of a narrative of political intrigue set in the Italian Renaissance. And then came 'something nobody counted on' – 'Moro Assassinato' – a poem with all the urgencies of a banner headline in the Italian press, yet haunted by the echo of those earlier times and the roar of distant beaches.

The Pazzi were an internationally eminent family of Florentine bankers and merchants who had been shaded by the rise to dominance of those fifteenth-century parvenus, the Medici. The Pazzi were old money. Their closest financial and ideological ties were with the ecclesiastical establishment; geopolitically, they looked to the Papal States and the Kingdom of Naples to the south. The Medici, by contrast, were bourgeois humanists, receptive to classical knowledge and independent thinking, and associated with new flows of capital. Their allies were Venice and Milan in the north. Florence in the late fifteenth century was nominally a republic, but little happened without the consent of its most powerful citizen, Lorenzo de' Medici. This humanist poet manipulated tax laws to confiscate Pazzi wealth, blocked their advancement and diverted patronage away from his rivals. When the Pazzi's relative, Pope Sixtus IV, appointed one of their cousins as Archbishop of Pisa, Lorenzo barred the prelate from entering the city. If you were a friend of the Medici, Lorenzo was magnificent; if you were connected to the Pazzi, the Medici had grown into tyrants. The scorned Archbishop Salviati and his Pazzi cousins, with the connivance of Sixtus IV and the Duke of Urbino, planned a *coup d'état* in Florence. The conspirators knew they had to remove the two foremost members of the Medici family in one stroke: if they got only Lorenzo, the Medici would rally round his younger brother Guiliano, and if they got only Guiliano, they would be leaving their most formidable opponent in play. Opportunity after opportunity fell through, until at last a favourable conjunction of events meant they could get enough armed mercenaries into Florence and have assassins ready to strike, if only Lorenzo and Guiliano could be brought together in one place. A diplomatic reception for a visiting Cardinal was first choice, but when Guiliano turned out to be indisposed, the conspirators opted for High Mass in the cathedral next morning.

As so often happens in Allen Curnow's poetry, the ostensible settings of 'In the Duomo' are overlaid with others in a 'ply-on-ply' pattern of loomings and palimpsest-like effects. Florence's cathedral morphs into Karekare's Cathedral Rock, a popular surf-casting spot, and the setting for the first poem in the sequence, 'Canst Thou Draw out Leviathan with an Hook?' Either of those great domes will at times suggest the shell of a snail – and dead snails feature in the sequence's second poem, 'A Balanced Bait in Handy Pellet Form', surely one of the few poems ever devoted to the subject of 'Slug-Slam'. 'Recitative', the first section of 'In the Duomo', looks back to the two preceding poems in a manner that will keep fishing from Cathedral Rock and shell shapes as active zones of reference in this opening description of Florence's cathedral. The time is not specified, but it appears to be the present day, and Mass is in progress.

> This is the rock where you cast your barbed wishes.
>> That is the clifftop where you hang by the eyes.
>> Here is where Leviathan lives.

> It is all in the walls of one great shell incised.
>> The instructions look simple, the trouble is the smoky
>> ambiguous morning sunlight, the heights inside

> the cathedral are blurred. So much for art, which only
>> comprehends the introversions of arches,
>> lunettes, capitals, where the sunlight slowly

> floats up towards their rock-hung perches
>> motes moths wings claws human hands fluttering
>> prayers kites clapping gustily to barefoot beaches,

> the tidiness of a carved by time discoloured
>> eminence being magnetic to such poor untidy
>> littles or nothings,

> bits and pieces, yet 'of such' is the highly
>> esteemed 'kingdom of heaven', what else?
>> Imagine an enormous face, conceive it smiling

> to an accompaniment of birds and bells
>> down blurred clifftops, makebelieve masonry,
>> by interior sunlight extinguished at eye level

> which is rock bottom. Here the linens, the sacred
>> silverware are arranged and the blood is poured
>> by experienced hands which do not shake

serving up to Messer Domeneddio god and lord
    the recycled eternity of his butchered son,
    this mouthful of himself alive and warm.

This is homoousianus, this is the cup
    to catch and keep him in, this is where he floats
    in a red cloud of himself, this is morning sun

blotting the columns, the ogives, the hollowed throne,
    smoking the kite-high concavity of the cliff.
    This is the question, *Caught any fish?*
                      Say, *No.*

I am teaching Leviathan to swim.[5]

'Homoousianus' means 'of the same essence': the wafer of bread transubstantiated into the body of Christ. A portion of the white host, dropped into the chalice, floats in red wine, and brings to mind these lines from the opening poem of the sequence:

A rockpool catches the blood,
so that in a red cloud of itself
the kahawai lies white belly uppermost. (11)

Kahawai bleed copiously. This image of a fish floating in a pool of its own blood is the second of what will soon be a three-term comparison. After the assassins in the cathedral strike,

Giuliano de' Medici
bled where he had to bleed,
bedrock flat on the church floor
in the cloud he made
of the strong bestial smell
of dissolving clay,
their offering to the oldest god
that holiest day. (20)

Blood, death and sacrifice are distributed in *An Incorrigible Music* through three orders of being – from the divine to the human to the natural – as if these realms were connected in a gory and impure version of the Great Chain of Being. There has earlier been a visual hint of that vertical line in the image of a drowned fisherman washed from Cathedral Rock: 'white belly to wetsuit black, swung copular / under the winching chopper's bubble' (10); and this vertical dimension registers more fully in the 'Recitative' section when the motes of dust floating upward in a shaft of light towards the cupola of the cathedral are compared to specks of humanity being drawn, as if by magnetic attraction, upwards towards the heavenly dome, to the enormous smiling face of 'Messer Domeneddio god and lord' (15), who in turn looks down through 'the kite-high concavity' (15) to the sacrifice enacted in the rite of the Eucharist on the altar below.

The next section begins with a quotation from Dante's *Inferno* describing Phlegethon, a river of boiling blood in the Seventh Circle of Hell, in which the bodies of those who committed crimes of violence are immersed. We are then introduced to Gian-Battista Montesecco, leader of the papal mercenaries seconded to the Pazzi family. The Count of Montesecco features in most histories of the conspiracy as its military advisor – a professional soldier whose sense of what was practicable was insufficiently heeded by the zealous and impatient leaders of the coup. In Curnow's poem, Montesecco becomes a hit-man with a conscience. His problem was 'believing / everything he read, the divinest poets / told the sublimest lies' (16), and – in the poem at least – he is convinced that the knights who ridded Henry of that turbulent priest, Thomas Becket, are stewing in Dante's river. 'I'll dagger you a dozen Medici at anybody's table / except Christ's' (17).

Curnow, we shall see, has another reason for introducing Dante, but in calling the next narrative section of his poem 'A Turning Point in History', he is developing a hint from that connoisseur of historical irony, Niccolò Machiavelli, who, in his *History of Florence*, argues that if Montesecco really was reluctant to commit sacrilege by killing the Medici brothers in a church, his unanticipated qualms altered the course of history, for the experienced assassin and man of action had to be substituted at short notice by two dim but obedient priests,

Maffei and Stefano – and even the author of the *Da Vinci Code* might have had trouble imagining them as a pair of ruthless killers. The poem picks up the story.

> *Ite missa est.*
> The rite being said and done,
> in a scarlet stir the hit-men edged
> each to his man.
> Lorenzo dropped his shoulder
> quicker than Maffei struck
> his fumbled blow [. . .]
>
> Stefano got no closer
> than a dagger's draw [. . .]
>
> and the two young Cavalcanti
> joined Il Magnifico,
> and they knifed it out in the sacristy
> to save Lorenzo,
> leaving his brother dead
> where he had to die
> face down, by the Pazzi's jabbing steel
> dancing wasp time. (19–20)

Curnow's focus is entirely on the murder in the Cathedral. In fact, the plotters also failed to storm the palace and raise the populace, and the whole sorry train of events might conceivably be told as farce. One of Guiliano's killers illustrated what is likely to happen to assassins who grip a knife the wrong way: with a downward thrust, Francesco Pazzi missed his mark and only succeeded in stabbing himself deeply in the thigh. Over in the palace, Montesecco's band of mercenaries had just begun their uprising when, on pulling shut the doors to a room, they found they had managed to lock themselves in. It might have been farce, but the aftermath was implacably grim and remorseless. Those immediately involved were quickly rounded up and unceremoniously hanged from the windows of the Palazzo Vecchio; Archbishop Salviati, dancing at the end of a rope, sunk his teeth into the chest of the conspirator hanging next to him. The mutilated bodies of the conspirators became playthings of the mob and instruments of terror; others with more distant Pazzi connections were hunted down and put to death in the cruellest of ways. Within a few months, hundreds of possible sympathisers had been tortured and executed, and over the coming years Medici assassins found their targets in distant cities.

For most historians, the significance of the Pazzi conspiracy lies in its violent aftermath. Machiavelli shrewdly observed that when a ruler creates the conditions in which conspiracy thrives, even the most liberal-minded of men will become cruel and tyrannical. More recent commentators have a quasi-tabloid, quasi-anthropological interest in uncovering the gangland underbelly of the High Renaissance, as Lorenzo, humanist poet and 'boss of bosses' survives a hit and rubs out his rivals.[6] The scandal, the mystery, is that so much art and so much violence should co-exist at a time and place reputed to be a pinnacle of Western civilisation.

It strikes me that Allen Curnow is unsurprised by all this, and that this is why his version of the story of the Pazzi conspiracy is told the way it is, with those glances at Dante and that peculiar emphasis on Montesecco as a man with qualms, and with the foreshortened focus on a single corpse on the cathedral floor. And I think it is also why the poem does not tell us what happened next, but switches its location to another cathedral.

> I tried from the cathedral
>   yesterday and had no luck,
>   Mrs Dragicevic said.

> Slaty grey strata
>   angled and squared abutted
>   the clubfoot of the cliff

> where she perched, this plump
>   vigilant bird, in her blue
>   quilted parka, pointing her

4.0 m. fibreglass pole
> over each big wave that walked
>> white from the west

with a long bearded howl,
> broke roaring into a run
>> for the rocks to come.

And the spot was a good one,
> the cathedral, so long as you kept
>> your head for heights

and the big ones came,
> il magnifico and his brothers
>> to the turn of the tide,

having to, having to come
> leaping to the holy lure,
>> an acceptable offering

to the blooding hand, the scaling,
> the scarlet clouded pool,
>> the necessary knife. (20–21)

One of the most striking things about this closing section of the poem is the way it converts the chances of surf-casting into the language of necessity. 'Having to, having to come / leaping to holy lure'. But every fisherman knows there's no 'having to' about it – if there were, as the old saying goes, it would be called catching not fishing. But when a big one does bite, when the rod bends and the adrenalin rushes, when the exhausted fish is played out and landed, one must 'never let them die of the air':

pick up your knife and drive it
through the gills with a twist,
let the blood run fast,
quick bleeding makes best eating. (10)

The phrasing of that last line has the unanswerable force of proverb. While most fishermen do deal with kahawai in this age-old way, I am told a revisionist school is scornful of the practice. The flesh of kahawai is suffused with a reddish black discolouration along the spinal column, but the revisionists argue that 'quick bleeding' will neither reduce its extent nor make a difference to the succulence of the white meat: the belief that it does so is a type of magical thinking.[7] Or so I gathered when I heard the skipper of a charter boat putting one of his customers right on the barbarity of that practice. 'How would you like to be stabbed through the lungs?', he asked, as he reached instructively for an instrument known as the priest and demonstrated how a *coup de grâce* is more humanely administered with one to two decisive blows to the head. As most fish caught on that boat went straight into the chilly bin where they did 'drown of the air', I suspect the skipper's sensitivities were outraged not through tender-heartedness but because his customer had swallowed an old saying hook, line and sinker. The words sounded right but they perpetuated a needless cruelty.

This is an example of the example the poem itself makes. I will say more about this recursive quality shortly, but for the moment it is enough to notice that Curnow is once again involving questions of how words relate to the world and how mind relates to matter – topics that had long been of interest to him. Put schematically, many of Curnow's poems explore problems of connection and disjunction between two levels of reality: there is the human world of language and culture, and there is the world as it exists apart from our symbolisations of it. Let us also suppose there are two orders of morality: the humane and the inhumane. Those levels and orders might line up (as if to be human were to be humane) but they almost never do: there is slippage between them. Thus, in the lines quoted above, a fisherman catches a kahawai and drives a knife through the gills with a twist; the poet then gives that twist a turn away from gory reality through the simple linguistic parallelism that gives so many of our aphorisms their sticking power: 'quick bleeding makes best eating'.

A phrase like this, and the condition of language generally, is the theme of the poem's next section.

An insult in the form of an apology
is the human answer to the inhuman
which rears up green roars down white,
and to the fish which is fearless. (10)

The poet goes on to imagine that only a human who is no longer human can be acquainted with the world on the world's own terms – the poem's drowned fisherman is 'fluent at last / in the languages of the sea' (11) – but that, of course, is also to know nothing, to be fearless as a fish is fearless. Imagining a language of the actual makes the human and the non-human seem very far apart. Yet many fishermen, many people, immersed as we are in a sub-branch of Dante's river, do spare a humane thought for any life we are taking. Why call a small heavy wooden club a priest? It goes with administering last rites and our liking for incongruity, but the phrase also signals our human inclination to shape inhuman actions and events by means of ritual. Ritual is a mode of conversion and re-contextualisation: that which is profane becomes sacred, that which is corporeal becomes transcendent, that which is contingent becomes necessary. And the hinge, the still point of conversion, is often a moment of violence or a substitution for one.

The third of the poems initially published in *Islands*, 'Bring Your Own Victim', emphasises this.

For Isaac the ram,
        for Iphigeneia the goat,
under the knife in the nick
        was the substitute.

The rule was never to notice
        what had taken place
by the sea, in the thicket, the thing
        was your sacrifice.

Agamemnon didn't inquire
        nor did Abraham,
would the highest settle for a goat
        or oblige with a ram?

The heavens might be humane
but you never knew,
you sharpened your knife, you did
what they said to do. (27)

'History', adds Curnow in the next section, 'began to be true / at a later time' (27).

On 9 May 1978, the bullet-riddled body of Aldo Moro was found crumpled up in the boot of a Renault 4 in Rome's Via Caetani. Fifty-four days earlier, Moro, President of the National Council of Christian Democrats, had been kidnapped by members of the Red Brigade. His police escort of five men were all murdered. The same evening, after the news had broken, the new Christian Democrat government, which had been facing collapse, and which Moro had been endeavouring to shore up through a series of delicate negotiations with the Communist Party, had its mandate confirmed by a sizeable majority that included support from the far left. One act of violence had done more to unify Parliament than Moro's fragile web of diplomacy, but that unified front would go on to demand the sacrifice of individuals. The police had been unable to find any trace of Moro or his captors. Within a few days, a communiqué from the Red Brigade declared their intention of putting Moro on trial before a 'People's Court of Justice'; the Brigade's leader was at that time on trial in Turin. After several weeks, another communiqué indicated that the Brigade was prepared to release Moro in exchange for the liberation of a certain number of 'political prisoners' but Andreotti's government refused to negotiate with terrorists, even though similar deals had been brokered in the past. Many have speculated why the deputy leader of the Christian Democrats should have done so little to aid the president of his own party. In the end, both the Red Brigade and the government sacrificed Moro for political ends: the former hoped to foment a crackdown that would re-radicalise the quiescent Communist Party; the latter cited the security of the state and, in a bizarre explanation of the legal situation in respect of Brigade members already convicted by the courts, cited a 'moral obligation to honour the sufferings of those families which mourn the tragic consequences of the terrorists' crime'.[8]

Moro wrote to his former colleagues in these terms:

With profound bitterness and amazement I have seen you adopt, without any serious, humane or political appreciation, an attitude of rigid finality . . . . Can you really all agree in wanting my death for a so-called reason of State, which someone treacherously presents to you as a solution to all the nation's problems? . . . . I plainly declare that for my part I cannot absolve nor justify anyone . . . . Say at once that you refuse to make an immediate stark reply, a reply that involves death. Dispel at once the image of a party unanimously determined to kill . . . . I am sentenced to death. The execution of this sentence depends on you. I ask no more than that my reprieve be granted – that it be granted for none other than the vital reason, . . . that my family needs my care, help, and guidance.[9]

Moro's letters of captivity were written in a way that constantly affirmed he was a person, a member of a family, a friend appealing to friends, not only in response to the impersonal violence of revolutionary fanatics but more particularly in response to the depersonalising violence of the state. Ironically, the more candid and direct his letters, the more his political colleagues allowed themselves to suspect that the letters were not Moro speaking, to imagine that their old friend wrote under duress, or had been betrayed into the pitiful register of the personal through an understandable weakness of character, the more readily, one imagines, they grasped at the iron principles by which they found themselves compelled to inaction.

In a 1987 investigation of the Moro affair, the Italian journalist Leonardo Sciascia made what has come to seem a prescient observation.

Two Stalinisms are in conflict – and I use the handy, contemporary word for something far older, 'something' which has always served a few inhuman human beings to indoctrinate the minds and emotions of men and wring suffering and blood from them. Or rather, it is the two halves of one and the same thing which are in conflict. And they are slowly, inexorably joining up again to squash anyone who happens to stand between them. The conscious, overt, violent and ruthless Stalinism of the Red Brigades . . . . and the insidious crafty Stalinism [of the state] which treats individuals as palimpsests, erasing what was written and rewriting it to serve their cause.[10]

Caught between those forces is the 'prisoner of the people', Aldo Moro – someone who 'doesn't want to be squashed'.[11]

Moro was courageous and lucid in his determination not to accept the assigned role of victim and, in a letter quoted in the poem, explicitly ruled out any participation by members of the government in his funeral. As it happened, his wishes were bypassed; his small private funeral was eclipsed by a state memorial service in which the Pope himself celebrated Mass. It is perhaps difficult for anyone writing about his predicament or the circumstances of his death to avoid finding in them a larger or more ritualistic significance. Moro – despite his own horror at and resistance to interpretative scenarios in which his death stands for something other than itself – is sacrificed, perhaps to the cruelty of a principle, perhaps to something else we would find difficult to name. Sciascia, whom I have quoted with approval, saw a man crushed between two forms of 'Stalinism' that bind the state to its enemies in an age of terrorism – but he also connected this to a primordial inhumanity, to a 'something' obscure or peculiar enough to require, in his repetition of that indeterminate word, the mantle of a set of inverted commas.

Allen Curnow must have faced a difficulty of tact when, with a finished sequence that was rather short for a book, circumstances presented him with the poetic equivalent of a scoop. The Moro affair was ripe for development within the terms already set by such poems as 'In the Duomo' and 'Bring Your Own Victim', but that is not to say that history was repeating itself. It is unlikely that anyone else following the news of Moro's kidnapping and murder in the Italian papers would have been reminded ineluctably of the Pazzi conspiracy, or noted an uncanny conjunction of dates in the 500 years between 1478 and 1978. All the similarities were willed similarities. Consider, for example, the way Curnow imagines the moment of Moro's death from the point of view of one of his executioners.

> . . . Gesù! he saw them
>
>   coming, the rods in our hands,
>   at one metre's range

the Beretta 7.65s
had to hit the left hunch-breast

eleven times, the grey head
whiplashed, nodding to the shots

yes yes yes yes
            yes yes yes
yes yes yes yes. (47)

The word 'rod' is Chicago gangster for gun, but it is the Cathedral
Rock sections of the poem that have determined this particular word
choice. This is the kind of subtle embroidery that makes the poems
into a sequence, but two other details also owe their existence to the
already scripted poems: the bullets 'had' to hit their target presumably because at that distance it would have been difficult to miss, but
the word choice is clearly designed to echo those verbs of necessity
– 'having to, having to come' – from the end of 'In the Duomo'. In his
letters, Moro made the countervailing point over and over: there was
no 'had to' about it; the Brigade should have let him go, the government
should have acted. And there is a perhaps questionable poetic licence
in the conversion of Moro's personal and unequivocal 'No' into the
string of eleven yeses that constitute what an earlier section of the
poem calls, 'the victim's / yes to the crime' (40).

Moro's assassination, which already involved a questionable sacrificial logic, becomes the subject of ritual over again in the poem – and
readers might well be repulsed by the figure of the poet brandishing
the bloody bandages of history and bewailing the evil that men do for
his own bookish ends. The opening lines of 'Moro Assassinato' indicate why such a response is not without foundation.

All the seas are one sea,
the blood one blood
and the hands one hand.

Ever is always today. (34)

The trouble with this rhetorically powerful frame is that it risks turning all acts of violence into an endless repetition of the same – but are 'the tales [. . .] all one tale' (34), as the poem goes on to assert? Only when viewed from an inhuman distance. The implication of Curnow's pronouncements about the ubiquity of violence – 'merely to exist being even for the gentlest / the rape of another's breath or bread' (16) – is that if we look hard at reality we will not like what we see: life is a killing floor, and it's ghastly. Why set one's compass by that point? Andrew Johnston, in a searching and powerful essay, has argued that Curnow's 'furiously knowing self' is committed to finding what it knows wherever it looks.[12] If 'ever is always today', there is no room for contingency, no openness to the new experience of the new moment. 'Curnow's denial of contingency', he concludes, 'leads to his ahistorical focus on human cruelty, rather than its obverse, shared historical suffering. The consequence of such essentialism . . . is to close off the possibility of solidarity.'[13]

There is an older argument behind this one. As Johnston himself points out, the charges he makes against Curnow reprise Keats's response to what the younger romantic poet called 'Wordsworth's egotistical sublime'.[14] And the qualities of openness to the experience of others that Johnston finds missing in Curnow are the very qualities Keats commends in his association of imaginative achievement with 'negative capability' – the power to empathise, to be transfixed by beauty, to remain 'in uncertainties, mysteries, doubts, without any irritable reaching after fact and reason'.[15] It may be true that few poets are less like John Keats than the un-chameleonlike Allen Curnow, but there is another side to this implied comparison too. Where Johnston associates the phrase that gives this sequence its title – *An Incorrigible Music* – with 'our capacity for evil', in reading the collection and the title poem, I am more inclined to recall 'the still sad music of humanity' that Wordsworth wrote of in 'Tintern Abbey'.[16] Curnow, like Wordsworth, is a tireless phenomenologist of his own feelings and sensations, but it is a mistake to charge either poet with solipsism on that account, with a lack of interest in how things seem to others, or with the bleak inflexibilities projected by a controlling ego. On the contrary, there is much empathy in the way both Curnow and Wordsworth write about themselves not so much from a perspective that is personal as from a perspective that is representative. Curnow has a special fondness for the pronouns 'you' and 'your' – he means himself, of course, but also us too. It is a voice that is not saying 'this is special', but 'this is ordinary' – which is why there is that odd tendency, noted earlier, for him to find that 'all the seas are one sea, / the blood one blood'.

The most insistent word in 'Moro Assassinato' is the word 'normality'. Each of the opening four stanzas of the fourth section of the poem, dealing with the kidnapping, begin with it.

> Normality was the moment's
> mixture, moment by moment
> improvising myself,
> ideas, sensations, among them
> the lacquered acridities
> of ducted air in the car,
> accelerations, decelerations,
> nothing to be trusted further
> than the mixture's moment. (39)

The very next moment – 'the ambush, / the crashed cars and the guards / gunned down dead in the street' (39) – is not what anyone would consider to be normal, but the speaker of the poem, in Moro's voice, insists on a connection: 'Normality is, do you follow? / a condition very like mine' (39). Immured in the 'Prison of the People', the sensations, memories and thoughts that constitute the 'mixture's moment' of individual consciousness roll on. To overlook the normality of this is to overlook the ordinary fact that Moro's own consciousness also continues through the hours and minutes of his imprisonment; and to overlook that is already to begin to discount his existence – a notion explored in another key in 'Things to do with Moonlight'. In this poem, the poet, simply by thinking about Descartes while piddling, conjures up the old philosopher's ghost in an encounter that playfully wonders whether the *ergo sum* of the famous *cogito* ought to have been *sumus* (I think, therefore *we* are). The other side of Cartesian sympathy is that thinking about Aldo Moro is necessarily to think the mixture's moment of one's self, which is why the kidnapped politician's line about 'normality being a condition very like mine' modulates into the personal voice of the poet in another of the sequence's stunningly effective hemispheric shifts.

> The child I was would have known
> better than the man I am,
>
> when they tripped him, trapped him,
> ripped his shirt, emptied his bag,
>
> caught him, laughed him to tears,
> rubbed cowshit into his hair,
>
> the irreversible justice
> of the wrong once done, the victim's
>
> yes to the crime. Who knows
> he had to be punished knows
>
> how the women who wipe away
> the tears and shit
>
> heal no hurt but their own.
> Tell the bullet to climb
>
> back up the barrel and close
> the wound behind it. They carried me,
>
> carrying the child who could teach me
> my case was not so special. (40)

Empathy is not undone just because it has limits. The problem for the poet, as I remarked earlier, is more one of maintaining a tactful balance between being able to sympathise with another's common reality, and keeping the distance appropriate to the traveller, to the onlooker deciphering the news in the Italian papers, to the poet for whom these events have propitiously fallen to hand. If the best antidote to the perils of indifference is to keep one's eye on the ordinary – every child knows what it is like to be bullied – the best antidote to the perils of over-identification lies with ordinary moments too. 'Moro Assassinato' ends with a gesture of solidarity with those who continued to leave flowers in the Via Caetani and with the written memorials of the poor, whose modest death notices – just a name on a small piece of newsprint, a black bar printed above and below – are 'run off at the *tipografia* / round the corner'(50) and pasted up on doors and doorways. There is a finely judged distance in the instance of sympathy with which 'Moro Assassinato' ends: a tourist sees an old woman in a doorway, the inscription 'Per Aldo Moro' pasted above; the words having rolled off the platen much as the published poem, repeating the typographical gesture, 'strikes off one more' (50).

An Incorrigible Music began as a study of the place of ritual in scenarios of violence, and of the way ritual, like language, is a system of arbitrary signs that articulates a real world. Curnow was able, later on, to find he had set himself a series of parameters within which he could see the ordinariness in an act of extreme political violence, and see through to its far side, in the spontaneous rituals of grief and sympathy with which that poem closes. When I think of the role Italy played in this book's inception, I am reminded of another of those first-time visitors to Italy who found the old world had anticipated his own. When Freud looked at the paintings we see in the treasure houses of Rome, Florence and Venice, at the Adoration scenes, at the portraits of Madonna and Child, it was to find that his counter-intuitive hunches and speculations had always had a simple and unaffected expression. Something old loomed in something he thought was new.

'Landfall in Unknown Seas', written by Curnow in 1942, commemorates the three-hundredth anniversary of the 'discovery' of our new world by the Dutch explorer Abel Tasman in 1642. It is perhaps the most ambitious and fully realised poem on a national theme ever written in this country – and is often performed with the fine 'Suite for String Orchestra' that Douglas Lilburn composed to go with it. The last section of the poem derides the fatuous celebration of national identity – 'speeches / Pinning on the Past like a decoration / For merit that congratulates itself' – and invokes as a counter-memory the violence of that first encounter between our European and Maori forebears at Golden Bay, and the protraction of that moment in 'the stain of blood that writes an island story'.[17] Another of his poems, 'Spectacular Blossom', begins with a picture-postcard Auckland scene: pohutukawa in blossom, their branches dipping in the incoming tide, red filaments collecting in rock pools, and from that everyday beach setting other realities loom. The tree is a young woman 'shuffling red petals' and tossing flowers as she walks towards a scene of ritual slaughter where 'the shallows kiss like knives'; in an astonishing last stanza, Curnow imagines the December wind as the 'Wristiest slaughterman' who 'smooths / the temple bones and parts the grey-blown brows / With humid fingers', so that, from bark to blossom, 'woody tumours burst in scarlet spray [. . .] On beaches where the knees of light crash down' – like cattle in an abattoir. At Governor's Bay, in the poem 'At Dead Low Water', the sea goes out a long way, leaving in the 'Sump of opulent tides' such emblems of transience as a holed dingy, 'bolt and strake frilled' with trailing weed, or the poet's own footprint 'Brimming and fading, vanishing'. In 'You Will Know When You Get There' – a poem from the 1982 collection – the beach is a place to imagine one's journey to death, as a man goes down 'the last steep kilometre' to the beach to pick mussels, as the earth 'rolls back and away' from the setting sun, and:

> A door
> slams, a heavy wave, a door, the sea-floor shudders.
> Down you go alone, so late, into the surge-black fissure.

For Curnow, the beach is a place of first things and last things, of transience and transubstantiation. I suspect he saw something of everything that beaches meant to him in the cathedrals and galleries of Italy, too, in the crucifixions, the martyrdoms, the Last Judgements, and found looming in those masterpieces and in the sacrificial rituals of the Church the reverberation of a darker and persistent reality: the stain of blood that writes a human story.

CHAPTER TWELVE

Placing Frame

The human race is an elsewhere race . . .
– Dinny Wheatstone in The Carpathians

EVERY TIME I GO INTO MY GARDEN TO PICK A FEW STALKS OF rhubarb', wrote Janet Frame, 'I like to think of Marco Polo's travels and the chapter headed, "Of the district of Succuir, where the rhubarb is produced, and from whence it is carried to all parts of the world".'[1] Rhubarb, she went on to observe, is also the word actors mumble to each other when miming meaningless sociable patter. Her remarks on its circulation come from the essay 'Departures and Returns' (1981), which begins with Frame contemplating a visiting celebrity author being interviewed for local television: 'And why have you chosen to visit this country? . . . . Oh, I've come here to gather material for a book.' The answer, received like a compliment, flatters our sense of good fortune in possessing what a visiting writer would come *all this way* to find: 'atmosphere, material, and a view while working'. And when such a book comes out, offering a 'kind of taste' of elsewhere, its readers are likely to feel they too have been taken on a journey, one which 'licenses [them] to say, proudly . . . "I've read about it, I know the people and their customs"'. In contrast to the rhubarb of these 'mutually valued supermarket recognitions', Frame posits the case of a visiting poet who fails to take advantage of our atmosphere, our material or the view out the writer's window. When the poems are eventually published, the media gets wind of a criticism: '"Poet Says Our Country is . . . thus . . . and thus . . .".'. The citizens protest indignantly, "It's not true. Libellous!"' But a group of aslant-looking poems written from afar may well have gone 'right to the heart of the place'. 'It's hard', Frame says, 'to change the idea of truth as an exterior geographical conception, limited to the eye's seeing.'

Frame herself was a traveller, and many of her books tell the story of a journey to a distant place and an alien experience of life, of characters in exile or confinement who must weigh the perils and attractions of a return home. And yet this writer, with her evident attachment to the country of her birth, goes on in 'Departures and Returns' to report a conversation with a friend who asks: why all this gallivanting to Manhattan and Baltimore and Berkeley – 'Why don't you stay at home like Jane Austen? . . . . You can travel to foreign lands without moving from your own backyard.' Frame concedes the point only to insist, bluntly, 'But I have no backyard. I have lost it.'[2]

It seems an odd comment from a writer who spoke of picking rhubarb from her own garden only a moment before. The contradiction has an explanation, but for the moment let us take it as if she had brandished a passport from 'Elsewhere' – from an ordinary garden in which a writer might look up from 'earnestly digging' to see the camel trains of Marco Polo winding through the mountain passes of the Tararuas. It is a backyard opening onto an elsewhere she has sometimes called 'Mirror City', or 'the room two inches behind the eyes', or 'the Manifold' or 'the Kingdom by the Sea'.[3] We hear rumours about what that place is like. Some suppose it is reached on Janet's own special wavelength, and – like the canvasses of Vincent Van Gogh – is just how things would look if you were a creative genius with abnormal sensitivities. An equally naïve view of art and art-making underpins the findings of medical researchers who have recently replaced Frame's early misdiagnosis of schizophrenia with a posthumous verdict of 'high-functioning autism' – a condition apparently detectable from the pages of her books, since her creative genius cannot help but express it.[4] This is no more scientific than a diagnosis of witchcraft, but there is a nice irony in the way these researchers have focused so fixatedly on autism that they were unable to detect the manifest signs of insight, empathy and solidarity that ought to have precluded their findings. More fully than most, Frame lived a paradox of the writing life: she needed both isolation and discipline to communicate at a high level, and she managed her life in the concentration of that end, not merely as a reflex of shyness and anxiety.

Critics have responded to Frame's predilection for an elsewhere world 'not limited to the eye's seeing' in very different ways. Her novels are sometimes linked to philosophical traditions that posit the existence of an ultimate but ungraspable reality on a higher plane, such as Plato's pure forms or Kant's noumenal world. Others maintain that her elsewhere is a utopia or a no-place, of no ontological significance but important because we have the capacity to imagine things differently; still others feel the most essential quality of her elsewhere is that we are cut off from it, that the words that would take us there can never arrive, although they are the only magic carpet we have.[5] Approaches like these are largely indifferent to the question of place in her texts. I share Frame's disdain for our tendency to take a false pride in writing simply because it comes from New Zealand, but neither can I read her books as if they were set just anywhere. The significance of our 'exterior geographical conceptions' may indeed be overrated, but I believe there is room for a more grounded reading of the place of imagination and the imagination of place in Frame.

I come back to this business of rhubarb. In her novels and autobiographies, Frame focuses time and again on the predicament of the person who, away from home, feels separated as if by glass from the performance of a sociable dumb-show beyond. Istina Mavet, in *Faces in the Water*, says: 'I was put in hospital because a great gap opened in the ice floe between myself and the other people whom I watched, with their world, drifting away through a violet-coloured sea.'[6] In *Towards Another Summer*, Grace Cleave, an expatriate novelist experiencing her first winter in a London bedsit, has looked forward to a weekend as the house guest of a sophisticated literary couple only to find herself tongue-tied with awkwardness. A record is put on – does she like Bach? Her host waits for Grace to send back the conversational ball but the enormity of her feelings makes her stumble: 'Yes, I like Bach. He's . . . His music's . . . I like him. When I listen to Bach – It was no use; she could not explain without tripping and falling headlong over clichés.'[7]

Several things generally happen to a character in Grace's situation. First, her sense of language vitrifies. It is as if the easy lightness of words had fused into strange lumps and shards. Phrases normally used to set an expression going – 'By the way', 'I'm afraid', 'You know' – take on a hard glaze and are immobilised by the burden of their literal meaning.[8] Or perhaps by the meaning locked within a word: 'Industrial School' becomes 'In*dust*rial School' – a 'vast hall', supposes Grace, where you were 'caged inside a skeleton and forced to revolve with it in a fury of black dust . . . and if people visited . . . they wouldn't even realize you were imprisoned there; they wouldn't be able to see you, and if you had any voice and tried to speak to them they would never hear you' (99). The thought frightens her, but once again, there is distance from other people and the prospect of not being able to communicate across a gap to them – a threat which is also a fantasy of refuge from the rhubarb of the world. Grace's shyness makes her feel acutely on display, but as she inwardly squirms, she likes to contemplate words as if they were the ones in a display case. It is her way of absorbing and containing their power.

Second, Grace experiences a sense of time expanding into the pauses and vacancies of sociable speech. Philip, her host, tells a good anecdote about a visit to the northwest of Scotland – 'so like the West Coast of New Zealand' – where he meets an ancient clansman who speaks of the Jacobite rebellion of 1745 as if it happened only recently. 'The Enterrrrprrrise was hopeless from the starrrrt', says Philip, imitating his informant, and drawing an appreciative laugh from his listeners (183–85). In a film, the represented action would take only seconds of screen time, but it takes the reader several minutes to follow Grace on a distracted speculation in which she imagines Philip with a baby's face, then as bald and ancient as old Dugald, and then to associate the '45 with her father's experience of the Great War, and to reinterpret the subtext of a story genially told round the breakfast table in terms of a scared voice saying: 'he didn't want to die, he didn't want to die' (184). Time slows, Grace's imagination darts like a kite, an existential urgency tugs her back to the present moment; sequences like these repeat in Frame's writing, establishing a pattern of riff and return as regular as the blues. Grace is also typical of many of Frame's characters in that her reveries trend homewards, towards childhood.

Grace Cleave, whose name means both to sunder and to join, thinks of herself as one of Charles Brasch's godwits 'vanishing towards another summer' – 'So I, a migratory bird, am suffering from the need to return to the place I have come from before the season and sun are right for my return' (59). At this stage – 1963 – the expatriate novelist is clearly occupied with what it means to have a home to return to and the problems of inhabiting it as an artist. Curnow's *Book of New Zealand Verse* is a touchstone. 'All the poets are writing about *my* place', Grace recognises; 'Even if they were not writing of New Zealand they would be writing of my place' (61). And so:

> As [Curnow] had commanded, she laid 'a more faithful memory' upon the scene of her country, omitting for once the spellbinding outward landscape, the tourist glaciers, mountains, rivers, plains, bush, so often referred to as if they had been planned glories of a human workshop; concentrating on the personal scenery, the truly human constructions of habit, opinion, prejudice. She watched the smooth golden people with their clear sight, perfect limbs, brains bouncing with sanity and conformity; it seemed they were Life-Guard angels marching from tiny Waipapa beach in the south . . . to the Northland coast burning with pohutukawas; while the massed bands played . . . and the sun shone, the day surged with light, while offshore the tidal wave, restrained for the moment or day or year, bided its drowning time, played its blue patience of wave overlapping numbered wave. Grace observed, with terror, the fanatical innocence of the march, the acceptance of it, the reverence towards it . . . (134)

It seems hard for Grace to separate the literary injunction to 'know one's place' from the prospect of having to keep step in the nation's regimented feel-good parade. The tension between these versions of 'home' – the place she needs to be and the place that won't let her be – registers in the way Grace's imagination is drawn to catastrophic scenarios, to the waiting tidal wave that will not only engulf everything but also still the agitation that throws up these images of doom as desirable release. The alternative is to be both at home *and* elsewhere.

Towards Another Summer was completed in London in 1963 and never offered to a publisher; it appeared posthumously in 2007. Michael King reports that Frame withheld the manuscript because it was 'embarrassingly personal', and because it had been written largely in order to clear her mind of material that was threatening to lodge inappropriately in her novel-in-progress, *The Adaptable Man* (1965).[9] It is uncanny how closely the 1963 draft, the work of only three months, not only anticipates the autobiographies – Grace's childhood turns out to be Frame's own – but also *Living in the Maniototo*, a novel about hosts and guests and fiction taking over, as well as her final novel, *The Carpathians*, which is much concerned with the powers of distance and features a linguistic apocalypse in which – as Frame forecast in 1963 – 'unintelligible words . . . blossom into the new language'.[10] The earlier book summons up its sense of elsewhere in an oracular poetic prose which, though extraordinary and powerful, could be parodied with words selected from a fridge magnet set one might call 'Framish'; the measure of a good player might be to combine – as Frame herself does – the words night, thought, creeps, furred, animal, secret, glass, light, crakes, hollow, mirror and dancing in a single sentence.[11] The genius of her later masterpieces is that the looming presence of elsewhere can be carried not only by words and images but also by the possibilities of narrative itself.

Living in the Maniototo, Janet Frame's penultimate novel, was published in 1979, in the years before pinot noir and the Central Otago Rail Trail, when the title could still suggest 'living in a really remote and isolated place'. An entry from *An Encyclopaedia of New Zealand* (1966), cited in an epigraph, explains how the 'unforgettable landscapes' and 'stark geometry' of this part of Central Otago reveal an 'undermass' from which 'most of the cover has been stripped' – as if an underlying reality, not visible elsewhere, had been laid bare.[12] The name is compounded from the Maori – 'mania, a plain: toto, bloody' – though in the Kiwi vernacular, 'bloody plain' also means featureless, boring. A famous New Zealand writer, a second note informs us, 'lived all his life in the Maniototo', in this nowhere, without ever leaving the district.[13] The reader might reasonably expect a novel called *Living in the Maniototo* to inform us about life on that backcountry plateau, but the book we read seems mislabelled: on the surface, it has nothing to do with the Maniototo at all. Instead, we follow a character named Mavis on her journeys to Baltimore and California, and the New Zealand settings of primary importance are the Auckland suburb of 'Blenheim', a South Island name that designates Glenfield's patch of the North Shore; and Stratford, the Taranaki town whose name also points elsewhere, and from which Mavis ostensibly writes the novel we are reading. A few years later, Janet Frame told an interviewer:

'For me, one of the fascinations of writing … is in the coding of what is written to describe what is not written. I like to think of the contents of a book as a signpost to a world not even mentioned.'[14]

The Maniototo Plain is only one of several voids or absences signposted in this book. Early in the novel, on her first trip to Baltimore, Mavis and her host visit the apartment of an artist named Tommy who has recently had to dispose of a loved pet – there is no backyard in which to bury the poor thing so the body goes out with the trash. Ever since, Tommy has been persecuted by the 'Blue Fury' – a mythical creature like the advertiser's 'white tornado' that used to whirl out of a bottle of Ajax household cleanser. The three characters, an American and two Kiwis, are exchanging the inevitable small talk of distance and location – 'what do you do with all that space?' asks Tommy – when, 'with a fearful look in his eyes he turned towards some apparition beside him':

> 'Got you', he cried, grasping the air.
>   There was a flash of light, a smell of laundry and the penetrating fumes of a powerful cleanser, then a neutral nothing-smell, not even the usual substituted forest glade or field of lavender or carnation, and all that remained of Tommy were two faded footprints on the floor. (38)

Most readers of the novel are so taken aback by this occurrence that they read the above paragraph at least twice. 'That can't have happened', we say to ourselves, but sure enough, it has. And the characters in the novel can't believe their eyes either. 'Things like that don't happen', says Brian, who decides it would be best not to mention Tommy's death to anyone. Mavis, however, has a theory: 'It was the result of an inevitable break in the surface of things, as if a fire from the centre of the earth or a volcano beneath its skin had at last been forced through into an overtaking of the visible world' (38). We no longer believe in the tricksters of myth and fable like Tom Thumb or Maui or Ariel or Loki (although Mavis, with her many aliases, claims to be the sister of each), but we can all picture the 'Hungry Enzymes' in our washing powder or the 'Germs' who lurk like street-corner thugs below the rim of the toilet bowl; these hidden agents unfold the mysteries of our world as surely as the goddess Iris explained rainbows to the ancient Greeks. Or consider the metaphor 'a clean death', which is literalised in the expunction of Tommy as well as in the disposal of his dog. Mavis's idea is that a sort of crack in the surface of things might allow figures of speech and creatures of dream and myth to 'overtake' our everyday literal reality; by the same logic, reasons Brian sceptically, Tommy has 'returned beneath the surface of an apparent reality' (39). Suppose both are right: given her recourse to geomorphology in describing this 'break in the surface of things' (38), we might guess that Tommy, vanished from view, has been translated to a stratum below this one, to an original undermass or plain, and is now 'living in the Maniototo'.

Tommy's encounter with the 'Blue Fury' is a first-act 'MacGuffin' that helps divert the reader's attention from larger eruptions of unreality happening elsewhere in the novel. Mavis's second trip to the United States involves a second visit to her friend Brian in Baltimore, after which she travels to San Francisco to house-sit for a couple named Garrett while they are abroad in Italy. Whilst there, she expects to work on a novel about the pilgrimage of the Watercress family to Menton, where the famous New Zealand writer Margaret Rose Hurndell spent the last days of her short life. Soon after settling into the house, Mavis learns that the Garretts have not only been killed by an earthquake in Italy, they have also bequeathed the house and all its contents to her in their will. There is one snag, explains the lawyer: the Garretts had earlier invited four guests to stay, and it now seems proper for Mavis to respect their invitation and host the guests herself. Both couples turn out to have New Zealand connections, though neither Doris and Roger nor Theo and Zita live there now. And so, over the two weeks of their visit, and over a number of chapters, the guests tell stories about the country they are from. These sections are narrated with acute psychological and geographical realism; we feel we get to know each of the guests well, as if they were characters from *Middlemarch* – the novel, that is, rather than the Central Otago township. The visit takes its course, the guests leave and Mavis is just on the point of locking the door when, surprise, surprise, the taxi that had been called to take her to the airport unexpectedly delivers the Garretts to the driveway. 'You've timed it well', says Irving. 'Did you enjoy your stay? Did you get your novel written?' (235). If Tommy's disappearance is a six on the Richter scale, the book is so written that the return of the householders rates a ten. In some shock, and perturbed to find that the Berkeley addresses associated with the lawyer and the guests have no counterpart in reality, Mavis flies out to Baltimore only to discover that Brian died of a heart attack the day after her departure. An unusual contents page, skimmed on a first reading, gives these sections of the book enigmatic titles like 'Attending and Avoiding in the Maniototo' and 'Avoiding Bound by the Present Historic'; only now does the reader gather that in *attending* to her guests, Mavis has *avoided* the reality of Brian's death.

Attending and avoiding are components of all reading and all writing. The first edition, and all subsequent editions of this text published in Frame's lifetime, have no chapter 22. Should this catch be attended to? If it is another signpost towards an unmentioned world, something looms from that space: Mavis's 'repressed' chapter must concern a missing week in her life, when she first arrived at the Garretts' house, when she would have received the telegram announcing Brian's death, when the novel she had been writing first began to be hijacked by her preoccupation with the guests. And if we prefer to believe chapter 22 is misnumbered rather than significantly absent, that a full complement of chapters has been attended to, second-time readers of the novel will nonetheless be astonished at how much 'avoiding' accompanied their initial reading of the novel: how many hints they hurried past, how many apparently obscure paragraphs about calculating the unknown side of a triangle, or about hosts and guests in the 'house' of fiction, or the artist living in her 'garret', were showing exactly what was happening even while misdirecting the reader. Then, paying more attention, the second- or third-time reader discovers that Brian's death, though never mentioned, has all along been a subtle under-shape contouring the stories of the guests, with their experiences of dislocation, of language loss and loss of footing, of erosion and erasure. As Mavis herself puts it, the book concerns 'journeys toward that are believed to be journeys away from, and journeys away that are really journeys within' (42).

An often quoted sentence in the novel runs: '. . . I feel that language in its widest sense is the hawk suspended above eternity, feeding from it but not of its substance and not necessarily for its life and thus never able to be translated into it; only able by a wing movement, so to speak, a cry, a shadow, to hint at what lies beneath it on the untouched, undescribed almost unknown plain' (43). If the hawk is language, the sky would be what the hawk moves through; Mavis's word is 'eternity': everything that was and will be, everything and anything that might have an existence in words. But a mist obscures the ground. We know the plain, the real on its own terms, only indirectly, through mediation, by the way the hawk's wing movements respond to air currents, to the topography of what we can't see. Just as Brian's death underpins the story of the guests, just as we can read the missing chapter 22 (if it was missing), so too is the novel about 'Living in the Maniototo' while not being set there.

Other names and places come unstuck in this book. Blenheim, we recognise, ought to be Glenfield, Margaret Rose Hurndell ought to be Katherine Mansfield, the Watercress family off to Menton are possibly the Steads, and so on – though most names are placed and most places are named right where we think they should be. The effect is of an imperfect fit between language and the people and places referred to, as if the lining of a familiar jacket had become bunched and misshapen. For the novel's several stroke victims, also, words and concepts no longer line up as they ought. Mavis says of her husband:

All beautiful words that people have but seldom used, the wide, rich tapestry of language that could cover the whole earth like a feasting-cloth or a golden blanket – these were lost. Lewis had been struck by lightning that burned great holes in his language and scorched the rest so as to make the pattern unintelligible; he had no more sustenance or warmth from language. (26)

And Theo's doctor explains:

'It's something we take for granted. Think a thought and a word is there, a phrase, a definition. Like throwing out a line and hooking a fish every time . . . . But with this vascular accident, the line is out and baited, and the fish are there, as they've always been, but they no longer take the bait or are aware of its existence; the two worlds have separated.' (206)

As stroke victims, Theo and Lewis experience damage to the interface between the world of language and the world of people, places and things. Just as a psychologist learns about the place of language by investigating it in a damaged state, so too might we learn about place when the verbs and nouns of belonging and location no longer automatically function. A recurrent concern of the *Autobiography* helps explain what I mean. Theo and Lewis's problem of separate worlds has a correlative in a defining problem of all settler literatures: a misalignment between the writer's own sense of place and the literary places of an ancestral homeland. In her *Autobiography*, for example, Frame recalls how, as a beginning writer, she could be led astray by her desire to please and produce work larded with the poeticisms of another place and another time. But she realised early on that those 'two worlds' had to be one.

> I wanted an imagination that would inhabit a world of fact, descend like a shining light upon the ordinary life of Eden Street, and not force me to exist in an 'elsewhere'. I wanted the light to shine upon the pigeons of Glen Street, the plum trees in our garden, the two japonica bushes (one red, one yellow), our pine plantations and gully, our summer house, our lives, and our home, the world of Oamaru, the kingdom by the sea. I refused to accept that if I were to fulfil my secret ambition to be a poet, I should spend my imaginative life among the nightingales instead of the wax-eyes and the fantails. I wanted my life to be the 'other world'. (101)[15]

Elsewhere, for Frame, is her own place lit up by the imagination. 'Not Dunedin or London or Ibiza or Auckland or any other cities I have known' – but the 'Mirror City before my own eyes' (435). Place is central to her poetics primarily because the imagination, as she puts it, 'depends on the substance transported there', on 'the transformation of ordinary facts and ideas into a shining palace of mirrors' (434). Her theory may sound transcendental, but she is describing an experience familiar to most of us. To an Aucklander, for example, the words 'Dominion Road' denote a street that runs straight as an arrow from the centre of the city all the way to Mt Roskill. I know a great dumpling restaurant halfway down, but in this context the words 'Dominion Road' have no special resonance. Put those same words into the song by Don McGlashan and the Mutton Birds, and I get a ridiculous kick out of it. 'Dominion Road', or so I would understand Frame to say, has been nudged 'elsewhere' by the songwriter's imagination. As Mavis herself puts it, when thinking of the attractions that America might hold for a teenager, and the power of 'the songs with the names' – Highway 61, Memphis, the Tallahatchie Bridge –

> . . . names with which Palmerston North, Marton, Foxton, couldn't hope to compete unless a spark of imagination, kindled somewhere (by Peter Wallstead, Margaret Rose Hurndell?) set the place alight like a bushfire. The Maori names – Wanganui, Waikato, Tuatapere, Taranaki – were more powerful because they were welded to the place by the first unifying act of poetry and not stuck on like a grocery label; nevertheless, the real triumph would be to set the spark raging in the mundane places. (96–97)[16]

But suppose there is a negative to this positive: suppose the ordinary capacity to irradiate place with the transforming light of the imagination becomes damaged, as a stroke victim's language is damaged, by a sort of spatial aphasia. The 'two worlds' would come asunder (but not wholly separate), and trauma would be registered though voids, through the vitrification of language, and through what Mavis, in her description of the suburb of Blenheim, calls 'an insinuation of Elsewhere' (23). The suburb where Mavis has 'buried two husbands' is as dystopian as any in New Zealand fiction. She thinks of it as twice removed from the real, and draws an intricate series of parallels between the loss of the primeval forest and the withering of language's power to articulate the space of settlement, between the psychic deprivation of its inhabitants and the absence of a relation of host to guest and guest to host. 'If you, a stranger, stay in Blenheim, you stay in a motel on the way to your "real" destination' (21).

There are no hosts and no guests when people are just passing through; all the delicate questions of tact, of negotiation, of appropriation, of possessiveness, of giving, of receiving, of how and how far one should make oneself at home, all these questions of settlement that feature so prominently in the novel, and that press through like mouldings from the underside of 'a world not even mentioned', have no purchase in Blenheim. Children born there feel a sense of loss, as if 'they had truly been children of the native forest which, like a father, has abandoned them by dying' (21); a loss also evident in the irony by which those 'who take part, however remotely, in destruction, . . . also take pleasure in recreating what [they] have destroyed' (22) – hence the proliferation of plant nurseries in the grim industrial belt known as Kaka Valley. Most Blenheim streets are named after 'British Lords and Estates, and battles of wars recent and long ago', but this older form of colonial dislocation has been overtaken by a newer 'insinuation of Elsewhere' in the shape of 'Heavenfield Mall': a shopping centre 'built for a climate of blizzards, intense heat, meagre daylight filtered through smog; for a city where the stars and the sun and the sky are no longer part of the human view' (22). Blenheim is the damaged space of settlement: at once anywhere and nowhere. It is the wrong kind of elsewhere, as yet barely modified by the powers of distance and of art. But a poet has died there (reminding the reader of James K. Baxter's heart attack on a Glenfield doorstep) and his death nourishes a legend which, to adapt the novel's own metaphor, becomes an upholstery button fixing the 'golden feasting blanket' of language to the plain beneath.

If there is a flaw in the faceted perfection of *Living in the Maniototo*, it might be that Blenheim, that pointedly abject suburb, is airily supplemented by Stratford as a countervailing good space of settlement, where Shakespearean associations loom benignly, where Mavis is both at home and the 'guest, as all who live there are, of the Taranaki mountain' (133). Without perhaps intending to, Frame has left us with a 'two-world' structure when, by her own lights, the signpost ought always to have been to the one place: 'Blenheim' and 'Stratford' inhabited together, not separated out as positive and negative registers of Pakeha settlement. She gets the balance right in her next novel, *The Carpathians*, set in the unremarkable small town of Puamahara, and in which her interest in the relation of persons to place, and in the potential reversibility of concepts like near and far, host and guest, is continued.

Etymologically, a host was once a guest, a guest was once a host and a parasite was someone you shared food with rather than something you were consumed by. Mattina, hosting a cancer, is herself a guest in Puamahara, where – much like the visiting writer in 'Departures and Returns' – she has travelled from her home in Manhattan with the aim of knowing the local inhabitants and collecting material about the Memory Flower that gives the town its name. Her journey doubles that of the young woman of the legend who was 'chosen by the gods as collector of the memory of her land', who meets helpers on the way at 'corners, crossroads, shores, boundaries' and is the first to pick and taste the Memory Flower and release the power of story-telling (11). One day, the listeners find she has gone, leaving only a tree with one bloom 'from which, it is said, fruit invisible to most eyes from time to time may grow' (11). A sculpture of a tree with one large pendant plaster blossom marks the spot, a tourist 'attraction' drawing no crowds in a town unselfconsciously blessed by orchards and blos-soming fruit trees.

Mattina's 'helpers' are the residents of Kowhai Street. Encountering them, Mattina encounters doorways or crossroads between the con-cepts of near and far, here and there. For Hercus Millow, a former POW, the war years seem closer than the events of the previous week; he looks through binoculars at the Tararuas – 'changing unattainable distance to palpable closeness' (64) – and recalls how, in camp, the POWs conspired to keep invisible pets as a way of bringing domes-tic space into their barbed-wire lives. Ed Shannon, computer-store owner, has a flight simulator programme that collapses distance with flights in 'reality mode'; while Joseph and Gloria James, piano tuners with perfect pitch and practised in wordless knowing, have an autistic daughter named Decima, who, says Gloria, 'could be thousands of miles away, in the Andes or the Carpathians, . . . for all the signs she gives that she's here and knows us' (106). On a marae visit with the Hanuere family, Mattina, a stranger, feels right at home, but not – as had been her practice – by absorbing others into her orbit through gifts and money, but by finding the distance appropriate to a guest. Conversely, Connie Grant has travelled from the UK to be closer to her son's family but finds herself more isolated than ever, while Mattina, separated from her husband Jake, finds that, 'like the Gravity Star she had achieved closeness through distance' (131).

The Gravity Star, itself unseen, bends light from a galaxy seven bil-lion light years away so that the far star system looms and appears closer. When Mavis and the residents of Kowhai Street become focused in the Gravity Star's beam, characters – and readers – face 'the prospect of the sudden annihilation of the usual perception of distance and closeness . . . . Near and far, then and now, here and there, the homely words of the language of space and time appear useless, heaps of rubble' (14). One night, towards the end of her stay, the metaphor literalises: in the dry tiny shapes of an alphabet soup, letters and punctuation marks from all the languages of the world fall from the sky in a typographical rain, and the residents of Kowhai Street stand at the end of their driveways calling and howling in a disarticulated language that is instinctively rebooting itself to be born. They may have become our future or returned to our evolutionary past; or perhaps the Gravity Star may have hoovered up their store of signifiers and signifieds and is restocking their faculty of speech with words and concepts from a galaxy light years away – whatever the disturbance to space and to time, these residents are now unknown and unknowable: they have surrendered their point of view. Two characters remain unaffected: Mattina and Dinny Wheatstone, 'the imposter novelist', who – so far as we can tell – may host Mattina and everyone else in this fiction, or herself be the guest of the novel's 'frame narrator', John Henry Brecon, who writes the book from Lake George, New York, in 1987. The 'outside' narrator becomes an 'inside narrator' – or vice versa – in a discursive involution like a Klein bottle folding in on itself.

A Klein bottle, mathematicians say, is non-orientable. As a work of metafiction, *The Carpathians* may look as hermetically sealed as that strange topological object, but revolve it, feel for the right surface and a globe will spring open: the book takes its shape from a backyard and a gap in the rhubarb patch. When Janet Frame was a girl, her backyard was 'a small square of concrete at the back door'.[17] It was neither a 'back garden' nor coextensive with the entire back section of the property – she would have crossed her backyard to reach an outside laundry, lavatory or washing-line. Later, the title of Walt Whitman's poem 'When Lilacs Last in the Dooryard Bloom'd' puzzled her: how could flowers bloom from a slab of concrete? Only after visiting friends in the United States and admiring plants in their dooryard did Whitman's line clarify for her. She concludes: 'I have no word for the space at the backdoor of my New Zealand home, for time transactions have removed the word backyard, while the newly learned dooryard can only be used in visits to the United States and its poetry; and so one word which was rich in my life is now in literary limbo and . . . I have a slightly undernourished personal culture as well as a slightly enriched one.'[18] A word's meaning goes, a new meaning arrives: it is the work of the Gravity Star, yet the Memory Flower still blooms, even as a plaster sculpture with its roots under concrete.

The blue furies and annihilating galaxies that figure in Janet Frame's fictional worlds serve to remind us that our human capacity for language and for memory is at once ordinary, momentous and fragile. Her obliterating agents are the mythical counterparts of the strokes and tumours all flesh is heir to, but their entropic force can also be personified by two types of characters. There are figures like Albion Cook, the bland realtor in *The Carpathians*, who has a 'large supply of useless, sparkless words that he was determined to use' (180), who is platitudinously indifferent to the past – 'It can't matter to you who lived here. Things change. People come and go' – and whose spatial aphasia reduces place to mere real estate (183). And there is also Decima, the adolescent without words, who Jake also meets on his pilgrimage to Puamahara in the wake of Mattina's death. People like Decima, Jake feels, 'would always be like special touchstones, gauges set with diamonds, to measure human possibilities and impossibilities, . . . and . . . to measure the usual need and dependence on spoken words against an infinite silence where the buffeting, battling, hurting world is met with no castle and keep of spoken language' (185).

But where to build one's cairn or pitch one's tent or purchase one's estate, and with what consequences? Insofar as we speak, remember and imagine, 'the human race', as Dinny Wheatstone says, 'is an else-where race' (51); but her perception, I feel, only intensifies our relation to place, and that is likely to be the case no matter whether, like John Mulgan or Robin Hyde, we number ourselves among the un-returning godwits, or, like Janet Frame, are pulled homewards by an inner compass. For Frame, the decision to return was literary. Home was where the language – though always changing, though always likely to reconfigure her backyard – was in place.

In her autobiography she recalls a review of *The Adaptable Man*, in which an English critic protested the barbarity of her calling the River Orwell the Orwell River – a mistake, inaudible to her ears and to mine, but to a Suffolk man as odd as the Thames River would sound to a Londoner. 'Unless the writer embraces the language of the new land', she writes, 'there are constant betrayals of language' (416). And she also has a sense that her place – a new land, older to some of its inhabitants, but still the last landmass to be settled by humans – had been less densely imagined than those older ancestral homelands. 'Living in New Zealand would be for me', she writes, 'like living in an age of mythmakers; with a freedom of imagination among all the artists because it is possible to begin at the beginning and to know the unformed places and to help form them, to be a mapmaker for those who will follow nourished by this generation's layers of the dead' (415). Earlier generations, and not only here, would recognise those composting sentiments. Overlaying the oral maps of the Maori, colonists envisaged a literature budding into the future like prosperous farms from the bush; nationalist writers, embarrassed by bluster, founded their own forward-looking anti-myths of settlement. Frame, drawing on all these traditions, brings a half-old and half-new sense of elsewhere to the map, overturning our accustomed sense of near and far, then and now, with a looming that is both illusion and marvel.

NOTES

Chapter One: Nature and the Question of Pakeha Turangawaewae

1   Wayne Mason's song was recorded by the Formyula in 1969 and by the Mutton Birds in 1992; the song was voted New Zealand's best song by members of the Australasian Performing Right Association (APRA) in 2001. The top-ranking songs were released in a compilation CD: 'Nature's Best: New Zealand's Top 30 Songs of All Time', Epic, 5054952000.

2   William Wordsworth, 'Lines Composed a Few Miles above Tintern Abbey, on Revisiting the Banks of the Wye during a Tour, July 13, 1798', *Selected Poems*, p. 72.

3   Most of those examples would make the point more implicitly than, say, A. R. D. Fairburn's 'Elements': 'Land of mountains and running water / rocks and flowers / and the leafy evergreen, O natal earth, / the atoms of your children / are bonded to you forever', ... 'let us come to you / barefoot, as befits love, / as the boy to the trembling girl, / as the child to the mother': *Collected Poems*, p. 28.

4   Mary Anne Barker, *Station Life in New Zealand*, p. 125. Subsequent page references are given in the text.

5   For a discussion of scenes where a traveller becomes monarch of all he surveys, see Mary Louise Pratt, *Imperial Eyes*, pp. 197–204.

6   Baughan writes: 'What we want is beauty is it not? rather than mere mileage, and satisfaction, not satiety?': *Studies in New Zealand Scenery*, p. 159.

7   After 'The Finest Walk in the World' appeared in the *Spectator* in 1908, local publishers Whitcombe & Tombs reprinted it as a booklet in 1909 and commissioned more of the same. 'Snow Kings' and 'A River of Pictures and Peace' were published in both venues (1910 and 1913 respectively), and subsequently collected with several other essays as *Studies in New Zealand Scenery* (1916), which was reprinted with an additional essay as *Glimpses of New Zealand Scenery* (1922). All page references cited in my text are valid for both the 1916 and 1922 volume.

8   See, for example, Bethell's 'Pause', Baxter's 'Poem in the Matukituki Valley', Allen Curnow's 'The Unhistoric Story' and Charles Brasch's 'The Silent Land'.

9   Wystan Curnow, *Putting the Land on the Map*, p. 49.

10   The process of cultural change I have in mind is well described by Philip Fisher. Commenting on the role of *Uncle Tom's Cabin* in enabling Americans to recognise that blacks were people rather than property, he writes: 'Where culture installs new habits of moral perception, . . . it accomplishes, as a last step, the forgetting of its own strenuous work so that what are newly learned habits are only remembered as facts. Once what had only recently been a risky and disputable claim has come to seem obvious, the highest work of culture has been done, but because the last step involves forgetting both the process and its very openness to alternatives or to failure, the history of culture has trouble in later remembering what it is socially and psychologically decisive for it to forget': *Hard Facts*, p. 4.

11   'Historical Model for Gardens Occupation', *New Zealand Herald*, 17 April 1995, 1, p. 6.

12   James K. Baxter, 'Te Whiori O Te Kuri', *Collected Poems*, p. 568. Subsequent page references to Baxter's poetry are given in this edition and are given in the text.

13   I am grateful to Margaret Edgcumbe for showing me her husband's inscribed copy of *Jerusalem Sonnets*. The inscription is reproduced as the frontispiece to John Newton's superb account of the relationship between Baxter, the young members of the commune and the local community: *The Double Rainbow*.

14   Bill Oliver traces the expression to an occasion when Baxter saw a double rainbow appear over Whanganui: the prophet 'interpreted the outer arc as Maori and the inner as Pakeha, and affirmed his readiness to die for "te wairua Maori" (the Maori spirit)': *James K. Baxter*, p. 150.

15   Cited in Frank McKay, *The Life of James K. Baxter*, p. 279.

16   The campaign was launched in 1999.

17   'The Royal Tour' was first screened in the US on the Travel Channel in December 2002, and appeared worldwide through the Discovery Channel the following year. All quotations from the programme are my own transcriptions from the soundtrack. It might be noted that the Queen is head of state in New Zealand.

18   Richard White, 'Are You an Environmentalist or Do You Work for a Living?', in William Cronon (ed.), *Uncommon Ground*, pp. 171–85.

19   Geoff Park, 'Our Terra Nullius', *Landfall*, 204, pp. 53–67.

20   White, 'Are You an Environmentalist or Do You Work for a Living?', p. 174.

21   Philip Fisher, *Still the New World*, pp. 1–30.

PART II: LANDING

1   Greg Dening has made 'crossing the beach' a central metaphor for the processes of cross-cultural transformation in the Pacific; see *Beach Crossings* for a book-length discussion. The phrase 'middle ground' echoes Richard White's classic American study of early contact, *The Middle Ground*.

2   'At Jacky Marmon's Grave', *Uncollected Northland Poems*, pp. 19–49.

3   Marmon's memoirs were first serialised in the *New Zealand Herald*, 9 October–11 December 1880. Other versions subsequently appeared in the *Auckland Star* and the *Otago Witness* in 1882.

4   Arthur Thomson, *The Story of New Zealand*, vol. I, p. 301.

5   Ibid.

6   Ibid, pp. 302–3.

7   Nathaniel Hawthorne, unsigned notice, in the Salem, Massachusetts, *Advertiser*, 25 March 1846: in Watson G. Branch (ed.), *Melville: The Critical Heritage*, p. 67.

Chapter Two: Augustus Earle and the Secret of Cannibalism

1   In common usage, 'cannibals' are people who cook and eat other humans. Unless otherwise specified, I use the term in a common, non-judgemental and non-technical way. When I wish to imply an especially value-laden set of connotations (such as the ferocity of cannibals or the savage gusto of their appetite), either my wording or the context will make those connotations plain. Conversely, I use the term 'anthropophagy' if a scientific understanding is intended.

2   William Arens' *The Man-Eating Myth* is the path-breaking work. For more recent studies, see Laurence Goldman (ed.), *The Anthropology of Cannibalism*; and Francis Barker, Peter Hulme and Margaret Iversen (eds), *Cannibalism and the Colonial World*. Peter Hulme's introduction to the latter volume is the best single overview of the debate.

3   Ian Barber's detailed local assessment of early New Zealand reports is informed by Arens' work, but concludes that 'a compelling case emerges for the occasional practice of cannibalism among late 18th century Maori communities' ('Archaeology, Ethnography, and the Record of Maori Cannibalism', *Journal of the Polynesian Society*, vol. 101, no. 3, p. 280). The postcolonial critics I refer to are Gananath Obeyesekere and Geoffrey Sanborn, both discussed elsewhere in this chapter. The former has written widely about Polynesian cannibalism, the apotheosis of Captain Cook and other European 'myths' of the Pacific. For a rebuttal of his views, see Marshall Sahlins, *How 'Natives' Think*; for an account of the Obeyesekere–Sahlins debate, see the introduction to Alex Calder, Jonathan Lamb and Bridget Orr (eds), *Voyages and Beaches*, pp. 4–11. Sanborn writes about Augustus Earle in the introduction to *The Sign of the Cannibal* – I am grateful for his provocative reading.

4   Edward Said, *Orientalism*, p. 94.

5   Reay Tannahill, *Flesh and Blood*, pp. 208–9.

6   Michael Pickering, 'Consuming Doubts: What Some People Ate? Or What Some People Swallowed?', in Goldman (ed.), *The Anthropology of Cannibalism*, pp. 51–74.

7   See my edition of F. E. Maning's *Old New Zealand and Other Writings*, p. 65. As it happens, bits of the late Captain Grant may have been ritually eaten after the battle of Ohaeawae, but we owe the notion that his flesh was *dried* to a misprint introduced in the 1864 edition. The correct word is 'used'.

8   Cited in Barber, 'Archaeology, Ethnography, and the Record of Maori Cannibalism', p. 256.

9   Ibid.

10   Augustus Earle, *Narrative of a Residence in New Zealand*, E. H. McCormick (ed.), pp. 60–61. Subsequent page references are included in the text.

11   Gananath Obeyesekere, 'British Cannibals', *Critical Inquiry*, vol. 18, 1992, p. 653. My emphasis.

12   Ibid.

13   Ibid.

14   Gananath Obeyesekere, 'Cannibal Feasts in Nineteenth-Century Fiji', in Barker, et al. (eds), *Cannibalism and the Colonial World*, p. 63.

15   Greg Dening, *Islands and Beaches*, p. 34.

16   Cited by Paul Lyons, 'Lines of Fright', in Barbara Creed and Jeanette Hoorn (eds), *Body Trade*, p. 126.

17   Augustus Earle, *Distant View of the Bay of Islands, New Zealand*. The original is held in the National Library of Australia (PIC T108 NK12/70 LOC Box B6) and is reproduced with permission. Like his *Narrative*, which was based on journal entries and revised for publication

in 1832, the painting was probably sketched at the time of his visit in 1827 and completed later. For a parallel reading of the painting, see W. J. T. Mitchell, 'Imperial Landscape', in W. J. T. Mitchell (ed.), *Landscape and Power*, pp. 5–34.

18   Sanborn, *The Sign of the Cannibal*, p. 6.

19   Ibid, p. 8.

20   Sanborn does not mention Titokowaru who, forty years after Earle's time, in very different circumstances, used cannibalism to terrorise the British. His letter to colonists is reproduced in James Belich, *I Shall Not Die*, pp. 56–57.

21   Homi Bhabha is well known for his idea that natives manipulate the stereotypes of their colonial masters in a manner that 'terrorises authority with the *ruse* of recognition, its mimicry, its mockery'. Cited in Sanborn, *The Sign of the Cannibal*, p. 9.

22   William Williams, Journal, 1827–8, 1834, typescript copy in the Algar Williams Collection, MS 91/75, Auckland Museum.

23   Sanborn, *The Sign of the Cannibal*, p. 5.

24   For information on Brian Boroo's travels, see Peter Dillon, *Narrative of La Pérouse's Expedition*; J. W. Davidson, *Peter Dillon of Vanikoro*; and E. H. McCormick's introduction to Earle's *Narrative*. Brian Boroo's identity is difficult to determine. He is said by all and sundry to be the son of 'the principal Thames chief' – Thames in this context is not necessarily the area around the present township but might also mean the river and its environs more generally. We know that Boroo's people had been allies of Ngapuhi, but their association with the death of Pomare in 1826 made them enemies and victims of several retaliatory raids; we also know that Boroo's father freed two of Pomare's sons who had been taken as slaves, in the hope of ensuring his son's safety when he arrived at Kororareka. These details may suggest a Ngati Maru connection. However, Dillon reports that reaching 'Boroo country' requires a journey up the river, and a march by land (1, p. 232); Davidson tentatively identifies Boroo's father as Tokoroa, or Te Toko, of the Uriohau branch of Ngati Whatua, who were then living at Horotiu (p. 103).

25   The full chronology of Brian Boroo's inadvertent travels is as follows. He first returned from a planned voyage on the *Research* (with muskets obtained in Calcutta) in July 1827, about a year after the death of Pomare I. On that occasion, Whetoi tried to lure him ashore with the captured Shelagh as bait; Hongi Hika and Te Whareumu also made threats; Shelagh remained ashore when the ship departed. Bad weather prevented the *Research* from landing at Thames, and the ship continued on its cruise to Tonga, Tikopia and Vanikoro, returning to the Bay of Islands for the second time on 6 November 1827. Once again, the Ngapuhi chiefs tried to detain him, and Dillon reports that Whetoi was enraged when both Shelagh and Brian left for Thames on the chartered *Governor Macquarie* in December. Boroo somehow failed to get himself ashore at Thames yet again, and returned to Kororareka (via Tonga and Tikopia) for the third time in February 1828. He then travelled on to Sydney with Earle on the *Governor Macquarie* and was there two months before Earle and others procured his passage home.

26   Ngapuhi, the large iwi encompassing the many hapu of the Hokianga and the Bay of Islands, have fluid affiliations in this period. The people Earle refers to as 'Narpooee' are the northern Bay of Islands hapu associated with Hongi; they are the allies of, but also in fierce competition with, the southern hapu of Ngati Manu associated with Te Whareumu, the late Pomare and Whetoi; the combined Ngapuhi of the Bay of Islands are allies of, but can also be in fierce competition with, the many eastern hapu of Ngapuhi from the Hokianga.

27   Earle's rendering of Te Whareumu's speech preserves a convention in Maori whereby a pronoun (he) can be understood metonymically (his relatives).

28   See Dillon, *Narrative of La Pérouse's Expedition*, vol. 2, pp. 350–52.

29   Ibid, p. 352.

30   See Earle, *Narrative*, pp. 106–9.

31   Obeyesekere, 'Cannibal Feasts in Nineteenth-Century Fiji', p. 64.

Chapter Three: Maning's Demons

1   F. E. Maning to Donald McLean, 25 October 1862, in *Old New Zealand and Other Writings*, Alex Calder (ed.), p. 214. Unless otherwise specified, all further Maning references are to this edition and are cited in my text.

2   Cited in Walter Jackson Bate, *John Keats*, p. 665.

3   Edward Markham, *New Zealand or Recollections of It*, p. 32.

4   Markham, *Recollections*, p. 57.

5   See T. L. Buick, *The Treaty of Waitangi*, pp. 170–74.

6   Felton Mathew and Sarah Mathew, *The Founding of New Zealand*, p. 53.

7   Te Hikutu, Maning's hapu, fought with the Crown, but his Te Ihutai friends across the harbour at Kohukohu were allies of Heke – they and their chief, Te Kahakaha, are conspicuously praised in the narrative.

8   Maning's biographer notes that while two judges sat on the Te Aroha case, it was Maning who delivered the judgment: R. M. Burdon, *New Zealand Notables*, p. 101.

9   F. E. Maning, 'Aroha', in F. D. Fenton (ed.), *Important Judgments*, p. 110.

10   Ibid, p. 112.

11   Ibid, p. 127.

12   Ibid, p. 130.

13   Muru, as Maning describes it, is a form of socially licensed plunder, allowing restitution for offences and failures (such as accident or sickness). Samuel Butler develops this perspective on 'muru' in *Erewhon*.

14   A more insightful observation would concern the relation of tapu and noa; the latter is not a concept Maning directly explores.

15   Anon., 'Musings on Manning's [*sic*] "Old New Zealand"', *Temple Bar*, vol. 5, no. 18, p. 527.

16   Anon., 'Musings', p. 526.

17   Cited in Patrick Brantlinger, *Rule of Darkness*, p. 187.

18   Letter from Maning to T. F. Cheeseman, 30 November 1878, Auckland Institute and Museum Library, MS 419.

19   Like his commentator, Maning does allow that 'European diseases also assisted, but not to any serious degree' (p. 187). His emphasis on the danger of 'noxious exhalations' is in keeping with a belief in the deleterious effects of 'bad air'. Microbes were not discovered until later in the century.

20   Joan Fitzgerald, 'Images of the Self', *Journal of Commonwealth Literature*, vol. 23, no. 1, 1988, pp. 16–41.

21   Quoted in James Cowan, *Sir Donald Maclean*, pp. 125–8.

22   Letter from Maning to J. Webster, 24 April [1879?], Auckland Public Library, MS 4/42.

23   Walter Benjamin, 'On the Concept of History', *Selected Writings*, p. 392.

24   Catherin Servant, *Customs and Habits of the New Zealanders*. Other details about Papahurihia are from Judith Binney's entry 'Papahurihia, Penetana' in the *Dictionary of New Zealand Biography*, vol. 1; and her essay, 'Papahurihia: Some Thoughts on Interpretation', *Journal of the Polynesian Society*, vol. 75, no. 3, 1966, pp. 321–31.

25   Edward Shortland, *Traditions and Superstitions of the New Zealanders*, p. 84.

26   Ibid, p. 95.

27   See *History of the War in the North*, pp. 46–47.

28   Servant, *Customs and Habits*, p. 55.

29   John 3:14–15.

30   Servant, *Customs and Habits*, p. 57.

31   Evelyn Stokes, *Wiremu Tamihana: Rangatira*, p. 27. Tarapipipi is sometimes known as Wiremu Tamihana or William Thompson.

32   A report by the missionary, Charles Davis, cited in Lady Mary Martin, *Our Maoris*, p. 35.

33   Shortland, *Traditions and Superstitions*, p. 93.

34   Ibid, p. 96. As for the meaning, perhaps 'shitbum' comes close.

35   Stokes, *Wiremu Tamihana: Rangatira*, p. 52.

36   Ibid, pp. 73–74.

37   James Cowan, 'The Wahoo Man', in Alex Calder (ed.), *Tales of the Maori Bush*, pp. 67–74.

38   Ibid, p. 70.

39   Ibid, p. 1.

Chapter Four: A Small Plot at Orakau

1   *The Last Stand* (Videorecording), Hayward Historical Film Trust, Auckland, 1990.

2   Geoffrey Sanborn, *Whipscars and Tattoos*, pp. 40–45.

3   For a discussion of Scott, see Franco Moretti, *Atlas of the European Novel*, pp. 33–47. The *Atlas* is a wonderfully fertile attempt to imagine what a geography of literature might be like, and prompted me to ask whether historical novels written by settler novelists in the colonies would vary in essential ways from the European model Moretti describes.

4   Moretti, *Atlas*, pp. 38–40.

5   William Satchell, *The Greenstone Door*, p. 174. Subsequent page references are given in my text.

6   In A. W. Reed's novel *Rewi's Last Stand*, which is based on Rudall Hayward's film scenario,

Ariana is saved by Bishop Selwyn, and hero and heroine live happily ever after on land gifted by the government and Ariana's roving father, but which Reed neglects to mention has been confiscated from her Maori relatives. It should be remembered that there are soft-headed alternatives to the difficulties of Satchell's ending.

7   Joseph Conrad, *Heart of Darkness*, p. 71.

PART III: SETTLING

1   Anon. (ed.), *Letters from Settlers and Labouring Emigrants*, p. 1. Subsequent page references are given in the text.
2   Allen Curnow, 'The Unhistoric Story', *Early Days Yet*, pp. 235–36.
3   Frederick Jackson Turner, 'The Significance of the Frontier in American History'. Turner's legacy is discussed in the essay 'Becoming West' noted below.
4   William Cronon, George Miles and Jay Gitlin, 'Becoming West: Toward a New Meaning for Western History', a jointly written introduction to William Cronon, George Miles and Jay Gitlin (eds), *Under an Open Sky*, pp. 11–22. I am indebted to perspectives developed in this essay.
5   Ibid, p. 13.
6   'It is nationalism which engenders nations, and not the other way round': Ernest Gellner, *Nations and Nationalism*, p. 55.
7   According to Anthony Smith, ethnic and national identities are a compound of 'myths, memories, values, symbols'. Cited in Brook Thomas, 'Placing Literature Written in English', *REAL Yearbook*, vol. 14, p. 6.
8   For an early critique emphasising the mediation of stylistic concerns, see Francis Pound, 'Harsh Clarities', *Parallax*, vol. 1, no. 3, Winter 1983, pp. 263–69.

Chapter Five: Taking Place

1   Report of the Select Committee on the Disposal of Land in the British Colonies, Parliamentary papers/House of Commons; no. 512, 1 August 1836, p. 108.
2   Roland Barthes describes the 'inoculation' of collective imagination in *Mythologies*, trans. Annette Lavers, p. 150.
3   Old Land Claim OLC 1/311, National Archives.
4   See Margaret Mutu, '*Tuku Whenua* and Land Sale in New Zealand in the Nineteenth Century', in Alex Calder, et al. (eds), *Voyages and Beaches*, pp. 317–28.
5   Old Land Claim OLC 1/311, National Archives.
6   In contrasting a 'Crown' position with a 'revisionist' position, I trust it will be understood that I am using a pair of shorthand descriptors for sides of a complex problem rather than identifying contesting parties as they might appear, say, on different sides before the Waitangi Tribunal.
7   The story appears in *Summer Fires and Winter Country* (1963), and is reprinted in Witi Ihimaera (ed.), *Where's Waari?*, pp. 140–62. Subsequent page references are to this collection and appear in the text.
8   Jane Campion, *The Piano*, pp. 142–43. One of those cross-cultural advisors, Waihoroi Shortland, though welcoming the opportunity for Maori involvement and collaboration, was somewhat more reserved about the cross-cultural credentials of the film. 'There is no way you could interpret this as being the ultimate Maori movie. I think the kindest description might be that we brush Maoridom at the time very gently – we're the backdrop against the main action of the movie . . . . There's still some distance to go . . . but people are actually taking the time out to consult with us, to talk with us. The big job of telling Maori stories is still something in the future for us to do.' Transcribed from an interview on the making of the film for the Maori television programme *Marae* (1994).
9   Linda Hardy, 'Natural Occupancy', in Suvendrini Perera (ed.), *Asian and Pacific Inscriptions*, pp. 213–27.
10   Campion, *The Piano*, pp. 104–5.
11   Ibid, p. 116.
12   Ibid, p. 141.
13   Ibid, p. 122.

Chapter Six: The Plots of Tutira

1   Herbert Guthrie-Smith, *Tutira*, third edition, p. 37. A fourth edition published in 1969 preserves the text of the third edition and adds an appendix noting changes in botanical and zoological nomenclature. A facsimile fifth edition, with a foreword by William Cronon, appeared in 1999. It is published as a Godwit Book by Random House in New Zealand and by the University of Washington Press in the United States. Pagination is constant for the textual matter of the third, fourth and fifth editions; unless otherwise specified, all subsequent page references in this essay are from the third edition, and are valid for subsequent editions. Page numbers are given in the body of my text.

2   I am indebted to William Cronon's discussion of these discursive structures in 'A Place for Stories: Nature, History, and Narrative', *Journal of American History*, vol. 78, no. 4, March 1992, pp. 1347–76. He writes: 'The upward and downward lines of these stories are everywhere apparent . . . . Their very familiarity encourages us to shape our story telling to fit their patterns', p. 1352.

3   Thomas Bracken, 'The Canterbury Pilgrims', *Musings in Maoriland*, pp. 84–85.

4   Cronon, 'A Place for Stories', p. 1352.

5   I prefer this slight variation on Cronon's original choice of terms. He writes: 'The one group of plots might be called "progressive", given their dependence on eighteenth-century Enlightenment notions of progress; the other might be called "tragic" or "declensionist", tracing their historical roots to romantic and anti-modernist reactions against progress': 'A Place for Stories', p. 1352.

6   The poem was published as an appendix to *The Long White Cloud*, pp. 380–82. A 1925 revision appears in Jenny Bornholdt, et al. (eds), *An Anthology of New Zealand Poetry in English*, pp. 499–500.

7   Ursula Bethell, 'Pause', in Vincent O'Sullivan (ed.), *An Anthology of Twentieth Century New Zealand Poetry*, p. 10. The poem, one of her most widely anthologised, was first published in *From a Garden in the Antipodes* (1929).

8   Henry David Thoreau is a notable American example. 'It would', he proposed in *Walden*, 'be of some advantage to live a primitive and frontier life, though in the midst of an outward civilization, if only to learn what are the necessaries of life and what methods have been taken to obtain them.' In the course of his re-enactment of the settling of America, of his exercise in reality testing, he likes to envisage the return of wilderness: 'Let wild Nature reign here once more . . .', pp. 12, 215.

9   'Current State of New Zealand's Biodiversity', http://www.biodiversity.govt.nz, accessed 15 June 2010.

10 According to the New Zealand government's 1994 'Environment 2010 Strategy' report, 'The possum population is around 70 million. They eat around 21,000 tonnes of vegetation every 24 hours, causing serious damage to canopies of indigenous species.' See http://www.cyberplace.org.nz/environment/env2010.html#2, accessed 15 June 2010.

11 Michael André Bernstein, *Foregone Conclusions*, p. 16 (his emphasis).

12 Andrew Hill Clark, *The Invasion of New Zealand by People, Plants and Animals*, p. v.

13 Guthrie-Smith was confident that had the earthquake occurred after Maori settlement of the lake, a record of the event would have been preserved in oral tradition.

14 Keri Hulme, *the bone people*, p. 157.

15 The reserve is now called Boundary Stream Mainland Island. For further information and links, see the New Zealand Department of Conservation's webpages for Parks and Recreation: http://www.doc.govt.nz/templates/PlaceProfile.aspx?id=34856, accessed 15 June 2010.

Chapter Seven: Suburbs, Settlers, Souls

1   Katherine Mansfield, 'To Stanislaw Wyspianski', in Vincent O'Sullivan (ed.), *An Anthology of Twentieth Century New Zealand Poetry*, p. 18.

2   Ibid.

3   'The Canon's Yeoman's Prologue', lines 104–7.

4   Katherine Mansfield, *The Collected Stories*, p. 23. Subsequent page references are given in the text.

5   Greg McGee, *Foreskin's Lament*, p. 53.

6   Allen Curnow, 'House and Land', in *Early Days Yet*, pp. 234–35.

7   In 1901, the population of Wellington was 49,344 people, half of whom were born in New Zealand: Chris Maclean, 'Wellington Region – Population', *Te Ara: the Encyclopedia of New*

Zealand. It is worth noting that Mansfield's one story to portray Wellington as a small town – 'Daphne' – is narrated by a bohemian artist on a temporary visit.

8   Jean Bartlett (ed.), *Takapuna: People and Places*, p. 46.
9   Letter from Frank Sargeson to the State Advances Corporation, 3 June 1947, MS-Papers-0432-140, Alexander Turnbull Library.
10 Frank Sargeson to John Lehmann, 22 January 1941, John Lehmann collection, Harry Ransom Humanities Research Center, University of Texas at Austin.
11 'Almost penthouse', Frank Sargeson to John Lehmann, 17 November 1948, Lehmann Family Papers Box 44 Folder 77, Department of Rare Books and Special collections, Princeton University Library; 'I really must send you', Frank Sargeson to William Plomer, 5 September 1949, MS-Papers-0432-187, Alexander Turnbull Library.
12 Frank Sargeson, *The Stories of Frank Sargeson*, pp. 284–85. Subsequent page references are given in the text.
13 Ian Wedde, 'Frank's Secret Army', *How To Be Nowhere*, pp. 25–29.
14 This point is made in Catherine Jurca's fine study of suburban fiction, *White Diaspora*.
15 Linda Hardy, 'Natural Occupancy', p. 214.
16 Jurca offers this definition: 'Sentimental dispossession refers to the affective dislocation by which white middleclass suburbanites begin to see themselves as spiritually and culturally impoverished by prosperity.' She adds: 'Literary representations of the suburb propose that white middleclass identity is not grounded in safe havens or homes but in its alienation from the very environments, artifacts, and institutions that have generally been regarded as central to its affect and identity': *White Diaspora*, p. 7.
17 Maurice Gee, *Going West*, p. 2. Subsequent page references are given in the text.
18 Rex writes these poems from a lifestyle block in Waimauku – beyond the suburbs, technically speaking, but the property with its creek recalls suburban Loomis.
19 Allen Curnow, *Early Days Yet*, p. 235.
20 'I have found myself piecing together the record of an adventure, or series of adventures, in search of reality . . .': Allen Curnow, 'Introduction', *The Penguin Book of New Zealand Verse*, p. 17. Harvey McQueen succinctly describes the controversy: 'The [Wellington] group defined itself in relation to their perception of Auckland-based Allen Curnow. Accordingly its interests were claimed to be what his were not – less concern about physical landscape and the New Zealand identity, more about universal issues which transcend borders. As a group . . . they wrote about actual life, society and the city suburbs with their state houses and backyard vegetable gardens. In retrospect the dispute was personal, regional and intergenerational rather than ideological': Roger Robinson and Nelson Wattie (eds), *The Oxford Companion to New Zealand Literature*, p. 269.
21 James K. Baxter, *Collected Poems*, p. 213.
22 Louis Johnson, *Selected Poems*, p. 92.
23 'Not I, some child, born in a marvellous year, / Will learn the trick of standing upright here': Allen Curnow, 'The Skeleton of the Great Moa in the Canterbury Museum, Christchurch', *Early Days Yet*, p. 220.

Chapter Eight: Glorious Phantoms: Frank Sargeson in Bohemia

1   'Mander, Mary Jane', in A. H. McLintock (ed.), *An Encyclopaedia of New Zealand*.
2   Wystan Curnow (ed.), *Essays on New Zealand Literature*, pp. 155–71.
3   The author's double-barrelled surname is a friendly wink in the direction of two of Sargeson's 'bodgie' friends and informants: Andy Coleman and Leo Thompson.
4   Oswald Mazengarb, et al., *Report of the Special Committee on Moral Delinquency in Children and Adolescents*, p. 7.
5   *The Stories of Frank Sargeson*, p. 246. Subsequent page references are given in the text.
6   W. L. C. Bakewell to Frank Sargeson, 8 February 1957, MS-Papers-0432-143, Alexander Turnbull Library.
7   Frank Sargeson, *Never Enough*, p. 85. Subsequent page references in this paragraph are given in the text.
8   Frank Sargeson, *Memoirs of a Peon*, p. 13. Subsequent page references are given in the text.
9   Allen Curnow, 'Introduction', *The Penguin Book of New Zealand Verse*, p. 56.
10 Melissa Gniadek, 'The Art of Becoming', *Journal of New Zealand Literature*, vol. 23, no. 2, 2005, pp. 21–35.
11 Ronald Hugh Morrieson, *The Scarecrow*, p. 1.
12 Maurice Duggan, 'Along Rideout Road that Summer', in *Collected Stories*, p. 196. Subsequent

page references are given in the text.

13   Bake's letter alludes to a favourite theory of Sargeson's: 'doesn't it occur to people that we must be naturally bisexual? .... No doubt you get the absolutely pure heterosexual. At the other end you get – well we've all seen pure homosexuals. But all the rest of us are somewhere in between': *Conversation in a Train*, p. 166.
14   *The Tempest*, act 3, scene 2, lines 133–34.
15   Sargeson, *Never Enough*, p. 104.

PART IV: LOOMING

1   C. K. Stead, 'For the Hulk of the World's Between', in Keith Sinclair (ed.), *Distance Looks Our Way*, p. 81.
2   Ibid. Stead's emphasis.
3   Maori war stories, by contrast, follow the 'national pattern' described below in their tendency to register the impact of the war on the domestic front.
4   Although the quotation is widely understood in this way, its original context involves her returning to Oakland and finding that her childhood home no longer exists: Gertrude Stein, *Everybody's Autobiography*, p. 289.
5   Janet Frame, *The Carpathians*, p. 8.
6   John Brocklesby, *Elements of Meteorology* (1853), cited in a discussion of looming by John R. Stilgoe, *Alongshore*, p. 25.
7   Ibid.

Chapter Nine: There and Back: Robin Hyde's Passport to Hell

1   For an Australian example, see Peter Weir's blockbuster film *Gallipoli* (1981); local instances include Maurice Shadbolt's play *Once on Chunuk Bair* (1982), which was adapted into the movie *Chunuk Bair* (1992). Comprehensive bibliographic essays on New Zealand war literature appear in Terry Sturm (ed.), *The Oxford Companion to New Zealand Literature in English*, pp. 566–75.
2   Stephen Fender, *Sea Changes*, pp. 342–43.
3   Janet Frame, *Intensive Care*, p. 27.
4   For background information on the life of Stark, on Hyde's relationship with him and on the composition of *Passport to Hell*, I am indebted to D. I. B. Smith's introduction to his edition of *Passport to Hell*. Smith's edition also provides annotations checking Hyde's narrative against Starkie's own journal and official war records, enabling the reader to identify points where Hyde has relied on her own imagination. The background to *Passport to Hell* is also covered in Derek Challis and Gloria Rawlinson, *The Book of Iris*, pp. 272–73.
5   Letters by John Tait to the *Southland Times* are cited and discussed by D. I. B. Smith (ed.), in Robin Hyde, *Passport to Hell*, pp. xiv–xvii.
6   Cited by Smith (ed.), in Hyde, *Passport to Hell*, p. xi.
7   Editors' 'Introduction' to Robin Hyde, *Nor the Years Condemn*, p. xxiii.
8   From Hyde's unpublished 1934 Autobiography (NZ MSS 412, Auckland Public Library), cited by Smith (ed.), in Hyde, *Passport to Hell*, p. xxi.
9   Freud links 'war neuroses' to the 'compulsion to repeat' in his essay 'Beyond the Pleasure Principle' (1920). Some readers will wonder why, after all these years, Freud's theories are trundled out as if they had not been overtaken by advances in psychology. But Freud has had, and continues to have, cultural (rather than scientific) influence because – like a good novelist – he offers compelling descriptions and interpretations of unconscious behaviour. Whether he is more than a certain kind of storyteller is another matter.
10   The correlation between 'real men' and an idealised nature has often been commented on: see, for example, Jock Phillips, *A Man's Country?*; and Kai Jensen, *Whole Men*.
11   While Starkie's colour is important in the novel (originally titled 'Bronze Outlaw'), Hyde's biographers suggest that the Delaware Indian Father and the Spanish mother are made up, probably by Starkie himself (Challis and Rawlinson, *The Book of Iris*, p. 274). Even so, an obituary of Starkie's father, cited by Smith, refers to Wyald Stark's 'dark' complexion: *Southland Daily News*, 5 November 1910; Hyde, *Passport to Hell*, p. xiii.
12   Robin Hyde, Letter to Eileen Duggan, 12 April 1935, http://www.nzepc.auckland.ac.nz/authors/hyde, accessed 15 June 2010.

13   'Her way to print was through the byways of daily and weekly journalism, where there was enough taste to perceive her talent, and enough booksy vulgarity almost to destroy it . . . . By incessant writing, incessant change, she fought to free her vision from its literary swathings – and in verse her worst enemy was the passionate crush on poetry with which she began. Her writing was near hysteria, more often than not, and she was incurably exhibitionistic': Allen Curnow, *The Penguin Book of New Zealand Verse*, p. 57.

14   See Alexander Aitken, *Gallipoli to the Somme*, pp. 41–42.

15   From Allen Curnow, 'The Skeleton of the Great Moa in the Canterbury Museum, Christchurch', *Early Days Yet*, p. 220.

16   Challis and Rawlinson, *The Book of Iris*, p. 18. As the cited passage comes from *The Godwits Fly*, p. 68, the biographical connection should be treated with caution.

17   'Introduction', *The Penguin Book of New Zealand Verse*, p. 17. Curnow's critics are perhaps unaware they use a similar trope when they complain of cultural nationalists 'overlooking' the significance of Maori.

18   Hyde, unpublished ms, cited by Smith (ed.), in Hyde, *Passport to Hell*, p. xxi.

19   Several chapters are narrated by Starkie. Hyde uses his voice partly for immediacy, partly to distance herself from his point of view – allowing, for example, racist comments about Egyptians to be given directly, without her corrective overlay.

20   A lengthy description is cited in Challis and Rawlinson, *The Book of Iris*, pp. 15–16. The source is incorrectly given as *The Godwits Fly*, which includes a briefer description of the embarkation.

21   The standard translation of Freud's term: *Nachträglichkeit*.

22   Wilfred Owen, 'Dulce Et Decorum Est', *Collected Poems*, p. 55.

23   Letter to J. H. E. Schroder, 27 March 1935, cited by Smith (ed.), in Hyde, *Passport to Hell*, p. ix.

24   Journal entry for 5 April 1935: cited in Challis and Rawlinson, *The Book of Iris*, p. 281.

Chapter Ten: Western Swing: John Mulgan's Man Alone

1   John Mulgan to Richard Mulgan, 8 July 1944, cited in Vincent O'Sullivan, *Long Journey to the Border*, p. 303. 'I've Got Spurs that Jingle Jangle Jingle' is not a song one associates with Ellington's Band. It was a hit for Kay Kyser's big band in 1942, and while I've found no Ellington recording, it may well have been covered by the band on radio shows and broadcasts to troops. Gene Autry's version of the song is readily available on *The Ultimate Gene Autry* (Columbia), as is his rendition of 'Deep in the Heart of Texas', which he first recorded in 1942.

2   James Belich, *Replenishing the Earth*, pp. 221–22 and passim. While I very much admire Belich's analysis and comparative overview of Anglophone settlement in the new world, it seems to me he has chosen an unfortunate term for a late phase of the process. 'Recolonization' misleadingly suggests renewed dependence rather than increasing interdependence between the former colony and homeland, and the maintenance of a single axis of relation between the two rather than a multiplication of lines of connection from a former colony to a globalising world. Even if one were to concede that New Zealand's economic/agricultural history from, say, 1910 to 1970 follows a dependent and single axis 'recolonization' model, our cultural history does not. Relations that were predominantly homeland focused (the publishing industry) soon become multiply stranded (movies from Hollywood, music from Tin Pan Alley, radio and television from the American and Australian networks as well as the BBC).

3   Cowan, *Tales of the Maori Bush*, p. 90.

4   Biographies of Tex Morton appear in the *Dictionary of New Zealand Biography* and in the 'heroes' section of nzedge.com, a website conceived, funded and maintained by Brian Sweeney and Kevin Roberts. Morton had an amazing career: as well being a top Country and Western singer – probably the first person to record country music outside the USA – he was a circus performer, stuntman, roustabout, hobo, television host and a stage hypnotist with a PhD in hypnotherapy from McGill University. I am not sure about the 100,000 copies of that comic strip; the round number has a Tex Mortonish ring of hyperbole to it. Morton maintained that he toured America with Hank Williams for six months in the early 1950s – the extent of that association is questioned in some online sources, but both singers had the same manager, and the two are likely to have performed on the same bill from time to time over that period. Historic recordings are available on the Tex Morton Regal Zonophone Collection, Vols 1 & 2 (EMI, 1993).

5   John Mulgan, *Man Alone*, p. 205. Subsequent pages references are given in the text.

6   For a discussion along these lines, see Stuart Murray, *Never a Soul at Home*, pp. 199–219.

7   The map and the route are mentioned by O'Sullivan, *Long Journey*, p. 194.

8   A partial exception: Mulgan at one point describes a bush full of birdsong – a chorus these days not often heard outside a bird sanctuary. Even so, we still know the 'same' bush as Johnson.
9   O'Sullivan, *Long Journey*, p. 196.
10   Ibid.
11   C. K. Stead, 'John Mulgan: A Question of Identity', *In the Glass Case*, pp. 67–98.
12   Ibid, p. 82.
13   Jean Laplanche and Jean-Bertrand Pontalis, *The Language of Psychoanalysis*, p. 205.
14   Cited by Lawrence Jones in his entry on Alan Mulgan in *The Oxford Companion to New Zealand Literature*, p. 384.
15   O'Sullivan, *Long Journey*, p. 15, citing Alan Mulgan's *The Making of a New Zealander* (1958).
16   Ibid, pp. 137–38.
17   Ibid, p. 125, citing a letter from JM to his parents, 13 September 1934.
18   Ibid, pp. 213–14, citing a letter from JM to his parents, 15 April 1940.
19   Ibid, p. 214.
20   Ibid, p. 159.
21   Ibid, p. 112, citing a letter from JM to his parents, 29 May 1934.
22   Ibid, p. 260.
23   Ibid, p. 197.
24   Ibid, p. 186.
25   Ibid, p. 56.
26   Louis L'Amour, *Radigan* (1958), cited in Jane Tompkins, *West of Everything: The Inner Life of Westerns*, p. 47. My discussion of the 'inner life' of Westerns is indebted to hers – though the inner life of that genre is also a matter of introspection for men of a certain age.
27   Tompkins, *West of Everything*, p. 3.
28   Ibid, p. 4.
29   My wording draws on Tompkins's phrase, 'the fully saturated moment': ibid, p. 14.
30   Owen Wister, *The Virginian*, p. 294.
31   As Tompkins writes, 'Town always threatens to entrap the hero in the very things the genre most wishes to avoid': *West of Everything*, p. 86.
32   Ibid, pp. 8–9.
33   Lawson's story is included in Witi Ihimaera (ed.), *Where's Waari?*, pp. 17–25.
34   Glover, *Selected Poems*, p. 65.
35   Ibid, p. 45.

Chapter Eleven: Cathedral Rock, Allen Curnow in Italy

1   Letter to Madame Strauss, 16 June 1906, cited in Ronald Hayman, *Proust: A Biography*, p. 147.
2   Letter to John Murray, 25 November 1816, *The Letters of Lord Byron*, p. 138.
3   Allen Curnow, 'The Unhistoric Story', *Early Days Yet*, pp. 235–36.
4   I am grateful to Allen Curnow's biographer, the late Terry Sturm, who kindly provided me with these details.
5   Allen Curnow, *An Incorrigible Music*, pp. 14–15. Subsequent page references included in my text are to this first edition. The full sequence is also reprinted in *Early Days Yet*, pp. 101–32.
6   The best modern account is Lauro Martines, *April Blood*, published long after Curnow's poem, and from which I have derived any details of the conspiracy that are not commonly known. The quoted phrase 'boss of bosses' comes from the blurb of *April Blood*.
7   I have consulted several more knowledgeable friends about this, and the consensus seems to be that the practice is not entirely a myth. One fish scientist informs me that a build-up of lactate in the blood of a struggling active fish like kahawai might affect the taste, while another suggests the practice has less to do with edibility than the visual appearance of the meat: since the white muscle of active fishes has more blood vessels than less active fishes, quick bleeding would prevent black vein-like markings from appearing. The red muscled flesh is richer in blood vessels and is generally regarded as poor eating – but 'quick bleeding' does not change that.
8   From a government memorandum responding to the pleas of Moro's family, thought to have been penned by Andreotti himself, cited in Leonardo Sciascia, *The Moro Affair*, p. 82.
9   This letter received by the party secretary, Senator Zaccagnini, on 21 April, was also made available to Italian newspapers. Cited in Sciascia, *The Moro Affair*, pp. 64–67.
10   Sciascia, *The Moro Affair*, p. 50.
11   Sciascia's phrase, in description of Moro, ibid.

12   Andrew Johnston, 'Late, Late Curnow: A Mind of Winter', *Journal of New Zealand Literature*, vol. 25 (2007), p. 64.
13   Ibid, pp. 64–65.
14   Keats refers to Wordsworth's 'egotistical sublime' in a letter to Richard Woodhouse, 27 October 1818.
15   The remarks on 'negative capability' are from a letter to his brothers, George and Tom Keats, 21 or 27 December 1817.
16   Johnston, 'Late, Late Curnow', p. 55. I might add that Curnow's extraordinary precision in describing places and things, which Johnston notes and admires, is another quality he would share with the author of 'Lines Composed a Few Miles above Tintern Abbey, on Revisiting the Banks of the Wye during a Tour, July 13, 1798' rather than with Keats.
17   Curnow, *Early Days Yet*, pp. 226–29. A point sometimes lost on our cultural entrepreneurs. On one occasion, to Curnow's half-bemused horror, Sir Edmund Hillary was invited to be the poem's narrator. Sir Ed was warmly admired for many reasons, but the reading of verse was not among his attainments, and the hoopla of a gala performance inadvertently emphasised the distinction between the poet's fascination with national themes and a 'rah-rah New Zealand' celebration of 'icons'.

Chapter Twelve: Placing Frame

1   All quotations in this paragraph are from 'Departures and Returns', in Guy Amirthanayagam (ed.), *Writers in East–West Encounter*, pp. 85–88.
2   Janet Frame, 'Departures and Returns', p. 91.
3   These recurring phrases are associated with the following texts: 'Mirror City' and 'the Kingdom by the Sea' with *An Autobiography*; 'the room two inches behind the eyes' with *State of Siege*; 'the Manifold' with *The Carpathians*.
4   See, for example, Sarah Abrahamson, 'Did Janet Frame have High-functioning Autism?', *Journal of the New Zealand Medical Association*, 12 October 2007, vol. 120, no. 1263; and Hilary Stace, 'Janet Frame and Autism', *Journal of the New Zealand Medical Association*, 26 October 2007, vol. 120, no. 1264.
5   My gestures towards these possible avenues of interpretation are not to be associated with any particular studies, as the best work resists easy summary. For a sampling of recent criticism, see Jan Cronin and Simone Drichel (eds), *Frameworks*. Drichel writes: 'what . . . are we to call Frame's seemingly insatiable desire for a *beyond*? Although perhaps not always recognizable as such, this question has (in one form or another) animated Frame criticism from the outset, with different critical approaches attaching markedly different meanings to this *beyond*', p. 183.
6   Janet Frame, *Faces in the Water*, p. 10.
7   Janet Frame, *Towards Another Summer*, p. 191. Subsequent page references are given in the text.
8   These phrases vitrify as Grace mentally rehearses how she is going to announce an intention to curtail her visit: *Towards Another Summer*, p. 160.
9   Frame's own words are cited without further reference in Michael King, *Wrestling with the Angel*, p. 245.
10   Frame, *Towards Another Summer*, p. 159.
11   Ibid, p. 13.
12   Janet Frame, *Living in the Maniototo*, p. 8. Subsequent page references are given in the text. For the *Encyclopaedia* entry, see under 'Otago Region'.
13   The epigraph is represented as coming from a biography of Peter Wallstead. The subject of this non-existent work inevitably recalls Ronald Hugh Morrieson, who seldom left his home town of Hawera.
14   Janet Frame, 'Alone on a River of Words: Interview with Rosemary Vincent', *New Zealand Times*, 2 October 1983, p. 9.
15   Janet Frame, *An Autobiography*, p. 101. The lines quoted appear in chapter 22 of *To the Is-Land*, published separately in 1982. Subsequent pages references to *An Autobiography* are provided in the text.
16   Frame's bushfire metaphor inevitably recalls the 'burn-offs' that made land available for settlement.
17   Frame, 'Departures and Returns', p. 91.
18   Ibid.

BIBLIOGRAPHY

Abrahamson, Sarah, 'Did Janet Frame have High-functioning Autism?', *Journal of the New Zealand Medical Association*, vol. 120, no. 1263, 12 October 2007, p. 2747.

Agnew, Vanessa and Jonathan Lamb (eds), *Settler and Creole Re-enactment*, Palgrave Macmillan, Basingstoke, 2009.

Aitken, Alexander, *Gallipoli to the Somme: Recollections of a New Zealand Infantryman*, Oxford University Press, London, 1963.

Amirthanayagam, Guy (ed.), *Writers in East–West Encounter*, Macmillan, London, 1982.

Anon. (ed.), *Letters from Settlers and Labouring Emigrants in the New Zealand Company's Settlements of Wellington, Nelson, & New Plymouth*, Smith, Elder & Co., London, 1843.

Anon., 'Musings on Manning's [sic] "Old New Zealand"', *Temple Bar*, vol. 5, no. 18, pp. 526–27.

Arens, William, *The Man-Eating Myth*, Oxford University Press, New York, 1979.

Armstrong, Philip, 'Dis/coveries: Allen Curnow's Later Poems', *Journal of Commonwealth Literature*, vol. 7, no. 2, 1999.

Ballantyne, David, *Sydney Bridge Upside Down*, Whitcombe & Tombs, Christchurch, 1968.

Barber, Ian, 'Archaeology, Ethnography, and the Record of Maori Cannibalism Before 1815: A Critical Review', *Journal of the Polynesian Society*, vol. 101, no. 3, pp. 241–92.

Barker, Frances, Peter Hulme and Margaret Iversen (eds), *Cannibalism and the Colonial World*, Cambridge University Press, Cambridge, 1998.

Barker, Mary Anne, *Station Life in New Zealand*, Macmillan and Co., London, 1870.

Barrowman, Rachel, *A Popular Vision: The Arts and the Left in New Zealand 1930–1950*, Victoria University Press, Wellington, 1991.

___, *Mason: The Life of R.A.K. Mason*, Victoria University Press, Wellington, 2003.

Barthes, Roland, *Mythologies*, trans. Annette Lavers, Paladin, St Albans, 1972.

Bartlett, Jean (ed.), *Takapuna: People and Places*, Takapuna City Council and North Shore Historical Society, Auckland, 1989.

Bate, Walter Jackson, *John Keats*, Harvard University Press, Cambridge, 1979.

Baughan, Blanche, *Studies in New Zealand Scenery*, Whitcombe & Tombs, Auckland, 1916.

Baxter, James K., *Collected Poems*, J. E. Weir (ed.), Oxford University Press, Wellington, 1979.

___, *James K. Baxter as Critic: A Selection from his Literary Criticism*, Frank McKay (ed.), Heinemann, Auckland, 1978.

Belich, James, *I Shall Not Die: Titokowaru's War*, Allen & Unwin, Wellington, 1989.

___, *Making Peoples: A History of the New Zealanders from Polynesian Settlement to the End of the Nineteenth Century*, Penguin, Auckland, 1996.

___, *Paradise Reforged: A History of the New Zealanders from the 1880s to the Year 2000*, Penguin, Auckland, 2001.

___, *Replenishing the Earth: The Settler Revolution and the Rise of the Anglo-World, 1783–1939*, Oxford University Press, New York, 2009.

___, *The New Zealand Wars*, Penguin, Auckland, 1998.

Bell, Claudia and Steve Matthewman (eds), *Cultural Studies in Aotearoa New Zealand*, Oxford University Press, Melbourne, 2004.

Benjamin, Walter, 'On the Concept of History', in Howard Eiland and Michael W. Jennings (eds), *Selected Writings*, vol. 4, Harvard University Press, Cambridge, 2003.

Bernstein, Michael André, *Foregone Conclusions: Against Apocalyptic History*, University of California Press, Berkeley, 1994.

Binney, Judith, 'Historical Model for Gardens Occupation', *New Zealand Herald*, 17 April 1995, 1, p. 6.

___, 'Papahurihia, Penetana', *Dictionary of New Zealand Biography*, vol. 1, Allen & Unwin, Wellington, 1990, pp. 329–31.

___, 'Papahurihia: Some Thoughts on Interpretation', *Journal of the Polynesian Society*, vol. 75, no. 3, 1966, pp. 321–31.

Bornholdt, Jenny, Gregory O'Brien and Mark Williams (eds), *An Anthology of New Zealand Poetry in English*, Oxford University Press, Auckland, 1997.

Bracken, Thomas, *Musings in Maoriland*, Arthur T. Kierle, Dunedin, 1890.

Branch, Watson G., *Melville: The Critical Heritage*, Routledge & Kegan Paul, London and Boston, 1974.

Brantlinger, Patrick, *Rule of Darkness: British Literature and Imperialism, 1830–1914*, Cornell University Press, Ithaca, 1988.

Buick, T. L., *The Treaty of Waitangi*, 2nd ed., Thomas Avery and Sons, New Plymouth, 1933.

Burdon, R. M., *New Zealand Notables: Series Three*, Caxton, Christchurch, 1950.

Burke, Gregory and Ian Wedde (eds), *Now See Hear! Art, Language, Translation*, Victoria University Press, Wellington, 1990.

Burman, E., 'The Culminating Sacrifice: An Interpretation of Allen Curnow's "Moro Assassinato"', *Landfall*, vol. 39, March 1985, pp. 22–36.

Butler, Samuel, *Erewhon*, Peter Mudford (ed.), Penguin, Harmondsworth, 1970.

Byron, George Gordon, *Letters of Lord Byron*, R. G. Howarth (ed.), Everyman, London, 1962.

Calder, Alex, 'My Katherine Mansfield', *Landfall*, vol. 43, no. 4, 1989, pp. 503–11.

___, 'Sacrifice and Signification in the Poetry of Allen Curnow', in Mark Williams and Michele Leggott (eds), *Opening the Book*, Auckland University Press, Auckland, 1995, pp. 83–104.

___, 'Unsettling Settlement: Poetry and Nationalism in Aotearoa/New Zealand', *REAL Yearbook of Research in English and American Literature*, vol. 14, 1998, pp. 165–82.

Calder, Alex, Jonathan Lamb and Bridget Orr (eds), *Voyages and Beaches: Europe and the Pacific, 1769–1840*, University of Hawai'i Press, Honolulu, 1999.

Campion, Jane, *The Piano*, Bloomsbury, London, 1993.

Challis, Derek and Gloria Rawlinson, *The Book of Iris*, Auckland University Press, Auckland, 2002.

Chapman, Robert, 'Fiction and the Social Pattern', *Landfall*, vol. 25, 1953, pp. 26–52.

Clark, Andrew Hill, *The Invasion of New Zealand by People, Plants and Animals*, Rutgers University Press, New Brunswick, 1949.

Conrad, Joseph, *Heart of Darkness*, Folio Society, London, 1997.

Cowan, James, *Sir Donald Maclean: The Story of a New Zealand Statesman*, A. H. & A. W. Reed, Wellington, 1940.

___, *Tales of the Maori Bush*, Alex Calder (ed.), Reed, Auckland, 2006.

Creed, Barbara and Jeanette Hoorn (eds), *Body Trade: Captivity, Cannibalism and Colonialism in the Pacific*, Routledge, New York, 2001.

Cronin, Jan and Simone Drichel (eds), *Frameworks: Contemporary Criticism on Janet Frame*, Rodopi, Amsterdam, 2009.

Cronon, William, 'A Place for Stories: Nature, History, and Narrative', *Journal of American History*, March 1992, pp. 1347–76.

___ (ed.), *Uncommon Ground*, Norton, New York, 1996.

Cronon, William, George Miles and Jay Gitlin, 'Becoming West: Toward a New Meaning for Western History', in William Cronon, George Miles and Jay Gitlin (eds), *Under an Open Sky: Rethinking America's Western Past*, Norton, New York, 1993, pp. 11–22.

___ (eds), *Under an Open Sky: Rethinking America's Western Past*, Norton, New York, 1993.

Curnow, Allen, *An Incorrigible Music*, Auckland University Press, Auckland, 1979.

___, *Early Days Yet: New and Collected Poems 1941–1997*, Auckland University Press, Auckland, 1997.

___, *Look Back Harder: Critical Writings 1935–1984*, Peter Simpson (ed.), Auckland University Press, Auckland, 1987.

___ (ed.), *The Penguin Book of New Zealand Verse*, Blackwood and Janet Paul, Auckland, 1966.

Curnow, Wystan (ed.), *Essays on New Zealand Literature*, Heinemann, Auckland, 1973.

___, 'High Culture in a Small Province', in Wystan Curnow (ed.), *Essays on New Zealand Literature*, Heinemann, Auckland, 1973, pp. 155–71.

___, *Putting the Land on the Map: Art and Cartography in New Zealand since 1840*, Govett-Brewster Art Gallery, New Plymouth, 1989.

Davidson, J. W., *Peter Dillon of Vanikoro*, Oxford University Press, Melbourne, 1975.

Davis, Leigh, 'Solo Curnow', *And*, vol. 3, 1984, pp. 49–62.

Day, Paul, *John Mulgan*, Twayne, New York, 1968.

Delrez, Marc, *Manifold Utopia: The Novels of Janet Frame*, Rodopi, Amsterdam, 2002.

Dening, Greg, *Beach Crossings: Voyaging Across Times, Cultures and Self*, Miegunyah Press, Melbourne, 2004.

___, *Islands and Beaches*, Dorsey Press, Chicago, 1980.

Devanny, Jean, *The Butcher Shop*, Heather Roberts (ed.), Auckland University Press, Auckland, 1988.

Dillon, Peter, *Narrative of La Pérouse's Expedition* (1829), 2 vols, Da Capo Press, New York, 1972.

Drichel, Simone, 'Signposts to a World that is Not Even Mentioned: Janet Frame's Ethical Transcendence', in Jan Cronin and Simone Drichel (eds), *Frameworks: Contemporary Criticism on Janet Frame*, Rodopi, Amsterdam, 2009, pp. 181–212.

Dudding, Robin (ed.), *Beginnings: New Zealand Authors Tell How They Began Writing*, Oxford University Press, Wellington, 1980.

Duggan, Maurice, 'Along Rideout Road that Summer', in Witi Ihimaera (ed.), *Where's Waari? A History of Maori Through the Short Story*, Reed, Auckland, 2000.

___, *Collected Stories*, C. K. Stead (ed.), Auckland University Press, Auckland, 1981.

During, Simon, 'Postmodernism or Postcolonialism?', *Landfall*, vol. 155, 1985, pp. 366–80.

___, 'What was the West? Some Relations between Modernity, Colonisation and Writing', *Sport*, vol. 4, 1990, pp. 63–89.

Earle, Augustus, *Narrative of a Residence in New Zealand*, E. H. McCormick (ed.), Clarendon Press, Oxford, 1966.

Evans, Patrick, 'Janet Frame and the Art of Life', *Meanjin*, vol. 44, Sept 1985, pp. 375–83.

___, 'Living and Writing in the Maniototo', *Span*, vol. 18, April 1984, pp. 76–88.

___, *The Long Forgetting*, Canterbury University Press, Christchurch, 2007.

Fairburn, A. R. D., *Collected Poems*, Pegasus Press, Christchurch, 1966.

Fairburn, Miles, *The Ideal Society and its Enemies: The Foundations of Modern New Zealand Society, 1850–1900*, Auckland University Press, Auckland, 1990.

Fender, Stephen, *Sea Changes: British Emigration & American Literature*, Cambridge University Press, New York, 1992.

Fenton, F. D. (ed.), *Important Judgments Delivered in the Compensation Court and Native Land Court, 1866–1879*, Auckland Native Land Court, 1879.

Fisher, Philip, *Hard Facts: Setting and Form in the American Novel*, Oxford University Press, New York, 1985.

___, *Still the New World: American Literature in a Culture of Creative Destruction*, Harvard University Press, Boston, 2000.

Fitzgerald, Joan, 'Images of the Self: Two Early New Zealand Autobiographies', *Journal of Commonwealth Literature*, vol. 23, no. 1, 1988, pp. 16–41.

Frame, Janet, 'Alone on a River of Words: Interview with Rosemary Vincent', *New Zealand Times*, 2 October 1983, p. 9.

___, *An Autobiography*, Century Hutchinson, Auckland, 1989.

___, 'Departures and Returns', in Guy Amirthanayagam (ed.), *Writers in East–West Encounter*, Macmillan, London, 1982, pp. 85–94.

___, *Daughter Buffalo*, Reed, Wellington, 1972.

___, *Faces in the Water*, The Women's Press, London, 1980.

___, *Intensive Care*, Century Hutchinson, Auckland, 1987.

___, *Living in the Maniototo*, George Braziller, New York, 1979.

___, *Owls Do Cry*, Pegasus Press, Christchurch, 1957.

___, *Rainbirds*, W. H. Allen, London, 1968.

___, *Scented Gardens for the Blind*, Pegasus Press, Christchurch, 1963.

___, *State of Siege*, Pegasus Press, Christchurch, 1967.

___, *The Adaptable Man*, Pegasus Press, Christchurch, 1965.

___, *The Carpathians*, Century Hutchinson, Auckland, 1988.

___, *Towards Another Summer*, Vintage, Auckland, 2007.

___, *Yellow Flowers in the Antipodean Room*, George Braziller, New York, 1969.

Freud, Sigmund, 'Beyond the Pleasure Principle', in Angela Richards (ed.), The Pelican Freud Library, vol. 11: *On Metapsychology*, Penguin Books, Harmondsworth, 1984.

Gee, Maurice, *Crime Story*, Penguin Books, Auckland, 1994.

Gee, Maurice, *Going West*, Viking, Auckland, 1992.

___, *Meg*, Faber, London, 1981.

___, *Plumb*, Faber, London, 1978.

___, *Sole Survivor*, Faber, London, 1983.

Gellner, Ernest, *Nations and Nationalism*, Cornell University Press, Ithaca, 1983.

Gibbons, Peter, 'Cultural Colonisation and National Identity', *New Zealand Journal of History*, vol. 36, no. 1, 2002, pp. 5–17.

___, 'Non-Fiction', in Terry Sturm (ed.), *The Oxford History of New Zealand Literature in English*, 2nd ed., Oxford University Press, Auckland, 1998.

Glover, Denis, *Selected Poems*, Bill Manhire (ed.), Victoria University Press, Wellington, 1995.

Gniadek, Melissa, 'The Art of Becoming: Sherwood Anderson, Frank Sargeson and the Grotesque Aesthetic', *Journal of New Zealand Literature*, vol. 23, no. 2, 2005, pp. 21–35.

Goldman, Laurence (ed.), *The Anthropology of Cannibalism*, Bergin and Garvey, Westport, CT, 1999.

Gombrich, Ernst, *Art and Illusion: A Study in the Psychology of Pictorial Representation*, Princeton University Press, Princeton, 2000.

Guthrie-Smith, Herbert, *Bird Life on Island and Shore*, William Blackwood & Sons, Edinburgh and London, 1925.

___, *Birds of Tutira*, Christine Cole Catley (ed.), Cape Catley, Whatamongo Bay, 1990.

___, *Birds of Water, Wood and Waste*, 2nd ed., Whitcombe & Tombs, Wellington, Christchurch and Dunedin, 1914.

___, *Mutton Birds and Other Birds*, Whitcombe & Tombs, Christchurch, Wellington and Dunedin, 1914.

___, *Sorrows and Joys of a New Zealand Naturalist*, A. H. & A. W. Reed, Dunedin and Wellington, 1936.

___, *Tutira: The Story of a New Zealand Sheep Station*, 3rd ed., William Blackwood & Sons, Edinburgh and London, 1953.

Hardy, Linda, 'Natural Occupancy', in Suvendrini Perera (ed.), *Asian and Pacific Inscriptions*, Meridian, Bundoora, Victoria, 1995, pp. 213–27.

___, 'The Ghost of Katherine Mansfield', *Landfall*, vol. 43, no. 4, 1989, pp. 416–32.

Hayman, Ronald, *Proust: A Biography*, HarperCollins, New York, 1990.

Hilliard, Chris, *The Bookmen's Dominion: Cultural Life in New Zealand 1920–1950*, Auckland University Press, Auckland, 2006.

Horrocks, Roger, 'Natural As Only You Can Be: Some Readings of Contemporary New Zealand Poetry', *And*, vol. 4, 1985, pp. 101–24.

___, 'The Invention of New Zealand', *And*, vol. 1, 1983, pp. 9–30.

Hulme, Keri, *the bone people*, Hodder and Stoughton, Auckland, 1985.

Hyde, Robin, *Nor the Years Condemn*, P. Bunkle, L. Hardy and J. Matthews (eds), New Women's Press, Auckland, 1986.

___, *Passport to Hell*, D. I. B. Smith (ed.), Auckland University Press, Auckland, 1987.

___, *The Godwits Fly*, Gloria Rawlinson (ed.), Auckland University Press, Auckland, 1970.

Ihimaera, Witi (ed.), *Bulibasha: King of the Gypsies*, Penguin, Auckland, 1994.

___ (ed.), *Where's Waari? A History of Maori Through the Short Story*, Reed, Auckland, 2000.

Jensen, Kai, *Whole Men: The Masculine Tradition in New Zealand Literature*, Auckland University Press, Auckland, 1996.

Johnson, Louis, *Selected Poems*, Terry Sturm (ed.), Victoria University Press, Wellington, 2000.

Johnston, Andrew, 'Late, Late Curnow: A Mind of Winter', *Journal of New Zealand Literature*, vol. 25, 2007, pp. 46–69.

Jones, Lawrence, *Barbed Wire & Mirrors: Essays on New Zealand Prose*, University of Otago Press, Dunedin, 1987.

___, 'New Zealand Realism: Retrospect and Prospect', *Landfall*, vol. 160, December 1986, pp. 472–86.

___, *Picking Up the Traces: The Making of a New Zealand Literary Culture 1932–1945*, Victoria University Press, Wellington, 2003.

Jurca, Catherine, *White Diaspora: The Suburb and the Twentieth Century American Novel*, Princeton University Press, Princeton, 2001.

Kavka, Misha, Jenny Lawn and Mary Paul (eds), *Gothic New Zealand: The Darker Side of Kiwi Culture*, Otago University Press, Dunedin, 2006.

King, Michael, *Frank Sargeson: A Life*, Viking, Auckland, 1995.

___, *Pakeha: The Quest for Identity in New Zealand*, Penguin, Auckland, 1991.

___, *Wrestling with the Angel: A Life of Janet Frame*, Viking, Auckland, 2000.

Lamb, Jonathan, 'A Sublime Moment off Poverty Bay, 9 October 1769', in Graham McGregor and Mark Williams (eds), *Dirty Silence: Aspects of Language and Literature in New Zealand*, Oxford University Press, Auckland, 1991, pp. 97–115.

___, *Preserving the Self in the South Seas*, University of Chicago Press, Chicago, 2001.

___, 'Problems of Originality: or Beware of Pakeha Baring Guilts', *Landfall*, vol. 159, 1986, pp. 352–59.

___, 'The Idea of Utopia in the European Settlement of New Zealand', in Klaus Neumann, Nicholas Thomas and Hilary Erickson (eds), *Quicksands: Foundational Histories in Aotearoa New Zealand*, University of New South Wales Press, Sydney, 1999, pp. 79–97.

___, 'The New Zealand Sublime', *Meanjin*, vol. 49, no. 4, 1990, pp. 663–75.

Laplanche, Jean and Jean-Bertrand Pontalis, *The Language of Psychoanalysis*, The Hogarth Press, London, 1973.

Lee, Jack, *Hokianga*, Reed, Auckland, 1996.

___, *The Bay of Islands*, Reed, Auckland, 1996.

Levin, Joanna, *Bohemia in America: 1858–1920*, Stanford University Press, Stanford, 1979.

Lyons, Paul, 'Lines of Fright: Fear, Perception, and the "Seen" of Cannibalism', in Barbara Creed and Jeanette Hoorn (eds), *Body Trade: Captivity, Cannibalism and Colonialism in the Pacific*, Routledge, New York, 2001, pp. 126–48.

McGee, Greg, *Foreskin's Lament*, Price Milburn, Wellington, 1981.

McKay, Frank, *The Life of James K. Baxter*, Oxford University Press, Auckland, 1990.

McLintock, A. H. (ed.), *An Encyclopaedia of New Zealand*, Government Printer, Wellington, 1966.

Maclean, Chris, 'Wellington Region – Population', *Te Ara: the Encyclopedia of New Zealand*, updated 31 May 2010; http://www.TeAra.govt.nz/en/wellington-region/12.

Mander, Jane, *Allen Adair*, Hutchinson, London, 1925.

___, *The Story of a New Zealand River*, Godwit, Auckland, 1994.

Maning, F. E., 'Aroha', in F. D. Fenton (ed.), *Important Judgments Delivered in the Compensation Court and Native Land Court, 1866–1879*, Auckland Native Land Court, 1879.

___, *Old New Zealand and Other Writings*, Alex Calder (ed.), Leicester University Press, Leicester, 2001.

Mansfield, Katherine, *The Collected Stories*, Penguin Books, London, 2007.

Maritnes, Lauro, *April Blood: Florence and the Plot against the Medici*, Oxford University Press, Oxford, 2003.

Markham, Edward, *New Zealand or Recollections of It*, E. H. McCormick (ed.), Government Printer, Wellington, 1963.

Martin, Mary, *Our Maoris*, E. & J. B. Young, New York, 1884.

Mathew, Felton and Sarah Mathew, *The Founding of New Zealand*, J. Rutherford (ed.), A. H. & A. W. Reed, Dunedin, 1940.

Mazengarb, Oswald, et al., *Report of the Special Committee on Moral Delinquency in Children and Adolescents*, Government Printer, Wellington, 1954.

Mercer, Gina, *Janet Frame: Subversive Fictions*, University of Otago Press, Dunedin, 1994.

Mitchell, W. J. T. (ed.), *Landscape and Power*, University of Chicago Press, Chicago, 1994.

Moretti, Franco, *Atlas of the European Novel*, Verso, London, 1998.

Morrieson, Ronald Hugh, *The Scarecrow*, Heinemann, Auckland, 1976.

Mulgan, John, *Man Alone*, Penguin Books, Auckland, 1990.

___ (ed.), *Poems of Freedom*, Gollancz, London, 1938.

___, *Report on Experience*, Peter Whiteford (ed.), Victoria University Press, Wellington, 2010.

Murray, Stuart, *Never a Soul at Home: New Zealand Literary Nationalism and the 1930s*, Victoria University Press, Wellington, 1998.

Mutu, Margaret, '*Tuku Whenua* and Land Sale in New Zealand in the Nineteenth Century', in Alex Calder, Jonathan Lamb and Bridget Orr (eds), *Voyages and Beaches: Pacific Encounters, 1769–1840*, University of Hawai'i Press, Honolulu, 1999, pp. 317–28.

Neumann, Klaus, Nicholas Thomas and Hilary Erickson (eds), *Quicksands: Foundational Histories in Aotearoa New Zealand*, University of New South Wales Press, Sydney, 1999.

New, W. H., *Land Sliding: Imagining Space, Presence, and Power in Canadian Writing*, University of Toronto Press, Toronto, 1997.

Newton, John, 'Colonialism Above the Snowline: Baughan, Ruskin and the South Island Myth', *Journal of Commonwealth Literature*, vol. 34, no. 2, 1999, pp. 85–96.

___, 'Homophobia and the Social Pattern: Sargeson's Queer Nation', *Landfall*, vol. 199, 2002, pp. 91–107.

___, *The Double Rainbow: James K. Baxter, Ngati Hau and the Jerusalem Commune*, Victoria University Press, Wellington, 2009.

O'Sullivan, Vincent (ed.), *An Anthology of Twentieth Century New Zealand Poetry*, Oxford University Press, Auckland, 1988.

___, *Long Journey to the Border: A Life of John Mulgan*, Penguin Books, Auckland, 2003.

Obeyesekere, Gananath, 'British Cannibals: Contemplation of an Event in the Death and Resurrection of James Cook, Explorer', *Critical Inquiry*, vol. 18, Summer 1992, pp. 630–54.

___, 'Cannibal Feasts in Nineteenth Century Fiji: Seamen's Yarns and the Ethnographic Imagination', in Frances Barker, Peter Hulme and Margaret Iversen (eds), *Cannibalism and the Colonial World*, Cambridge University Press, Cambridge, 1998, pp. 63–86.

Oliver, W. H., *James K. Baxter: A Portrait*, Port Nicholson Press, Wellington, 1983.

Owen, Wilfred, *The Collected Poems of Wilfred Owen*, New Directions, New York, 1965.

Park, Geoff, *Nga Uruora: The Groves of Life: Ecology & History in a New Zealand Landscape*, Victoria University Press, Wellington, 1995.

___, 'Our Terra Nullius', *Landfall*, vol. 204, November 2002, pp. 53–67.

___, *Theatre Country: Essays on Landscape and Whenua*, Victoria University Press, Wellington, 2006.

Paul, Mary, *Her Side of the Story: Readings of Mander, Mansfield, & Hyde*, University of Otago Press, Dunedin, 1999.

Pearson, Bill, *Fretful Sleepers and Other Essays*, Heinemann, Auckland, 1974.

Perry, Nick, 'Flying by Nets: The Social Pattern of New Zealand Fiction', *Islands*, vol. 23, 1987, pp. 161–77.

Phillips, Jock, *A Man's Country? The Image of the Pakeha Male: A History*, Penguin, Auckland, 1987.

Pickering, Michael, 'Consuming Doubts: What Some People Ate? Or What Some People Swallowed?', in Laurence Goldman (ed.), *The Anthropology of Cannibalism*, Bergin and Garvey, Westport, CT, 1999, pp. 51–74.

Pound, Francis, 'Harsh Clarities', *Parallax*, vol. 1, no. 3, Winter 1983, pp. 263–69.

Pratt, Mary Louise, *Imperial Eyes: Travel Writing and Transculturation*, 2nd ed., Routledge, New York, 2008.

Reed, A. W., *Rewi's Last Stand*, Reed, Dunedin, 1939.

Reeves, William Pember, *The Long White Cloud*, George Allen & Unwin, London, 1950.

Ricketts, Harry, 'Looking Back at Curnow, Harder', *Journal of New Zealand Literature*, vol. 5, 1987, pp. 29–44.

Roberts, Hugh, 'The Same People Living in Different Places: Allen Curnow's Anthology and New Zealand Literary History', *Modern Language Quarterly: A Journal of Literary History*, vol. 64, no. 2, 2003, pp. 219–37.

Robinson, Peter, 'Allen Curnow Travels', *English: the Journal of the English Association*, vol. 49, Spring 2000, pp. 39–63.

Robinson, Roger and Nelson Wattie (eds), *The Oxford Companion to New Zealand Literature*, Oxford University Press, Auckland, 1998.

Sahlins, Marshall, *How 'Natives' Think: About Captain Cook, for Example*, University of Chicago Press, Chicago, 1995.

Said, Edward, *Orientalism*, Penguin, Harmondsworth, 1991.

Salmond, Anne, *Between Worlds: Early Exchanges Between Maori and Europeans 1773–1815*, Penguin Books, London and New York, 2003.

Sanborn, Geoffrey, *The Sign of the Cannibal*, Duke University Press, Durham and London, 1998.

___, *Whipscars and Tattoos:* The Last of the Mohicans, Moby-Dick, *and the Maori*, Oxford University Press, New York, 2010.

Sargeson, Frank, *Conversation in a Train*, Auckland University Press, Auckland, 1983.

___, *Joy of the Worm*, MacGibbon & Kee, London, 1969.

___, *Memoirs of a Peon*, Godwit, Auckland, 1994.

___, *More than Enough*, A. H. & A. W. Reed, Wellington, 1975.

___, *Never Enough*, A. H. & A. W. Reed, Wellington, 1977.

___, *Once is Enough*, Martin Brian & O'Keefe, London, 1973.

___, *The Hangover*, MacGibbon & Kee, London, 1967.

___, *The Stories of Frank Sargeson*, Penguin, Auckland, 1982.

___, *Wrestling with the Angel: Two Plays*, Caxton Press, Christchurch, 1964.

Satchell, William, *The Greenstone Door*, Golden Press, Auckland, 1973.

___, *The Land of the Lost*, Kendrick Smithyman (ed.), Auckland University Press, Auckland, 1971.

___, *The Toll of the Bush*, Kendrick Smithyman (ed.), Auckland University Press, Auckland, 1986.

Sciascia, Leonardo, *The Moro Affair*, trans. Sacha Rabinowitz, Carcanet, Manchester, 1987.

Servant, Catherin, *Customs and Habits of the New Zealanders 1838–42*, D. R. Simmons (ed.), Reed, Wellington, 1973.

Shadbolt, Maurice, *Once Upon Chunuk Bair*, Hodder and Stoughton, Auckland, 1982.

___, *Summer Fires and Winter Country*, Eyre and Spottiswoode, London, 1963.

___, *The Lovelock Version*, Hodder and Stoughton, London, 1980.

Shieff, Sarah, 'The Varieties of Cultural Nationalism: "Landfall in Unknown Seas" 1942–1995', *Span*, vol. 39, 1994, pp. 29–55.

Shortland, Edward, *Traditions and Superstitions of the New Zealanders*, Longman, London, 1856.

Simmons, Laurence, 'Bridging the Wild', *Landfall*, vol. 204, 2002, pp. 95–208.

Simpson, Peter, 'Allen Curnow Talks to Peter Simpson', *Landfall*, vol. 44, no. 3, 1990, pp. 296–313.

Smith, Anna and Lydia Wevers, *On Display: New Essays in Cultural Studies*, Victoria University Press, Wellington, 2004.

Smithyman, Kendrick, *Atua Wera*, Auckland University Press, Auckland, 1997.

___, 'Uncollected Northland Poems', Jack Ross (ed.), *brief*, 26 January 2003, pp. 19–49.

Solnit, Rebecca, *Savage Dreams: A Journey into the Landscape Wars of the American West*, University of California Press, Berkeley, 1999.

Stace, Hilary, 'Janet Frame and Autism', *Journal of the New Zealand Medical Association*, vol. 120, no. 1264, 26 October 2007, p. 2791.

Stafford, Jane, 'Fashioned Intimacies: Maoriland and Colonial Modernity', *Journal of Commonwealth Literature*, vol. 37, no. 1, 2002, pp. 31–48.

___, 'The Ashram at Akaroa: Blanche Edith Baughan, India and the Literature of Maoriland', *Kunapipi: Journal of Post Colonial Writing*, vol. 22, no. 2, 2000, pp. 44–53.

Stafford, Jane and Mark Williams, *Maoriland: New Zealand Literature 1872–1914*, Victoria University Press, Wellington, 2006.

Stead, C. K., *All Visitors Ashore*, Godwit, Auckland, 1994.

___, *Answering to the Language: Essays on Modern Writers*, Auckland University Press, Auckland, 1989.

___, 'For the Hulk of the World's Between', in Keith Sinclair (ed.), *Distance Looks Our Way: The Effects of Remoteness on New Zealand*, Paul's Book Arcade, Auckland, 1961.

___, 'John Mulgan: A Question of Identity', *In The Glass Case*, Auckland University Press, Auckland, 1982, pp. 67–98.

___, *In the Glass Case: Essays on New Zealand Literature*, Auckland University Press, Auckland, 1982.

___, *Kin of Place: Essays on Twenty New Zealand Writers*, Auckland University Press, Auckland, 2002.

___, *Mansfield*, Harvill, London, 2004.

Stein, Gertrude, *Everybody's Autobiography*, Exact Change Books, Boston, 2004.

Stilgoe, John R., *Alongshore*, Yale University Press, New Haven, 1994.

Stokes, Evelyn, *Wiremu Tamihana: Rangatira*, Huia, Wellington, 1992.

Sturm, Terry, *An Unsettled Spirit: The Life and Frontier Fiction of Edith Lyttleton*, Auckland University Press, Auckland, 2003.

___, 'Fictions and Realities: An Approach to Allen Curnow's *Trees, Effigies, Moving Objects*', *World Literature Written in English*, vol. 14, 1975, pp. 25–50.

___ (ed.), *The Oxford History of New Zealand Literature in English*, 2nd ed., Oxford University Press, Auckland, 1998.

Tannahill, Reay, *Flesh and Blood: A History of the Cannibal Complex*, Abacus, London, 1996.

Taylor, Alister (ed.), *James K. Baxter, 1926–1972: A Memorial Volume*, Alister Taylor Publishers, Wellington, 1972.

Thomas, Brook, 'Placing Literature Written in English', *REAL Yearbook of Research in English and American Literature*, vol. 14, 1998, pp. 1–32.

Thomas, Nicholas, *Colonialism's Culture: Anthropology, Travel, and Government*, Polity Press, Cambridge, 1994.

Thomson, Arthur, *The Story of New Zealand: Past and Present, Savage and Civilized*, 2 vols, John Murray, London, 1859.

Thoreau, Henry David, *Walden*, Stephen Fender (ed.), Oxford University Press, Oxford, 1997.

Tompkins, Jane, *West of Everything: The Inner Life of Westerns*, Oxford University Press, New York, 1992.

Turner, Frederick Jackson, 'The Significance of the Frontier in American History', *The Frontier in American History*, Holt, Rinehart & Winston, New York, 1920.

Turner, Stephen, 'Compulsory Nationalism', *Moving Worlds*, vol. 8, no. 2, 2008, pp. 7–19.

___, 'Cultural Plagiarism and the New Zealand Dream of Home', *Landfall*, vol. 214, 2007, pp. 85–90.

___, 'Inclusive Exclusion: Managing Identity for the Nation's Sake in Aotearoa New Zealand', *Arena*, vol. 28, 2007, pp. 87–106.

___, 'Living Law', *Landfall*, vol. 212, 2006, pp. 128–41.

___, 'Settlement as Forgetting', in Klaus Neumann, Nicholas Thomas and Hilary Erickson (eds), *Quicksands: Foundational Histories in Aotearoa New Zealand*, University of New South Wales Press, Sydney, 1999, pp. 20–38.

Wallace, Lee, 'Queer, Here: Sexuality and Space', in Claudia Bell and Steve Matthewman (eds), *Cultural Studies in Aotearoa New Zealand*, Oxford University Press, Melbourne, 2004, pp. 66–83.

Wallace-Crabbe, Chris, 'That Second Body: An Australian View of Allen Curnow's Progress', *Ariel*, vol. 16, no. 4, 1985, pp. 67–75.

Wedde, Ian, *How To Be Nowhere*, Victoria University Press, Wellington, 1995.

___, *Making Ends Meet: Essays and Talks*, Victoria University Press, Wellington, 2005.

___, *Symmes Hole*, Penguin, Auckland, 1986.

Wevers, Lydia, *Country of Writing: Travel Writing and New Zealand 1809–1900*, Auckland University Press, Auckland, 2002.

___, *Reading on the Farm: Victorian Fiction and the Colonial World*, Victoria University Press, Wellington, 2010.

White, Richard, 'Are You an Environmentalist or Do You Work for a Living?: Work and Nature', in William Cronon (ed.), *Uncommon Ground*, Norton, New York, 1996, pp. 171–85.

___, *The Middle Ground: Indians, Empires, and Republics in the Great Lakes Region, 1650–1815*, Cambridge University Press, New York, 1991.

Williams, Mark, *Leaving the Highway: Six Contemporary New Zealand Novelists*, Auckland University Press, Auckland, 1990.

Williams, Mark and Michele Leggott (eds), *Opening the Book: New Essays on New Zealand Writing*, Auckland University Press, Auckland, 1995.

Williams, William, Journal, 1827–8, 1834, MS 91/75, Auckland Museum.

Wilson, Janet, 'Post-modernism or Post-colonialism? Fictive Strategies in *Living in the Maniototo* and *The Carpathians*', *Journal of New Zealand Literature*, vol. 11, 1993, pp. 114–31.

Wister, Owen, *The Virginian*, Wordsworth, Ware, 1996.

Wordsworth, William, *Selected Poems*, Nicholas Roe (ed.), Folio Society, London, 2002.

INDEX